WEATHERING THE STORM

WEATHERING THE STORM

Women of the American Revolution

BY ELIZABETH EVANS

CHARLES SCRIBNER'S SONS * NEW YORK

TO
SARA PICK EVANS

LIBRARY OF CONGRESS CATALOGING IN PUBLICATION DATA
Evans, Elizabeth.
  Weathering the storm.
  Bibliography: p.
  1. United States—History—Revolution, 1775–1783—
Women. 2. United States—History—Revolution, 1775–
1783—Biography. I. Title.
E276.E93   917.3'03'30922 [B]   74-10524
ISBN 0–684–13953–7

1 3 5 7 9 11 13 15 17 19 H/C 20 18 16 14 12 10 8 6 4 2
Printed in the United States of America

List of Illustrations

Acknowledgments

To me, the most gratifying aspect of writing about history is the time spent reading original manuscripts and letters. It requires humility, and a great respect for people who preserve them. I am very grateful to Nicholas B. Wainwright, director of The Historical Society of Pennsylvania, Peter J. Parker, chief of manuscripts, and to Lucy Hrivnak, for their considerable aid. In the charming atmosphere of Newport, Theodore E. Waterbury, executive director of the Newport Historical Society, and Gladys E. Bolhouse, curator of manuscripts, graciously enriched my research. I am particularly grateful to Edwin B. Bronner, curator of the Quaker Collection of the Haverford College Library, and to Barbara L. Curtis and Elizabeth B. Tritle for hours spent at their beautiful, peaceful campus. In working at the Massachusetts Historical Society, I cannot sufficiently thank Stephen T. Riley, director, and Gertrude A. Fisher, for their untiring assistance. I am also grateful to Robert M. Lunny, director of The New Jersey Historical Society, to Robert C. Morris, the society's keeper of manuscripts, to Clark A. Elliott, assistant curator of the Harvard University Archives, and to Leo Flaherty, curator of the Archives, Commonwealth of Massachusetts. The Microfilm Division of the National Archives assisted my search into military pension files. Roy P. Basler, chief of the Library of Congress's reference department, Manuscript Division, and Paul G. Sifton, specialist of early American history, revealed material never before published. For the seemingly endless amount of material available at the New York Public Library, I am indebted to Maud Cole in the Rare Book Division, John Miller in the American History Division, Elizabeth Roth in the Prints Division, and Gunther Pohl in the Local History and Genealogy Division. The Antiquarian and Numismatic Society and the Institut d'histoire de l'amérique française, Canadian societies, graciously sent copies of material in their collection, as did Margaret Cook, curator of manuscripts, Earl Gregg Swem Library, Williamsburg, Virginia. Warm appreciation is also due Thomas Harry, who alleviated many of the difficulties involved in research. Quotes from the following have been used with permission: *The American Campaigns of Rochambeau's Army, 1780–1783,* by Anne S.K. Brown and Howard C. Rice, Jr. copyright 1972 by Princeton University Press and Brown University Press; *Moreau de St. Mery's American Journey,* translated and edited by Kenneth Roberts and Anna M. Roberts, copyright 1947 by Doubleday and Company, Incorporated; *Adams Family Correspondance,* and *Diary and Autobiography of John Adams,* edited by L.H. Butterfield, copyright 1963, 1961 by The Belknap Press of Harvard University Press.

Contents

WEATHERING THE STORM

October 1, 1774: It seems we have troublesome times a coming, for there is great disturbance abroad in the earth and they say it is tea that caused it. So then if they will quarrel about such a trifling thing as that, what must we expect but war. I think or at least fear it will be so.

—*Jemima Condict Harrison*

December 20, 1777: General Washington's army have gone into winter quarters at the Valley Forge. We shall not see many of the military now. We shall be very intimate with solitude. I am afraid stupidity will be a frequent guest.

—*Sarah Wister*

August 6, 1778: Exceeding foggy morning; all terrified with apprehension that when the weather cleared, our destiny would be known; all the shops still kept shut, no business of any kind done, only carting and fortifying. . . .

—*Mary Gould Almy*

December 1779: War with its iron hand corrupts manners and invades the mind as much as it destroys the body, and all ranks of people are more or less affected by it . . . in short, America is not the same. The very climate seems changed.

—*Grace Growdon Galloway*

March 1802: Many have seen, and many can contemplate, in the field of imagination, battles and victories amidst garments rolled in blood; but it is only one of my own sex, exposed to the storm, who can conceive of my situation.

—*Deborah Sampson Gannett*

Introduction

I can not say that I think you very generous to the ladies, for whilst you are proclaiming peace and good will to men, emancipating all nations, you insist upon retaining an absolute power over wives . . . we have it in our power not only to free ourselves but to subdue our masters.

Abigail Smith Adams to her husband
John Adams, 1776.

It was unthinkable to men of the eighteenth century that virtuous and modest women would cheapen themselves by publicly attacking male authority. John Adams was adamant when he wrote in 1778: "From all that I had read of history and government, of human life and manners, I had drawn this conclusion, that the manners of women were the most infallible barometer, to ascertain the degree of morality and virtue in a nation. . . . The Jews, the Greeks, the Romans, the Swiss, the Dutch, all lost their public spirit, their republican principles and habits, and their republican forms of government, when they lost the modesty and domestic virtues of their women.

"What havoc said I to myself, would these manners make in America? Our governors, our judges, our senators, or representatives and even our ministers would be appointed by harlots for money, and their judgments, decrees and decisions be sold to repay themselves, or perhaps to procure the smiles (and embraces) of profligate females."

Yet, judging from the writings of those who lived during the second half of the eighteenth century, women could have bettered the nation had they shared political power with men. Instead, they were relegated to the role of housewife, laboring over the hearth and breast-feeding a seemingly endless procession of babies. Typical was the wife of Christopher Marshall, druggist and member of the Committee of Observation and

Inspection of the Provincial Congress in Philadelphia. In 1778 her husband wrote in his journal: "From early in the morning till late at night, she is constantly employed in the affairs of the family, which for some months has been very large, for besides the addition to our family in the house, a constant resort of comers and goers, which seldom go away with dry lips and hungry bellies. This calls for her constant attendance, not only to provide, but also to attend at getting prepared in the kitchen, baking our bread and pies, meat, etc., but also on the table. Her cleanliness about the house, her attendance in the orchard, cutting and drying apples, of which several bushels have been procured, add to which her making of cider without tools, for the constant drink of the family, her seeing all our washing done, and her fine clothes and my shirts, the which are all smoothed by her. Add to this her making of twenty large cheeses, and that from one cow, and daily using milk and cream, besides her sewing, knitting, etc. Thus she looketh well to the ways of her household, and eateth not the bread of idleness."

The archaic marriage laws, nearly identical with those of England, were intolerable. Deprived of economic resources and education, denied political positions, stigmatized with "spinsterhood" if they remained single, not surprisingly most women chose marriage. By law a wife was identified with her husband, as one person. Her legal existence was suspended. She was called in law a "femme-covert," and was said to be "covert-baron," which meant she was under the protection of a baron or master. If she lived in a colony other than Connecticut her husband had complete legal control over her children. He could send them away wherever and whenever he wished. Not only was the wife placed under her husband's protection, but all of her property, personal as well as real estate, was also under his control during his lifetime, after which it reverted back to his wife or her heirs. All profits and income derived from this property went to her husband. This "apron-string hold," as it was then termed, gave him the right to sell her property. Creditors could seize it. She could not even will it to anyone. If she wished to change title ownership of her land both she and her husband had to execute the deed jointly. A justice then spoke with the wife, alone, to verify her consent to the transaction. In cases where women lived separately from husbands who were unable, for various reasons, to provide for them, the courts protected women's rights to their own property. However, during the Revolution both the Continental Congress and the state assemblies passed acts allowing the government to confiscate and sell estates belonging to Loyalists attainted of treason, including real estate their wives had inherited. The Pennsylvania General Assembly passed an act in the spring of 1778 allowing property owned by Joseph Galloway to be seized and sold by the Commissioners of Forfeited Estates. Included was the estate belonging to his wife Grace Galloway (Galloway diary, page 185), property she had inherited from her father, Lawrence Growdon. This was taken from her despite the fact that she had committed no act of treason. Furthermore, she was horrified to learn that her husband had sold part of this inherited estate before he fled to England, and had her name removed from another property deed. The Assembly "graciously" permitted her to purchase the remaining shares of her estate, which she refused to do.

Women fortunate not to have husbands blacklisted for treason were allowed to manage their husbands' business affairs, acting as agents, in cases where the men were away at sea or fighting for the American cause during the Revolution. A colonial improvement over English law was the legal recognition of antenuptial and postnuptial contracts. These private documents were created and signed by both wives and husbands. They permitted wives to retain control of their own property and real estate. Postnuptial contracts were effective in avoiding distasteful divorce proceedings. Though a woman could refuse to marry a man unless he co-signed such a document, her stand actually meant very little, for he could have it contested at any time by taking court action. She could not. In addition, not all of the colonies gave legal recognition to such contracts. Another advantage in being male was that a husband could safely sleep with other women, knowing that his wife could not take legal action in divorce. If he caught his wife committing adultery he could prosecute her lover for abduction, because the wife was not supposed to possess a power of consent. He could also obtain a divorce, in most colonies, in which case his wife would be forbidden by law to marry her lover. In New York, divorce was prohibited until 1787, when the state enacted its first divorce statute. Even in the case of bigamy, a first wife could not take action to dissolve her marriage, because in court nothing was decreed that tended to bastardize the issue born in wedlock. Illegitimacy was recognized by law only when a woman was unfaithful to her husband.

"Spinsters" and widows, though usually poorer than married women, had legal rights. They could take court action, sue, administer their own estates, purchase as they wished, inherit and will property, make business transactions, and keep earnings received from employment. Widows could have jurisdiction over their children.

Women made no incursions into politics, small breakthroughs in religious sects, and only illegal and accidental inroads into the military establishment. While Americans were shouting "Taxation without representation is tyranny!" against the British they were denying political positions and the vote to women who paid taxes. The only state in which women did vote during the last half of the century was New Jersey. On July 2, 1776—two days before the Declaration of Independence was adopted—the New Jersey state constitution was passed, granting the vote to women. In 1807 this law was invalidated by state legislators, largely because women were not voting for them. The other states clearly stated in their constitutions that the vote was to be given to white males only, plugging any loopholes that existed in the early colonial charters. Men believed, inflexibly, that rakish voting places were much too undignified for women to be seen in. This view was shared by Thomas Jefferson. Despite the fact that Jefferson was an extraordinary man, with versatile accomplishments, he nevertheless opposed women's involvement in politics. Jefferson wrote from Paris in September 1788—while the federal Constitution was under discussion in Philadelphia—to Angelica Church, daughter of Philip Schuyler, the New York delegate to Congress: "You see by the papers, and I suppose by your letter also, how much your native state has been agitated by the question on the new constitution. But that need not agitate you. The tender breasts of ladies were not formed for political convulsion." From Monticello Jefferson wrote to Samuel Kerchival on September 5, 1816: "Were our State a pure democracy, in which all its inhabitants should meet together to transact all their business, there would yet be excluded from their deliberations . . . women, who, to prevent deprivation of morals and ambiguity of issue, could not mix promiscuously in the public meetings of men."

The most famous advocate of women's rights was Abigail Smith Adams, wife of John Adams, member of the Continental Congress and later President of the United States. Her considerable knowledge of political and social problems was revealed in her prolific correspondence to her husband. Refusing to be an obscure mouthpiece for her husband's views, she influenced many of his political decisions. Nevertheless, John was quite bullheaded about women's rights and refused to take the subject seriously. During the Revolution she explained why so many women lacked interest in patriotism, "the most disinterested of all virtues. Excluded from honors and from offices . . . deprived of a voice in legislation, obliged to submit to those laws which are imposed on us, is it not sufficient to make us indifferent to the public interest?" On March 31, 1776, Abigail asked her husband to have women's legislation enacted. "In the new code of laws which I suppose it will be necessary for you to make I desire you would remember the ladies, and be more generous and favorable to them than your ancestors. Do not put such unlimited power into the hands of the husbands. Remember all men would be tyrants if they could. If particular care and attention is not paid to the ladies we are determined to foment a rebellion, and will not hold ourselves bound by any laws in which we have no voice, or representation.

"That your sex are naturally tyrannical is a truth so thoroughly established as to admit of no dispute, but such of you as wish to be happy willingly give up the harsh title of master for the more tender and endearing one of friend. Why then, not put it out of the power of the vicious and the lawless to use us with cruelty and indignity with impunity. Men of sense in all ages abhor those customs which treat us only as the vassals of your sex." Her husband replied: "As to your extraordinary code of laws, I cannot but laugh. We have been told that our struggle has loosened the bands of government every where; that children and apprentices were disobedient; that schools and colleges were grown turbulent; that Indians slighted their guardians and negroes grew more insolent to their masters. But your letter was the first intimation that another tribe more numerous and powerful than all the rest were grown discontented. This is rather too coarse a compliment; but you are so saucy, I won't blot it out.

"Depend upon it, we know better than to repeal our masculine systems. Altho they are in full force, you know they are little more than theory. We dare not exert our power in its full latitude."

This infuriated the "lioness," whose growls turned into a roar. She unleashed an angry letter to Mercy Otis Warren, historian, dramatist, and sister of James Otis, asking for her support. "He is very saucy to me in return for a list of female grievances which I transmitted to him. I think I will get you to join me in a petition to Congress. I thought it was very probable our wise statesmen would erect a new government and form a new code of laws. I ventured to speak a word in behalf of our sex, who are rather hardly dealt with by the laws of England which give such unlimited power to the husband to use his wife ill. . . . It would be bad policy to grant us greater power, they say, since under all the disadvantages we labour we have the ascendancy over their hearts and charm by accepting, by submitting."

In nearly all religious denominations women were denied authoritative positions of power. Christian women were expected to sit quietly in their pews and act according to the biblical writings of Saints Paul and Peter, "But I would have you know, that the head of every man is Christ; and the head of the woman is the man." "Likewise, ye wives, be in subjection to your own husbands." "But I suffer not a woman to teach, nor to usurp authority over the man, but to be in silence. For Adam was first formed, then Eve. And Adam was not deceived, but the woman being deceived, was in the transgression." Never mind that he kept on plucking ripe fruit, she continued to be castigated as a "fallen woman." There were three religious sects in which women were prominent: the Society of Friends (Quakers), the society of Ann Lee (Shakers), and the society of Jemima Wilkinson.

The first Friends to arrive in America to spread the good word were women: Mary Fisher and Ann Austin in Massachusetts, and Elizabeth Harris in Maryland. Mary and Ann were immediately arrested, imprisoned, and deported by Puritan authorities. By the eighteenth century, Quakers were numerous in the colonies, particularly in Pennsylvania and New Jersey, though they were also found in large numbers elsewhere. Many wealthy and prominent families were Quakers. The Society rejected symbolic rituals and abstract doctrines of other Christian sects. Instead, they emphasized simplicity, the conscientious intuition of each individual, and equality of the sexes. Their male and female ministers denounced war and slavery. No church authority pronounced a couple man and wife. The two stood alone before gathered Friends and declared their love and faithfulness toward each other. A third person, of either sex, then rose and legalized the marriage by proclaiming that no one had objected to it during the three announcements made in previous meetings. Everyone assembled signed the marriage contract as witnesses; those unable to attend signed it later.

During regular services Quaker women not only asked questions and expressed opinions from seats in the congregation, they preached in front of it as well. When sixty ministers and elders met in Burlington, New Jersey, on February 22, 1767, twenty-five were women. Women preachers traveled great distances on horseback, over dirt roads and forest paths, in freezing weather and sweltering heat, to preach at Meeting Houses and comfort the ill in their homes. A few ebullient eccentrics among them made interesting copy for local newspapers. In the spring of 1775 in Philadelphia, "Mary Harris, a Quaker preacher from Wilmington, Delaware visited the three Quaker Meeting Houses in this city, in a very odd manner, by walking through each of the preacher's galleries, then down, passed amongst the people backwards and forwards, seemingly in great affliction and distress, uttering, it's said, words to this effect—'See to your standing, for that thus the Lord was about to search and examine his camp,' etc. and then said 'I shall have peace in having thus discharged and done my Lord's errand. So farewell.' " Quaker women gathered in separate meetings to discuss financial problems, marriage, being single, pregnancy, childbearing, work, community problems, war, and their children's education. Quakers had equal educational facilities for both boys and girls, as opposed to the common American practice of suppressing female education.

Ann Lee's society began not long after she and her followers, six men and three women, sailed into the port of New York from England in August 1774. "Mother and the Elders" purchased property at Neskeyuna, New York, not far from Albany, and founded the Church of Christ's Second Coming. Onlookers called them Shakers because they shook a lot during their services. Ann Lee's father and husband were blacksmiths; yet, from this humble beginning, she with the Elders accumulated a following of thousands of people in New England and New York and so threatened the male establishment that law officials and militia officers aroused mob violence against them and had them arrested. She preached that Jesus Christ "ascended to his Father, that the way might be prepared for his second coming, in the female part of his manhood . . . and when the time was fully come, according to the appointment of God, Christ was again revealed, not in Judea, to the Jews, nor in the person of a male, but in England . . . and in the person of a female'' (Ann Lee); that married people "must forsake the marriage of the flesh." Prior to this sexual enlightenment Ann Lee had borne four children, all of whom had died in infancy. Her rejection of sexual relations greatly disturbed her husband; he schlumped in and around taverns on drunken bouts and left her. New England judges and militiamen became alarmed when she preached, before large gatherings, that people cannot follow Christ by fighting a revolution. In 1780 she and the Elders were arrested and imprisoned in Albany. In 1781 the militia broke up her meeting in Petersham in an attempt to seize her. Later that day about thirty men fought with her followers who were guarding the house where she was staying. Three men burst into her room, "seized her by the feet, and inhumanely dragged her, feet foremost, out of the house, and threw her into a sleigh with as little ceremony as they would the dead carcass of a beast, and drove off, committing at the same time, acts of inhumanity and indecency which even savages would be ashamed of." Two of the assailants, a county sheriff, and a deacon's son, confessed they had taken her to find out whether she was a woman or not. They were paid to "knock her" by a militia captain, Samuel Peckham. While militiamen were organized during the Revolution to fight for American liberty, in 1782, militiamen, under the command of Captain Phineas Farnsworth, forced Ann Lee to leave Harvard. Later the same year, while she was preaching in New Lebanon, militia mobs again had her arrested.

Jemima Wilkinson was born of Quaker parents in the town of Cumberland, Rhode Island, in 1751. During the summer of 1775 she complained of illness and for about two months secluded herself in her home. She did not appear again in public until the fall when she sidetracked people going into the Meeting House and told them she had experienced mystical revelations, her past self had died, and she was rejuvenated in Christ. She converted enough people at public gatherings and private burial services to hold her own scheduled religious meetings. When she preached throughout Rhode Island, Connecticut, and Massachusetts, people began speaking of her all over New England. After preaching in Philadelphia and opening a branch in Worcester, Pennsylvania, she established a settlement called New Jerusalem in Genesee County, New York, in 1788. While soliciting funds for the settlement, two Rhode Island women stole two thousand dollars from the state treasurer. This ended the Rhode Island society. Until her death in 1819, Jemima Wilkinson dedicated herself to the conversion of Indians in New York State.

The Continental Army, authorized by Congress, began recruiting January 1, 1776. Twenty-six infantry regiments, one rifle regiment, and one artillery regiment were to be organized, consisting of 20,373 men. A woman could break through this male bastion either by enlisting, illegally, as a man—a few women did—or by replacing a fallen husband on the battlefield —a few did that, too. The courage and strength of women were proven on the battlefield by at least three women, unquestionably there were more. Deborah Sampson Gannett (Gannett manuscript excerpts and speech, page 303), under the assumed name of Robert Shurtleff, served with the 4th Massachusetts Regiment, fighting against the British, Tories, and Indians. Margaret Cochran Corbin ("Captain Molly") and Mary Hays ("Molly Pitcher") fired artillery cannons against Hessians and bloodybacks (scarlet-coated British).

During the Battle of Fort Washington, on the northern end of Manhattan in New York, November 16, 1766, Margaret Corbin aided her husband, John Corbin, a private in the Pennsylvania State Regiment of Artillery. Under fire, she doused a sponge into water, swabbed the cannon bore, and helped her husband ram the gun with cannon shot. When he was killed by enemy fire she took over, until her own body was torn with grapeshot. She was maimed for life and permanently lost the use of one arm. As compensation, the military assigned her to the Invalid Regiment, stationed at West Point. On July 6, 1779, the Continental Congress resolved "that Margaret Corbin, who was wounded and disabled in the attack on Fort Washington, whilst she heroically filled the post of her husband who was killed by her side serving a piece of artillery, do receive, during her natural life, on the continuance of the said disability, the one-half of the monthly pay drawn by a soldier in the service of these states; and that she now receive out of the public stores, one complete suit of cloaths, or the value thereof in money." This was amended the following year to read one complete outfit of clothing each year. She was also entitled to a monthly rum or whiskey ration at West Point, denied her by the commissary because it wasn't their custom to issue liquor to women. She prodded the brass into putting pressure on the commissary until she was able to walk out of the building carrying all of the bottles forbidden her for months. Most people treated her with affection and respect. Women looked after her; West Point supply officers gave her unauthorized blankets and bedding. For years she was seen fishing along waterfronts, dressed in an old artillery coat and vest. Long after her death, her body was disinterred from an obscure spot and placed, with military honors, in the West Point cemetery.

At the time of the Revolution, Mary Hays was married to William Hays, a gunner in the Pennsylvania State Regiment of Artillery. During his seven years' service she remained with him at camp and battle sites, lugging buckets of water, aiding the wounded, and helping at the cannons. Private Joseph Martin of the 8th Connecticut Regiment watched Mary Hays during the Battle of Monmouth, New Jersey, on June 28, 1778. He recorded in his journal that she "attended with her husband at the piece the whole time. While in the act of reaching for a cartridge and having one of her feet as far before the other as she could step, a cannon shot from the enemy passed directly between her legs without doing any other damage than carrying away all the lower part of her petticoat. Looking at it with apparent unconcern, she observed that it was lucky it did not pass a little higher, for in that case it might have carried away something else, and continued her occupation." When her husband was wounded that day Mary took his place at the cannon. Some witnesses claimed she had fired several rounds; others said she had only loaded and fired once. Following the war the couple settled in

Carlisle, Pennsylvania, where a son, John, was born. When William died, she married John McCauly. On February 21, 1822, one year before her death, the government granted her "the sum of forty dollars immediately and the same sum yearly during her life" as a pension for her services during the war.

Hundreds of women followed their husbands, brothers, sons, and lovers to camps and battle areas, where they cooked, washed and mended clothes, nursed the wounded, and boosted the soldiers' morale. General George Washington, a harsh disciplinarian, was always nettled by the presence of these women. The feisty leader rebuked those who were not nurses for refusing to grow food crops on farms for his troops. He was compelled, however, to allow a limited number of women on these marches, well aware that many of his soldiers would either desert or refuse reenlistment if their women were not allowed with them. The best Washington could do was grumble in his written orders:

> *Mid-July 1777*: "Women are to march with the baggage."
> *August 4, 1777*: "The multitude of women in particular, especially those who are pregnant, or have children, are a clog upon every movement."
> *August 27, 1777*: "Women are especially forbid any longer, under any license at all, to ride in the waggons, and the officers earnestly called upon to permit no more than are absolutely necessary, and such as are actually useful, to follow the army."
> *September 13, 1777*: "No woman under any pretence whatever to go with the army, but to follow the baggage."
> *June 7, 1779*: "The General was sorry to see thro'out the march a much greater proportion of men with the baggage than could possibly be necessary."
> Ironically, a 1788 dictionary defines baggage as "a familiar epithet for a woman."

It is impossible to give exact percentages of women who were for American independence (Patriots, Whigs, Rebels), those who were neutral, or those who opposed severance from England (Loyalists, Royalists, Tories). Allegiances shifted as atrocities and American victories occurred. Nevertheless, prior to 1776 the majority of women did not wish independence from Great Britain. A large number opposed it after that time. Nor did women always side with their husbands: Loyalist wives had husbands who fought in the American army, and Patriot wives had husbands who fought with the British.

Patriots were scorned as the "tyrannical and arbitrary rabble of America" by Loyalists, who looked upon their radicalism as a threat to the peaceful and prosperous society. Yet many reputable women aided the cause. They protested importation taxes by boycotting English products, including tea, a popular item in America; they spun and wove their own cloth and fashioned their own clothes; they made coats and shirts for the American army out of blankets, sheets, and linen; they relinquished their shining pewter services so that bullets could be made from them; they supplied food and medical aid; and they took over farmwork and managed their husbands' businesses while the men were away fighting. In Mecklenburgh and Rowan counties, North Carolina, and in Amelia County, Virginia, women assembled and vowed not to become attached to men who refused to take up arms against the British. By 1780 the spirit of patriotism was so kindled among women in Pennsylvania and Maryland they collected large sums of money and quantities of linen for Washington's troops. "Emulating the noble example of their patriotic sisters of Pennsylvania," the women of Trenton, New Jersey, gathered pledges and funds from organized groups throughout their state. A Providence, Rhode Island, woman was successful in having her recipe for soap printed in a number of newspapers so that people would be able to make it for the troops. The superior British soap was very scarce. "Take eight quarts of common family soap, and put to it about half a pint of common sea salt; boil this for a few minutes, then set it by and let it cool. The soap will remain on top. This must be taken off and thrown into clean, cold water. After remaining in it twelve hours it must be taken out, melted, and poured into any moulds that may be chosen. When it is cold it will become hard, and can be carried in packs as well as crown [British] soap."

During the British occupation of Philadelphia in 1778 a free, black woman, "having received two hard dollars for washing, and hearing of the distress of our prisoners in the gaol, went to market and bought some neckbeef and two heads, with some green, and made a pot of as good broth as she could; but having no more money to buy bread, she got credit of a baker for six loaves, all of which she carried to our unfortunate prisoners, who were much in want of such supply. She has since then paid the baker, and says, she never laid out money with so much satisfaction.—Humanity is the same thing in rich or poor, white or black."

When their homes were threatened by Loyalists, British, or Hessian (German mercenaries) soldiers, women fought to keep them at a distance, even killing a few with rifles or muskets. In a frontier cabin along the Wahatche (War Woman) Creek in Georgia, Nancy Hart shot two armed Tories and held others at gunpoint until help arrived. Elsewhere, wives hid husbands in grain barrels, cellars, and concealed rooms to keep them from being arrested, and worked for their release when they were. Women intercepted important enemy documents. Rachael and Grace Martin, sisters-in-law, armed with pistols and dressed in men's clothing, stood watch on a dark South Carolina road. When a mounted courier and escorts trotted into view they were halted, their dispatches confiscated. The men were forced to turn their horses around in retreat. Feeling disgusted and fatigued they requested a night's lodging in a nearby home. They told the woman who owned the house they were rather harmless individuals on parole, having been held up unexpectedly by two armed men. Mrs. Martin (Grace's mother) listened with amused compassion. In Massachusetts, between Pepperell and Groton, a group of women wearing their husbands' clothes and armed with muskets and pitchforks hid behind the thickets at Jewett's Bridge, over the Nashua River. Captain Leonard Whiting galloped over the bridge with valuable papers, from Canada to the British in Boston, hidden in his boots. After shoving the Tory off his horse, the women jabbed him with their weapons, pulled the documents out, and marched their prisoner to the Groton jail.

In some cases women didn't have to resort to weapons; they used their wits. Lydia Darrah charmed British officers into holding a late night conference in her Philadelphia home. Pretending to retire for the night, she crept back and listened as the enemy planned an attack against the American army at Whitemarsh, north of Philadelphia. The following morning she told her husband that flour was needed from the mill at Frankford, southeast of Whitemarsh. With permission from General Howe to pass through British lines, she walked the four or five miles, through snow, to the mill. After depositing her empty sack, she walked further, toward American outposts. An American officer on a scouting mission listened attentively as she gave him the information. She then returned to the mill, picked up the flour, and trudged through snowdrifts to Philadelphia. When the British army approached Whitemarsh they found Washington's troops alerted and prepared for them. Being the weaker force, the British returned to Philadelphia without a conflict.

Women who were neutral during the Revolution were either apathetic toward and unconcerned with political and military problems or were pacifists having religious convictions of nonviolence. Those disinterested believed they were neither persecuted nor harassed under British rule, that is, not until British troops marched through their towns and abused them. Then, too, women did not wish to commit themselves to a cause that might well replace a stable government with a radical one. Most pacifists were members of the Society of Friends (Quakers). Though many Quaker men sympathized with the Patriot cause, they refused to violate Christ's teachings by killing or by holding government positions which would give aid to violence. Quakers who refused to adhere to pacifist principles were turned out of the Society. Men and women who remained Quakers allowed their belongings to be taken by foragers without resistance and permitted their Meeting Houses to be seized for hospitals or barracks and their homes to be used for quartering soldiers and the sick and wounded. The Wister family (Wister diary, page

110) of Gwynedd, Pennsylvania, graciously fed and sheltered several American officers. Among them were Major Benjamin Stoddert, later appointed Secretary of the Navy under John Adams; Colonel James Wood, later Governor of Virginia; and General William Smallwood, later Governor of Maryland. Yet, despite Quaker generosity toward them, most Patriots loathed these nonconformists for refusing to take oaths of allegiance, for not actively participating in the war, and for refusing to deal in Continental currency. It was also unsettling to Patriots when Philadelphia Quakers remained in their homes while large numbers of the city's inhabitants, including members of the Continental Congress, fled in 1777 as the British army was about to occupy the city. Patriots feared that Quakers would aid the enemy. And the British had the same fear.

Loyalist women, who were generally conservative, opposed severance from Great Britain. Though many protested unjust tax laws imposed by the British Parliament, none had any intention of helping the revolutionaries, radicals who they were certain would bring chaos to America's stable economy. In addition, many of their husbands earned income from English clients and products. Many clergymen of the Anglican Church sided with the British because the church hierarchy was in England. Loyal were many wives of large landowners, members of colonial councils, lawyers, doctors, office holders, and merchants—people who had much to lose if the Revolution succeeded. Loyalism also had support among wives of small farmers, artisans, tradesmen, innkeepers and others who feared losing what little income they had. Loyalism was strongest in the Middle States, North and South Carolina, and Georgia. It was weakest in New England, Maryland, and Virginia.

"Every Tory is a coward, for a servile, slavish self-interested fear is the foundation of Toryism." "A Tory is a thing whose head is in England, and its body in America, and its neck ought to be stretched," shouted Patriots against Loyalists. In September 1777 a group of frustrated and angry Loyalists who struck back were jailed in Poughkeepsie, New York. They were "charged

with robbing several houses, and putting the families in fear
. . . they were all painted and dressed like Indian men . . . five
of them proved to be women, three of whom are a mother and
two daughters."

Patriots violated or changed the law to suit their own interests.
Committees of Safety, groups particularly fond of inflicting harm
upon Loyalists, were formed early in the Revolution. They
burned homes and barns, plundered people's possessions,
slaughtered animals, and after tarring and feathering men made
them ride poles until their genitals were damaged. They relished
attacks upon Loyalists who harbored tea. One woman's supply
was confiscated by committeemen who then "proceeded with
some ceremony and exultation before the house, to destroy it by
fire." When a Patriot broke into her house seeking flame to
ignite the tea, the woman soused him with a kettle full of scalding
water. In Brooklyn Ferry, New York, during the spring of 1776,
Mrs. John Rapalie sipped her tea contemptuously one afternoon
during her regular tea hour. Angry militiamen fired their cannon
through her window. The shot smashed the window glass,
soared over the tea table, and lodged itself in the wall, close to
where Mrs. Rapalie was sitting. Afterwards, she took great pride,
as she continued sipping tea, in pointing out the projectile to
friends. Refusing to be intimidated, she sent a message to the
British informing them of Washington's plans for escaping Long
Island. The message arrived too late.

While their husbands fought in such corps as Patrick Ferguson's American Riflemen, Robert Roger's Queen's Rangers,
John Butler's Loyal Rangers, Cortlandt Skinner's New Jersey
Volunteers, and about twenty-three others, wives lived in areas
for the most part protected by the British. New York City was
the safest place in the colonies, for it was occupied by the British
during most of the war. In 1779 a number of New York women
collected large sums of money "for the purpose of fitting out
immediately a formidable, fastsailing privateer, to be called *The
Fair American.* Rivington's *Royal Gazette* argued that the women's
action "ought to be considered by the rebels as a proof of the

flagrancy of their own insolence and obstinacy in rejecting such generous offers of reconciliation as to excite the indignation of the fair sex, whose natural characteristics are gentleness and benevolence."

Patriots denied Loyalists the same rights they later had amended to the Constitution: freedom of speech, the right to assemble peaceably, the right "to be secure in their persons, houses, papers, and effects against unreasonable searches and seizures." Women were imprisoned without any evidence that they had violated the law and without benefit of trial. Family estates were confiscated by state assemblies, an action sanctioned by the Continental Congress. Property and valuable objects were seized as tax payments to support the Patriot war effort. Livestock and grain were stolen, trees taken for firewood and shacks for the American army. Patriot farmers refused to sell provisions to Loyalists; millers refused to grind their grain. Even the British army inflicted serious damage upon Loyalist property. British troops, under orders, burned several Loyalist mansions in Philadelphia, afraid that Patriots would fire upon them from these unoccupied homes. During the British occupation of Boston, General John Burgoyne lived in the home of Samuel Quincy, a Loyalist who was then in England. A woman living opposite this mansion reported she had seen "raw meat cut and hacked upon her [Mrs. Quincy's] mahogany tables, and her superb damask curtains and cushions exposed to the rain, as if they were of no value." Apparently when Burgoyne was about to enter Boston for the first time and said, "Well, let us in, and we shall make elbow room," he didn't have just the town in mind.

By the war's end between seventy-five and one hundred thousand Loyalists had fled the country. Many began life anew in the wilderness regions of Canada, Nova Scotia, and the West Indies, much as their ancestors had done in America. Many sailed to England where they were, for the most part, not well received, and where they experienced loneliness for their native country. Some of them managed to return. Most did not.

All who remained in America during the Revolution—Patriots, neutralists, and Loyalists—suffered from the scarcity of staple products. Along with rampant inflation came the shortage of such items as tea, coffee, and sugar. Letters and newspapers vented women's wrath over such scarcities. The *Pennsylvania Journal* of March 1, 1775, reported that a petition, written by elderly women would soon be sent to either the Assembly or the next Congress in Philadelphia to change the current policy toward tea, stated: "Your petitioners, as well spinsters as married, having been long accustomed to the drinking of tea, fear it will be utterly impossible for them to exhibit so much patriotism as wholly to disuse it. . . . Your petitioners are also informed there are several old women of the other sex, labouring under the like difficulties, who apprehend the above restriction will be wholly insupportable; and that it is a sacrifice infinitely too great to be made to save the lives, liberties, and privileges of any country whatever. Your petitioners, therefore, humbly pray the premises may be taken into serious consideration, and that they may be excepted from the resolution adopted by the late Congress, wherein your petitioners conceive they were not represented; more especially as your petitioners only pray for an indulgence to those spinsters, whom age or ugliness have rendered desperate in the expectation of husbands; those of the married, where infirmities and ill behaviour have made their husbands long since tired of them, and those old women of the male gender who will most naturally be found in such company." From Boston Abigail Adams wrote her husband on July 31, 1777, that many women attributed the scarcity of sugar and coffee to the merchants having hoarded them. "Some stores had been opened by a number of people, and the coffee and sugar carried into the market and dealt out by pounds. It was rumoured that an eminent, wealthy, stingy merchant (who is a bachelor) had a hogshead of coffee in his store, which he refused to sell to the committee under 6 shillings per pound. A number of females, some say a hundred, some say more, assembled with a cart and trucks, marched down to the warehouse and demanded the keys, which he refused to deliver. Upon which, one of them seized him by his neck and

cool air." Elizabeth Drinker (Drinker diary, page 152), mother of nine children, spoke for most women when she wrote, "I have often thought that women who live to get over the time of childbearing, if other things are favourable to them, experience more comfort and satisfaction than at any other period of their lives."

Life was rarely favorable to black women, however. Abigail Adams believed it hypocritical that Americans should be fighting for freedom, while denying it to blacks. "It always appeared a most iniquitous scheme to me to fight ourselves for what we are daily robbing and plundering from those who have as good a right to freedom as we have." Denied the vote, even though free blacks paid taxes, separated from white people in churches that preached the humility, compassion, and love of Christ, denied burial in "white only" cemeteries, and oppressed by white work-men, who didn't want them as apprentices, it was extraordinary that most blacks remained decent and compassionate. As slaves, husbands were sometimes sold separately from wives, and chil-dren from parents. As servants, black women usually fared toler-ably, though there were incidences of depraved cruelty. One such occurrence involved a servant and her six-month-old infant in Charleston, South Carolina. According to the Philadelphia diarist Moreau de St. Mery, "when this Negress appeared wear-ing a rather clean skirt, the mistress questioned her on this new aquisition. She made an answer at which the mistress was so angry that she threw herself on her and beat her. Afterwards she had her taken to prison by a constable, and there she was given ten lashes of a whip every day. At the end of six days, the mistress allowed her to be moved by the entreaties of several persons and had this woman released from jail. The unhappy creature, whose breasts, grown big with milk, had caused her severe pain, has-tened to empty them so that they would fill with a more recent milk. Then, having washed them, she nursed her child, whom the mistress had made drunk with Madeira wine in order to stop the infant's cries during the six days of her mother's detention."

A young black woman who achieved national and European

acclaim was Phyllis Wheatley. Born in Africa, torn from her mother at an early age, and sold to Boston's Wheatley family, this precocious child attracted the attention of Massachusetts's literary figures. Treated as a daughter by the family, Phyllis avidly absorbed history, geography, Latin, science, and the Bible, all of which inspired a profusive outpouring of poetic verse. Recovering from an illness at the age of nineteen, the family sent her to London, along with the Wheatley's son, who was traveling on business. In London her volume *Poems on Various Subjects, Religious and Moral* (1773) was first published and translated into several languages. Following her return to America, Phyllis wrote poems honoring many prominent people, including George Washington. The general wrote in reply, "The style and manner exhibit a striking proof of your poetical talents; in honor of which, and as a tribute justly due to you, I would have published the poem, had I not been apprehensive that, while I only meant to give the world this new instance of your genius, I might have incurred the imputation of vanity." Phyllis Wheatley married, mothered three infants, only one of which survived, and died poverty-stricken at an early age in an obscure part of Boston.

The medical profession had made little progress since the landing of the Pilgrims, though there were a number of doctors with European degrees. Surgical instruments were primitive; anesthesia, other than opium and alcohol, was unknown. Doctors frequently performed operations , even for the removal of cancer tumors, while the patient sat in an arm chair at home. Quacks were paid for attaching snails to people suffering from skin cancer as a precaution against its spreading or for coating the areas with plaster in an attempt to remove the disease. The most reputable doctors in the colonies prescribed medicine concocted originally by quack practioners. Dr. Rush acknowledged, before members of the American Philosophical Society in 1786, that "it was from the inventions and temerity of quacks that physicians have derived some of their most active and useful medicines."

Yellow fever and smallpox epidemics raged throughout the

colonies. The worst yellow fever devastation was in Philadelphia, where the 1793 epidemic caused about 4,000 deaths, or one person out of every ten; the 1798 epidemic, 3,500 deaths. The disease infested the city during hot summer months when vast swamp areas nearby were thick with mosquitoes, when exposed piles of garbage in the city stenched with rot. Mosquitoes fed upon diseased passengers or crewmen from ships, who lay in squalid hotel rooms near the wharves. Infected insects then spread the disease among the city people. Smallpox and yellow fever were so prevalent in the colonies that it was not unusual to see people on the street or in carriages holding to their nostrils sponges soaked with boiled wine, vinegar, and herbs, or to see pots of these boiling ingredients in homes to ward off the foul disease. Smallpox inoculation centers were set up in every major city, using the primitive method of puncturing the skin with live virus. In Boston on July 8, 1776, Hannah Winthrop wrote Mercy Warren that "the reigning subject is the smallpox. Boston has given up its fears of an invasion and is busily employed in communicating the infection. Straw beds and cribs are daily carted into the town. That ever prevailing passion of following the fashion is as predominate at this time as ever. Men, women and children eagerly crowding to inoculate is, I think, as modish, as running away from the troops of a barbarous George [King George III] was the last year," following the battles of Lexington and Concord.

Hypochondriasis was a disease prevalent among slaves. Dr. Rush wrote in a published paper: "It occurs soon after their importation and often proves fatal, with a train of painful and distressing symptoms which are ignorantly ascribed to the effects of slow poison taken by themselves or given to them by others. This disease, with all its terrible consequences, is occasioned wholly by grief and therefore stands justly chargable upon slavery."

Newspaper accounts and Congressional reports during the war make it easy to assume that acts of rape and murder against women were committed only by the British and Hessians. However, most newspapers sided with Patriots and members of the Continental Congress were biased. Rape attacks by American soldiers or militiamen were hushed either before news of them reached the press or by members of the press themselves. Great copy material was provided for the American cause when the British violated women. Unquestionably most rape assaults were made by British soldiers. Not on home ground—many resented being in America—they looked upon most American women as their enemy. Few British rapists were punished. Lord Rawdon (Captain Francis Rawdon) wrote his uncle, the Earl of Huntington, on August 5, 1776, that he appreciated southern women because they did not publicly take issue after being raped by British soldiers. Rawdon viewed Staten Island, New York, women with caustic disdain: "A girl cannot step into the bushes to pluck a rose without running the most imminent risk of being ravished, and they are so little accustomed to these vigorous methods that they don't bear them with the proper resignation, and of consequence we have most entertaining courtsmartial every day. To the southward they behaved much better in these cases, if I may judge from a woman who, having been forced by seven of our men, made a complaint to me 'not of their usage,' she said—'No, thank God, she despised that'—but of their having taken an old prayer book for which she had a particular affection.

"A girl on this island made a complaint the other day to Lord Percy of her being deflowered, as she said, by some grenadiers. Lord Percy asked her how she knew them to be grenadiers, as it happened in the dark. 'Oh, good God,' cried she, 'they could be nothing else, and if your Lordship will examine I am sure you will find it so.'"

Late in 1776 sixteen young women and a mother with her ten year old daughter fled to a wooded area near Pennytown, New Jersey, fearful of the ravages and plundering of British soldiers stationed in that town. The soldiers searched the forest and sexually assaulted the group. Not far away, a girl of thirteen "was taken from her father's house, carried to a barn about a mile, there ravished, and afterwards made use of by five more of these Brutes." In December, British officers confiscated estates within a five mile area of Princeton, ordering other estates plundered and burned. Two dragoons quartered at Pensneck, about two miles from Princeton, forced a farmer's daughter into her barn, and lied when they told her they only wished to flush out Rebels. As one soldier stifled her cries the other raped her. The two men then exchanged places, and she was raped a second time.

On April 18, 1777, a committee appointed by the Continental Congress to inquire into the conduct of British troops read their report. A portion concerned "the lust and brutality of the soldiers in abusing women." The committeemen had "authentic information of many instances of the most indecent treatment, and actual ravishment of married and single women; but, such is the nature of that most irreparable injury that the persons suffering it, though perfectly innocent, look upon it as a kind of reproach to have the facts related and their names known. . . . Some complaints were made to the commanding officers on this subject, and one affidavit made before a justice of the peace, but the committee could not learn that any satisfaction was ever given, or punishment inflicted, except that one soldier in Pennington was kept in custody for part of a day." Congress ordered the report published. Four thousand English and two thousand German copies were ordered printed, to be distributed among the enemy. No copy is known to exist. Although affidavits made by raped women were in the committee's possession, it is probable that the committee's report and these affidavits were never published. They are now in the possession of the Library of Congress. There is documentation that Benjamin Franklin had been assigned the task of having the report printed; that as late as 1780 Franklin was still procrastinating over whether or not it should be published. He believed the section on American prisoners to be too harsh against the British. The enemy continued raping women. That same year an American officer entered Connecticut Farms, New Jersey, shortly after its being burned and pillaged by soldiers of the 22nd British Regiment and a group of Hessians. He came across a young girl who "could only answer in broken accents of the most excessive grief." She said "that she was ruined and wished never again to be spoken to." She had been "forcibly subjected to the brutal violence of seven or eight different officers of that army."

Colonial and state laws stated that in cases where there is sufficient evidence a felony indictment of rape (the legal term was "rapuit" or ravished) must be placed against the aggressor and an impartial trial by jury held. Upon conviction a rapist was usually sentenced to life imprisonment, though this was rarely the penalty in southern colonies when a black woman was involved. Under law no other witness to the act except the woman violated was necessary. She gave testimony under oath, as did other people who took the stand to give testimony regarding her moral integrity, or lack of it, and evidence of any other kind that might be helpful in the trial. The offence of rape was in no way mitigated by showing that the woman at last yielded to the violence, if such consent was forced by fear of death or duress. A complete and fascinating report, published verbatim, of a rape trial held in New York City is the *Report of the Trial of Richard D. Croucher on an Indictment for a Rape on Margaret Miller,* printed in 1800.

As frontiersmen pushed westward during the 1770s, they arrogated Indian property and murdered natives. In 1774 Captain Michael Cresap and Daniel Greathouse slaughtered the wife and children of a Mingo chief, Logan, near the Ohio River. Thomas Jefferson, horrified, wrote that Logan was "a chief celebrated in peace and war, and long distinguished as the friend of the whites." A rampage of murder by the British in 1775 brought a scathing reaction from Mercy Otis Warren: "The unparallel barbarity in the late action at Lexington evinces that they had forgotten the laws and usages of civilized nations. We have reason to believe that no reports of their cruelty have been exaggerated; their brutal fury has certainly led them to perpetuate the most savage acts. I saw yesterday a gentleman who conversed with the brother of a woman cut in pieces in her bed with her new born infant at her side." As the war became more violent, acts of savagery occurred more frequently. In Rye, Connecticut, the daughter of Jonathan Kniffin was shot to death in early April 1777 by Patriots hidden behind a stone wall. She was carrying clothes to her father along a country road. The Patriots stole her bundle, severed her finger for a ring, and abandoned her body. In 1778 Indians revenged the slaughter of tribal brothers killed at the Battle of Oriskany, the year before, by joining Tories in a series of grisly raids in the Wyoming and Mohawk valleys: men, women, and children were burned alive at Fort Wilkesbarre when the enemy sealed and set fire to homes; thirty-two people of Cherry Valley, nearly all of whom were women and children, were butchered (Ferguson journal, page 271).

Two of the grimmest murders involved Jane McCrea of New York and Hannah Caldwell of New Jersey. During the summer of 1777 Jane McCrea was staying with a family near Fort Edward, where her fiancé David Jones was stationed as a volunteer in General Burgoyne's Loyalist contingent. Indians, unaware that she was a Loyalist and encouraged to bring in prisoners for a reward, seized Jane and brought her toward the fort. Along the way, a heated dispute arose between this and another group of Indians as to who should receive the reward. A chief then cleaved the sharp ridge of his tomahawk deep into Jane's skull, slicing off part of her scalp. News of this despicable act reached the fort, where Jones was shown her severed skin. It was also quickly related to the American general, Horatio Gates, who wrote Burgoyne a letter of outrage. Burgoyne replied that it had not been premeditated barbarity, that the Indian responsible had been brought before him and that "he should have suffered an ignominious death had I not been convinced by circumstances and observations beyond the possibility of a doubt, that a pardon, under the forms which they accepted, would be more efficacious than an execution to prevent similar mischiefs."

Hannah Ogden Caldwell, mother of nine children, lived in the rustic village of Connecticut Farms, New Jersey. Her husband, James Caldwell, was a clergyman who preached in Elizabeth

Town's First Presbyterian Church. He was also a chaplain with New Jersey troops. On Sundays he nestled loaded pistols on both sides of his Bible while preaching for armed rebellion against the British; on weekdays he shouldered a musket and clutched his Bible while marching with the troops. In June 1780 the 22nd British Regiment, reinforced with Hessians, invaded New Jersey from New York in a devastating sweep toward Springfield. Mr. Caldwell left his home to fight with New Jersey troops. Forced to retreat from Springfield, the British and Hessians returned by way of Connecticut Farms, sacking the countryside, firing upon people, and pillaging and burning stores and homes along the way. Hannah Caldwell lowered a well bucket with valuable articles, filled hidden pockets in her clothing with jewelry, and gathered her children in a far bedroom, where an infant suckled her breast. Breaking from ranks, a British soldier crept over the yard and fired through the window. As glass shattered against a young daughter's face, the shot ripped through Mrs. Caldwell's left breast and lung. Soldiers smashed the back door and looted her home. The officers remained silent. Before the house was engulfed in flames neighbors carried Hannah's body outdoors, though the British had tried to prevent it. The following day, Mr. Caldwell told the townspeople he was certain his wife's death had been planned beforehand, encouraged by higher British officers, and directed against him because of his involvement with the American army. He said the soldiers were afraid to show his wife any mercy because they well knew the will of their superiors. Caldwell was slain the following year at an American outpost on Elizabeth Town Point by an American sentry named Morgan. Many people believed that Morgan had been paid by the British to kill him. The sentry was convicted by a jury and hung at Westfield.

Mercy Otis Warren and Abigail Smith Adams never waivered in their dedication to the principles of freedom, to the rebellion against British oppression, despite the ravages and sufferings of war; yet both feared that ambitious, selfish politicians would tread on people's rights and liberties. Mercy wrote to Hannah

Winthrop in 1778 that "the capital friends of America in every colony look with indignation and disgust on a man, whose prime object is the applause of the multitude, and whose vanity leads him to sacrifice the best interests of his country at the shrine of flattery. . . . While Caesar meditated triumph over the citizens, and trampled on the liberties of Rome, he squandered gratuities and scattered largesses among the people. . . . Is not America tainted with all the vices that stained that ancient Republic? It is easy to give a long list of the absurd follies that are rampant among us; but where are the virtues that will make a balance sufficient to support a happy commonwealth. . . . The statesman is plotting for power, and the courtier practising dissimulation without checks, while the rapacious are growing rich by oppression, and fortune throwing her gifts into the lap of fools." From London in 1787 Abigail wrote to her sister, Elizabeth Shaw, "When I reflect upon the advantages which the people of America possess over the most polished of other nations, the ease with which property is obtained, the plenty which is so equally distributed, their personal liberty and security of life and property, I feel grateful to Heaven who marked out my lot in that happy land; at the same time I deprecate that restless spirit, and that baneful pride ambition, and thirst for power which will finally make us as wretched as our neighbours."

THE DIARIES
AND JOURNALS

Jemima Condict Harrison

✳ Nestled among valleys and mountains northwest of Newark, New Jersey, in the eighteenth century were rustic settlements of the Mountain Society. River streams, disturbed only by darting fish and fallen leaves, were unpolluted; the air, nightly carpeted with a mass of clear stars, was clean and fresh; the landscape, splashed with clusters of purple-white apple blossoms, was heavily forested. One-and-a-half-story homes, barns, and shops were made of oak cut from the woods and red sandstone quarried from the mountains. Sharply pitched roofs kept snow and rainwater from accumulating and rotting the shingles. Winding through the countryside were narrow dirt roads, icy in the winter, muddy and easily rutted in the spring and fall. People on horseback, farmers with wagons, and visitors in fancy carriages rode through the main thoroughfare. "On a knoll in the midst of the travelled road, which on either side retired like the parting Jordan making way for the Ark," was the two-story meeting house—the Mountain Society church, where Jemima Condict's father occasionally preached and her grandfathers managed church affairs. An aunt and uncle, too poor to own horses or a carriage, rode to church in an ox cart, and hid their poverty by tying their cattle to a tree at the village outskirts, before walking to services. People from far off packed their lunches and ate them in the building's milk room.

The mountain people's livelihood depended upon the area's natural resources. Men, women, and flocks of children were paid to pick and sort apples for local cider mills and distilleries. Apple cider, apple whiskey, and apple brandy were sold to city wholesalers, countryside taverns, and anybody who bothered to knock on the front door. Saw mills sold oak to builders and coopers, who made air-tight barrels, tubs, kegs, and pipe staves without the use of nails. Farmers bought these containers for packing butter, cheese, and lard for commercial sale. New York merchants purchased pipe staves and kegs for shipment to the West Indies where they were used for construction and rum. Speckled over the countryside were sheep herds, their wool sold to cloth producers. Farmers sold food products; tan yards made leather, and local stores made shoes.

These simple, earthy people were acclimated to harsh winters. Homes were heated by a large fireplace in the living room, a room that also served as the kitchen. In the late afternoon one's horse dragged a large log to the door. Placed in the rear of the fireplace and cradled in embers, the log kept the house reasonably warm during the night. An iron crane hung in the fireplace supported a large kettle of hot water and cooking pots. The smell of bread, biscuits, and pies permeated the room during daylight hours, while they were baking in a brick Dutch oven adjacent to the fireplace.

In 1678 John Condit, Jemima's Welsh great-great-grandfather, emigrated to Newark from England, along with his son Peter, who married Mary Harrison and settled in the Newark mountains. Their son, Samuel Condit (Jemima's grandfather), was born in 1696. While in his twenties Samuel bought three-hundred acres of land from the Indians—an area spanning both sides of the Second Mountain. He later gave each of his children, including Jemima's father, Daniel, fifty acres and a house. Daniel, a farmer and preacher, married Ruth Harrison, a distant cousin. Jemima, the third of eight children, was born August 24, 1755. Much of her youth was spent working the fields of her parents' farm and helping in the house, though she managed to spend hours struggling over textbooks at a small schoolhouse east of the mountains, where emphasis was placed upon the Bible and deportment. Despite pressures made upon her to conform, Jemima retained an individualistic, impulsive nature, and a sensitive compassion toward others.

Large numbers of the mountain people perished from epidemics of dysentery, smallpox, and throat distemper between 1773 and 1777. For many years Dr. Matthias Pierson (physician, surgeon, and dentist) had been the only doctor available for many miles around; but in the mid-1770s Pierson acquired a young colleague, Dr. John Condit, one of Jemima's cousins who became a United States Senator after the Revolution. Many people's lives were cut short early in life; others lived very long lives:

Jemima's grandfather, Samuel Harrison, lived to be ninety-three; his sister, Eleanor, died when one-hundred; and his son, Samuel Harrison, Jr., lived to be ninety-two.

Inbreeding was prevalent among Newark mountain settlers during the seventeenth and eighteenth centuries. People often married relatives, though there was some concern over the marriage of first cousins. Jemima married a first cousin, Aaron Harrison—her mother's nephew. Nor was it unusual for members of a family, or members of related families having the same last name, to spell the family name differently. Jemima's parents spelled their last name Condit; Jemima used Condict, as did other relatives.

As a result of British and American hostilities at Lexington and Concord, Massachusetts, in April 1775, the New Jersey Provincial Congress provided for a colony militia. All male inhabitants between the ages of sixteen and fifty, capable of bearing arms, were formed into companies. A few of the many Newark mountain men who joined the militia, later joined the Continental Army. Responding to Congress's call were many of Jemima's relatives: Daniel, father, private in both the militia and Continental "Jersey Line"; David Condit, uncle, lieutenant colonel in the Continental "Jersey Line"; John Condit, cousin, militia surgeon; Aaron Harrison, husband, militia private; Nathaniel Condict, cousin, militia private; Samuel Condit, brother, militia private; Jonathan Condict, uncle, militia captain. Jemima frequently rode horseback to the training ground, where she watched men armed with muskets, rifles, tomahawks, and pitchforks, and attired in a variety of farm clothes, awkwardly attempt to be part of the military. After breaking ranks, these militiamen gathered at Samuel Munn's tavern to read the latest war news and training schedules, and carouse over whiskey and ale.

In November 1776 General Washington's army of about 3,500 men was forced to retreat southward from New York. Crossing the Passaic River over the Aquackinack Bridge, his troops marched over sticky river marshes until they reached Newark. The bedraggled, badly equipped men camped outside the town, before continuing their retreat. Ten thousand British troops seized Newark only hours after the American soldiers had packed their gear, fleeing in a southwestwardly direction. A contingent trudged through the mountain settlement, swinging south at the Mountain Society's burying ground. British soldiers in pursuit encamped for the night among the tombstones, pressing against the sandstone slabs to shield themselves from a biting winter wind. Later in the war the British used this cemetery to set up an artillery battery, firing cannons at Rebels hidden on the First Mountain. The Mountain Society manned a series of signal stations along the crest, keeping a sharp watch over British troop movement.

In September 1777 Jemima Condict wrote in her diary of a skirmish at Wardgesson (now Watsessing) about four miles from her home. Three British detachments on a foraging expedition ferried across to Elizabeth Town from New York, marching through Newark to the Second River region. At Wardgesson they were battered by the New Jersey militia: eight Britishers were killed, nineteen wounded, ten missing, and five were captured. Those who escaped took four hundred sheep, horses, oxen, and cows.

Although the mountain region was a hotbed of anti-British intrigue, many inhabitants remained loyal to the Crown. Patriots referred, derisively, to a cluster of Loyalist homes as "Tory Corner." Assaults were not uncommon, particularly at the church, where both factions attended services. Jedediah Chapman, pastor, boldly defended the Revolution from the pulpit, though he scurried up the mountain each time word reached him that he was about to be seized and given to the British.✻

Wednesday, August 24, 1774: This day I am entering another year. I hope I may live and spend it better than I did the last, or any that is past. There seems to be a great alteration among the young people this year. Some that was before bad enough is now, I hope, become new creatures. What! Am I still going on in sin, growing worse, instead of better. What reason have I to be ashamed! *Saturday, October 1*: It seems we have troublesome times a coming, for there is great disturbance abroad in the earth and they say it is tea that caused it. So then if they will quarrel about such a trifling thing as that, what must we expect but war. I think or at least fear it will be so.

This day is Tuesday, and I moping all day. I suppose you'll say I am lazy, but let that be as it will. I have just now received a letter, and who should it be from but my old friend Ruth Williams from Smoaking. I hear some of our old neighbours is a coming down. Ah good! Lackaday! Here they come. I was so glad to see them that I felt all fool. I knew not what to say. They say they left our cousins all well, which is very good news. But I hope to hear more about them, for they will tarry three weeks before they go back. So I will quit and lay my pen aside for tonight.

Monday: I went to Samuel Condit's and worked perditiously hard all day, for they had roast meat and baked puddins, but we got little of it! But however, I come off and got home about sunset, and took to my bed. Was glad when I got there, for upon my word, which you may believe at this present juncture, I was tired enough. But stop, I've said enough.

Tuesday: Well, how is it with you my friends? I think I feel somewhat stiff in the joints. But I hope to have some respect, for today there is going to be a meeting at our house. Well, the meeting is over, and these was the words of the text: "Ye who believe in God believe also in me." Oh I think this is a troublesome world, for I a poor miserable wicked creature find but little comfort. 'Tis because my mind is taken up in vanity, and I am a discontented mortal. I am so indeed.

Friday, October 14: Went to see my cousin Jemima Williams. She being not well and I don't think ever will be. Oh what a fine thing is health!

Sunday was sacrament and there was numbers took in to the full communion, mostly young people. Mr. Chapman preached on that day from these: "Then said Jesus to them 'Yet a little while am I with you. Then I go unto him that sent me.' " John, 7th chapter, 33rd verse.

Sunday night: Just now received a letter and having perused it found it came from my cousin W. Condit. I wrote an answer and then retired to bed, bidding myself goodnight. Monday is come and the Lord in his goodness has spared me to see it. I being all the first part of this week very much toxicated in my mind about that affair, for I don't know what to do.

But boast not mistaken swain of thy art,
To please my partial eyes.
The charms that have subdued my heart,
Another may despise.

Thursday: Spent the whole afternoon with my friends that came from West Branch. I heard them tell so much about it that I long to see it. They been at me to go up with them and stay there this winter. I told them if it was but a day's journey I would go; but I could not bear the thought of going so far from my father's house. They told me there was young men plenty there for me; but I thought I was in no hurry for a husband at present. And if I was I thought it was too far to go upon uncertainties. So I concluded to stay where I was. I believe I shan't repent it. A husband or not, for I am best off in this spot. But they are going. I must now take my leave of them and I don't know but for the last time. So I wished them well. But they said that want enough, I must write to them. I promised I would, and after having taken our leaves of each other, we parted. But I believe they felt pretty heavyhearted. But they are gone. So I will leave them.

Thursday: I had some discourse with Mr. Chandler. He asked me why I did not marry. I told him I want in no hurry. "Well," said he, "I wish I was to marry you." I told him he would soon wish himself unmarried again. "Why so?" "Because," says I, "you will find that I am a cross, ill-contrived piece of stuff." I told him that I would advise all the men to remain as they was, for the women was bad, and the men so much worse that it was a wonder if they agreed. So I scared the poor fellow and he is gone.

Sunday: Mr. Chapman preached for these words: Timothy, 1st chapter and 12th verse. I spent this evening in writing, but the worst of it is, what I write is nonsense. If I did write what would be instructive or what would do me any good, or anyone else, 'twould be some sense in spending time and paper. But no wonder I can write nothing that's good, for I don't do anything that's good. I hope I may live to spend my time better and have better employment for my pen, for I must be scrabbling in leisure time, tho' I find but very little time now. Sometimes after our people is gone to bed I get my pen, for I don't know how to content myself without writing something.

Tuesday I went up to Swinefield, a number of us, to get eat. I can't say but a hundred men all passed us in the wilderness, which was something of a pleasing sight to behold. Went down the same night to watch with my poor old grandfather, and so by that means got sight at my, what shall I say, friend matter. I went to singing the next night and rid home with "Mr. Maturity." I spent the week and it's gone. I can't recall it for all the world.

New Year's Day, 1775: Went to meeting and Mr. Chapman preached from Romans, 14th chapter, 8th verse. We come home, tho' not without some difficulty, for it was very bad going and we'd a young horse. When I got home I found Mr. M.W. the tailor there at work. The next day I had to work with him. We had a great deal of discourse about old times, and concluded our chat with wishing each other well. He is a nice young man, worthy of good wishes; he said he hoped I would be suited but he never should be. I think his fortunes good, and I will tell you a reason why—because he wants to have such a creature as I. Friday and Saturday I felt very melancholy to think what life I had lived.

Wednesday, January 11: My dear father went to town, came home at night, and gave me a fine present. It was a long cloak, a present indeed. Such a one as I did not deserve. But you can't think how I felt when he gave it to me. I was both glad and sorry I had not been more deserving and that I had not been more thankful and behaved myself better in the service of so kind a father. I wanted my sister to have one.

Monday, February 5: Was my cousins inoculated. I am apt to think they will repent their undertaking before they done with it, for I am sure 'tis a great venture. But since they are gone, I wish them success. And I think they have had good luck so far, for they have all got home alive. But I fear cousin Nancy Dod won't get over it well.

Wednesday: Being full of thoughts about what to do, as I have this year past. Sometimes I think I will certainly bid him farewell forever. But I thought I would talk to my mother and see if I could be convinced one way or tother, for I want to hear the ground of what they have to say. So one day my mother says to me "Your father is going to get you a chest." I told her I should be glad of one but would not have her think 'twas because I thought to marry. "Why," says she, "Don't you never intend to marry?" I told her people said I was a going to have Mr._____[Aaron Harrison, her future husband] "But they tell me they don't think it is a right thing, and it is forbid. But can't none of them as I can find out tell me where 'tis forbid. So," says I, "what do you think of it mother?" She said she did not think it was right unless I thought it was myself. I asked her if she thought my thinking it was right would make it so. She said my thinking so would cause a contented easy mind. "Well," says I, "but that ain't telling what you think about it." She said she had heard his mother talk about it, and she [his mother] was against his coming here. Mother said, moreover, that she was apt to think I would live a dog's life amongst them. This made me think I would not have him. But I still insisted upon hearing what she had to say. At last she told me that she had thought a great deal about it and for her part could not see but that it was right. As far as its being forbid, she did not think there was such a place in the Bible. She said likewise that she did not see what ministers should marry them for, if 'twas forbid. So after this and much more being said, I turned it off with a laugh, and said "What a fool am I. I talk as if I was going to marry a cousin in good earnest, but I did not know as I had one that would have me. But if I hold my tongue and say nothing, others will have all the talk." They talk to me, but convince they don't. I could wish with all my heart I knew the right way and could be made to choose it; but if it be wrong, then what a fool was I while young to place my mind on such a one as a cousin. It's very true. It's oh poor me, what shall I do? Why, I tell you what a conclusion I made and I hope I may hold to it. That is to trust in Him who knows all things, for He knows what is best for me, what I ought to do, and what I ought not to do, and will, I hope, order things in mercy for me. Tuesday I went up to my sister Ogden's and there was a houseful of people. We had a great sing indeed, for the Horse Neckites and the Newarkites were both assembled together. There was the newly married couple, and you may be sure they cut a fine figure, for she is a bouncer Joan and he a little cross snipper snapper snipe. They tell me he cried when he was married; at which I don't a bit wonder, for I think twas enough to make the poor fellow bellow, if he had his wits about him, for I am sure she can beat him. I don't know though. He is like roast pork, more strengthening. His wife said that he was less so than she was. But, then, he was more strengthening. So I will leave them to make the best of their bargain. I don't know as anyone has lost, for she had a doleful, long nose and he a conceived chin like myself.

Monday morning I resolved, if possible, to have my tooth out. So down I went to Dr. Condit and he got his cold iron ready. My tooth was easy, and I told him I dare not venture. I now had hurt; but I could not make him promise he would not, tho' I thought he began to pity me a little, and that was what I did it for. For it's true I believe I want so afraid as I pretended to be. I was in hopes he'd draw it easier for it and I don't know but he did, for he was mighty careful. But when he put his contrivances in my mouth I pulled them out again. At last they fell a laughing at me, and said if I do not have a tooth drawn I never would be fit to marry. I told them I never reckoned to be if twas as bad as to have a tooth drawn. At which they all fell a laughing, for I was a fool for them. But it want long before I could put my tooth in my pocket and laugh with the best of them. So I come home, but I got such a cold in my face that it ached all the rest of the week. When I got home I went to bed for I had slept but little for some time before. I had not been there long before I was surprised with an unusual pounding at the door. At last they opened the door and in come an old woman dressed in rags, an object of pity to behold, and a little dog following after. Oh, she told a sorrowful story enough, if twas true. I can't say but it was; but it looked a little strange to me how she would travel so far in a day as she said she had. But she had her dog for a bedfellow. In the morning we got breakfast, and don't you think she took as good care of her dog as she did of herself. I could not but laugh to see her, for she would chew the victuals, and then he must eat it out of her hand. What a nasty piece of stuff she is, sure enough. But she is going and I can't help but pity her. What reason have I to give thanks unto the Lord that I am thus provided for, when I don't deserve the breath I draw.

Yesterday Mr. [Aaron Harrison] come again and wanted me to go with him to Elizabeth Town. I made several excuses, for I was resolved not to go. But he would hear to none of them. At last I told him mother would not let me go. So I winked to her to say no, for she was present. So she told him it would not do. Then he fell to coaxing her, but she said "No, I won't let her go." So he went off, gentleman-like, but I thought when he got upon his little nag that he did not want a button behind him, for he almost covered him himself. But he has gone off. I believe he's mad with all, but I can't help it now.

Sunday: Mr. Chapman preached from Romans, 6th chapter, 23rd verse. I stayed at my uncle's that night, and on Monday my cousin Jeams Harrison and I went to see our old grandfather. I found that old saying to be true: "Once a man and twice a child." for he is very childish, and tho' he is the highness of a man, yet he is a child. We stand there a spell and then went back again. I was a little put to it to get away from poor old grandfather. I pitied him, for I thought he would think he was old and despised. He says to me "You are tired a staying with me already." I made some excuse so that I got away, and don't expect ever to spend so much time with him again, for the old must die. Yet I may die before him for ought I know.

Monday at night I did not know how to contrive it to get away without they knowing. How at last I schemed it; for I had told them all day that if Jeams Harrison was down I would go up with him. So it answered very well for they knew no better. But I got safe home, and glad of it too, for I like home the best, and 'tis a great mercy that I have such a home to go to. The old saying is "Home, is home, let it be ever so homely." I think so, though I count not my father's a homely home. Neither would I have you think so my friends.

Monday, which was called training day. I rode with my dear father down to see them train, there being several companies met together. I thought it would be a mournful sight to see if they had been fighting in earnest. How soon they will be called forth to the field of war we cannot tell, for by what we can hear, the quarrels are not like to be made up without bloodshed. I have just now heard said that all hopes of conciliation between Britain and her colonies are at an end, for both the king and his Parliament have announced our destruction. Fleet and armies are preparing with utmost diligence for that purpose.

April 23: As every day brings new troubles, so this day brings news that yesterday, very early in the morning, they began to fight at Boston. The regulars [British troops] we hear, shot first. They killed thirty of our men. A hundred and fifty of the regulars were killed.

Sunday, April, the last day: Did Mr. Bradford preach, and in the afternoon preached from these words: "He that is unjust shall be so still, and he that is rightous shall be rightous still, and he that is holy shall be holy still." What fine privileges we now have; but I am one of them that makes not a good use of what I hear. Yes, I am one of that foolish sort whose folly will not depart from him; or that do not depart from my foolishness.

Monday, May 1: This day I think is a day of mourning. We have word come that the fleet is coming into New York. Also, today the men of our town is to have a general meeting to conclude upon measures which may be most proper to be taken. They have chose men to act for them. I hope the Lord will give them wisdom to conduct wisely and prudently in all matters.

Sunday, May 7: Being not very well, stayed home in the forenoon and got partly ready to go in the afternoon, but through pride stayed at home, thinking I did not look well enough. Besides, I thought if I went I would not go to hear. I had not a heart to receive. So, instead of going and praying to God for a heart, I gave way to my wicked thoughts and spent the day in idleness. I cannot tell what was the matter. All that afternoon I felt very uneasy in my mind. I thought I never deserved to have another opportunity to go, because I did not improve them was given me. Then again, thinks I, what is all this, for how many Sabbaths have I stayed at home when I have been better in health than I am now. To my shame I have been a great many, and never attended to the word, but trifled the day away in sin and folly. I went out with no better end than to serve the devil. I had no such uneasiness of mind neither, but then again it came into my head that I had never spent one day aright, never yet done anything for the glory of God, nor for my poor never dying soul. My whole life time had been taken up in vanity.

Monday, July: I had considerable of the fever all day, and continued so all the week. Me thinks I am in a very poor way. I am ready to think sometimes I shall never be well again, and I don't deserve to have another minute's health while I live. Sunday I felt somewhat better. I went to meeting. Mr. Chapman preached from Psalms, 62, 8th and 9th verses: "Trust in Him at all times. Pour out our hearts before Him. God is a refuge for us."

Sunday, August 20: Did Mr. Chapman begin his journey to New England to take a visit among his friends and relations.

September 4: There was an Indian preached at our meeting house.

September 28: Was Thomas Crane very suddenly and in an awful manner taken out of time and into eternity. He was plowing in the field. His father was cutting a tree that was turned up by the roots. That instant he had cut it off his son passed by. The root flew back and took him under, which killed him immediately. He was a young and lively youth and 'tis hoped he served the Lord in truth. This is a warning to small and great to prepare for a future state.

October 4: Was I taken sick, tho' not bad. But through the mercy of God I am so that I can sit up some part of the time now. How soon I shall be deprived of that privilege I cannot say, for surely it is too great a mercy for such a wreck as I to enjoy, unless I spend my time better than I do. During the time of my being sick the Lord was dealing mercifully with me. My affliction was lighter than the least of my sins deserved. Tho' I had long abused and made a mockery of the preaching of the word, yet the Lord was pleased to show me his goodness there also.

Sunday, December 20: The Lord was pleased in mercy to restore health to me, so I think I am as well as before. He also shows great mercy as to grant me another opportunity to go to His house to hear the preaching of the gospel. But oh how forgetful of His mercies, how unthankful under so great favours! Not withstanding my great sins, the Lord is pleased to grant mercy. He is giving me space to repent. He in mercy has spared me another week, and tho' I sinned away the last Sabbath I am brought to see the light of another. Sing praises to the Almighty!

July 23, 1776: Did that distressing disorder, the bloody flux, begin to rage in this neighborhood. Rubin Harrison lost his son Adonijah on the 29th. He was the second he had lost of that name.

August 6: Then died John Ogden's child, and was buried on the 8th day.

August 16: Then died Jered Freeman. He was taken sick at New York among the soldiers, was brought home, and died soon after. Isaac Freeman also lost two of his children with the same distemper. John Freeman lost his child August the 17th.

August 25: Died Sam Smith's child.

August 29: Amos Burrel lost his child. The same month Sam Crane lost one with fits.

August 30: Then died Timothy Crane with the same distemper. The same day died Joseph Peirson's child.

September 2: Did Thomas Freeman's daughter die.

September 3: Did John Freeman depart this life.

September 4: Jonathan Smith lost his child. The same night Jonathan Condict's daughter died.

Both few and evil are the days of man,
They quick away do pass.
Just like a hand's breath on a span,
All flesh is like the grass.

September 8: Did Jabez Williams' child die. Abel Freeman also has lost one of his children, and the widow of John Freeman has lost one of hers. John Dod lost one about the same time.

September: We hear news from our army at Montague, and several of them we hear is dead. Since their departure, Benjamin Canfield, Steven Morris, and David Lewis died with the camp disorder. William Acorn, we hear, was killed by the Indians. Sen Jabez Freeman, the son of the late deceased John Freeman, is dead. Also, Sias Heady died up there with the sick men. When we are at home we think ourselves secure.

But at home or abroad we are never sure
When or what our end will be.
Thus in viewing others we daily may see.

Tuesday, September 9: Then died another of Jonathan Condict's daughters. Enock Beach has lost three of his children in about a fortnight.

Wednesday, September 10: Then died Joseph Williams' wife. She has been many years confined with the rheumatism.

Sunday, September 15: Then departed this life grandfather Harrison, aged ninety-three years.

Tho' he is old, age will not save
Him, nor others, from the grave.

Sunday, the 15th day died Jabes Regs. Sunday, the 22nd they buried his third child, two of them; a son and daughter was in their prime cut off in the full bloom of youth. Tuesday the 24th then died his wife also. The rest of the family is left, tho' of so many they are bereft. Joseph Freeman also lost two of his children with the same disorder. Thaniel Taylor lost one about the same time. Isaac Smith lost one of his children. Jonathan Tomkins lost his wife the same month with the consumption.

September 21: Then died Ruth Williams' child.

September 27: Jean Jones lost his child. Died Thomas Stage.

September 28: Died Moses Crane.

September 29: Departed this life John Spear.

October 4: Amos Dod lost his child.

October 5: Amos Tomkins lost his child. Then died Moses Freeman.

October 9: Then died Martha Harrison. Thomas Codamas has lost one child. Benjamin Baldwin lost one of his children.

October 10: Jonah Ward lost his child.

October 13: Then died Elisabeth Crane.

October 14: Then died Eleanor Baldwin. Did Eli Williams' child die.

October 21: Died Sam Ward's child, and soon after lost another.

October 25: Then died Amos Harrison's child.

The dear delights we here enjoy,
And fondly call our own,

Are but fond pleasures lent us now,
To be repaid anon.

November: Then Samuel Condict, my father's brother, died, and in December died another Perry.

Begins the year 1777: It is now the 2nd of January and as I have not had time to write any this winter I thought this is a proper season—as I am up with my sick sister—to take pen in hand and recollect a little of what is past. I intended to keep a strict account of the times; but as providence has ordered matters, I have my hands full by night and day, so that I shall now only just tell you in broken language what troubles we have had in our family since I saw you last. My dear mother was taken sick the 25th of October and was so bad we did not much expect her recovery. It was then I thought I would be deprived of that great blessing I had so long undeservedly enjoyed. My youngest brother also lay very bad, so that we did not expect him to live for many days. Dear father was taken sick quick after. But through the goodness of God they soon recovered, so that we were in hopes of having health in our habitation. But at Christmas my sister was taken sick and was extremely bad. She had a strange disorder. It lay in her throat and stomach. Sometimes she would be so choked that we never expected she would come to again. Another of my brothers likewise, at the same time, was very sick. But it has pleased a holy God to show us His power in raising them to a state of health.

January 20: Then died Jane Soverel. Well, my dear friends. What a time is this! A sickly time and a very dying time, the people fleeing before their enemies.

January 29: Samuel Ogden, my brother-in-law, was taken sick at Newark and was brought up to his uncle Abram's where, after a short tho' tedious fit of sickness, died, his mother being there to tend him. She was taken sick the next night and died the week following. So they both died from home, yet not from friends. And so we all must go
When God His summons sends.

February 10: Died grandmother Condict.

April 10: Died David Condict, my father's brother. The next day died Caleb Condit with the smallpox. Caleb Hatfield's wife died the same month.

June 25: Died Jeams Harrison with the smallpox.

July 10: Died grandfather Condict.

September 12: On Friday there was an alarm. Our militia was called. The regulars [British] came over into Elizabeth Town where they had a brush with a small party of our people, then marched quietly up to Newark and took all the cattle they could. There was five of the militia at Newark. They killed Samuel Crane and took Zadock, Allen Leady and Samuel Freeman prisoners. One out of the five ran and escaped. They went directly up to Second River, and on Saturday morning marched up towards Wardgesson. Our people attacked them there, where they had a smart scrimmage. Some of our people got wounded there; but I do not learn that any was killed. There was several killed of the regulars, but the number is yet uncertain.

September: Died Captain Pierson's child.

September 25: Died Nathanial Ogden.

October 2: Did Raftus Pierson's child die.

October 4: Died the widow Brown.

October: Did Amos Tomkin's child die.

November 16: Stayed at home. I suppose it want right. Monday, well. My cousin John is at work at our house, and he can make great shoes, tho' he be a little man. Tuesday we heard that Ruth William's oldest child was taken with the sorethroat distemper and is dead. Died the 10th of November, which ought to put us in mind of our mortality.

Friday: It is most terrible cold and I am forced to be in the shop, for I have to weave. I can't get along with it. Sunday I felt not very well, so I stayed at home in the forenoon. In the afternoon Mr. Chapman preached from Corinthians, 1st chapter, 21st verse. It pleased God by the foolishness of preaching to save them that believe. Monday I still felt very little work done by me that day, I think. Tuesday my cousin (B. Harrison) came here to see me. She was greatly altered from what she was, but I, a poor miserable creature, could talk but little with her. She begged to talk with me. I did not know what to say. How do you think I felt? Why, I can't tell, for I thought I would talk with her, and talk I suppose as good as she. But I am sure I should have been a hypercritic indeed, if I had. Well, it's almost night. Doctor Condit come here and so I did not go to meeting. He tells me that one of our cousins has fell out of the chair, and that Nefer Carpenter and wife just died. I think I never heard the like of daily hearing of one and others being hurt or killed!

Now begins a new year, the year 1778: New Years Day my sister and I went down to see our cousin, Mary Harrison, who is sick. From there went to meeting. Chitchats and, after leave of them, betook myself to rest, intending tomorrow to get out my wear. So I went to work and finished it, then went to bed. The next day I went to a frolic at Mr. Thomas Williams' and of all the frolics that ever I was at I never was at such a one; for there was old folks and children by numbers and, upon my word, they carried on so that I left them and come off home. But being very much pleased with their contrivance I thought it not much harm to make a song about them. So one day to please the devil I went to work and made one, but I did it in such a hurry that it did not go very well. However, it answered the end. But I don't think I did right, as it was not doing as I would be done by. However, it is done and I can't help it.

The 7th day of April: I went up to see my sister, she being not very well. So I stayed there 'til next morning, and then she came home with me. And now I think to stay at home, for the measles is about and I intend to keep clear of it as long as I can. One of my cousins (Jemima Williams) is very sick and I fear never will get well. She was to get married to one of my uncles (Samuel Condit) that week he was taken. I hope she will soon recover, so I will leave her to trust in providence. The 16th day of this month was my cousin Jonathan Condit taken sick with the measles. He held poorly, but it was not thought he was dangerous 'til the 22nd day and then he was took bad and the 23rd day of the month he was struck with the nervous fever. Oh, may I be anobled to prepare for such a time. Lord help me!

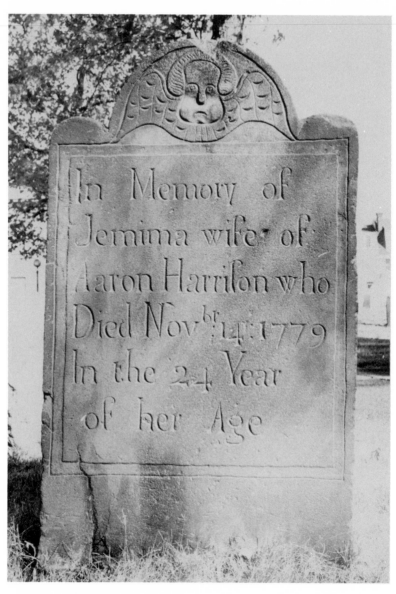

Jemima Condict Harrison lies buried in the old burying ground, beside the First Presbyterian Church in Orange, New Jersey, near the road where, on a windy day, "the dirt flew and there was chairs and waggons a rattling."

Summer: When I was but a child my dear parents sent me to school, to Mrs. D.W. where there was some children that I now think was none of the cleverest. I don't write this to excuse myself, for I know I wasn't sent to learn of them; but, oh how ready I was to idle!

[Jemima Condict married Aaron Harrison early in 1779.]

[*Later in 1779*]: Dear and loving parents. I am about to leave you and do beg your forgiveness for all I have done amiss while in your service. I confess I have been a grief to you all my days, instead of a comfort, which is now a grief to me. I am going where I shall have no father to pray night and morning. I have lived this four and twenty years under great mercies, but I have made so poor use of them, it is just I should be deprived of them all. Yet, dear father, I beseech of you not to forget me. Pray for me, oh pray for me daily. So after once more asking your forgiveness and blessing, I remain yours. My dearest and loving sister, you and I have lived many years together, but now we must part, which is a hard thing to me. Oh, how can I? My dear sister, I have not been such a sister to you as I ought to a been, yet. Can't you forgive me? Yes, pray, forgive all, and don't forget me. We have spent many pleasant hours together and I hope we shall as many more, better than any we have before. So farewell my dear sister, farewell.

* Jemima Condict Harrison died November 14th at the age of twenty-four, shortly after giving birth to an infant son, Ira. She was buried in the Mountain Society's burying ground, near the road she had often used while riding horseback. Her husband, Aaron, later married Phebe Crane and named one of their four children Jemima; her son, Ira, never reached the age of twelve. Jemima's grave has withstood two centuries of snow blizzards and rainstorms, and has been spared the ravages of excavation— the site was placed under the care of the First Presbyterian Church in Orange. Perhaps it will never be known why she was buried in a secluded area, distant from clusters of Condit, Condict, and Harrison graves.*

Martha I'ans Walker

✳ Sometime in the late 1740s or early 1750s an English Indiaman—a three-masted merchant sailing vessel, armed with cannon and well-built to withstand dangerous voyages to the Far East—came up into the wind in the Boston harbor. After the ship's fore and aft sails had been furled, and dock workers had made cable secure, three young English sisters disembarked and took their first carriage ride through Boston. The ship's captain, Robert Parker, accompanied his stepsisters.

Boston was a town the elderly Bostonian Samuel Sewall viewed with alarm "Affectation and use of gayety, costly buildings, stilled and other strong liquors . . . rageth with great impetuosity," all of which, Sewall believed, bred "sensuality, effeminateness, unrighteousness, and confusion." Prostitutes, many of them mariners' wives, poised near the wharves like mute dolls propped behind glass cabinets. As the carriage clattered over cobblestones Martha I'ans and her sisters saw flashes of brick stores, with windows displaying costly "women's shoes and pattoons, fine macklins and English laces and edgings, mantua silks, paderina and fine cambricks." Leaving the bumpy cobblestones behind at the northern outskirts of Boston, the travelers passed over uneven dirt roads, until they reached Nahant, about twelve or fourteen miles northeast of Boston.

Little is known of Martha I'ans' childhood in England. Her mother had thrice married: to a Parker, an I'ans, and a third person—probably an army officer, for one of her sisters remembered having eaten dinner while listening to the tunes of an army band.

A few years after her arrival in America, Martha married Thomas Walker, a Boston trade merchant who had emigrated from England in 1752. She bore two sons, James and Thomas, before the family moved to Montreal, Canada, in 1763. Jane Walker was born the following year. Their prosperity in Canada

"An East View of Montreal, in Canada," c. 1768, *engraved by Pierre Canot after a drawing by Thomas Patten. Armed British ships, like the eighteen-gun vessels in the foreground, must have bristled Thomas Walker, who resisted British rejection of French-Canadian self-determination.*

enabled the family not only to own an attractive house and stores in Montreal, but a farm and potash factory in l'Assomption as well.

Thomas Walker was appointed a justice of the peace in 1764, when hostility existed in Quebec Province between the Canadian army and French-Canadians seeking political power. The latter were particularly enraged over enforced measures requiring citizens of the province to lodge troops in their own residences where ever there was a shortage of barracks. Several of Montreal's magistrates, including Thomas Walker, protested that this was an illegal imposition. Tempers flared when Captain Fraser, officer in charge of lodgings, pressured a landlord into ejecting a magistrate from his rented rooms in order to replace him with Captain Payne of the 28th Regiment. Walker instigated Payne's eviction, and the officer was removed. Fraser retaliated by complaining bitterly to the governor-general of Quebec, General Murray.

Shortly afterwards, Walker's household was violently attacked by thugs. Walker accused the military, and accumulated enough evidence to have a trial held in February and March of 1767. Daniel Disney—captain of a company in His Majesty's 44th Regiment of Foot, and town major of the garrison of Montreal—was indicted on two charges: "one for burglary and felony in breaking and entering Thomas Walker's house at Montreal, on the night of the 6th day of December, in the year 1764, with the intention to murder the said Thomas Walker; the other for feloniously and of malice of forethought cutting off the right ear of the said Thomas Walker, with intention thereby to disfigure him." The presiding judge, Chief Justice William Hey, reported to authorities in London after the trial that Walker had testified the following:

On the 6th of December 1764 at half past 8 in the evening Mrs. Walker looked at her watch and said it was time to go to supper—that the cloth was laid in the hall but that he not having been very well that day she was persuading him to stay and eat his supper in the parlour—that they staid about 10 or 15 minutes in this and other conversation, and then went into the hall to supper—that he sat with his back to, and very near the street door—that he had been but a very little time at supper when he heard a rattling of the latch of the door as of persons wanting to come in in a hurry—that Mrs. Walker said "Entré," upon which the outward door was thrown open, and thro' the sash of the inward one he saw a great number of people disguised in various ways, some with little round hats, others with their faces blacked, and others with crapes over their faces—that he had time to take so much notice of them as to distinguish two persons whose faces, tho' blacked, he was sure he should know again if he saw them—that they burst the inward door and several of them got round to the doors leading to the parlour as designing to cut off his retreat into that room—that upon turning his head towards that room he received from behind a blow which he believes was given with a broad sword,—that he passed thro' them into the parlour, receiving many wounds in the passage, got to the further end of the room near the chamber door before which stood 2 men who had got before him and prevented his entrance into it—that these 2, with others who had followed him, striking and wounding all the way, set upon him and forced him from the door into the window, the curtains of which entangled itself round him and he believes prevented their dashing his brains out against the wall: that he received in the whole no less than 52 contusions, besides many cuts with sharp instruments—that he believes during the struggle in the window he was for some little time deprived of his senses, sunk in stupefaction or stunned by some blow, till he heard a voice from the opposite corner of the room say "Let me come at him. I will dispatch the villian with my sword"; that this roused him and determined him to sell his life as dear as he could—that 'till this time, tho' he had apprehended and experienced a great deal of violence, he did not think they had intended to murder him —that he broke from the persons who held him in the window and advanced toward the part of the room from whence the voice came, where two persons were standing with their swords in a position ready for making a thrust at him. But he does not know whether they actually made a pass at him or not, that he put by one of their swords with his left hand, upon which they both retreated into the corner—that his eyes at this time being full of blood, he was not capable of distinguishing the features of a face with great accuracy, but from the size and figure and gesture of the person whose sword he parried, and from whom he believes the words came, he thought it to be Major Disney—that several of them then seized him at once (one of them in particular taking him up under the right thigh) and carried him towards the fireplace with the intention, as he believed, to throw him upon the fire—that the marks of his bloody fingers were upon the jamb of the chimney—that he turned himself from the fire with great violence, and in turning received a blow on his head which the surgeons say must have been given with a tomahawk—which felled him to the ground, and after that a blow upon his loins, which he feels to this day—that one of them sat or kneeled by him (he lying at his length upon the floor), endeavoring to cut his throat—that he resisted it by inclining his head upon his shoulders, and putting his hand to the place, a finger of which was cut to the bone—that it was a fortnight before he knew that he had lost his ear, his opinion all along having been that in that operation they intended to cut his throat, and believed they had done it —that one of them said "The villian is dead," another, "Damn him. We have done for him," and a third uttered some words, but his senses then failed him, and he does not recollect what they were.

Charles Ainslie, a Canadian government official, had written Governor Murray a week after the assault that Walker had been so badly beaten that he was "as black as a hat, and so swelled up that you barely can know the remains of his face or the color of his skin."

When the assailants broke into her home, Martha Walker fled through the kitchen and back yard shrieking "This is murder!" before hiding in a cowhouse. Justice Hey recorded that Martha Walker testified at the trial "that she saw Major Disney among a group of figures very distinctly with a crape over his face and dressed in a Canadian cotton night gown." Major Disney had several witnesses testify that he was elsewhere at the time of the attack. After hearing their testimony, the jury left the courtroom and returned in an hour with the verdict of not guilty.

In 1767 Walker led a radical movement for the establishment of an elective assembly composed of French-Canadians, an assembly that would allow the people of Quebec Province a strong voice in the solution of their problems. This was rejected by the Canadian government. Walker continued to organize and train French-Canadian and Anglo-American rebels. In 1775 Walker, passionately aroused by the explosive conflict of the American colonists in Massachusetts against the British, furtively organized a strong rebel group. Guy Carlton, Canada's governor, made no attempt to have these men arrested.

Meanwhile, members of the Continental Congress in Philadelphia, apprehensive of a British invasion from Canada, sent American agents to Quebec on a clandestine mission to organize an effective network of American, Anglo-American, and French-Canadian secret agents. After receiving the men from Philadelphia in his home, Walker used every means to incite a revolt among the people of Montreal and surrounding towns against the Canadian government. Many of those he spoke to, however, refused to fight for Americans, though they were willing to give provisions to an American army should it pass through.

Walker exchanged letters with General Benedict Arnold and Ethan Allen, using Indians from the village of Sault-Saint-Louis as messengers. Both Walker and Allen urged the Caughnawaga Indians not to fight for the English King, to kill his soldiers instead. The Indians were promised rum in payment. On the 24th of May, Arnold sent a letter to Walker from Crown Point, New York, asking him to send, periodically, an account of the number of British troops in the Montreal area, their movements, and if they were joined by any Canadians or Indians. "If any number of the former," wrote Arnold, "you may assure them they will soon see an army of Bunker's Hill men in the heart of the country. I have here and at Ticonderoga about one-thousand men, and expect to be joined in a few days by two-thousand more." Rashly, Walker spread the news in towns and villages that an American force was on its way, that American soldiers would harm no one who kept silent, but those who would fight them would suffer for it. In July, Walker promised arms, powder, and money to French-Canadians; his outspokenness and blatancy irritated Martha Walker, and she warned him that his behavior would do him great harm.

On July 27, 1775, the Continental Congress concluded that the time had arrived to invade Quebec. Carleton's army consisted of only about 800 men. John Brown, an officer under General Arnold, summoned Walker to Chambly, where a secret meeting was held. On the 17th of September the American general, Richard Montgomery, with a force of about one thousand, began his attack upon St. Johns. Late in September, Ethan Allen and John Brown were sent to Canada to enlist the support of the Canadians, including Indians. Violating orders, the two men split forces and attempted to sack Montreal. However, Saint-Luc de La Corne's men—about thirty British regulars leading a force of over three-hundred Canadians—smashed through Allen's group, forcing him to surrender. Allen later recorded in his journal that prior to his defeat he had "dispatched two messengers, one to Laprarie to Col. Brown, and the other to l'Assomption, a French settlement, to Mr. Walker who was in our interest, requesting their speedy assistance, giving them, at the same time, to understand my critical situation. In the meantime, sundry persons came to my guards, pretending to be friends, but were by them taken prisoners and brought to me. These I ordered to confinement until their friendship could be further confirmed; for I was jealous they were spies, as they proved to be afterwards. One of the principal of them, making his escape, exposed the weakness of my party, which was the final cause of my misfortune; for I have been since informed that Mr. Walker, agreeably to my wishes, exerted himself, and had raised a considerable number of men for my assistance, which brought him into difficulty afterwards, but upon hearing of my misfortune, he disbanded them again."

Martha Walker's journal begins in May 1775, several months before General Montgomery's invasion of Quebec Province. The marble bust of King George III that she refers to was given by His Majesty to the people of Montreal, in recognition of their suffering during the great fire in the city May 18, 1765. One-hundred-and-eight houses were destroyed in this blaze, and two-hundred-and-fifteen families rendered homeless. The bust "graced" the Place d'Armes square where, each morning, Canadian soldiers took roll call.*

May, 1775: Morning and evening on the neck of the bust and hanging in the form of a rosary—at the end of which was suspended a label—were some potatoes cut and strung like beads, with the words "Voici le Pape de Canada ne le sous de l'Engleterre" [Behold the Pope of Canada and the English Sot], which occasioned great confusion, much ill blood, and many menaces from the officers and soldiers.

A drum was sent round the town, with offers of a reward for the discovery of the perpetrators. But notwithstanding this, the bust was the following night, or soon after, broken to pieces and thrown down a privy. Suspicion of Mr. Walker and his party ran high; happily for him, Dr. Beaumont of the 26th Regiment was his physician, and visited him every day, or the soldiery would have acted over again the tragedy of 1764.

As soon as Mr. Walker's health would permit, whilst he was still under a course of medicine, he went down to our farm at l'Assomption—distant about thirty miles from Montreal—both to recover his health and to withdraw from the clamour and confusion of the times, which rather increased rather than diminished. It was said by his enemies that Mr. Walker was gone to his farm as a more convenient and more private situation to carry a correspondance with the rebels. Before he went down to the farm, he conversed one day with a Monseigneur Rouville—who was soon after made a judge—something being said to Mr. Walker about its being the duty of all the King's subjects to obey their master; to which he replied: "An Englishman owns not the King for his master. The King is not my master, as I don't eat his bread. Were I an officer I should own him for my master and obey his commands as such. At present I am his subject only, and am ready to obey the laws." This conversation was immediately communicated to the governor [Sir Guy Carleton] and the person thanked, as we were told, for his zeal.

Soon after this, Lieutenant H_____n, then on half pay, called at our house and, as he sat in his carriage, handed me a letter which came from General Arnold. Not suspecting the contents were of consequence or knowing they had taken the fort [Ethan Allen took Fort Ticonderoga, New York, on May 10th] I opened it and found in it nearly these words (I write from memory): "I breakfasted here, and expect to see you and my friends at Montreal. Dated Ticonderoga."

This was put into my hands before many witnesses. After this my house was constantly watched. Reports were spread of letters being found upon savages [Indians] and others, directed to Mr. Walker from the rebels. The governor was heard frequently to say that there were persons who absented themselves from town whom it would better become, to come to town and set an example of loyalty to the Canadians by taking up arms; that no protection should screen a traitor—all of which was applied to Mr. Walker.

About this time (the summer of 1775) parties starting from the colonies were frequently seen about Lake Champlain and on the borders of Canada. In particular, a famous partizan, Capt. Baker, was frequently talked of. A scouting party of some, if not all savages, was sent out after him. They returned with a report that they had come up with and fired upon them; that they believed they had killed the chief [Baker]—they thought they saw him fall behind a tree. They, the Indians, dared not go ashore to see, for fear of an ambuscade, but said could the party be reinforced they would conduct them to the spot. They found the body of Capt. Baker, whose party had, as it appeared, retreated with the greatest precipitation after he fell, leaving him unburied, with all his papers in his pocket book. In it, it was said, were some for Mr. Walker. They brought the body in great triumph to St. Johns, where General Prescott and all the military force then was in garrison. Prescott gave it, as was then practiced, to the savages, who treated it too shockingly to be related. [The Indians severed Baker's head and sold it to British officers.]

About this time scalps were brought in every day. The savages passed frequently under my window with them bleeding; yelling as they passed, sometimes numbers of them would sit down on the steps before my door and under my windows, as if they were sent to terrify me. My acquaintances forsook me; dealers left our store; our business was entirely at a stand. Reports were industriously spread that parties, sometimes of savages, sometimes of Canadians, were sent to bring up Mr. Walker, dead or alive. Our servants were insulted by the soldiery; persons continually watched my motions.

A person whose name was Stanley, who, after having quitted the army had been our domestic (and was at the time I am speaking of on a small farm of ours, just without the town), came to ask after his master, and to tell the reports of the town and his apprehensions. He was, when he went out the door, seized by a man who looked like a gentleman, was carried to the main guard, and threatened to be hung up immediately if he did not divulge all he knew of his master's and my correspondance. They kept him there some time, reiterating their threatenings to hang him up if he did not discover all he knew, and, at last, dismissed him upon his promising never to come into our house again, or to go on any errand, or carry any billet for me.

All this time Mr. Walker was ignorant of what was passing at his own house in town; but he had flying reports that things did not go right. He sent a note by a country man who was his neighbor to request me to come down, to which I readily consented and wrote to him to come and meet me as usual half way on a particular day. But before the appointed day St. Johns was beseiged [November 3rd] or invested by General Montgomery. Confusion and animosity was increased. Many threats were thrown out against the supposed partizans of the rebels, particularly against Mr. Walker. I dared not write and was afraid to go lest the house should be rifled. I concluded it would be most expedient to send a message to Mr. Walker to acquaint him with the confused situation of affairs in general and particularly with my reasons for not meeting him, and to desire him to return back to the farm.

To do this the messenger must walk 15 miles [the mid point between Montreal and l'Assomption] for I sent him on foot that he might not raise any suspicion of his being gone out of town. But he was not half a mile out of town before he was stopped by the town mayor, Mr. Hughes, who followed him on horseback, carried him into the first barn they came to, and stript him from head to foot. Even the linings of his shoes were ripped up to search for letters which he was supposed to be carrying to his master. He was threatened, as the other person had been, with instant death if he did not disclose all he knew of his master's correspondance with the rebels. He urged his innocence in vain. In vain he told his errand; still they threatened him, and kept him confined.

Now my servants left me, upon being told that their master would certainly be hanged for treason and his fortune confiscated. They, of course, would lose their wages. Driven at last to desperation, I wrote a billet to General Carlton requesting to know the cause of the steps he was taking with our people, and what crime had been alledged against them. His answer was verbal, by an officer, to this effect: that the proceedings with my clerk and farmer were by his order; that I should be made acquainted with their crime and punishment in due time. Upon which I wrote a very submissive billet to his Excellency requesting I might be permitted to wait on him. He appointed an hour.

I went and requested, as above, to be made acquainted with his Excellency's motives for such extraordinary proceedings. He said that he had as yet done nothing that he should have done had he attended to the representations, and followed the advice, of many people; that there were many and heavy charges against Mr. Walker and, though he knew he had the protection of some great men, and had been particularly recommended to him, no protection should screen a traitor; that Mr. Walker ought to have set an example to the Canadians by taking up arms in defense of the country. That, I observed, ought not yet to be imputed to him. I was persuaded he was a loyal subject. I presumed to ask what else he was charged with. He replied that he had sufficient proof for his condemnation but was not at liberty to tell of what nature it was; but that he had corresponded with the rebels was well known; and that he, his Excellency, was accountable to the King for his conduct, he was under a necessity of doing what was very disagreeable to him.

I assured his Excellency that the charge of correspondance was without foundation; that it was true that a letter had been received from a person of that description, but that he, Mr. Walker, had never seen it; that I was sure he did not correspond with the rebels; that having lived many years in Boston, he felt a disinclination to doing anything against those people whom he had always considered as some of the most loyal subjects his Majesty had; that he was grieved to hear of the cruelties that were permitted to be exercised by savages and others upon their frontiers; and that he kept out of the way, that he need not be under the necessity of taking an active part against them. This had no effect on the governor and, in fine, he said many severe things, in very soft and polite terms. He concluded by saying Mr. Walker was a dangerous man, that he, the governor, was accountable to the King for his conduct, and the safety of the province required that Mr. Walker should quit the country immediately. To which I replied with the utmost astonishment: "Quit the country, sir! 'Tis impossible! Mr. Walker cannot quit the country at present, were he so disposed. When he came here he was in a situation to choose his place of residence, but his substance is at present out of his hands, scattered all over the Indian countries. It would be his ruin and that of his connections, were he to take such a step."

"He must go. You may stay and take care of his affairs. You shall be protected."

"Your Excellency knows that Mr. Walker's dealings are very extensive, so much so, that I could by no means undertake to superintend them."

"I am very sorry madam to be forced to use severity against Mr. Walker, but he must go, and go by the way of Quebec, and not over the Lakes."

"As Mr. Walker knows nothing that is passing here, your Excellency will permit me to go to him to acquaint him."

"Yes. I will send some person with you to guard you from insult. Name any officer you wish should accompany you. Capt. Crawford?"

"Yes sir."

"You shall go in my carriage."

"I thank your Excellency, I prefer my chaise."

We set out in about an hour, two in the afternoon. Arrived at the village at 10 of the clock where I left Capt. Crawford at the house of Mr. F. Cy, who accompanied me to the potasserie (as it is called) about half a mile from the village of l'Assomption. Mr. Walker's surprise at seeing me at that time of night was great. But what were his feelings when he heard that I came accompanied by a King's officer who came in the governor's name to be informed of his [Walker's] reasons for staying in the country, and to acquaint him that he must quit Canada? He would not suffer the officer to come to the house; nor would he see him 'til the next morning. So great was his indignation at his errand that he would scarcely be prevailed upon to see him at all and hear his message. However, he went the next morning to Mr. Cy's house at the village, where he heard the governor's message. To the first part he replied that he was as much at home there as in his home in town; that he knew no person to whom he was as to that matter accountable; that he was a British subject, and had a right to reside anywhere; that where he had property he thought his right unquestionable; that he came down there to superintend the erecting of some additional out buildings that were necessary on his farm, and for some other business, and when that was accomplished he should return to town; that it would be very inconvenient to quit Canada in the present situation of the publick and of his private affairs. But, if Governor Carleton would give him an order in writing to quit, and endemnify him for any subsequent loss to him and his connections, he would obey his order, upon which we took our leave. He returned to the potasserie. I came with the officer to town. I left him to report the answer to the governor, I went to our own house, and never saw nor heard from Mr. Walker for three weeks or more.

All this time I passed under the most alarming apprehensions in dreary solitude in the midst of a large and populous town, alone; forsaken by every individual acquaintance, who dared not look at, much less enter my house for fear of falling under suspicion of being accomplices in the supposed treason. Everyone was forbidden on pain of imprisonment to carry a scrip of paper for me to my husband. I am expecting every moment to hear he was taken or killed in his house. I took the resolution of locking up the house and stores, and went down to l'Assomption. I fled like a bird escaped from the snares of the fowler, but expecting every moment to be pursued.

I arrived without accident or alarm at l'Assomption. My husband received me with the most cordial and lively affection, which the sense of our danger had increased to the highest degree that human nature is capable of. I told him I came to share his fate.

I employed every opportunity and used every argument that prudence and affection could suggest to persuade him to go, if not quite away, then to go to some friend's house at a distance, or to secure a part of the moveable property which we had there by putting it into the hands of some person in the neighborhood; particularly some money and valuables which I brought down with me, expecting the house in town would be rifled. All this was to no purpose. His answer was: "I am able to defend my property. I will never leave that to another that I can do myself."

About this time a rash attack was made upon the city of Montreal by a handful of men under Ethan Allen [September 25, 1775] who were defeated, himself taken and sent to England with some of the people. Some saved themselves by flight.

About 9 o'clock in the evening on the 5th of October we were alarmed by the barking of our dogs (of which we had several about the farm) and sent one of the servants upstairs to look out of our window to see what it was. He came down saying there was a number of men in a canoe, or canoes, who rowed up the stream as if the devil was in them. Still Mr. Walker would not be warned. They were, he said, habitants returning in a noisy vein from the mill, and advised me to drive away womanish apprehensions, to compose myself and go to rest. [Carleton sent men to arrest Mr. Walker. They broke into the house, which brought him immediately to the top of the stairs] with his coat on, which with great agility he had put on, as his firearms were —some of them—in his pockets. He placed himself at the head of the staircase, then got up to a place above the rooms, and heard them come in yelling and swearing, calling for the damned traitor to come out. Finding no person (for the servants all fled instantly) they attempted the staircase; but a blunderbuss fired by Mr. Walker dispersed them in a moment. The officers—a corporal, a captain of militia and some others—were wounded. They immediately held a council amongst themselves, with the sergeant who succeeded to the command, and concluded to load and fire as fast as they could into the house; first setting fire to the four corners of it; which they did by placing combustibles on poles, as well as at the bottom.

Whilst this was doing, I laid myself down on my face by a stack of chimneys. [Overcome by smoke, she was taken to a window by her husband, through which they were planning to escape.] But Sergeant McFall, who had succeeded to the command of the party, prevented him by telling him that when a gentleman had surrendered himself, he was under the protection of the party.

They, notwithstanding, handled him very roughly and almost strangled him by the collar of his shirt.

I observed that the season had been rainy for some time past; the land was rich. I stood up to the mid-leg in mud, without shoe or stocking, or any other covering on me for some time. Deaf to my entreaties, this "humane" officer would neither order the soldiers to give me my own apparel (which they distributed amongst themselves before my face) nor suffer me to go into a neighbor's to borrow some. When they were distributing the plunder they divided, amongst other goods, pieces of handkerchiefs. I entreated them to give me one, but they refused. At last my negro woman pulled off her shoes and lent them to me, and gave me a piece of an old sheet which, being thrown over my head, covered me all over. Soon after, Sergeant McFall, perceiving my situation, kindly took off his blanket coat and put it on me.

The house was by this time nearly consumed and the plunder distributed amongst the party. When the wounded officer ordered horses for himself and others, Sergeant McFall said "bring a carriage for your mistress too," to which the officer said "No, damn her, let her walk."

We were hurried into a batteau [small boat], and put on board this vessel, where we stayed about an hour. Then we were reconducted to the batteau, where we found one or two officers who had not made their appearance before. A corporal who had been wounded was laid in the bottom of the boat, on a mattress taken from our beds. The sight of this man and his groans were intended no doubt to increase the horror of our situation.

There were two other batteaus which set off directly after us. The apprehended rescue was still in view when the soldiers, in liquor and not used to that river, instead of keeping close within shore, where the current is less violent, went out into the stream. They were, of course, hurried down with the current from rock to rock, oftentimes at the risk of their lives. For a long time they found themselves just in the same place from whence they had set out.

At the junction of the River Assomption with the River St.

Lawrence we were joined by more batteaus filled with soldiers, which, for the safety of the party, had been sent up the former river to intimidate and prevent the people rising. Thus we proceeded up the river and arrived within about 4 miles from town.

[They ordered Mr. Walker] to be pinioned; it was done instantly. Then they ordered his irons should be put on and riveted well. "Take this unhappy man. Put him in such a place, and give him a straw bed and a blanket. We will show you sir, what military justice is." They led him from me and I never saw him 'til I procured his liberty through the assistance of General Montgomery.

"Where is the other prisoner? Where is Mrs. Walker? Come forward in this affair of the rebellion."

"What have I done sir, to merit this treatment?"

"Oh! We know what you have done." Then, imitating my voice and manner, he said, "Esperez mes enfants, esperez; nous verrons! However, the governor, in consideration of your sex, allows you to go to your own house, under guard, where you will not be permitted to see any person. Capt. Anstruther, will you conduct Mrs. Walker to her house?" I went, on his arm, and found a man and maid servant whom I had left with the care of the house.

The third day, thinking I knew the voice of the sentinel who was at the portico at the back door of the house, I ventured to open the door and speak to him. It turned out to be as I thought, a Monseigneur Fromanteau, who but two years before was our clerk and overseer at the farm and potasserie at l'Assomption. To pretend to describe his surprise, mixed with horror, at seeing me would be in vain. I desired he would go to the governor and request me to let me have my keys and some food, and that some person might be sent, whom they could trust, to fetch me water, of which I had none but what was stale to drink. He returned with my keys and an assurance that he, the governor, had not been made acquainted; that it was not his desire that either of us should suffer anything but confinement. Mr. Jones, the deputy provost who had charge of Mr. Walker, came to me and offered me provision from his own table.

The pleasure of preparing a repast for my beloved, unfortunate husband was soon embittered and the end defeated by the insolence of the sentinels, upon various pretexts: It was sent too soon, or too late for the guard who had made his report, and the door could not be opened. Add to this that the dishes were uncovered to look for letters, etc. and the food was spoiled and cold before he got it. Despairing to raise the seige of St. Johns, they began now to think of making good their retreat, with all their effects, to Quebec before they capitulated.

About this time I had a negro boy (who, with two men negroes and a woman, had deserted from the farm at the time of our misfortune) come to wait on his master. He brought me word that I must send as much provision as would last three days, for that they would not open the door every day. Words are wanting to describe my consternation! The measure of my affliction was now full. I perceived their designs in a moment and communicated my fears—which proved to be but too well grounded —to a confidential friend, who procured a person to watch the place where Mr. Walker was confined day and night. They intended to steal him away from me; but I found out on the third day that, taking advantage of a stormy day, they had hurried him on board a vessel in the government service, commanded by one Lisotte.

The town was now in the greatest confusion. St. Johns capitulated [November 3] to General Montgomery, everything having been as I observed above put on board the vessels (11 in number). The inhabitants were told that if they did not engage to defend the town he, the governor, would set it on fire. However, they refused. The vessels with all the troops and partizans that were not at St. Johns sailed without firing the town. The same night, General Montgomery landed his troops on an island just above the town, called Isle St. Paul. This night a faithful friend came to me and offered me any service or to do anything towards liberating Mr. Walker that I could suggest. I told him I had planned in my own mind a probable scheme, and wanted only so faithful and active a friend as himself to execute it. It was this: I have read somewhere that a single gun in a retired situation, placed on an eminence at a certain distance would do great execution on a vessel that is passing. You know that the passage somewhere near the Point of Sorrel is very narrow, so that a vessel can only pass near the shore.

＊Mrs. Walker's scheme was not carried out, and her husband was confined in solitary confinement for thirty-three days. His irons were "riveted in so cruel a manner as to jar the bone," Martha revealed, "and were twice the usual size and weight." Walker was then transferred to Lisotte's armed schooner, and placed in the hold prison. In the middle of November General Montgomery's force seized Montreal and eleven British vessels on the St. Lawrence River, including the schooner Walker was on. Returning to l'Assomption, he and James Price tried to rouse the people into joining Montgomery's attack against the city of Quebec. Most of the inhabitants, however, feared British reprisals; many felt that Montgomery would be defeated. Impatiently, Walker made his way up the St. Lawrence to Pointe aux Trembles, within fifteen miles of Quebec, where he waited for Montgomery's troops. General Montgomery and General Arnold's combined attack against the city's fortress ended in a fiasco on December 31st; Montgomery was slain by artillery fire and Arnold suffered a leg wound; thirty Americans were killed, four hundred fifty taken prisoner. Few of those who retreated toward Fort Ticonderoga survived. The paths were strewn with rigid, icy bodies of soldiers who had died of smallpox and starvation. Abandoned along the way, these men were buried by snowdrifts, until the spring thaw.

In February 1776 the Continental Congress appointed a commission of three—Samuel Chase, Benjamin Franklin, and Charles Carroll—to go to Montreal and convince Canadians that the American invasion of Canada was not only necessary for the defense of American freedom, but also for the liberation of the province from Canadian oppression. The commissioners reached Montreal in April and lodged in the Walker home. Carroll liked the house because it was "the best built, and perhaps the best furnished in this town." The trio made their headquarters at the Château de Ramezay, nearby.

The ravages of smallpox, and American naval defeat on May 9th at Quebec caused numerous Anglo-Americans in and around Montreal to flee southward. Mrs. Walker, Mrs. Price, and Benjamin Franklin left the city by boat at 8 A.M. on May 11th. In order that Mrs. Walker might pass through guard posts on her way to Philadelphia, she had in her possession the following letter, written by the commissioners:

Dear Sir

We desire that you will show to Mrs. Walker every civility in your power and facilitate her on her way to Philadelphia; tho' fear of cruel treatment from the enemy on account of the strong attachment to, and zeal of her husband in the cause of the united colonies induces her to depart precipitately from her home, and to undergo the fatigues of a long and hazardous journey. We are sorry for the occasion of writing this letter and beg your attention to alleviate her distress; your warm politeness and humanity, we are sensible, without this recommendation from us, would prompt you to perform the friendly office. We are with great esteem and sincere regard for yourself and family,

> *Samuel Chase*
> *Charles Carroll*
> *Benjamin Franklin*

Benjamin Franklin took her safely to Albany, and then traveled southward without her. Somewhere in New York State, Franklin wrote a letter to Chase and Carroll, who were still in Canada. The letter is dated May 27, 1776:

Dear Friends—We arrived here safe yesterday evening, having left Mrs. Walker with her husband at Albany, from whence we came down by land. We passed him on Lake Champlain; but he returning overtook us at Saratoga, where they both took such liberties in taunting at our conduct in Canada, that it came almost to a quarrel. We continued our care of her, however, and landed her safe in Albany with her three waggon loads of baggage, brought thither without putting her to any expense, and parted civilly, though coldly. I think they both have an excellent talent at making themselves enemies, and I believe, live where they will, they will never be long without them.

Benjamin Franklin

It is probable the Walkers arrived in Philadelphia that summer or fall and left the city before the British seized it in 1777. They returned to Boston to live. In 1785 the Walkers, or Thomas Walker alone, visited London. Mr. Walker was seen dining in London with Pierre du Calvert, a French Protestant who had been a merchant, judge, and seigneur in Canada.

According to the *Boston Gazette* and *Massachusetts Sentinel,* Thomas Walker died in Boston on July 8, 1788, at the age of seventy. Following her husband's death, Martha Walker returned to Canada, where her son and brother's-in-law families lived. In 1816 Martha's niece, Mary Greenwood Gay of Dedham, Massachusetts, penned to her brother, John Greenwood: "If you go to Canada in July you can inquire if Madame Walker is still alive; she is mother's sister; her son was Judge Walker of Montreal; he is dead."*

Margaret Hill Morris

*Margaret Hill, born in 1737 near Annapolis, Maryland, was the eighth Quaker child of Richard and Deborah Moore Hill. Two years later, Richard, overburdened with financial problems as a physician and shipping merchant, was compelled to take his wife and son Richard to Funchal on the island of Madeira. Margaret—at an age when she was first learning to walk—her sisters, and a brother were left in Philadelphia to be looked after by a fifteen-year-old sister, Hannah Hill Moore, the wife of Dr. Samuel Preston Moore. When Margaret was fourteen she was told that her mother had died unexpectedly in Madeira. She sadly wrote in her diary that her mother's "body was attended by the merchants and other gentlemen of Madeira to the sea." Her father returned to Philadelphia shortly afterwards, but her brother died six months later in Madeira.

Philadelphia was a town of several thousand clapboard or brick houses, of cobblestone and dirt streets lined with elm and poplar trees and oil lanterns. Inhabitants scrubbed, religiously and twice-weekly, their doors, window ledges, and sidewalks, a habit which caused passersby to fall in freezing weather. Residential areas were languidly peaceful, save for the grating wheels of horse drawn carriages, and barrows pulled by peddlers hawking oysters. However, early in the morning on November 8, 1775, Philadelphians felt the shock of an earthquake.

In 1758 Margaret married William Morris, a drygoods merchant, and, following tradition, no longer wore her hair unrestrained. Judging from a diary entry the marriage, though brief, was a happy one: "My dear and aged parent preserved in health; my sisters, for whom I was anxiously concerned, happily married; myself still happy in the tender affections of a beloved husband, who, notwithstanding his youth, has been preserved from falling into the fashionable vices and follies of the town; and next, to crown all, I have to praise thy glorious name for my safe deliverance in childbirth." The little boy died the following autumn, shortly before his mother again endured labor pains and breast-fed an infant girl. During eight years of marriage Margaret bore seven, perhaps eight, children—four survived childhood. Two unbearable tragedies struck the family in 1765: her daughter Mary died in February, her husband in December, when Margaret was one month pregnant. In a moment's solitude she penned in her diary: "Thou, oh Lord has seen good to try me divers times with the loss of dear parents, children and friends; and at none of thy dispenses has my heart murmured or repined; I have constantly and daily endeavoured to say, thy will be done in me. But, oh, the awful and trying stroke which thou now hast permitted to overtake me is almost too much for frail nature to bear without thy assistance. Had it been thy will to have accepted of my willing soul as a sacrifice for the life, the precious life of my dearly beloved husband, my poor infants would then have had a father and a friend to direct their steps, and to lead them as it were thro' the rugged road of life." Her son was born August 18, 1766: "Distressing situation," she wrote, "no husband to comfort with the voice of love my languishing state."

As a widow her social life was meager, and she was very lonely. "Every friend that is taken from me leaves me more destitute in a world that has really no charms for me. I have none to lean upon; no earthly friend, and none in Heaven but thyself that is able to remove the difficulties that surround me, and appear to my shortsighted view to be insurmountable." In June 1770 she moved her family to Burlington, New Jersey, where two sisters had made their homes: Sarah Dillwyn, wife of George Dillwyn, a Quaker preacher, and Milcah Martha Moore, wife of Dr. Charles Moore. Due to the accommodations Margaret chose to live with the Dillwyns. "I fear I shall not be able to make it agreeable to them to remain with me. Yet if thou strengthen me, oh God! to overcome the vileness of my own evil nature, we shall be comforts and supports to each other. For I know the goodness of my darling sister's heart, and if causes of uneasiness arise between us the fault must be mine. Sickness and sorrow have so

Margaret Hill Morris's portrait, painted in Philadelphia when she was sixteen, reveals perceptive intelligence and maturity.

soured and fretted my temper that I feel and grieve at the change. Oh, be pleased to unite us in thy love, and let not my poor orphans be a bar to our union. If I love anything on earth above them it is the dear inmates who have condescended to take up their abode with me."

Burlington, about twenty miles north of Philadelphia on the Delaware River, consisted of about two hundred clapboard, stone or brick houses, many of which were on an island. Scattered over the riverbanks were numerous buttonwood trees, their massive trunks of white bark once used by early settlers for

Years later, in Burlington, New Jersey, Margaret Hill Morris attended the Friends Meeting House, arriving in a "chair" similar to the one shown here. When Hessian troops were quartered in the hexagonal house they damaged both the interior and surrounding fences, using the latter for firewood. The building was torn down in 1784, for a larger one containing a schoolhouse.

securing river vessels. Burlington was one of the earliest Quaker settlements in the colonies; by 1776, one hundred thirteen men and women were gathering at the Society of Friends' hexagonal Meeting House.

From their riverside home on Green Bank the Dillwyn and Morris families could leisurely watch the billowing sails of passing cargo and passenger boats. The house, rented by the Dillwyns, had been occupied previously by William Franklin, the last Royal Governor of New Jersey, and son of Benjamin Franklin. While a large portion of the nation's youth was heatedly aroused by the intrusion of British soldiers, Margaret valued one advantage of rural solitude. Writing to Milcah Martha (Patty), who had moved with her family to Montgomery Square, Pennsylvania, she said, "The weighty duty of taking care of my precious charge engrosses my most earnest thoughts, and I hope it may be permitted, if it is right it should be so, to keep them in this place till they are fixed in their principles, and then there will be less danger in launching them out in the world."

Margaret Morris's diary, written for Patty, began on December 6, 1776, when Sir William Howe's British troops arrived in New Brunswick, New Jersey, thirty-five miles north of Burlington. The following day, Major General Cornwallis's British division (including Hessian units) marched southward through New Jersey, threatening Philadelphia. Simultaneously, a British fleet on the Delaware River, below Philadelphia, blockaded American passage. Cornwallis arrived at Trenton, New Jersey, on December 8 as the last of Washington's troops were crossing over the Delaware River into Pennsylvania. Opposed to violence, Margaret looked forward "to the desirable period when the now contending parties shall shake hands, and all be friends once more; this is the height of my politics, and the wish next my heart."*

December 6, 1776: Being on a visit to Haddonfield, I was preparing to return to my family, when a person from Philadelphia told us the people were in great commotion, that the English fleet was in the river, and hourly expected to sail up to the city; that the inhabitants were removing into the country; and that several persons of considerable repute had been discovered to have formed a design of setting fire to the city, and were summoned before the congress and strictly enjoined to drop the horrid purpose. When I heard the above report my heart almost died within me, and I cried that surely the Lord will not punish the innocent with the guilty, that I wished there might be found some interceding Lots and Abrahams amongst *our people.* On my journey home I was told the inhabitants of our little town were going in haste into the country, and that my nearest neighbors were already removed. When I heard this I felt myself quite sick; I was ready to faint. I thought of my Sarah Dillwyn (the beloved companion of my widowed state)—her husband at the distance of some hundred miles from her. I thought of my own lonely situation, no husband to cheer with the voice of love my sinking spirits. My little flock, too, without a father to direct them how to steer. All these things crowded into my mind at once, and I felt like one forsaken. A flood of friendly tears came to my relief, and I felt an humble confidence that He who had been with me in six troubles would not forsake me now. While I cherished this hope, my tranquility was restored, and I felt no sensations but of humble acquiescence to the Divine will. I was favoured to find my family in good health on my arrival, and my dear companion not greatly discomposed, for which favour I desire to be made truly thankful.

Dec. 7: A letter from my next neighbour's husband, at the camp, warned her to be gone in haste. Many persons coming into town today brought intelligence that the British army were advancing towards us.

Dec. 8: Every day begins and ends with the same accounts. We hear today that the regulars [British] are at Trenton. Some of our neighbours gone, and others going, makes our little bank look lonesome. But our trust in Providence still firm, and we dare not even talk of removing our family.

Dec. 9: This evening we were favoured with the company of our faithful friend and brother, Richard Wells [husband of Margaret's sister Rachel]. This testimony of his love was truly acceptable to us.

Dec. 10: Today our amiable friend Hetty Cox and her family bid us adieu. My brother also left us, but returned in less than an hour, telling us he could not go away just as the Hessians were entering the town. But, with no troops coming in, we urged him to leave us next morning, which he concluded to do, after preparing us to expect the Hessians in a few hours. A number of galleys [double-masted boats commanded by Commodore Thomas Seymour of the Pennsylvania Navy] had been lying in the river before the town, for two days past.

Dec. 11: After various reports from one hour to another of light-horse approaching, the people in town had certain intelligence that a large body of Hessians were come to Bordentown, and we might expect to see them in a few hours. About 10 o'clock of this day a party of about 60 men [Pennsylvania riflemen] marched down Main Street. As they passed along they told our doctor [Jonathan Odell, an Episcopal clergyman and doctor] and some other persons in the town that a large number of Hessians were advancing, and would be in the town in less than an hour. This party were riflemen who, it seems, had crossed the river somewhere in the neighbourhood of Bordentown to reconnoitre, and meeting with a superior number of Hessians on the road, were then returning, and took Burlington on their way back; from us they crossed to Bristol, and by the time they were fairly embarked, the Hessians—to the number, as we heard, of 4 or 500 —had passed what we call York Bridge. On the first certainty of their approach, John Lawrence and two or three others thought it best for the safety of the town to go out and meet the troops. He communicated his intention to one of the gondola [smaller boat in Seymour's fleet] captains, who approved of it and desired to be informed of the result. The gentlemen went out, and though the Hessian colonel spoke but little English, yet they found that upon being thus met in a peaceable manner on behalf of the inhabitants, he was ready to promise them safety and security, to exchange any messages that might be proper with the gentlemen of the galleys. In the meantime he ordered his troops to halt; they remained in their ranks between the Bridge and the corner of Main Street, waiting an answer from on board. John Lawrence and T. Hulings went down to report what had passed, and told Capt. Moore that the colonel had orders to quarter his troops in Burlington that night, and that if the inhabitants were quiet and peaceable, and would furnish him with quarters and refreshment, he would pledge his honor that no manner of disorder should happen to disturb or alarm the people. Capt. Moore replied that in his opinion it would be wrong in such a case to fire on the town, but that he would go down and consult the commodore, and return an answer as soon as might be. While this answer was waited for, Dr. Odell was told it would be a satisfaction, both to the Hessian commandant and to our own people, to have a person who could serve as interpreter between them. Not doubting the foreigner could speak French, the doctor went to him, and he had the satisfaction to find it probable, at least, that he might be of service to the people of the town. The commandant seemed highly pleased to find a person with whom he could converse with ease and precision. He desired the doctor to tell the gentlemen of the town to the same purport as above, with this addition: that he expected there would be found no persons in the town in arms; nor any arms, ammunition, or other effects, belonging to persons that were in arms against the king, concealed by any of the inhabitants; that if any such effects were thus secreted, the house in which they should be found would be given up to pillage; to prevent which, it would be necessary to give him a just and fair account of such effects, which account he would forward to the general, and that if we acted openly and in good faith in these respects, he repeated his assurances, upon the honour of a soldier, that he would be answerable for every kind of disorder on the part of his troops. They remained in profound silence in their ranks, and the commandant with some of his officers came into town as far as John Lawrence's, where they dined, waiting the commodore's answer. The doctor says, that as he thought he observed much of the gentleman in the commandant, and the appearance, at least, of generosity and humanity, he took an opportunity to inform him that there was an old friend of his [the doctor's] who was a colonel, and of some estimation in the Continental Army—that he was at present with Gen. Washington; that his lady, an amiable woman, had gone into the country with most of her effects;

that the doctor was ignorant of the place of her retreat, but that before her departure she had begged him on the footing of former friendship to take into his house, and if he might be permitted to keep as under his protection, some few things which she could not remove, and told the commandant, he was ready to give an exact account of such of her effects as he had thus taken charge of. At the same time, he confessed that when he took them it was in the hope of being suffered to preserve them for his friend. The commandant told him without a moment's hesitation, "Sir, you need not be at the trouble of giving any further account of those things you have so candidly mentioned. Be assured that whatever effects have been entrusted with you in this way, I shall consider as your own, and they shall not be touched." From this answer he was encouraged to hope he might be of still further service to his friends, in the full persuasion that nothing would happen to disconcert the peaceable disposition that was making. But as it happened, the commodore had received intelligence of a party of Hessians having entered Burlington, before Capt. Moore got down to him, and had ordered up four galleys to fire on the town wherever any two or three persons should be seen together. Capt. Moore met and hailed them, one after another, but the wind was so high that he was not heard or understood. The four gondolas came up; the first of them appearing before Main Street. John Lawrence, T. Hulings and William Dillwyn went down upon the wharf and waved a hat, the signal agreed on with Capt. Moore for the boat to come ashore and give the commodore's answer in peace. To the astonishment of these gentlemen, all the answer they received was first a swivel shot. Not believing it possible this could be designedly done, they stood still, and John Lawrence again waved his hat, and was answered with an 18 pounder. Both these fires, as the gondola people have since told us, were made with as good aim as could be taken, as they took it for granted it was at Hessians they fired. However, as it was impossible to conjecture how such conduct could have happened, or to suspect such a mistake, 'tis no wonder the town was exceedingly alarmed, looking upon it in the light of a cruel as well as unprovoked piece of treachery. Upon this news the commandant rose calmly from table, his officers with him, and went out to eight or ten men who had come to the door as a bodyguard. He turned to the doctor as he went into the street, and said he could easily dispose of his people out of the possibility of danger, but that much mischief might be done to the town, and that he would take a view of the gondolas and see what measures might be necessary on his part; but that he should be sorry to be the occasion of any damage or distress to the inhabitants. He walked down the street, and sent different ways three sentinels in Indian file together—to view and report to him what they saw. These being now and then seen at different times in divers parts of the town, induced the people on board to believe that the houses were full of Hessians. A cannonade was continued till almost dark in different directions, sometimes along the street, sometimes across it. Several houses were struck and a little damaged, but not one living creature, either man or beast, killed or wounded. About dark the gondolas fell down a little way below the town, and the night was passed in quiet. While all this tumult was in town we, on our peaceful bank, ignorant of the occasion of the firing, were wondering what it could mean, and unsuspecting of danger, were quietly pursuing our business in the family, when a kind neighbour informed us of the occasion, and urged us to go into the cellar as a place of safety. We were prevailed on by him to do so, and remained there till it ceased.

Dec. 12: The people of the galleys, suspecting that some troops were yet either concealed in town or in the neighborhood of it, have been very jealous of the inhabitants, who have been often alarmed with reports that the city [Philadelphia] would be set on fire. Many have gone in haste and great distress into the country, but we still hope no mischief is seriously intended. A number of men landed on our bank this morning, and told us it was their settled purpose to set fire to the town. I begged them not to set my house afire. They asked which was my house. I showed it to them, and they said they knew not what hindered them from firing on it last night, for seeing a light in the chambers they thought there were Hessians in it, and they pointed the guns at it several times. I told them my children were sick, which obliged me to burn a light all night. Though they did not know what hindered them from firing on us, I did. It was the guardian of the widow and the orphan, who took us into His safekeeping, and preserved us from danger. Oh, that I may keep humble, and be thankful for this, as well as other favours vouchsafed to my little flock.

Dec. 13: This day we began to look a little like ourselves again. The troops were removed some miles from town, as we heard, and our friends began to venture out to see us. But the suspicions of the gondola men still continued, and search was made in and about the town for men distinguished by the name of Tories. About noon of this day dear brother Richard Wells popped in upon us. He heard the firing yesterday, and being anxious for our safety, he ran the risk of venturing amongst us to see how we had fared. Surely this proof of his love will never be forgotten by me while my memory lasts. He left us soon after dinner.

Dec. 14: This day we began to feel a little like ourselves again. This day there was no appearance of the formidable Hessians. Our friends began to show themselves abroad. Several called to see us; amongst the number was one (Dr. Odell) esteemed by the whole family, and *very intimate* in it; but the spirit of the devil still continued to rove through the town in the shape of Tory-hunters. A message was delivered to our intimate friend, informing him a party of armed men were on the search for him—his horse was brought, and he retired to a place of safety. Some of the gentlemen who entertained the foreigners were pointed out to the gondola men. Two worthy inhabitants were seized upon and dragged on board. From the 13th to the 16th we had various reports of the advancing and retiring of the enemy. Parties of armed men rudely entered the houses in town, and a diligent search was made for Tories. Some of the gondola gentry broke into and pillaged Richard Smith's house on the bank. About noon this day (the 16th) a very terrible account of thousands coming into town [500 New Jersey militia and artillerymen] and now actually to be seen on Gallows Hill. My incautious son caught up the spyglass, and was running towards the mill to look at them. I told him it would be liable to misconstruction, but he prevailed on me to let him gratify his curiosity. He went, but returned much dissatisfied, for no troops could he see. As he came back poor Dick took the glass and, resting it against a tree, took a view of the fleet. Both of these were observed by the people on board, who suspected it was an enemy that was watching their motions. They manned a boat, and sent her on shore. A loud knocking on my door brought me to it. I was a little fluttered and kept locking and unlocking that I might get my ruffled face a little composed. At last I opened it, and half a dozen men, all armed, demanded the keys of the empty house. I asked what they wanted there; they said to search for a d———d Tory who had been spying at them from the mill. The name of a Tory, so near to *my own door* seriously alarmed me, for a poor refugee [Dr. Jonathan Odell], dignified by that name, had claimed the shelter of my roof, and was at that very time concealed, like a thief in an auger hole. I rung the bell violently—the signal agreed on if they came to search—and when I thought he had crept into the hole, I put on a very simple look, and cried out "Bless me, I hope you are not Hessians. Say, good men are you the Hessians?" "Do we look like Hessians," asked one of them rudely. "Indeed I don't know." "Did you never see a Hessian?" "No, never in my life; but they are *men,* and you are men, and may be Hessians, for anything I know. But I'll go with you into Col. Cox's house, though indeed it was my son at the mill. He is but a boy, and meant no harm. He wanted to see the troops." So I marched at the head of them, opened the door, and searched every place; but we could not find the Tory—strange where he could be. We returned—they, greatly disappointed—I, pleased to think *my house* was not suspected. The captain, a smart little fellow named Shippen, said he wished he could see the spyglass. Sarah Dillwyn produced it, and very civilly desired his acceptance of it, which I was sorry for, as I often amused myself in looking through it. They left us, and searched James Verree's and the next two houses, but no Tory could they find. This transaction reached the town, and Col. Cox was very angry and ordered the men on board. In the evening I went to town with my refugee and placed him in other lodgings. I was told today of a design to seize upon a young man in town, as he was deemed a Tory. I thought a hint would be kindly received and, as I came back, called on a friend of his, and told him. Next day he was out of the reach of the gondolas.

Dec. 17: More news, great news—very great news. The British troops are actually at Mount Holly. Guards of militia are placed at London and York bridges. Gondola men in arms are patrolling the street, and a diligent search made for firearms, ammunition, and Tories. Another attempt last night to get into R. Smith's house. Early this morning James Verree sent in, to beg I would let my son go a few miles out of town on some business for him. I consented, not knowing of the formidible doings up town. When I heard of it I felt a mother's pangs for her son all the day. When night came and he did not appear, I made no doubt of his being taken by the Hessians. A friend made my mind easy by telling me he had himself passed through the town where the dreadful Hessians were said to be playing the very mischief. It is certain there were numbers of them at Mount Holly, but they behaved very civilly to the people, excepting only a few persons who were in actual rebellion, as they termed it, whose goods and all they injured. This evening every gondola man was sent on board with strict orders not to set a foot on the Jersey shore again —so far so good.

Dec. 18: This morning gives us hope of a quiet day—but my mind is still anxious for my son, not yet returned. Our refugee has gone off today out of the reach of gondolas and Tory-hunters. Much talk of the enemy. Two Hessians had the assurance to appear in town today; they asked if there were any rebels in town, and desired to be shown the *men-of-war* [warships]—what a burlesque on *men-of-war!* My son returned at night, and to his mortification saw not one Hessian, light-horse, or anything else

Margaret Hill Morris /85

worth seeing, but had the consolation of a little adventure at York Bridge, being made to give an account of himself as he went out yesterday, his horse detained, and h ordered to walk back to town and get a pass from Gen. Reed [Col. Joseph Reed, Washington's adjutant general]. This he readily agreed to; but instead of a pass, Col. Cox accompanied him back to the bridge, and Don Quixote, jr. mounted his horse and rode through their ranks in triumph. Two field pieces are said to be mounted at Bristol.

Dec. 19: A man was met on the road, with a white rag tied to a stick—I suppose to represent a flag—but whence he came, or where he was going, the wisest head on the Bank (J.V.) cannot conjecture. A report prevails that Gen. Putnam with 1000 men are on their march. This put all into motion at Holly. The Hessians retire to the Black-Horse. Not one gondola man ashore all this day; we may burn a candle all night and sleep secure. This evening I received a letter from Dr. Charles Moore, inviting me to move into his neighbourhood, but my mind is easiest while I conclude to abide where Providence has cast my lot. He has preserved us in great dangers, and I dare not distrust His future care. A letter from the brother-in-law and friend of my heart, George Dillwyn, gives me hope of his return. His advice must determine my future movements. If I do remove, a friend in need is a friend indeed.

Dec. 20: A snow storm last night has almost stopped the navigation, and sent our guarda-costas out of our sight down the river. Surely this will be a quiet day. Methinks I will call for my work-basket, and set myself to sewing—but hark, a rap at the door—that face (James Verree) is full of intelligence. "Well what news neighbour?" "Oh, bless me, great news indeed. Why ha'nt you heard it?" "No, we have seen nobody from town today; do tell us." "Why the Hessians are actually just here. William Dillwyn and others are all gone out to see what they can do." "Well, and will they bring them all into town? I'm sure we are but poorly provided just now for a great deal of company." Verree still goes on—"Oh. Ah. You will have enough of them; I expect to have my house full. I saw a man from Holly yesterday who says he saw fifty of the light-horse, all very fine English horses. Oh it was a terrible sight to see how they all foamed at the mouth and pranced—and fifty Hessians all quartered at Holly. But Putnam is surely coming with 1500 men." "Well, but neighbour, I should suppose it was a very fine sight to see so many fine horses together, and prancing." "Oh no, bless my spirits, it is a terrible sight to see how they foamed at the mouth." Well, we shall hear by and by what the ambassadors have done. I hope they won't come in tonight with the Hessians, for I am quite unprovided to entertain company. Whip the fellows, I got supper enough for twenty of them the first night of the alarm, and I'm resolved I'll trouble myself no more about them till I see some of them in earnest. Seventeen Hessians in town today, and we were told the recorder was desired to prepare a dinner for five-hundred men. A friend from town called in about 4 o'clock and told us they were all a-coming. We asked if he had seen them; no, but he heard they were just here. We asked him how we, at this distance from town, should know of their coming; they might pop upon us here and scare us out of our wits, as we had no man in the house. He said "Oh you will know it fast enough I warrant. Why, the noise of the waggons and rattling of the cannon will be heard at a great distance. I advise you to make good use of your time till they do come, and put all things of gold and silver out of their way, and all linen too, or you will lose it." I said they pillaged none but rebels, and we were not such. We had taken no part against them. But that signified nothing; we should lose all. After he was gone, my Sarah Dillwyn and myself asked each other why it was that all those stories did not put us into a fright. We were not even discomposed; surely it is a favour never to be forgotten. We concluded to sit up a little later than usual tonight, but no rattling could we hear. Ambassadors returned—a report that the congress dollars will be allowed to circulate for a certain number of years—a battery talked of, to be raised at the point of the island. We are told the two pieces of cannon, said to be at Bristol, have disappeared.

Margaret Hill Morris /87

Dec. 21: More snow last night. No danger of gondolas now. More ambassadors gone out today to the Hessians. Not much to be expected from one of them. A great deal of talk in the neighbourhood about a neutral island; wish with great earnestness it may be allowed. Wonder the men in town don't think it worth while to step down here and tell us what they are after. I get quite in the fidgets for news. I sent Dick to town to collect some; he returned quite newsless. Good mind to send him back again. William Dillwyn comes at last and tells us all we expected to hear, pleases us by saying we shall have timely notice of their coming, and gives a hint that the feeble and defenseless will find safety and protection. We rank ourselves amongst the number having no man with us in the house. I am determined not to be unprovided again. Let them come or not, as the weather is now so cold provisions will keep good several days. We pity the poor fellows who were obliged to be out last night in the snow. Repeat our wishes that this may be a neutral island. Quite sleepy. Go to bed and burn a lamp all night; talk as loud as usual, and don't regard the creaking of the door. No gondola men are listening about the bank. Before we retired to bed this evening, an attempt was made to teach the children to pronounce "vegates" [How do you do?] like a Dutchman. Our good neighbour is a little concerned to think there is not one in the neighbourhood that will be able to interpret for us when the Hessians are quartered on us. At last, by dint of mere conjuration, I discover that his maid is a Dutch woman, and we resolve that she will be the interpreter of the bank, Her master thinks it will be a great thing to have one that can speak for us.

Dec. 22: It is said Putnam with 1000 men [600 New Jersey militia and Virginia artillerymen] are at Mount Holly. All the women removed from the town, except one widow of our acquaintance. This evening we hear the sound of much hammering at Bristol, and it is conjectured that a fortification is carrying on there. More cannon are said to be planted on the island. We hear this afternoon that the gentlemen who went last to the Count Donop [Col. Carl von Donop, Hessian] with a request that our town might be allowed to remain a neutral one, are returned, and report that he had too many affairs of greater consequence in hand to attend to them, or give an answer. I think we don't like the Count quite so well today as we did yesterday. We heard yesterday that Gen: Charles Lee [American general] was taken prisoner by a party of light-horse, who surrounded him and took him to New York (I hope privately that he will not escape). Today (22nd) we hear Gen. Howe is at Trenton, and it is thought there will be an engagement soon. A man who was at Mount Holly the other day tells us he saw a great many of the British troops, that some of them went to the magazine there (a small room over the court-house) and took out about 100 wooden canteens, the same number of broken firearms, and, calling for a guard of 100 men, piled them up in the street, and ordered the men in the division to take charge of them. This afternoon we hear of our refugee again, and that he has got a protection, as it is called. The rage of Tory-hunting a little subsided. We now hear only of the Hessian-hunters. But they make a poor hand of it; not one brought in that we know of. We hear this afternoon that our officers are afraid their men will not fight and wish they may all run home again. A peaceable man ventured to prophesy today that if the war is continued through the winter, the British troops will be scared at the sight of our men, for as they never fought with naked men, the novelty of it will terrify them and make them retreat faster than they advanced to meet them; for he says, from the present appearance of our ragged troops, he thinks it probable they will not have clothes to cover them a month or two hence. Several of the families who left the town on the day of the cannonading are returned to their houses. The intelligence brought in this evening is seriously affecting a party of our men. About 200 marched out of Mount Holly, and meeting with a party of Hessians near a place called Petticoat Bridge, an engagement ensued—the Hessians retreating rather than advancing. A heavy firing of musketry and some cannon were heard. We are informed that twenty-one of our men were killed in the engagement, and that they returned at

Margaret Hill Morris /89

night to their headquarters at Mount Holly, the Hessians to theirs at Black-Horse.

Dec. 23: This day twelve gondolas came up the river again, but we know not as yet the occasion of their coming. The troops at Mount Holly went out again today and engaged the Hessians near the same place where they met yesterday; 'tis reported we lost ten men and that our troops are totally routed and the Hessians in possession of Mount Holly. This evening a little alarm in our neighbourhood; a report reaching us that 3000 troops now at Bristol are to cross over in the night (and to land on our Bank) in order to join the routed party of yesterday. My dear Sarah Dillwyn's spirits for the first time forsook her on hearing this, and my heart grieved that I could offer nothing to compose her. We conjecture the gondolas are to lie here in readiness to receive our men should they be put to flight. Be that as it may, we don't like to see them so near us, and wish for another snow storm to drive them away.

Dec. 24: The gondolas have all gone out of sight—but whether up or down the river we know not. This morning we are told of a fearful alarm which was spread through the town last night: that the gondolas had orders to fire on it in the night, as it was said the Hessians were expected to come in after the rout of yesterday, and take possession here as they had done at Mount Holly. Happily this account did not reach us till it was proved to be false. It seems the commodore had sent one McKnight on shore, who informed the inhabitants of it. W. Smith and B. Helm went to Bristol in the evening, and acquainted Gen. Cadwalader with what they had heard, who signified to the commodore the necessity of the removal of the fleet, as the ice would probably make it difficult for them to sail a few days hence. When this was taken to the commodore, he denied having sent the information which so alarmed the inhabitants. It was thought he appeared to be a little disguised by liquor at the time. We hear the Hessians are still at Holly, and our troops in possession of Church Hill, a little beyond. The account of twenty-one killed the first day of the engagement, and ten the next, is not to be depended on, as the

Hessians say our men ran so fast they had not the opportunity of killing any of them. Several Hessians in town today. They went to Daniel Smith's and enquired for several articles in the shop, which they offered to pay for. Two were observed to be in liquor in the street; they went to the tavern, and calling for rum ordered the man to charge it to the King. We hear that two houses in the skirts of the town were broke open and pillaged by the Hessians. The gondolas have been lying down at Dunk's Ferry all this day. A pretty heavy firing was heard up the river today, but no account yet received of the occasion, or where it was.

Dec. 25: An officer is said to be gone to Bristol from the Count Donop at Holly, with a flag, and offers of letting our town remain a neutral port. Gen. Reed is at Philadelphia. An express was sent to him, and we hear he is to meet the Count tomorrow at John Antrim's, and settle the preliminaries.

Dec. 26: The weather is very stormy; we fear Gen. Reed will not meet the Count today. A great number of flatbottom boats have gone up the river; we cannot learn where they are going to.

Dec. 27: A letter from Gen. Reed to his brother, informing him that Washington had had an engagement with the regulars on the 25th early in the morning [Battle of Trenton], taking them by surprise; killed 50 and took 900 prisoners. The loss on our side is not known, or if known, not suffered to be public. It seems this heavy loss to the regulars was owing to the prevailing custom among the Hessians of getting drunk on the eve of that great day which brought peace on earth and good will to men. But, oh how unlike Christians is the manner in which they celebrate it. Can we call ourselves Christians, while we act so contrary to our master's rules? He set the example which we profess to follow, and here is a recent instance that we only profess it; instead of good will, envy and hatred seem to be the ruling passions in the breasts of thousands. This evening, the 27th, about 3000 of the Pennsylvania militia and other troops landed in the neck, and marched into town with artillery, baggage, and all, and were quartered on the inhabitants. One company were lodged at

James Verree's, and a guard placed between his house and ours. We were so favored as not to have any sent to our house. An officer spent the evening with us, and appeared to be in high spirits, and talked of engaging the English as a very trifling affair —nothing so easy as to drive them over the North River [Hudson River]; not considering there is a God of battle, as well as a God of peace, who may have given them the late advantage in order to draw them out to meet the chastisement that is reserved for them.

Dec. 28: Early this morning the troops marched out of town in high spirits. A flight of snow this morning sent the gondolas again down the river. My heart sinks when I think of the numbers, unprepared for death, who will probably be sent in a few days to appear before the Judge of Heaven. The weather is clearing up this afternoon. We observed several boats with soldiers [Brig. Gen. Thomas Mifflin and troops] and their baggage, making up to our wharf. As I looked at them, I thought I saw a face that was not strange to me, and taking a nearer view, found it was the well known face of my beloved brother[-in-law] and friend, George Dillwyn. When I saw the company he was among, I thought of what Solomon said of his beloved—that she was like an apple tree amongst the trees of the wood. When he came into the house my kindred heart bade him welcome to the hospitable roof, for so must I ever deem that roof which has sheltered me and my little flock—though our joy at meeting him was checked by the prospect before us, and around. A man who seemed to have some command over the soldiers just landed, civilly asked for the keys of Col. Cox's house, in which they stowed their baggage, and took up their quarters for the night, and were very quiet.

Dec. 29: This morning the soldiers at the next house prepared to depart, and as they passed my door, they stopped to bless and thank me for the food I sent them, which I received, not as my due, but as belonging to my Master who had reached a morsel to them by my hands. A great number of soldiers are in town today. Another company took possession of the next house when the first left it. The inhabitants are much straitened for bread to supply the soldiers and firewood to keep them warm. This seems to be only one of the many calamities of war.

Dec. 30: A number of poor soldiers sick and wounded brought into town today, and lodged in the court-house; some of them in private houses. Today I hear several of our town's men have agreed to procure wood for the soldiers; but they found it was attended with considerable difficulty, as most of the waggons usually employed to bring in wood were pressed to take the soldiers' baggage.

Dec. 31: We have been told of an engagement between the two armies, in which it was said the English had 400 taken prisoners, and 300 killed and wounded. The report of the evening contradicts the above intelligence, and there is no certain account of a battle.

January 1, 1777: This New Year's day has not been ushered in with the usual ceremonies and rejoicing; indeed, I believe it will be the beginning of a sorrowful year to very many people. Yet the flatterer—hope—bids me look forward with confidence and trust in Him who can bring order out of this great confusion. I do not hear that any messengers have been in town from the camp.

Jan. 3: This morning between 8 and 9 o'clock we heard very distinctly a heavy firing of cannon. The sound came from towards Trenton. About noon a number of [American] soldiers, upwards of 1000, came into town in great confusion with baggage and some cannon. From these soldiers we learn there was a smart engagement yesterday at Trenton, and that they left them engaged near Trenton Mill, but were not able to say which side was victorious. They were again quartered on the inhabitants, and we again exempt from the cumber of having them lodged in our house. Several of those who lodged in Col. Cox's house last week returned tonight, and asked for the key, which I gave them. At about bedtime I went into the next house to see if the fires were safe, and my heart was melted with compassion to see such a number of my fellow creatures lying like swine on the floor, fast asleep, and many of them without even a blanket to cover them. It seems very strange to me that such a number should be allowed to come from the camp at the very time of the engagements, and I shrewdly suspect they have run away—for they can give no account why they came, nor where they are to march next.

Jan. 4: The accounts hourly coming in are so contradictory and various that we know not which to give credit to. We have heard our people have gained another victory [Battle of Princeton], that the English are fleeing before them, some at Brunswick, some at Princeton. We hear today that Sharp Delany, Anthony Morris, and others of the Philadelphia militia are killed, and that the Count Donop is numbered with the dead; if so, the Hessians have lost a brave and humane commander. The prisoners taken by our troops are sent to Lancaster jail. A number of sick and wounded were brought into town—calls upon us to extend a hand of charity towards them. Several of *my* soldiers left the next house, and returned to the place from whence they came. Upon my questioning them pretty close, I brought several to confess they had run away, being scared at the heavy firing on the 3rd. There were several innocent looking lads among them, and I sympathised with their mothers when I saw them preparing to return to the army.

Jan. 5: I heard today that Capt. Shippen, who threatened to shoot my son for spying at the gondolas, is killed. I forgave him long ago for the fright he occasioned me, and felt sorry when I heard he was dead. We are told today that Gen. Mercer is killed, and Gen. Mifflin wounded. What sad havoc will this dreadful war make in our land.

Jan. 6: We are told today that 2000 New England men fell in the late engagement.

Jan. 7: This evening all the gondolas, which have been for several days past lying before Bristol, sailed down the river, except one which is stationed there for the winter, I suppose. An order arrived about five this evening for the remainder of the soldiers to march. They hurried away, but returned in less than an hour, the officers thinking it too late for them to reach Bordentown tonight.

Jan. 8: All the soldiers are gone from the next house—only one of the number stopped to bid me farewell; but I did not resent it, remembering that only one of the ten lepers cleansed by our Lord returned to give thanks—not that I would compare the few trifling services I was able to render those poor creatures, to that great miracle. But it rose in my mind at the time, perhaps, as a check to any little resentment that I might have felt for being neglected. I went into the house after they had left it, and was grieved to see such loads of provisions wastefully lying on the floor. I sent my son to desire an officer in town to order it away, and he returned his compliments and desired me "to keep it from spoiling"—that was, to make use of it; but as it was not his to give, and I had no stomach to keep it from spoiling, I sent it to another person, who had it taken to the sick soldiers.

Jan. 9: We hear today that our troops have driven the English to Brunswick, and some say there has been another battle. All the officers went out of town today. The report of poor Anthony Morris being killed is confirmed by an officer who was in the engagement. We hear that Washington has sent to buy up a number of stoves, from whence it is conjectured he is going into winter quarters. The weather is very cold; more snow falling has filled the river with ice, and we expect it will be strong enough to walk over in a day or two and give an opportunity to those inclined to escape, of crossing over, which for several days past has been attended with some difficulty, all the boats belonging to the town being seized upon by the gentlemen of the galleys, and either borne away or broke to pieces, which they said was done to prevent the Hessians from crossing the river. On the same pretence, a number of bridges have been taken up, and others so much damaged, as to make it difficult for travellers to pass from hence to Philadelphia. Several of the soldiers, who were brought into town sick, have died, and it is feared the disorder by which they were afflicted is infectious.

Jan. 11: The weather is very cold, and the river quite shut. I pity the poor soldiers now on their march, many of whom will probably lay out in the fields this cold night. What cause have I for gratitude that I and my household are sheltered from the storm. Oh that the hearts of my offspring may learn to trust in the God of their mother—He who has condescended to preserve us in great danger, and kept our feet from wandering from the habitation His goodness has allotted us.

Jan. 12: We are told today of the robbery of one of the Provincial commissaries. The sum is said to be £10.000. I have not heard who is suspected of committing the robbery. The Earl of B_____n [Earl of Burlington, Dr. Odell], who quitted his habitation on the first alarm of the Hessians coming in, is returned with his family. We have some hopes that our refugee will be presented with a pair of lawn sleeves, when dignities become cheap, and suppose he will then think himself too big to creep into his old auger hole. But I shall remind him of the place, if I live to see him created first B_____p of B_____n [Bishop of Burlington].

Jan. 13: Several of the Tories, who went out of town while the gondolas were here, are returned, on hearing there had been a general jail delivery at Philadelphia. One man who thought he was immovable has been compelled to swear or sign allegiance to the States.

Jan. 14: The *lie* of the day runs thus—that the New England men have taken Long Island, are in possession of King's Bridge; that Gen. Lee is retaken by his own men; that the regulars are in a desperate condition (intrenching at Brunswick, and quite hopeless of gaining any advantage over the Americans this campaign). A letter from my amiable friend Hetty Cox informs me her husband's battalion was in the front of the battle at _____ and behaved remarkably well. They took 200 prisoners, and left 80 on the field. He acknowledges the preserving hand of Providence in bringing him safe through such a scene of blood. I hear Gen. Howe sent a request to Washington desiring three days' cessation of arms to take care of the wounded and bury the dead, which was refused. What a woeful tendency war has, to harden the human heart against the tender feelings of humanity. Well may it be called a *horrid art,* thus to change the nature of man. I thought that even barbarous nations had a sort of religious regard for their dead. A friend from Trenton tells me poor Anthony Morris died three hours after he was wounded, and was buried in Friend's burying ground at Stony Brook. Also Capt. Shippen was buried by him. The same friend told us a man was killed in his bed at the house of Stacy Potts in Trenton, in the time of the engagement there, and that Potts' daughter, a young woman about the age of mine, went from home to lodge, the night preceding the battle, and returned in the morning. Just as she stepped into her father's door a ball met her (being directed by the unerring hand of Providence), took the comb out of her hair, and gently grazed the skin of her head, without doing her any further injury. Who shall dare to say they are shot at random? *Jan. 15:* I was a good deal affected this evening on seeing the hearse in which General Mercer's body was conveyed over the river on the ice, to be buried at Philadelphia. Poor Capt. Shippen's body was also taken over at the same time, to be reburied at Philadelphia. P. Reed gave us the following account of a report they heard from a man, whom her sister sent to Burlington to bring some things they were in want of (the night the last soldiers came into town). Reed's wife hired a waggon to come here, and got one of her neighbours to come and fetch some of her goods. Just as the man began to load the waggon, the soldiers came running into town, and the man whipped up his horses and drove away without the goods. When he got to Reed's house in the country he told them there was 10,000 waggons in Burlington—that Gen. Washington, Lee, Howe, and all the Americans were engaged in battle at Burlington,—that Washington was mortally wounded, and that the streets were full of dead bodies, and that the groans of the dying was still in his ears. They opened their letters in fearful haste, and found nothing relative to what the man told them, nor could they convince him that his fright had magnified the matter, till they sent a person up here to enquire.

Margaret Hill Morris /97

February 3: Today appeared in print a proclamation of Gen. Washington's, ordering all persons who had taken protections from the King's commissioners to come in thirty days and swear allegiance to the United States of America, or else to repair with their families to the lines of the British troops. What will become of our refugee now?

Feb. 4: Today eight boats full of soldiers sailed up the river to join the continental forces. They appeared to be very merry, with their drums beating and colours flying. This is said to be the day appointed for our Friends who are prisoners to have a hearing before Putnam. A man who is not a lover of the peace told us it was expected there would be bloody work on the occasion.

Feb. 6: Several hundred soldiers, returning from the camp, were quartered on the inhabitants, and in general, I hear, behaved well.

Feb. 7: All the soldiers quartered on the town last night went away today. The prisoners taken from our town and Mount Holly, discharged and returned home—several of them much fatigued, and some sick.

Feb. 11: This evening two doctors were brought into town and put into prison for inoculating in their families, contrary to the orders of Gen. Putnam, who had prohibited them from inoculating. They were discharged in a few days.

April 10: John Lawrence, Thomas Watson, and several other persons obnoxious to the state, were imprisoned here, and divers others bound over to their good behavior, and to appear at the next court, to be held—none knows where.

April 17: A number of flat-bottom boats went up the river and landed troops at Bristol. It is said 1500 men are billeted on the inhabitants there.

April 19: A report that there has been an engagement between the British troops and Americans—the latter victorious. B. Helm was summoned before the governor, and bound to answer at the next court for preferring silver dollars to paper. The English said to be in motion; the fleet is in the river.

May 7: Capt. Webb and his family came here in order to set off the next day for New York, having received orders from the governor to depart the state. Just as they were retiring to bed, a captain of light-horse arrived with a party of soldiers, and demanded the keys of his trunks—some of which they opened, and searched for letters. They took all they could find, and guarded him to his lodging at R. Smith's, where he was watched all night in his room. They set a guard over his goods, and in the morning returned and examined all his trunks, and then waited on him to Philadelphia, where he was to wait on the general and answer to sundry charges, one of which was, that he was suspected of being a spy. This he boldly cleared himself of. Another was that he had, in a sermon he preached about two years ago, told the people that if they took up arms against the King they would be d_____d. He likewise pleaded innocent to this charge, and finding they could not prove it on him, they referred him to the governor, who reproved him for not taking advantage of a pass he had granted him two or three weeks ago, and absolutely prohibited him from prosecuting his journey to New York, and ordered him to repair with his family to Bethlehem, there to remain during their pleasure, and confined him to a magic circle of six miles.

May 13: The court met here, when several persons confined to our jail (some Tories) were examined. John Lawrence was released, Daniel Ellis imprisoned, and J. Carty fined sixpence for contempt of court; several were ordered back to prison, and R. Smith, B. Helm, T. Hulings, and Collin Campbell examined; R. Smith was ordered to pay £100, or be confined in prison. He chose the latter, and accordingly took possession of the room John Lawrence quitted. The oaths were offered to the three others, which they refusing, were fined.

May 26: This day Capt. Webb and his family left us to go to Bethlehem.

May 28: William Dillwyn, who some days since received a passport from Gen. Washington, set out for New York with the widow Allen accompanying him.

June 7: The reports often coming in by express give us reason to believe the English army are in motion, and it is generally supposed they intend to bend their course to Philadelphia.

June 10: A person from the camp came to town to engage a number of guides (to go back with him) who were well acquainted with the different roads to Philadelphia, that in case our people should be obliged to retreat, they may not be at a loss.

June 11: Certain intelligence arrived, per express, that the English are at Bound Brook, the Americans at Morristown.

June 13: Early this morning the soldiers beat to march from Bristol, and in the course of the day several boats full of soldiers, with the Pennsylvania militia, sailed up the river.

June 14: Before daylight this morning, the alarm guns at Princeton, Trenton, Bordentown, and Bristol were fired, and answered by those below. About 9 o'clock the gondolas and barges began to appear in sight, and from that time to 9 at night there have gone up the river five or six gondolas. Several flat-bottom boats are also gone to Bristol. There is a report of a battle today, which seems probable, as we have heard much firing above. By a person from Bordentown we hear twelve expresses came in there today from camp. We were told by a woman who lodged in the same room where Gen. Reed and Col. Cox took shelter when the battle of Trenton dispersed the Americans that they, Reed and Cox, had laid awake all night consulting together about the best means of securing themselves, and that they came to the determination of setting out next day as soon as it was light, to the British camp, and joining them with all the men under their command. But when morning came an express arrived with an account that the Americans had gained a great victory—the English made to flee before the ragged regiments of Americans. This report put the rebel general and colonel into high spirits and they concluded to remain firm to the cause of America. They paid me a visit, and tho' in my heart I despised them, treated them civilly, and was on the point of telling them their conversation the preceeding night had been conveyed to me, as on the wings of the wind, but on second thoughts gave it up, tho' perhaps the time may come when they will hear more about it.

Some of the gondolas men and their wives being sick, and no doctor in town to apply to, they were told that Mrs. Morris was a skillful woman, and kept medicines to give to the poor. Notwithstanding their late attempt to shoot my poor boy, they ventured to come to me, and in a very humble manner begged me to come and do something for them. At first I thought they might have a design to put a trick on me, and get me aboard of their gondolas and then pillage my house, as they had done some others; but on asking where the sick folk were, was told they were lodged in the governor's house. So I went to see them. There was several, both men and women, very ill with a fever —some said the camp or putrid fever. They were broke out in blotches, and on close examination it appeared to be the itch fever. I treated them according to art, and they all got well. I thought I had received all my pay when they thankfully acknowledged my kindness; but lo, in a short time afterwards a very rough, ill-looking man came to the door and asked for me. When I went to him, he drew me aside and asked if I had any friends in Philadelphia. The question alarmed me, supposing there was some mischief meditated against that poor city. However, I calmly said, "I have an ancient father [-in-law], some sisters, and other near friends there." "Well," said the man, "do you wish to hear from them, or send anything by way of refreshment to them. If you do, I will take charge of it, and bring you back anything you may send for." I was very much surprised, and thought, to be sure, he only wanted to get provisions to take to the gondolas. When he told me his wife was one of those I had given medicine to, and this was the only thing he could do to pay me for my kindness, my heart leaped with joy, and I set about preparing something for my dear absent friends. A quarter of beef, some veal, fowls, and flour, were soon put up, and about midnight the man called and took them aboard of his boat. He left them at Robert Hopkins's, at the Point, from whence my beloved friends took them to town. Two nights after, a loud knocking at our front door greatly alarmed us. Opening the chamber window, we heard a man's voice saying, "Come down

softly and open the door, but bring no light." There was something mysterious in such a call, and we concluded to go down,
and set the candle in the kitchen. When we got to the front door
we asked "who are you?" The man replied, "a friend, open
quickly." So the door was opened, and who should it be but our
honest gondola man, with a letter, a bushel of salt, a jug of
molasses, a bag of rice, some tea, coffee, sugar, and some cloth
for a coat for my poor boys—all sent by my kind sisters. How
did our hearts and eyes overflow with love to them, and thanks
to our heavenly Father for such seasonable supplies. May we
never forget it. Being now so rich, we thought it our duty to
hand out a little to the poor around us, who were mourning for
want of salt. So we divided the bushel and gave a pint to every
poor person that came for it, and had great plenty for our own
use. Indeed it seemed as if our little store increased by distributing it, like the bread broken by our Saviour to the multitude,
which, when he had blessed it, was so marvellously multiplied.
One morning, having left my chamber at an earlier hour than
usual, and casting my eyes toward the river, was surprised to see
hundreds of boats, all filled with British soldiers. I ran to my dear
George Dillwyn's room and begged him to get up and see the
sight. He went to the window, and I waited to hear what he
would say; but as he said nothing, I called out to him, "Brother,
what shall we do, now?" He opened his door and sweetly and
calmly said, "Let us, my sister, keep still and quiet. I believe no
harm will happen to us." And indeed we were favoured with
remarkable stillness. Even the children's minds seemed to par-
take of it. The boats were ordered up the river to Bordentown,
to burn all the gondolas. Poor Robert Sutton and his son passed
my door. I stopped him and asked him where he was going. He
said to join the soldiers to march to Bordentown, for the English
were going to burn it, and on their return would do the same
to Burlington. I begged him not to go, and said perhaps he
would be killed. He said he would go for all that. Next day we
heard he was killed. The report was that some of the militia had
fired on the English boats as they were rowing up the river. The

fire was returned, and poor Sutton was one of the first, if not the only one killed. The last boat we saw was a small one, with only three men and the rowers in it. They were not soldiers. When they came opposite to the town wharf they stopped rowing, and pulled off their hats and bowed to the people on the wharf. We heard afterwards it was our poor refugee, Dr. S. Burling, and S. Stansbury, who intended to have come on shore and paid us a visit, but so many people appearing on the wharf and street, they thought it safest to take to their oars and follow the fleet. One large vessel, with cannon, was in the fleet, and when they returned, were ordered to fire if they saw soldiers on the wharf or about the streets. It seems the soldiers had notice of the time when they were to return, and they placed themselves along the shore, quite down to the ferry. It was First day afternoon, and all the family but myself gone to meeting. I was laying on the bed, and hearing a large gun, looked out of the window and saw the large ship so close to our landing that I thought they were coming ashore. When, behold, they fired two or three of their great guns, which shook the house and went through the walls of our next door neighbour, who was a captain in the rebel army. I still kept at the window, unapprehensive of danger, and seeing two men on the deck talking, and pointing to my house, one of them said, "In that house lives a woman to whom I am indebted for my life. She sheltered me when I was driven from my own home." This I was afterwards told by a person who heard it. It is needless to add that it was our poor refugee who made the above acknowledgement. I really think they have made an end of the gondolas; I hope never to see another. A rebel quartermaster, who had received some little civilities from my Sarah Dillwyn and myself, asked me one day if I did not wish to see my friends in Philadelphia. I said it was the wish nearest to my heart. He said he would accompany me as far as Frankford if I would promise to take no kind of provisions with me, and that he would meet me at the same place and conduct me home again. Such an offer was not to be slighted. I went to my friend A. Odell and asked her if she would venture to bear me company. She joyfully agreed, and we borrowed a horse and chair, and early next morning set out. Our quartermaster being our guard, and good neighbour James Verree went with us to the ferry to see us safe over. We got to Abel James's place in the afternoon, and sent notice to our friends in town. Next morning my father[-in-law], Moore and Wells, and my two sisters, with Dr. Odell and all, met us at Kensington, for they dared not go further, that being the British lines. I believe there never was a more heart-rendering meeting. I had not seen my father[-in-law] and sisters for many months. The dangers we were surrounded with, and the probability of this being the last time we might meet on earth, together with the reports of the great scarcity of provisions in town, and a thousand other things, all contributed to make it an awfully affecting meeting. My sisters went to Abel James's place and dined with me. A. Odell stayed with her husband till evening, when my dear sisters left me and returned to town. The parting with my beloved sisters was almost too much for me. I thought we were taking a last farewell of each other; but part we must. They went to town, and Nancy and myself retired soon to bed, expecting our quartermaster to call on us by daylight. But no news did we hear of him. A heavy firing in the morning made us fearful we should not get safe home. About nine o'clock some stragglers stopped at our quarters, and said there had been a skirmish between the English and Americans, and more terrible still, that parties were ordered out to bring in all they should meet with. This intelligence made us conclude to venture homewards without our guard. We got into our chair and whipped and cut our dull horse at a strange rate. Several parties passed and repassed, and questioned us about whence we came and where we were going. They said if we were going to Burlington we should be stopped at the ferry and taken to Washington's headquarters, for there was a report that women had been into town and brought out goods. We kept our minds pretty calm, hoping that if we got safe to the ferry, as we were so well known, we should meet no more dangers. We got along well till we got to the hill beyond the Red Lyon, which being very bad, and we still pressing our poor horse to make more haste, he made one violent exertion to reach the top of the hill, when, to our utter dismay, the swingletree broke, and the chair began to roll down the hill. We both jumped out at the same instant. Nancy held the horse while I rolled a stone behind the wheel. There we stood, afraid to stir from the horse, and thinking we should be obliged to leave the chair, and lead the horse home. At last we ventured to the door of a small house hard by and begged them to assist us. A man came out and with the help of Nancy's ribbons and my garters, fixed us off, and we once again mounted the chair, and walked the horse till we came near the Bristol road, where we heard the ferry was guarded, and none suffered to cross. However, we kept on and at length reached the ferry, where, instead of armed men, we could hardly find one man to put us over. At last we got over, and now being on our own shore, we began like people just escaped from shipwreck, to review the dangers past and congratulate ourselves on our arrival in a safe port; and I hope not without a sincere, though silent, acknowledgement of the good hand that had vouchsafed to bring us so far on our way to our lonely habitations. When we arrived at my door, my beloved Sarah Dillwyn had the neighbours and children all sitting with her; her tender anxious mind filled with apprehensions for our safety. As we had stayed a day longer than we intended, it was conjectured by our wise neighbour, James Verree, that some terrible thing had happened, nothing less than that the horse, which was his, had been seized, and we kept in Philadelphia. Richard Smith, who lent the chair, was equally alarmed for the fate of his carriage; and S.H., who loudly exclaimed against the expedition, said we were certainly carried to headquarters; and as Nancy's husband was in the British pay, it would go hard with her for his sake. But behold, all their wise conjectures proved like the croaking of the raven, an ill-omened bird that brings good tidings to none; for in the midst of it all we appeared before them in our proper persons, before our arrival was announced. Some cried out, where's the horse? where's the chair? where have you been? We gaily told them all was safe, then sat down to a good dish of tea, and rehearsed all we had seen, heard, and suffered. When we were seriously advised never to engage again in such a perilous undertaking, we as seriously assured them that if we did we would look out for a stronger horse and chair, and be our own guide, for that our late expedition, so far from being a discouragement, was like a whet to an hungry man, which gave him a better appetite to his dinner.

* America lacked medical colleges, and the best doctors were the few who had studied abroad. Margaret, whose medical knowledge equalled that of the average practitioner, doctored many wounded and sick soldiers, and numerous citizens around Burlington. The demands made upon her were such that each morning, following breakfast, a carriage was placed at the front door, awaiting her visits to patients. She once treated thirty people who were suffering from smallpox. In addition to possessing a number of medical textbooks, Margaret relied on various remedies she had jotted down in notebooks. Hers were peculiar, perhaps, in that they were interspersed with food recipes. One notebook contained the following: "To pickle hams," "To preserve cream and use it at sea," "For the rheumatism," "Ringworms to cure," "To make candles for the summer," "To cleanse the skin and prevent pimples," "To destroy bed bugs," "For the hooping cough," "For the piles," "For the bleeding piles," "For the jaundice," "Laxative pills," "For a cough," "Dough nuts," "To kill rats," "New Year cakes," "For preserving eggs," "For the dysentery," "For the itch," and a newspaper item for treating boils: "A roasted fig beat up with white sugar finely powdered is used as a suppurative to a plague boil at Constantinople." Because of the scarcity of medical supplies in Burlington, Margaret opened a small pharmacy, using medical ingredients shipped to her from friends in Philadelphia.

She treated her children's illnesses, and the accidental mishaps that children everywhere were prone to. To her sister Patty she wrote:

Poor, unlucky Dick had like to have committed a fatal mistake last night; he had eaten too many currants, and was very sick afterwards, and thirsty, and he thought a draught of the currant juice, with water, would settle his stomach, and went in the parlour to get it. There happened to be a bottle of antimonial wine on the sideboard, which he took up, and poured about a spoonful in, and then the currant juice; the vomiting increasing, I gave him chamomile tea. This settled his stomach, and I was going to bed, when he told me he believed the stuff he took with the currant juice had made him sick. This alarmed me, and I began to make strict inquiry, and found he had taken what might possibly finish him; so to work I went with milk and oil, and made him drink till, I dare say, there was not a particle left. Happily, these carried the dregs downwards. He was vomiting from eight o'clock till near eleven, before I knew the occasion, and was in great pain till two. This morning he looks weak and poorly, but, I dare say, will never take anything from a bottle that he don't know.

On another occasion "unlucky Dick" had his leg pierced by a sharp arrow while watching boys play at being Indians.

When the Dillwyns left Burlington to live in England, Margaret's brother purchased the house for her. In 1781 she sold it for 500 pounds sterling and moved her family to Philadelphia, where she sold an inherited waterside lot and wharf for 1,800 pounds, a lot on Race Street for 500 pounds, and a lot on 5th and Race Streets for 300 pounds. With this income she was able to live comfortably, and have her children educated—two pursued medical careers.

Summers in Philadelphia were unbearably hot, so much so that it led the French statesman and diplomat, Talleyrand, to remark, "At each inhaling of air, one worries about the next one." Flies and mosquitoes were so intolerable that families had to keep windows closed at night, making the heat more oppressive and sleep difficult. Furthermore, the fashionable feather beds in many homes induced bedbugs to multiply. Insects swarmed over food and it was not unusual after drinking to find one or more dead ones at the bottom of a goblet. Elder-flower powder was sprinkled liberally over rice, wheat, fruit, and bed sheets as an insecticide to kill ants, moths, and weevils.

Such inconveniences, however, were minor compared with the city's devastating yellow fever epidemics. When the disease infested Philadelphia during the summer and fall of 1793 Margaret's son, Dr. John Morris, and his wife died from it. About 4,000 people perished; fifty-two children were orphaned, and wet nurses had to be found for sixteen infants. Remaining in Philadelphia to help treat the inflicted, Margaret wrote her son Richard in September that "every person in the neighbourhood is sick and dying . . . we are in the midst of danger, and whose turn it may be next we know not . . . it is endless to say who are sick and dead; it seems as if the hearses were going by day and night. This day, we were told, 126 were buried, but the number has gradually lessened since that time, and though many are sick, yet fewer die now than in the beginning. As to myself, I dare not quit the post assigned me by Infinite Wisdom. Alas! wither should I go, and for what? I've heard of some who, in the moment they were putting the goods into a cart to remove from their own house, were seized with a fever, and before their goods were unloaded at another place have died." To ward off contamination and the foul odor of putrefaction people were advised by doctors to mix herbs—rue, sage, mint, wormwood, lavender, and rosemary—with white wine-vinegar and "snuff a little up your nostrils when you go into the air, and carry about you a bit of sponge dipped in the same, in order to smell to upon all occasions, especially when you are near any place or person that is infected."

Before the 1797 onslaught an estimated two-thirds of the city's inhabitants had fled. All houses and inn space for many miles outside the city were either purchased or rented. Margaret again witnessed the clattering of sickcarts, but this time resolved to move her family back to Burlington. "If I should, by resolving to remain here, detain my children," she reasoned, "and they should be taken away by the malignant fever, as the others were, who refused to go and leave me behind, it would be more than I could bear."

In Burlington the family lived in a pleasant three-story house on Main Street, where they remained until her daughter, Margaret, married Isaac Collins in 1810. Presumably, she moved to their lodgings. Though physically disabled during the last year or so of her life, Mrs. Morris insisted upon being carried in a sedan chair to gatherings at the Meeting House, a few doors away. There she was seated in a prominent place in the second gallery, and supplied in the winter with a charcoal-heated footstool.

She died at home on October 10, 1816, at the age of seventy-nine; her daughter recorded the final hours: "My brother Richard Morris went to her bedside—she looked earnestly at him and I asked her if she knew him. She said yes, fixing her eyes steadily upon him for some time. I then asked her if she had any pain. She said, intelligibly, 'not any'—and continued sensible 'till about 4 o'clock. After this she took no notice, laying entirely still in the same position I had placed her on . . . not having been moved at all for 54 hours. She continued to breathe shorter and shorter without any apparent pain until sixteen minutes past eleven at night, when she had a slight spasm, and in endeavoring to regain her respiration, uttered a groan twice—which closed the awful scene; but the sweetness that had prevailed still continued to be felt, and we were enobled in measure to rejoice that she was safely landed, when all tears are wiped away."*

Sarah Wister

∗On July 20, 1761 a tiny infant, dripping salty fluid, was abruptly thrust out of a dark, warm womb, only to be assailed suddenly by the starkness of light. In the Wister's Philadelphia home on Market Street, Sarah (Sally) was bundled by a midwife and snuggled next to Lowry Wister. Sally's father Daniel, a prosperous merchant, was the son of John Wister—a German emigrant from Baden who amassed a considerable fortune as a wine merchant. Her mother Lowry was the daughter of Owen Jones and was descended from Welsh planters, King Edward I of England, and the twelfth-century Welsh chieftain, Rhirid Flaidd of Penllyn.

The Wisters generally spent the summer months at their country estate in Germantown, avoiding the discomforts of Philadelphia. The city's intense, sudden changes of wind and sweltering heat spells, broken by sudden storms, weakened people's resistance to dysentery, fevers, smallpox, and other sicknesses. People who kept windows open for ventilation, despite the invasion of mosquitoes, were often assaulted by the racket of coaches, wagons, and drays clattering over cobblestone, and the reek of slop that seeped occasionally into brick gutters.

Their estate in Germantown, with its vast acres of field and woodland, included a large mansion, its walls fashioned from stone quarried from the hills, its joists of oak felled from "Wister's Woods." During winter visits and chilly fall nights the parlor, kitchen, and library were warmed by roaring fires, in hearths so large the entire family could sit inside them. Tiled German stoves, reaching almost to the ceiling, kept a few of the upper rooms heated.

On rainy days Sally could listen from her bedroom to the patter of water drops on foliage and wile away hours dipping a quill into an inkwell, scrawling letters to school chums. From Philadelphia in 1776 her friend Peggy Rawle wrote that she envied Sally's being able to get "out of the noise of the town in the cool, the silent shades. I set at the door by myself, with not a creature to speak to. I know I shall have your pity, which is one comfort." Peggy yearned for the time when Sally, Sally Burge and she would be together again. "As to the boys I fancy we must give them up willingly. I shall not, nor have I now, the most distant desire of being with them again. I think we pass our time more agreeably without them than with them." The three spent winters attending Anthony Benezet's Quaker school.

In 1776 war with Great Britain was inevitable; many Philadelphians feared that the city, with its hotbed of radicals in the Continental Congress, would be attacked by British troops. Anxieties increased when British and Hessian troops seized New York City in September. On the night of the 20th, Patriots foolishly took revenge by setting fire to the city. The British, fearing a Rebel attack, waited cautiously until daybreak before helping firemen and seamen fight the roaring blaze. An infuriated British officer wrote in his diary of "one villian who abused and cut a woman who was employed in bringing water to the engines and who was found cutting the handles of the fire buckets." The Rebel "was hung up by the heels on the spot by the seamen. One or two others who were found in houses with firebrands in their hands were put to death by the enraged soldiery and thrown into the flames. . . . The sick, the aged, women, and children, half naked were seen going they knew not where, and taking refuge in houses which were at a distance from the fire, but from whence in several instances driven a second and even a third time by the devouring element, and at last in a state of despair, laying themselves down on the common." When the fire was finally reduced to smoking embers one quarter of the city had been consumed.

News of the catastrophe reached Philadelphia, and rather than be victims of a similar ravage of their own city, the Wisters sought refuge in a remote country area northeast of Valley Forge. Near the Wissahickon Creek, among the rambling hills of Gwynedd (North Wales) they shared a farmhouse belonging to the Foulke family. When William Foulke died the year before, he left 700 acres, a farmhouse, and mill to his oldest son Jesse, though his widow, Hannah, had a life interest. Hannah and her three grown children—Jesse, Priscilla (Prissa), and Lydia (Liddy)—lived in one half of the house, the Wisters in the other half. Except for a few pieces of silver, china, and delftware, the rustic house was bereft of luxuries common to Philadelphia households. Sally ruminated over her boredom:

My residence at North Wales was at times almost insupport-able, especially when we were without company and in a suc-cession of rainy, disagreeable weather, and I sauntered through the house, upstairs, then down again, out of one chamber into the other, snatch up a book, find it old, throw peevishly down —take my work, this employs me a few minutes, toss it away —a sigh from the inmost recesses of my heart. Oh dear, oh dear, go to the door—a long lane very muddy, the barn, fences and trees as common as my fingers. I hate the country—where now ye poets are all your charming walks, your smiling scenes? Away to the south door—overflowed meadows, board fences, sloppy roads, woods, woods, woods, continually presented to my aching eyes. Philadelphia, dear Philadelphia, why am I absent from thee, and thy loved inhabitants? Why is not reason a resident in my heart? But what has reason to do with a discontented mind?—Obey a summons to dine—the meal over—run to my chamber, sometimes visited by someone, oftener intruding thoughts—jump up—in a stupid mood. Put on my cap, sometimes straight and tolerable, frequently crooked and intolerable. Adjust my dress, toss up the window, hearing a noise and fancing it some smart military or other swain. Disappointed, nothing but T. McGlathary driving a stray horse home—or the pigs running to the daily supplied trough—SLAM DOWN the sash in anger, provoking pigs and horses—walk very leisurely—or else, as fast as I can, down-stairs and into the parlour. Mama and Betsy [Sally's sister] at work. Silence reigns throughout the room, till broken by inquiry of Sally, where her work is—I do not know, perhaps lost. Throw myself in an armchair. A long pause ensues, mama intent upon her work, my sister vastly industrious. I rise from my seat, open a drawer, shut it, open another. "And where is our father, pray?" "Gone to the mill." "To the MILL," I exclaim, "tis disagreeable enough to walk there in fine weather. He must find great entertainment to go splashing in the mud—so would not I. Betsy would thee?" "Do Sally be still. I am engaged in imaginary pleasures." Every effort to dispell their amazing taciturnity proves ineffectual. I go to see if there is any prospect of clearing up again, visit the door, look up and down the lane, chicks and pigs in abundance, cast my eyes toward heavens, one compact cloud, no friendly beams of sun to cheer my gloomy thoughts. Rain, rain, rain, pat, pat, pat. Dropping off the eves on the broad flat stones. No variation, but one continued sound, much like the sane men in my days. I wish it would clear.

Yet for the people who remained in Philadelphia the environment was becoming increasingly more dangerous. Many people were dying of smallpox, dysentery, and fevers. The victims were largely the poor, who could not afford the cost of medical treatment. Sally's most cherished friend, Debby Norris, wrote her of the troubled city: "Philadelphia is not as it used to be. You can scarce walk a square without seeing the shocking sight of a cart with five or six coffins in it. Oh! it is too dreadful a scene to attempt to describe. The poor creatures die without numbers. Large pits are dug in the negroes' burying ground, and forty or fifty coffins are put in the same hole. This is really true. I do not exaggerate."

On July 23, 1777, two hundred fifty British warships, transports, and miscellaneous vessels had their sails hoisted in New York Harbor. Commanded by Sir William Howe, the ships veered southward for the invasion of Philadelphia. At the mouth of the Delaware River the fleet was blocked by an elaborate cheveaux de frise—strong iron-clad spikes placed menacingly below the water's surface. Howe's troops, forced to land along the Maryland coast, advanced to Brandywine, Delaware, where on September 11th they battered Washington's army. Unopposed, the British crossed the Schuylkill River near Valley Forge the night of the 22nd, and were then in an excellent position to launch an assault upon Philadelphia. On the day Sally began her diary, the British encampment was ten or twelve miles southwest of the Foulke farm. The diary was dedicated to Debby, by means of an attached letter. ✻

September 24, 1777: Two Virginia officers called at our house and informed us that the British army had crossed the Schuylkill. Presently after, another person stopped, and confirmed what they had said, and that General Washington and army were near Pottsgrove. Well, thee may be sure we were sufficiently scared; however, the road was very still till evening. About seven o'clock we heard a great noise. To the door we all went. A large number of waggons, with about three hundred of the Philadelphia militia. They begged for drink, and several pushed into the house. One of those that entered was a little tipsy, and had a mind to be saucy. I then thought it time for me to retreat; so figure me (mightily scared, as not having presence of mind enough to face so many of the military) running in at one door and out another, all in a shake with fear; but after a while, seeing the officers appear gentlemanly and the soldiers civil, I called reason to my aid. My fears were in some measure dispelled, tho' my teeth rattled and my hands shook like an aspen leaf. They did not offer to take their quarters with us; so, with many blessings, and as many adieus, they marched off.

Sept. 25: This day, till twelve o'clock, the road was mighty quiet, when Hobson Jones came riding along. He made a stop at our door, and said the British were at Skippack Road, that we should soon see the light horse. A party of Hessians had actually turned into our lane. My dadda and mamma gave it the credit it deserved, for he does not keep strictly to the truth in all respects; but the delicate, chicken-hearted Liddy Foulke and me were wretchedly scared. We could say nothing but "Oh! What shall we do? What will become of us?" These questions only augmented the terror we were in. Well, the fright went off. We seen no light horse or Hessians. Owen Foulke came here in the evening and told us that General Washington had come down as far as the Trappe, and that General McDougle's brigade was stationed at Montgomery, consisting of about 16 hundred men. This he had from Dr. Edwards, Lord Stirling's aide-de-camp; so we expected to be in the midst of one army or t'other.

Sept. 26: We were unusually silent all the morning. No passengers came by the house, except to the mill, and we don't place much dependence on mill news. About 12 o'clock, cousin Jesse heard that General Howe's army had moved down towards Philadelphia. Then, my dear, our hopes and fears were engaged for you. However, my advice is, summon up all your resolution, call Fortitude to your aid, don't suffer your spirits to sink, my dear. There's nothing like courage; 'tis what I stand in need of myself, but unfortunately have but little of it in my composition. I was standing in the kitchen about 12, when somebody came to me in a hurry, screaming, "Sally, Sally, here are the light horse!" This was by far the greatest fright I had endured. Fear tacked wings to my feet. I was at the house in a moment; at the porch I stopt, and it really was the light horse. I run immediately to the western door, where the family were assembled, anxiously waiting for the event. They rode up to the door and halted, and enquired if we had horses to sell. He was answered negatively. "Have not you, sir," to my father, "two black horses?" "Yes, but have no mind to dispose of them." My terror had by this time nearly subsided. The officer and men behaved perfectly civil; the first drank two glasses of wine, rode away, bidding his men follow, which, after adieus in number, they did. The officer was Lieutenant Lindsay of Bland's regiment, Lee's troop. They, to our great joy, were Americans, and but four in all. What made us imagine them British, they wore blue and red, which with us is not common. It has rained all this afternoon and, to present appearances, will all night in all probability. The English will take possession of the city [Philadelphia] tomorrow or next day. What a change will it be. May the Almighty take you under His protection, for without His divine aid all human assistance is vain.

May heaven's guardian arm protect my absent friends,
From danger guard them, and from want defend.

Forgive, my dear, the repetition of those lines, but they just darted into my mind. Nothing worth relating has occured this afternoon. Now for trifles. I have set a stocking on the needles, and intend to be mighty industrious. This evening some of our folks heard a very heavy cannon. We suppose it to be fired by the English. The report seemed to come from Philadelphia. We hear the American army will be within five miles of us tonight. The uncertainty of our position engrosses me quite. Perhaps, to be in the midst of war and ruin, and the clang of arms. But we must hope the best. Here, my dear, passes an interval of several weeks in which nothing happened worth the time and paper it would take to write it. The English, however, in the interim, had taken possession of the city.

October 19: Now for new and uncommon scenes. As I was laying in bed and ruminating on past and present events, and thinking how happy I should be if I could see you, Liddy came running into the room and said there was the greatest drumming, fifing, and rattling of waggons that ever she had heard. What to make of this we were at a loss. We dressed and down stairs in a hurry. Our wonder ceased. The British had left Germantown, and our army were marching to take possession. It was the general opinion they would evacuate the capital. Sister Betsy and myself, and George Emlen went about half a mile from home, where we could see the army pass. Thee will stare at my going, but no impropriety, in my opine, or I should not have gone. We made no great stay, but returned with excellent appetites for our breakfast. Several officers called to get some refreshments, but none of consequence till the afternoon. Cousin Prissa and myself were sitting at the door; I in a green skirt, dark short gown. Two genteel men of the military order rode up to the door. "Your servant, ladies," etc.; asked if they could have quarters for General Smallwood. Aunt Foulke thought she could accommodate them as well as most of her neighbors said they could. One of the officers dismounted and wrote "Smallwood's Quarters" over the door, which secured us from straggling soldiers. After this he mounted his steed and rode away. When we were alone our dress and lips were put in order for conquest, and the hopes of adventures gave brightness to each before passive countenance. Thee must be told of a Dr. Gould who, by accident, had made acquantance with my father; a sensible, conversible man, a Carolinian,—and had come to bid us adieu on his going to that state. Daddy had prevailed upon him to stay a day or two with us. In the evening his generalship came with six attendants— which composed his family—a large guard of soldiers, a number of horses and baggage waggons. The yard and house was in confusion and glittered with military equipments. Gould was intimate with Smallwood, and had gone into Jesse's to see him. While he was there, there was great running up and down stairs, so I had an opportunity of seeing and being seen, the former the most agreeable, to be sure. One person in particular attracted my notice. He appeared cross and reserved; but thee shall see how agreeably disappointed I was. Dr. Gould ushered the gentlemen into our parlour, and introduced them. General Smallwood, Captain Furnival, Major Stoddert, Mr. Prig, Captain Finley, and Mr. Clagan, Colonel Wood, and Colonel Line. Those last two did not come with the general. They are Virginians, and both indisposed. The general and suite are Marylanders. Be assured I did not stay long with so many men, but secured a good retreat, heart-safe, so far. Some supped with us, others at Jesse's. They retired about ten, in good order. How new is our situation! I feel in good spirits, though surrounded by an army: the house full of officers, yard alive with soldiers—very peaceable sort of men, tho'. They eat like other folks, talk like them, and behave themselves with elegance; so I will not be afraid of them. That I won't. Adieu. I am going to my chamber to dream, I suppose of bayonets and swords, sashes, guns, and epaulets.

Oct. 20: Morning—I dare say thee is impatient to know my

sentiments of the officers; so, while Somnus embraces them, and the house is still, take their characters according to their rank. The general is tall, portly, well-made. A truly martial air, the behaviour and manners of a gentleman, a good understanding, and great humanity of disposition constitute the character of Smallwood. Col. Wood, from what we hear of him and what we see, is one of the most amiable of men: tall and genteel, an agreeable countenance and deportment. The following lines will more fully characterize him.

How skilled he is in each obliging art,
The mildest manners with the bravest heart.

The cause he is fighting for alone tears him from the society of an amiable wife and engaging daughter. With tears in his eyes he often mentions the sweets of domestic life. Col. Line is not married, so let me not be too warm in his praise, lest you suspect. He is monstrous tall and brown, but has a certain something in his face and conversation very agreeable. He entertains the highest notions of honour, is sensible and humane, and a brave officer; he is only seven and twenty years old, but, by a long indisposition and constant fatigue, looks very older and almost worn to a skeleton, but very lively and talkative. Capt. Furnival —I need not say more of him than that he has, excepting one or two, the handsomest face I ever saw, a very fine person; fine light hair, and a great deal of it, adds to the beauty of his face. Well here comes the glory, the major, so bashful, so famous, he should come before the captain, but never mind. I at first thought the major cross and proud, but I was mistaken. He is about nineteen, nephew to the general, and acts as major of brigade to him; he cannot be extolled for the graces of person, but for those of the mind he may justly be celebrated. He is large in his person, manly, and an engaging countenance and address. Finley is wretched ugly, but he went away last night, so I shall not particularize him. Nothing of any moment today; no acquaintance with the officers. Cols. Wood and Line, and Gould dined with us. I was dressed in my chintz and looked smarter than night before.

Oct. 21: I just now met the major, very reserved: nothing but "Good morning," or "Your servant, madam;" but Furnival is most agreeable; he chats every opportunity; but luckily has a wife. I have heard strange things of the major. Worth a fortune of thirty thousand pounds, independent of anybody, the major moreover is vastly bashful; so much so he can hardly look at the ladies. (Excuse me, good sir; I really thought you were not clever; 'tis bashfulness only, we will drive that away.)

Oct. 25: Evening—Prepare to hear amazing things. The general was invited to dine, was engaged; but Colonel Wood, Major Stoddert, and Dr. Edwards dined with us. In the afternoon, Stoddert, addressing himself to mamma, "Pray, ma'am, do you know Miss Nancy Bond?" I told him of the amiable girl's death. This major had been at Philadelphia College. In the evening I was diverting Johnny at the table, when he drew his chair to it and began to play with the child. I asked him if he knew N. Bond. "No, ma'am, but I have seen her very often." One word brought on another one. We chatted the greatest part of the evening. He said he knew me directly as he seen me. Told me exactly where we lived. It rains now, so adieu.

Oct. 26: A very rainy morning, so like to prove. The officers in the house all day. Afternoon—The general and officers drank tea with us and stayed part of the evening. After supper I went into aunt's, where sat the general, Colonel Line, and Major Stoddert, so Liddy and me seated ourselves at the table in order to read a verse book. The major was holding a candle for the general, who was reading a newspaper. He looked at us, turned away his eyes, looked again, put the candlestick down, up he jumps, out of the door he went. "Well," said I to Liddy, "he will join us when he comes in." Presently he returned, and seated himself on the table. "Pray, ladies, is there any songs in that book?" "Yes, many." "Can't you favor me with a sight of it?" "No, major; 'tis a borrowed book." "Miss Sally, can't you sing?" "No." Thee may be sure I told the truth there. Liddy, saucy girl, told him I could. He begged, and I denied; for my voice is not much better than a raven. We talked and laughed for an hour.

He is very clever, amiable, and polite. He has the softest voice, never pronounces the "r" at all.

I must tell thee, today arrived Colonel Gist and Major Leatherberry; the former a smart widower, the latter a lawyer, a sensible young fellow, and will never swing for want of tongue. Dr. Diggs came Second day [Monday]; a mighty disagreeable man. We were obliged to ask him to tea. He must needs prop himself between the major and me, for which I did not thank him. After I had drank tea, I jumped from the table and seated myself at the fire. The major followed my example, drew his chair close to mine, and entertained me very agreeably. Oh Debby, I have a thousand things to tell thee. I shall give thee so droll an account of my adventures that thee will smile. "No occasion of that, Sally," methinks I hear thee say, "for thee tells me every trifle." But, child, thee is mistaken, for I have not told thee half the civil things that are said of us *sweet* creatures at "General Smallwood's quarters." I think I might have sent the gentlemen to their chambers. I made my adieus, and home I went.

Oct. 27: Morning—A polite "good morning" from the major, very sociable than ever. No wonder; a stoic could not resist such affable damsels as we are. Evening—We had again the pleasure of the general and suite at afternoon tea. He (the general, I mean) is most agreeable; so lively, so free, and chats so gaily that I had quite an esteem for him. I must steel my heart. Captain Furnival is gone to Baltimore, the residence of his beloved wife. The major and I had a little chat to ourselves this eve. No harm, I assure thee; he and I are friends. This eve came a parson belonging to the army. He is, how shall I describe him, near seven foot high, thin, and meagre, not a single personal charm, very few mental ones. He fell violently in love with Liddy at first sight; the first discovered conquest that has been made since the arrival of the general. Come, shall we chat about Col. Gist? He's very pretty; a charming person. His eyes are exceptional, very stern, and he so rolls them about that mine always fall under them. He bears the character of a brave officer; another admirer of Liddy's, and she of him. When will Sally's admirer's appear?

Ah, that indeed. Why, Sally has not charms sufficient to pierce the heart of a soldier. But still I won't dispair. Who knows what mischief I yet may do. Well, Debby, here's Dr. Edwards come again. Now we shall not want clack, for he has a perpetual motion in his head, and if he was not so clever as he is, we should get tired.

Oct. 29: I walked into aunt's this evening. I met the major. Well, thee will think I am writing his history; but not so. Pleased with the encounter, Betsy, Stoddert, and myself, seated by the fire, chatted away an hour in lively and agreeable conversation. I can't pretend to write all he said; but he shone in every subject that was talked of.

Oct. 31: A most charming day. I walked to the door and received the salutation of the morn from Stoddert and other officers. As often as I go to the door, so often have I seen the major. We chat passingly, as, "A fine day, Miss Sally." "Yes, very fine, major." Night—Another very charming conversation with the young Marylander. He seems possessed of very amiable manners; sensible and agreeable. He has by his unexceptional deportment engaged my esteem.

November 1: Morning—Liddy, Betsy, and a T.L. (prisoner of this state) went to the mill. We made very free with some Continental flour. We were powdered mighty white, to be sure. Home we came. Col. Wood was standing at a window with a young officer. He gave him a push forward, as much as to say, "Observe what fine girls we have here." For all I do not mention Wood as often as he deserves. It is not because we are not sociable; we are very much so, and he is often at our house. Liddy and I had a kind of adventure with him this morn. We were in his chamber chatting about our little affairs, and no idea of being interupted. We were standing up, each an arm on a chest of drawers. The door banged open—Col. Wood was in the room; we started, the colour flew into our faces and crimsoned us over; the tears flew into my eyes. It was very silly, but his coming was so abrupt. He was between us and the door. "Ladies, do not be scared, I only want something from my portmanteau; I beg you not to be disturbed." We ran by him, like two partridges, into mamma's room, threw ourselves into chairs, and reproached each other for being so foolish as to blush and look so silly. I was very much vexed at myself, so was Liddy. The colonel laughed at us, and it blew over. The army had orders to march today [to White-marsh]; the regulars accordingly did. General Smallwood had the command of militia at that time, and they being in the rear, were not to leave their encampment until Second day. Observe how militaryish I talk. No wonder, when I am surrounded by people of that order. The general, Colonels Wood, Line, Gist, and Crawford, Majors Stoddert and Leatherberry, dined with us today. After dinner, Liddy, Betsy, and thy smart journaliser put on their bonnets, determined to take a walk. We left the house. I naturally looked back; when behold, the two majors seemed debating whether to follow us or not. Liddy said, "We shall have their attendance;" but I did not think so. They opened the gate and came fast after us. They overtook us about ten poles from home and begged leave to attend us. No fear of a refusal. They inquired where we were going. "To neighbor Roberts's. We will introduce you to his daughters; you us to General Stevens." The affair was concluded, and we shortened the way with lively conversation. Our intention of going to Roberts's was frustrated; the rain that had fallen lately had raised the Wissahickon too high to attempt crossing it on foot. We altered the plan of our ramble, left the road, and walked near two miles thro' the woods. Mr. Leatherberry, observing my locket, repeated the lines with the energy of a comedian:

On her white breast a sparkling cross she wore,
That jews might kiss and infidels adore.

I replied my trinket bore no resemblance to a cross. "'Tis something better, madam." 'Tis nonsense to pretend to recount all that was said; my memory is not so obliging; but it is sufficient that nothing happened during our little excursion but what was very agreeable and entirely consistent with the strictist rules of politeness and decorum. I was vexed a little at tearing my muslin petticoat. I had on my white whim, quite as nice as a First day in town. We returned home safe. Smallwood, Wood, and Stoddert drank tea with us and spent the greater part of the evening. I declare this general is very, very entertaining, so good-natured, so good-humoured; yet so sensible I wonder he is not married. Are there no ladies formed to his taste? Some people, my dear, think that there's no difference between good nature and good humour; but according to my opinion, they differ widely. Good nature consists in a naturally amiable and even disposition, free from all peevishness and fretting. It is accompanied by a natural gracefulness—a manner of doing and saying everything agreeably; in short, it steals the senses and captivates the heart. Good humour consists in being pleased, and who would thank a person for being cheerful if they had nothing to take from them otherways. Good humour is a very agreeable companion for an afternoon, but give me good nature for life. Adieu.

Nov. 3: Morning—Today the militia marches, and the general and officers leave us. High ho. I am very sorry; for when you have been with agreeable people, 'tis impossible not to feel regret when they bid you adieu, perhaps for ever. When they leave us we shall be immured in solitude. The major looks dull. About two o'clock the general and major came to bid us adieu. With daddy and mammy they shook hands very friendly; to us they bowed politely. Our hearts were full. I thought major was affected. "Goodby, Miss Sally," spoken very low. He walked hastily and mounted his horse. They promised to visit us soon. We stood at the door to take a last look, all of us very sober. The major turned his horse's head, and rode back, dismounted. "I have forgot my pistols," passed us, and ran upstairs. He came swiftly back as if wishing, through inclination, to stay; by duty compelled to go. He remounted his horse. "Farewell, ladies, till I see you again," and cantered away. We looked at him till the turn in the road hid him from our sight. "Amiable major," "Clever fellow," "Good young man," was echoed from one to the other. I wonder if we shall ever see him again. He has our wishes for his safety. Well, here's Uncle Miles. Heartily glad of that am I. His family are well, and at Reading. Evening—Jesse, who went with the general, returned. I had by him a letter from my dear Polly Fishbourn. She is at George Emlen's. Headquarters is at their house. We had compliments from the general and major. They are very well disposed of at Evan Meredith's, six miles from here. I wrote to Polly Fishbourn, by Uncle Miles, who waited upon General Washington next morning.

Nov. 4: Morning—It seems strange not to see our house as it used to be. We are very still. No rattling of waggons, glittering of muskets. The beating of the distant drum is all we hear. Colonels Wood, Line, Gist, and Major Leatherberry are still here; the two last leave us today. Wood and Line will soon bid us adieu. Amiable Wood; he is esteemed by all that know him. Everybody has a good word for him. Here I skip a week or two, nothing of consequence occurring. Wood and Line are gone. Some time since arrived two officers, Lieutenants Lee and Warring, Virginians. I had only the salutations of the morn from them. Lee is not remarkable one way or another; Warring an insignificant piece enough. Lee sings prettily, and talks a great deal of how good turkey hash and fried hominy is (a pretty discourse to entertain the ladies), extols Virginia, and execrates Maryland, which, by-the-by, I provoked them to; for though I admire both Virginia and Maryland, I laughed at the former, and praised the latter. Ridiculed their manner of speaking. I took great delight in teasing them. I believe I did it sometimes ill-naturedly; but I don't care. They were not, I am certain almost, first-rate gentlemen. (How different from our other officers.) But they are gone to Virginia, where they may sing, dance, and eat turkey hash and fried hominy all day long, if they choose. Nothing scarcely lowers a man in my opinion more than talking of eating what they love and what they hate. Lee and Warring were proficients in this science. Enough of them.

December 5: Oh, gracious Debby, I am all alive with fear. The English have come out to attack (as we imagine) our army. They are on Chestnut Hill, our army three miles this side. What will become of us, only six miles distant. We are in hourly expectation of an engagement. I fear we shall be in the midst of it.

Heaven defend us from so dreadful a sight. The battle of Germantown and the horrors of that day are recent in my mind. It will be sufficiently dreadful, if we are only in hearing of the firing, to think how many of our fellow creatures are plunged into the boundless ocean of eternity, few of them prepared to meet their fate. But they are summoned before an all-merciful judge, from whom they have a great deal to hope.

Dec. 6: No firing this morning. I hope for one more quiet day. I was much alarmed just now, sitting in the parlour, indulging melancholy reflections, when somebody burst open the door. "Sally, here's Major Stoddert." I jumped. Our conjectures were various concerning his coming. The poor fellow, from great fatigue and want of rest, together with being exposed to the night air, had caught cold, which brought on a fever. He could scarcely walk, and I went into aunt's to see him. I was surprised. Instead of the lively, alert, blooming Stoddert, who was on his feet the instant we entered, he looked pale, thin, and dejected, too weak to raise a bow, and "How are you, Miss Sally?" "How does thee do, major?" I seated myself near him, inquired the cause of his indisposition, asked for the general, received his compliments. Not willing to fatigue him with too much chat, I bid him adieu. Tonight Aunt Hannah Foulke administered something. Jesse assisted him to his chamber. He had not lain down five minutes before he was fast asleep. Adieu. I hope we shall enjoy a good night's rest.

Dec. 7: Morning—I tripped into aunt's. There sat the major, rather more like himself. How natural it was to see him. "Good morning, Miss Sally." "Good morrow, major, how does thee do today?" "I feel quite recovered, Sally." "Well, I fancy this indisposition has saved thy head this time." Major: "No ma'am; for if I hear a firing, I shall soon be with them." That was heroic. About eleven I dressed myself, silk and cotton gown. It is made without an apron. I feel quite awkwardish and prefer the girlish dress. Afternoon—A Mr. Seaton and Stoddert drank tea with us. He and me had a little private chat after tea. In the evening Seaton went into aunt's; mamma went to see Prissa, who is poorly; papa withdrew to talk with some strangers. Liddy just then came in, so we engaged in an agreeable conversation. I begged him to come and give us a circumstantial account of the battle, if there should be one. "I certainly will, ma'am, if I am favoured with life." Liddy unluckily took it into her head to blunder out something about a person being in the kitchen who had come from the army. Stoddert, ever anxious to hear, jumped up. "Good night to you ladies," was the word, and he disappeared, but not forever. "Liddy, thee hussy; what business had thee to mention a word of the army? Thee sees it sent him off. Thy evil genius prevailed, and we all feel the effects of it." "Lord bless me," said Liddy, "I had not a thought of his going, or for ten thousand worlds I would not spoke." But we cannot recall the past. Well, we laughed and chatted at a noisy rate, till a summons for Liddy parted us. I sat negligently on my chair, and thought brought on thought. I got so low-spirited that I could hardly speak. The dread of an engagement, our dreadful situation (if a battle should ensue) we should be in, joined to my anxiety for Polly Fishbourn and family, who would be in the midst of the scene, was the occasion. And yet I did not feel half so frightened as I expected to be. 'Tis amazing how we get reconciled to such things. Six months ago the bare idea of being within ten, aye, twenty miles of a battle would almost have distracted me. And now, tho' two such large armies are within six miles of us, we can be cheerful and converse calmly of it. It verifies the old proverb that "use is second nature." I forgot one little piece of intelligence, in which the girls say I discovered a particular partiality for our Marylander, but I disclaim anything of the kind. These saucy creatures are forever finding out wonders, and for metamorphosing molehills into mountains.

> Friendship I offer pure and free;
> And who, with such a friend as ME
> Could ask or wish for more.

"If they charged thee with vanity, Sally, it would not be very unjust." Debby Norris, be quiet; no reflections, or I have done. "But the piece of intelligence, Sally." It is just coming, Debby.

In the afternoon we distinctly heard platoon firing. Everybody was at the door; I in the horrors. The armies, as we judged, were engaged. Very composedly says the major to our servant, "Will you be kind enough to saddle my horse? I shall go." Accordingly the horse was taken from the hospitable, quiet barn to plunge into the thickest ranks of war. Cruel change. Seaton insisted to the major that the armies were still; "nothing but skirmishing with the flanking parties; do not go." We happened (us girls I mean) to be standing in the kitchen, the major passing thro' in a hurry, and I, forsooth, discovered a strong partiality by saying, "Oh! Major, thee is not going!" He turned round. "Yes, yes, I am, Miss Sally," bowed, and went into the road; we all pitied him. The firing rather decreased; and, after persuasions innumerable from my father and Seaton, and the firing over, he reluctantly agreed to stay. Ill as he was, he would have gone. It showed his bravery, of which we all believed him possessed of a large share.

Dec. 8: Rejoice with us my dear. The British have returned to the city [Philadelphia]. Charming this. May we ever be thankful to the Almighty Disposer of events for his care and protection of us while surrounded with dangers. Major went to the army. Nothing for him to do; so returned. Third or Fourth day, I forget which, he was very ill; kept to his chamber most of the day. In the evening I saw him. I pity him mightily, but pity is a poor remedy.

Dec. 11: Our army moved, as we thought, to go into winter quarters, but we hear there is a party of the enemy gone over Schuylkill; so our army went to look at them. I observed to Stoddert, "So you are going to leave us to the English." "Yes, ha! ha! ha! leave you for the English." He has a certain indifference about him sometimes that, to strangers, is not very pleasing. He sometimes is silent for minutes. One of these silent fits was interrupted the other day by his clasping his hands and exclaiming aloud, "Oh, my God, I wish this war was at an end." Noon —The major gone to camp. I don't think we shall see him again. Well, strange creature that I am, here have I been going on without giving thee of an account of two officers,—one who will be a principal character; their names are Capt. Lipscomb and a Mr. Tilly; the former a tall, genteel man, very delicate from an indisposition, and has a softness in his countenance that is very pleasing, and has the finest head of hair that I ever saw; 'tis a light shining auburn. The fashion of his hair was this—negligently *tied* and waving down his back. Well may it be said,

Loose flowed the soft redundance of his hair. He has not hitherto shown himself a lady's man, tho' he is perfectly polite. Now let me attempt to characterize Tilly. He seems a wild, noisy mortal, tho' I am not much acquainted with him. He appears bashful when with girls. We dissipated the major's bashfulness; but I doubt we have not so good a subject now. He is above the common size, rather genteel, an extreme pretty, ruddy face, hair brown, and a sufficiency of it, a very great laugher, and talks so excessively fast that he often begins sentences without finishing the last, which confuses him very much, and then he blushes and laughs; and, in short, he keeps me in perpetual good humour; but the creature has not addressed one civil thing to me since he came. But I have not done with his accomplishments yet, for he is a musician—that is, he plays on the German flute, and has it here. Night—The family retired; take the adventures of the afternoon as they occurred. Seaton and Captain Lipscomb drank tea with us. While we sat at tea, the parlour door was opened; in came Tilly; his appearance was elegant; he had been riding; the wind had given the most beautiful glow to his cheeks, and blowed his hair carelessly round his face. Oh, my heart, thought I, be secure! The caution was needless, I found it without a wish to stray. When the tea equipage was removed, the conversation turned on politicks, a subject I avoid. I gave Betsy a hint. I rose, she followed, and we went to seek Liddy. We chatted a few minutes at the door. The moon shone with uncommon splendour. Our spirits were high. I proposed a walk; the girls agreed. When we reached the poplar tree we stopped. Our ears were assailed by a number of voices. "A party of light horse," said one. "The English, perhaps; let's run home." "No, no," said I, "be heroines." At last two or three men on horseback came in sight. We walked on. The well-known voice of the major saluted our hearing with "How do you do, ladies." We turned ourselves about with one accord. He, not relishing the idea of sleeping on the banks of the Schuylkill, had returned to the mill. We chatted along the road till we reached our hospitable mansion. Stoddert dismounted and went into Jesse's parlour. I sat there a half hour. He is very amiable. Lipscomb, Seaton, Tilly, and my father, hearing of his return, and impatient for the news, came in at one door, while I made my exit at the other. I am vexed at Tilly, who has his flute, and does nothing but play the fool. He begins a tune, plays a note or so, then stops. Well, after a while, he begins again; stops again. "Will that do, Seaton? Hah! hah! hah!" He has given us but two regular tunes since he arrived. I am passionately fond of music. How boyish he behaves.

Dec. 12: I ran into aunt's this morning to chat with the girls. Major Stoddert joined us in a few minutes. I verily believe the man is fond of the ladies, and, what to me is astonishing, he has not discovered the smallest degree of pride. Whether he is artful enough to conceal it under the veil of humility, or whether he has none, is a question; but I am inclined to think it the latter. I really am of opinion that there is few of the young fellows of the modern age exempt from vanity, more especially those who are blessed with exterior graces. If they have a fine pair of eyes, they are ever rolling them about; a fine set of teeth, mind, they are great laughers; a genteel person, forever changing their attitudes to show them to advantage. Oh vanity! vanity! how boundless is thy sway! But to resume this interview with Major Stoddert. We were very witty and sprightly. I was darning an apron, upon which he was pleased to compliment me. "Well, Miss Sally, what would you do if the British were to come here?" "Do," exclaimed I; "be frightened just to death." He laughed and said he would escape their rage by getting behind the representation of a British grenadier which you have upstairs. "Of all things, I should like to frighten Tilly with it. Pray, ladies, let's fix it in his chamber tonight." "If thee will take all the blame, we will assist thee." "That I will," he replied, and this was the plan. We had brought some weeks ago a British grenadier from Uncle Miles's on purpose to divert us. It is remarkably well executed, six feet high, and makes a martial appearance. This we agreed to stand at the door that opens into the road (the house has four rooms on a floor, with a wide entry running through), with another figure, that would add to the deceit. One of our servants was to stand behind them; others were to serve as occasion offered. After half an hour's converse, in which we raised our expectations to the highest pitch, we parted. If our scheme answers, I shall communicate it in the eve. Till then, adieu. Night—Never did I more sincerely wish to possess a descriptive genius than I do now. All that I can write will fall infinitely short of the truly diverting scene that I have been witness to tonight. But, as I mean to attempt an account, I had as well shorten the preface and begin the story. In the beginning of the evening I went to Liddy and begged her to secure the swords and pistols which were in their parlour. The Marylander, hearing our voices, joined us. I told him of my proposal. Whether he thought it a good one or not I can't say, but he approved of it, and Liddy went in and brought her apron full of swords and pistols. When this was done, Stoddert joined the officers. We girls went and stood at the first landing of the stairs. The gentlemen were very merry, and chatting on public affairs, when Seaton's negro (observe that Seaton, being indisposed, was apprized of the scheme) opened the door, candle in hand, and said, "There's somebody at the door that wishes to see you." "Who? All of us?" said Tilly. "Yes, sir," answered the boy. They all rose (the major, as he afterwards said, almost dying with laughing), and walked into the entry, Tilly first, in full expectation of news. The first object that struck his view was a British soldier. In a moment his ears were saluted with "Is there any rebel officers here?" in a thundering voice. Not waiting for a second word, he darted like lightning out of the front door, through the yard, bolted o'er the fence, swamps, fences, thorn-hedges and ploughed fields. No way impeded his retreat. He was soon out of hearing. The woods echoed with

On a shrouding, dank night in December 1777, Robert Tilly of Virginia "darted like lightning" out of the Foulke house at North Wales, "through the yard, bolted o'er the fence, swamps, fences," to flee from "a bit of painted wood."

"Which way did he go? Stop him! Surround the house!" The amiable Lipscomb had his hand on the latch of the door, intending to make his escape; Stoddert, considering his indisposition, acquainted him with the deceit. We females ran downstairs to join the general laugh. I walked into Jesse's parlour. There sat poor Stoddert (whose sore lips must have received no advantage from this), almost convulsed with laughing, rolling in an armchair. He said nothing; I believe he could not have spoke. "Major Stoddert," said I, "go to call Tilly back. He will lose himself —indeed he will;" every word interrupted with a "Ha!ha!"

Sarah Wister / 131

The Coldstream Guardsman, referred to by Sally Wister as a British grenadier, was believed to have been painted by Major John André for a play given by the British in Philadelphia during the city's occupation.

At last he rose and went to the door; and what a loud voice could avail in bringing him back, he tried. Figure to thyself this Tilly, of a snowy evening, no hat, shoes down at heel, hair untied, flying across meadows, creeks, and mud holes. Flying from what? Why, a bit of painted wood. But he was ignorant of what it was. The idea of being made a prisoner wholly engrossed his mind, and his last resource was to run. After a while, we being in rather more composure, and our bursts of laughter less frequent, yet by no means subsided,—in full assembly of girls and officers—Tilly entered. The greatest part of my risibility turned into pity. Inexpressible confusion had taken entire possession of his countenance, his fine hair hanging dishevelled down his shoulders, all splashed with mud; yet his bright confusion and race had not divested him of his beauty. He smiled as he tripped up the steps; but 'twas vexation placed it on his features. Joy at that moment was banished from his heart. He briskly walked five or six steps, then stopped and took a general survey of us all. "Where have you been, Mr. Tilly?" asked one officer. (We girls were silent.) "I really imagined," said Major Stoddert, "that you were gone for your pistols. I followed you to prevent danger,"—an excessive laugh at each question, which it was impossible to restrain. "Pray, where were your pistols, Tilly?" He broke his silence by the following expression: "You may all go to the Devil." I never heard him utter an indecent expression before. At last his good nature gained a complete ascendence over his anger and he joined heartily in the laugh. I will do him the justice to say that he bore it charmingly. No cowardly threats, no vengeance denounced. Stoddert caught hold of his coat. "Come, look at what you ran from," and dragged him to the door. He gave it a look, said it was very natural, and, by the singularity of his expressions, gave fresh cause for diversion. We all retired to our different parlours, for to rest our faces, if I may say so. Well, certainly, these military folks will laugh all night. Such screaming I never did hear. Adieu tonight.

Dec. 13: I am fearful they will yet carry the joke too far. Tilly certainly possesses an uncommon share of good nature, or he could not tolerate these frequent teasings. Ah, Deborah, the major is going to leave us entirely—just going. I will see him first. Noon—He has gone. I seen him pass the bridge. The woods which you enter immediately after crossing it hindered us from following him further. I seem to fancy he will return in the evening. Night—Stoddert not come back. We shall not, I fancy, see him again for months, perhaps years, unless he should visit Philadelphia. We shall miss his agreeable company. But what shall we make of Tilly? No civil things yet from him. Adieu tonight, my dear.

Dec. 14: The officers yet here. No talk of their departure. They are very lively. Tilly's retreat the occasion; the principal one, however. Night—Captain Lipscomb, Seaton, and Tilly, with cousin Hannah Miles, dined with us today. Hannah's health seems reestablished, to our great joy. Such an everlasting laugher as Tilly I never knew. He caused us a good deal of diversion while we sat at table. Has not said a syllable to one of us young ladies since Sixth day eve. He tells Lipscomb that the major had the assistance of the ladies in the execution of the scheme. He tells a truth. About four o'clock I was standing at the door, leaning my head on my hand, when a genteel officer rode up to the gate and dismounted. "Your servant, ma'am," and gave me the compliment of his hat. Went into aunt's. I went into our parlour. Soon Seaton was called. Many minutes had not elapsed before he entered with the same young fellow whom I had just seen. He introduced him by the name of Captain Smallwood. We seated ourselves. I then had an opportunity of seeing him. He is a brother to General Smallwood. A very genteel, pretty little fellow, very modest, and seems agreeable, but no personal resemblance between him and the major. After tea, turning to Tilly, he said, "So, sir, I have heard you had like to have been made a prisoner last Friday night." "Pray, sir, who informed you?" "Major Stoddert was my author." "I fancy he made a fine tale of it. How far did he say I ran?" "Two miles, and that you fell into the mill dam." He raised his eyes and hands and exclaimed "What a confounded falsehood." The whole affair was again revived. Our Tillian hero gave a mighty droll account of his "retreat," as they call it. He told us that after he had got behind our kitchen he stopped for company, as he expected the others would immediately follow. "But I heard them scream, 'Which way did he go? Where is he?' 'Aye,' said I to myself, 'he is gone where you shan't catch him,' and off I set again." "Pray," ask'd mamma, "did thee keep that lane between the meadows?" "Oh no, ma'am; that was a large road, and I might happen to meet some of them. When I got to your thorn hedge, I again stopped. As it was a cold night, I thought I would pull up my shoeheels and tie my handkerchief round my head. I then began to have a suspicion of a trick, and, hearing the major bellow, I came back." I think I did not laugh more at the very time than tonight at the rehearsal of it. He is so good-natured, and takes all their jokes with so good a grace, that I am quite charmed with him. He laughingly denounces vengeance against Stoddert. He will be even with him. He is in the major's debt, but he will pay him.

Dec. 15: Smallwood has taken up his quarters with us. Nothing worth relating occurred today.

Dec. 16–18: We chatted a little with the officers. Smallwood not so chatty as his brother or nephew. Lipscomb is very agreeable; a delightful musical voice.

Dec. 19: The officers, after the politest adieus, have left us. Smallwood and Tilly are going to Maryland where they live, Seaton to Virginia, and Lipscomb to camp to join his regiment. I feel sorry at this departure, yet 'tis a different kind from what I felt some time since. We had not contracted so great an intimacy with those last.

Dec. 20: General Washington's army have gone into winter quarters at the Valley Forge. We shall not see many of the military now. We shall be very intimate with solitude. I am afraid stupidity will be a frequent guest. After so much company, I can't relish the idea of sequestration.

Dec. 21: A dull round of the same thing over again. I shall hang up my pen until something offers worth relating.

February 3–4, 1778: I thought I never should have anything to say again. Nothing happened all January that was uncommon. Capt. Lipscomb and Moss stayed one night at Jesse's, and supped with us. How elegant the former was dressed, and how pretty he looked. Indeed, I have forgot to keep an exact account of the day of the month in which I went down to George Emlen's with Polly Fishbourn, but it was the 23rd or 24th of February. After enjoying a week of her agreeable company at the mill, I returned with her to Whitemarsh. We went on horseback—the roads bad. We however surmounted this difficulty, and arrived there safe.

Sarah Wister /135

Feb. 24: Eve—George Emlen brought us a charming collection of books—"Joe Andrews," "Juliet Grenville," and some ladies magazines. Polly Fishbourn sent us "Caroline Melmoth."

Feb. 25: I rose between eight and nine, breakfasted, read and worked by turns, chattered agreeably. I think Sally Emlen is one of the most beautiful women I ever seen, agreeable, affable, sensible, in the true sense of the words. Her conversation is so very lively and diverting that were her personal attractions less than they are she could not fail of being beloved. She has one lovely daughter.

Feb. 26: I thought our scheme of going to friend Fishbourn's was entirely frustrated, as Sally Emlen was much indisposed with the headache. About twelve she got better. We made some alteration in our dress, stepped in the carriage and rode off. Spent a most delightful day. As we approached the house on our return, we perceived several strangers in the parlour. Polly's face and mine brightened up at the discovery. We alighted. Polly swung open the door and introduced me to Major Jameson and Captain Howard, both of the dragoons, the former from Virginia, the latter a Marylander. We all seemed in penseroso style till after supper. We then began to be rather more sociable. About ten they bid us adieu. I dare say thee is impatient to know my sentiments of the swains. Howard has very few external charms; indeed I cannot name one. As to his internal ones, I am not a judge. Jameson is tall and manly, a comely face, dark eyes and hair. Seems to be much of a gentleman. No ways deficient in point of sense, or, at least, in the course of the evening, I discovered none.

Feb. 28: This day my charming friend and myself ascended the barren hills of Whitemarsh, the tops of which we had an extensive prospect of the country round. The traces of the army which encamped on these hills are very visible. Ragged huts, imitations of chimneys, and many other ruinous objects, which plainly showed they had been there. D. J. Shoemaker dined with us.

Feb. 29: Very cold and windy. I wonder I am not sent for. Read and worked by turns.

March 1: A raw, snowy day. I am sent for, nevertheless. Adieu.

North Wales, at my old habitation at the mill. Eve—Such a ride as I have had, O dear Debby. About two o'clock the sleigh came for me. Snowing excessively fast, though not sufficiently deep to make it tolerable sleighing; but go I must. I bid adieu to my agreeable friends, and with a heavy heart and flowing eyes, I seated myself in the unsociable vehicle. There might have as well been no snow on the ground. I was jolted just to pieces. But, notwithstanding these vexations, I got safe to my home, when I had the great pleasure of finding my dear parents, sisters, and brothers well, a blessing which I hope ever to remember with thankfulness. Well, will our nunnery be more bearable now than before I left it? No beaus since I left here, so I have the advantage of the girls. They are wild to see Major Jameson.

May 11: The scarcity of paper, which is very great in this part of the country, and the three last months producing hardly anything material, has prevented me from keeping a regular account of things; but today the scene begins to brighten, and I will continue my nonsense. In the afternoon we were just seated at tea —Dr. Moore with us. Nelly (our girl) brought us the wonderful intelligence that there were light horse in the road. The tea-table was almost deserted. About fifteen light horse were the vanguard of 16 hundred men under command of General Maxwell. I imagined that they would pass immediately by, but was agreeably disappointed. My father came in with the general, Colonel Brodhead, Major Ogden, and Captain Jones. The general is a Scotsman—nothing prepossessing in his appearance; the colonel, very martial and fierce; Ogden, a genteel young fellow with an aquiline nose. Captain Cadwallader Jones—if I was not invincible, I must have fallen a victim to this man's elegancies, but, thank my good fortune, I am not made of susceptibilities—tall, elegant, and handsome, white faced with blue regimentals, and a mighty airish cap and white crest; his behaviour is refined,— a Virginian. They sat a few minutes after tea, then bid us adieu. This brigade is encamped about three miles from us.

May 31: Evening—This afternoon has been productive of adventures in the true sense of the word. Jenny Roberts, Betsy, Liddy, and I, very genteelly dressed, determined to take a stroll. Neighbour Morgan's was proposed and agreed to. Away we rambled, heedless girls. Passed two picket guards. Meeting with no interruptions encouraged us. After paying our visit, we walked towards home, when to my utter astonishment, the sentry desired us to stop; that he had orders not to suffer any persons to pass but those who had leave from the officer, who was at the guardhouse, surrounded by a number of men. To go to him would be inconsistent with propriety; to stay there, and night advancing, was not clever. I was much terrified. I tried to persuade the soldier to let us pass. "No; he dared not." Betsy attempted to go. He presented his gun with the bayonet fixed. This was an additional fright. Back we turned; and, very fortunately, the officer, Captain Emerson, seeing our distress, came to us. I asked him if he had any objection to our passing the sentry. "None at all, ma'am." He waited upon us, and reprimanded the man, and we, without any further difficulty, came home.

June 2: I was standing at the back window, and an officer and private of dragoons rode by. I tore to the door to have a better view of them. They stopped. The officer rode up, and asked for Jesse, who was called. Afternoon—Oh, Deborah; what capital adventures. Jesse came. The idea of having light horse quarter'd at the farm was disagreeable; the meadows just fit to mow, and we had heard what destruction awaited their footsteps. This was the dialogue between Jesse and the officer: "Pray, sir, can I have quarters for a few horsemen?" "How many?" "Five and twenty, sir. I do not mean to turn them into your meadows. If you have any place you can spare, anything will do." And he dismounted, and walked into aunt's parlour. I, determined to find out his character, followed. "I have," replied Jesse, "a tolerable field that may perhaps suit." "That will do, sir. But if you have any objection to putting them in a field, my men shall cut the grass, and bring it in the road. I am under the necessity of quartering them here, but I was ordered. I am only an inferior officer." Some elegant corporal, thought I, and went to the door. He soon joined me, speaking to his man, "Ride off and tell Mr. Watts we rendezvous here." He inquired the name of the farmer, and went into aunt's; I into the back room. The troop rode up. "New scenes," said I, and moved upstairs, where I saw them perform their different maneuvres. This Mr. Watts is remarkably tall, and a good countenance. I adjourned to the parlour. The first officer marched up and down the entry. Prissa came in. "Good, now, Prissa. What's the name of this man?" "Dyer, I believe." Captain Dyer. Oh, the name! "What does he say?" "Why, that he will kiss me when he has dined." "Singular," I observed, "on so short an acquaintance." "But," resumed Prissa, "he came and fixed his arm on the chair I sat in: 'Pray, ma'am, is there not a family from town with you?' 'Yes.' 'What's their name?' 'Wister.' 'There's two fine girls there. I will go chat with them. Pray, did they leave their effects in Philadelphia?' 'Yes, everything, almost.' 'They shall have them again, that they shall.' " There ended the conversation. But this ugly name teased me. "Oh, Sally, he is a Virginian; that's in his favor greatly." "I'm not sure that's his name, but I understood so." Prissa left us. I stepped into aunt's for Johnny and desired him to come home. Up started the captain: "Pray, let me introduce you ma'am." "I am perfectly acquainted with him," said I, and turned to the door. "Tell your sister I believe she is not fond of strangers." I smiled, and returned to our parlour. Night, nine o'clock, aye, ten I fancy—Take a circumstantial account of this afternoon, and the person of this extraordinary man. His exterior first. His name is not Dyer, but Alexander Spotswood Dandridge, which certainly gives a genteel idea of the man; but I will be particular. His person is more elegantly formed than any I ever saw; tall and commanding. His forehead is very white, though the lower part of his face is much sunburned; his features are extremely pleasing; an even, white set of teeth, dark hair and eyes. I can't better describe him than by saying he is the handsomest man I ever beheld. Betsy and Liddy coincide in this opinion. After I had sat awhile at home, in came Dandridge. He entered into chat immediately. Asked if we knew Tacy Vanderen. Said he courted her and that they were to be married soon. Observed my sampler, which was in full view. Wished I would teach the Virginians some of my needle wisdom; they were the laziest girls in the world. Told his name. Laughed and talked incessantly. At last, "May I" (to mammy) "introduce my brother officer?" We assented; so he called him. "Mr. Watts, Mrs. Wister, young Miss Wister. Mr. Watts, ladies, is one of our Virginia children." He sat down. Tea was ordered. Dandridge never drank tea; Watts had done; so we set to the tea table alone. "Let's walk in the garden," said the captain; so we called Liddy, and went (not Watts). We sat down in a sort of a summer house. "Miss Sally, are you a Quaker?" "Yes." "Now, are you a Quaker?" "Yes, I am." "Then you are a Tory." "I am not, indeed." "Oh, dear," replied he, "I am a poor creature. I can hardly live." Then, flying away from that subject, "Will you marry me, Miss Sally?" "No, really; a gentleman after he has said he had not sufficient to maintain himself, to ask me to marry him." "Never mind what I say, I have enough to make the pot boil." Had we been acquainted seven years we could not have been more sociable. The moon gave a sadly pleasing light. We sat at the door till nine. Dandridge is sensible, and (divested of some freedoms, which might be called gallant in the fashionable world) he is polite and agreeable. His greatest fault is a propensity to swearing, which throws a shade over his accomplishments. I asked him why he did so. "It is a favorite vice, Miss Sally." At nine he went to his chamber. Sets off at sunrise.

June 3: Morning—I was awakened at four this morning with a great racket of the captain's servant calling him; but a lazy fellow never rose till about half an hour before eight. This his daylight ride. I imagined they would be gone before now, so I dressed in a green skirt and dark short gown. Provoking. So down I came, this captain, wild wretch, standing at the back door. He bowed and called me. I only looked, and went to breakfast. About nine I took my work and seated myself in the parlour. Not long had I sat, when in came Dandridge—the handsomest man in existence, at least that I had ever seen. But stop here, while I just say, the night before, chatting upon dress, he said he had no patience with those officers who every morning before they went on detachments would wait to be dressed and powdered. "I am," said I, "excessively fond of [hair] powder, and think it very becoming." "Are you?" he replied. "I am very careless, as often wearing my cap thus" (turning the back part before) "as any way." I left off where he came in. He was powdered very white, a pretty colored brown coat, lapelled with green, and white waistcoat, and small clothes, and his

Sword beside him negligently hung.

He made a truly elegant figure. "Good morning, Miss Sally. You are very well, I hope." "Very well. Pray sit down," which he did, close by me. "Oh, dear," said I, "I see thee is powdered." "Yes, ma'am. I have dressed myself off for you." Will I be excused, Debby, if I look upon his being powdered in the light of a compliment to me? "Yes, Sally, as thee is a country maid, and don't often meet with compliments." Saucy Debby Norris! 'Tis impossible to write a regular account of our conversation. Be it sufficient to say that we had a multiplicity of chat. About an hour since, sister Hannah came to me and said Captain Dandridge was in the parlour and had asked for me. I went in. He met me, caught my hands. "Oh, Miss Sally, I have a beautiful sweetheart for you." "Poh, ridiculous. Loose my hands." "Well, but don't be so cross." "Who is he?" "Major Clough. I have seen him. Ain't he pretty, to be sure? I am going to headquarters. Have you any commands there?" "None at all; but (recollecting), yes, I have. Pray, who is your commanding officer?" "Colonel Bland, ma'am." "Please give my compliments to him, and I should be glad if he would send thee back with a little more manners." He replied wickedly, and told me I had a little spiteful heart. But he was intolerably saucy; said he never met with such ladies. "You're very ill-natured, Sally." And, putting on the sauciest, sober face, "Sally, if Tacy Vanderen won't have me, will you?" "No, really; none of her discarded lovers." "But, provided I prefer you to her, will you consent?" "No, I won't." "Very well, madam." And after saying he would return tomorrow, among a hundred other things, he elegantly walked out of the room. Soon he came back, took up a volume of Homer's *Iliad,* and read to us. He reads very well, and with judgment. One remark he made, that I will relate, on these lines—

While Greece a heavy, thick retreat maintains,
Wedged in one body, like a flight of cranes.

"God knows our army don't do so. I wish they did." He laughed, threw down the book, left his sword, and went away. Four o'clock, afternoon—Major Clough, Captain Swan, and Mr. Moore, a Lieutenant of horse, dined with Dandridge. The latter, after dinner, came in to bid us adieu. He sat down and was rather saucy. I looked very grave. "Miss Betsy, you have a very ill-natured sister. Observe how cross she looks." He prayed we might part friends, and offered his hand. I gave him mine, which he kissed in a very gallant manner; and so, with truly affectionate leave, he walked to the parlour door, "God Almighty bless you, ladies," bowed, went into the road, mounted a very fine horse, and rode away; leaving Watts and the troop here to take care of us, as he said. "Mr. Watts, Miss Sally, is a very worthy man; but, poor soul, he is so captivated with you,—the pain in his breast all owing to you." He was caught by this beauty spot tapping my cheek. [Fashionable eighteenth century women attached small patches of various shapes to their faces as a mark of coquetry.] But he is gone; and I think, as I have escaped thus far safe, I am quite a heroine and need not be fearful of any of the lords of the creation for the future. Six o'clock, evening—Watts drank tea with us. A conversable man. Says that the Dandridges are one of the genteelest families in Virginia—relations of General Washington's wife. He appeared very fond of the captain, who has had a liberal education. Very sensible and brave. I sat in the entry all last evening with Watts, as did Betsy. But first, let me say, Fifth day morning we chatted on a variety of subjects; and amongst others, he mentioned the cruelty of the Britons, which, I agreed, were very great. He said he would retaliate whenever he had an opportunity. I strenuously opposed such a procedure, observing that it would be erring in the same way, and tho' they might deserve it, yet it would be much nobler to treat them with lenity. Remember the lines of Pope—

> That mercy I to others show,
> That mercy show to me.

"I perfectly remember them. Your sentiments are noble; but we must retaliate sometimes." A horseman delivered this message: "Let the troops lie on their arms, and be ready to march at a moment's warning." He immediately gave these orders to the sergeant. Every soldier was in motion. I was a good deal frightened, and asked Watts the reason. He fancied the British were in motion, tho' he had not received such intelligence. "What will thee do if they come here?" "Defend the house as long as I can, ma'am." I was shocked. "Bless my heart; what will become of us?" "You may be very safe. The house is an excellent house to defend; only do you be still. If the British vanquish us, down on your knees, and cry 'Bless the king.' If we conquer them, why you know you are safe." This added to my fright. I called my dear mamma, who was much indisposed. Dadda was gone to Lancaster. Mamma asked him the same questions; he gave her the same answers. I was in a fearful taking, and said if I thought such a thing would happen I would set off, tho' nine o'clock, and walk to Uncle Foulke's. "No, don't go tonight, Miss Sally. I will take you there tomorrow. Don't be uneasy. This is nothing. I often go to bed with my boots on upon some alarms." "But will thee take off thy boots tonight?" "Yes, I will, indeed." "Is thee really in earnest about defending the house?" "No, madam; for believe me, if I hear the enemy is in motion, depend upon it, I will immediately depart, bag and baggage." This dispelled my fears, and after wishes for a good night, he retired to his chamber. Imagine my consternation when our girl came running in, and said the lane was filled with light horse. I flew to the side door. It was true. My joy was great when I heard Major Clough ask if this was Captain Dandridge's quarters. I answered in the affirmitive. He rode round to the other door. Watts, though gone to bed, was called. He chatted apart with the major a while, then went off towards Skippack road, followed by a large party of horse and waggons. My fears were all renewed; and, as if we were to be in perpetual alarms, by came another party, much larger than the other, in dark clothes. These we all thought were British. They halted; all as still as death. The officer rode up to the door. "Does Mr. Foulke live here?" "Yes," said somebody. "Is there not a family from town here—Mr. Wister's?" I recollected the voice and said, "Captain Stoddard, I presume?" "Yes madam. Are you Mr. Wister's wife?" "No, his daughter." "Is your papa at home?" "No," I replied, but invited him in to see mamma. He agreed; dismounted, as did many other officers; but he alone came into our parlour. Watts followed to bid us adieu. They sat a few minutes; told us that two of their men had deserted, and when that was the case, they generally moved their quarters. Watts told him how I was frightened. He said I paid but a poor compliment to their cavalry. I only smiled. The alarm had partly deprived me of the power of speech. They sat about fifteen minutes, then rose, and after the politest adieus, departed. All the horse followed—about one hundred and fifty. I never saw more regularity observed, or so undisturbed a silence kept up when so large a number of people were together. Not a voice was heard except that of the officer who gave the word of command. The moon at intervals broke thro' the heavy black clouds. No noise was perceived save that which the horses made as they trotted o'er the wooden bridge across the race. Echo a while gave us back the sound. At last nothing was left but the remembrance of them. The family all retired to their respective chambers, and enjoyed a calm repose. This Captain Stoddard is from New England, and belongs to Colonel Sheldon's regiment of dragoons. He made an acquaintance with my father at Germantown whilst our army was at that place, and had been here once before. He is clever and gentlemanly.

June 4: Oh, gracious, how warm is this day; but, warm as it is, I must make a slight alteration in my dress. I do not make an elegant figure, tho' I do not expect to see a stranger today.

June 5: Morning, 11 o'clock—Last night we were a little alarmed. I was awakened about 12 o'clock with somebody's opening the chamber door. I observed cousin Prissa talking to mamma. I asked what was the matter. "Only a party of light horse." "Are they Americans?" I quickly said. She answered in the affirmitive, which dispelled my fears, and told me that Major Jameson commanded, and that Captains Call and Nixon were with him. With this intelligence she left us, and I resolved in my mind whether or not Jameson would renew his acquaintance; but Morpheus buried all my ideas, and this morning I rose by or near seven, dressed in my light chintz, which is made gown-fashion, kenting handkerchief, and linen apron. "Sufficiently smart for a country girl, Sally." Don't call me a country girl, Debby Norris. Please to observe that I pride myself on being a Philadelphian, and that a residence of twenty months has not at all diminished the love I have for that place (which is very much talked of at present), I expect to return to it with a double pleasure. Dressed as above, down I came, and went down to our kitchen, which is a small distance from the house. As I came back I seen Jameson at the window. He met me in the entry, bowed. "How do you do, Miss Sally?" After the compliments usual on such occasions had passed, I invited him in to our parlour. He followed me in. We chatted very sociably. I inquired for Polly Fishbourn. He said he had seen her last first day; that she was well. Her mamma had gone to Lancaster to visit her daughter Wharton, who, as I suppose you have heard, has lost her husband. I asked him whether Dandridge was on this side the Delaware. He said "Yes." I wanted sadly to hear his opinion, but he said not a word. The conversation turned upon the British leaving Philadelphia. He firmly believed they were going. I sincerely wished it might be true, but was afraid to flatter myself. I had heard it so often that I was quite faithless, and expressed my approbation of Pope's 12th beatitude, "Blessed are they that expect nothing, for they shall not be disappointed." He smiled and assured me they were going away. He was summoned to breakfast. I asked him to stay with us. He declined the invitation with politeness, adding that he was in a hurry, obliged to go to camp as soon as he could. He bowed, "Your servant, ladies," and withdrew immediately.

Sarah Wister / 145

After breakfast they set off for Valley Forge, where General Washington's army still are. I am more pleased with Major Jameson than I was at first. He is sensible and agreeable, a manly person, and a very good countenance. We girls differ about him. Prissa and I admire him, whilst Liddy and Betsy will not allow him a spark of beauty. Aunt's family are charmed with his behavior—so polite, so unassuming. When he disturbed them last night he made a hundred apologies—was so sorry to call them up—'twas real necessity obliged him. I can't help remarking the contrast between him and Dandridge. The former appears to be rather grave than gay—no vain assuming airs. The latter calls for the genius of a Hogarth to characterize him. He is possessed of a good understanding, a very liberal education, gay and volatile to excess. He is an Indian, a gentleman, grave and sad in the same hour. But what signifies? I can't give thee a true idea of him; but he assumes at pleasure a behavior the most courtly, the most elegant of anything I ever seen. He is very entertaining company, and very vain of his personal beauties; yet nevertheless his character is exceptional.

June 7: Evening—High-ho Debby! There's no little meaning in that exclamation, ain't there? To me it conveys much. I have been looking what the dictionary says. It denotes uneasiness of mind. I don't know that my mind is particularly uneasy just now. The occurrences of the day come now. I left my chamber between eight and nine, breakfasted, went up to dress, put on a new purple and white striped Persian, white petticoat, muslin apron, gauze cap, and handkerchief. Thus arrayed, Miss Norris, I ask your opinion. Thy partiality for thy friend will bid thee say I made a tolerable appearance. Not so, my dear. I was this identical Sally Wister, with all her whims and follies; and they have gained so great an ascendency over my prudence that I fear it will be a hard matter to divest myself of them: but I will hope for a reformation. Cousin Hannah Miles came about nine and spent the day with us. After we had dined, two dragoons rode up to the door; one a waiting man of Dandridge's, the faithful Jonathan. They are quartered a few miles from us. The junior sisters

(Liddy and Betsy), joined by me, ventured to send our compliments to the captain and Watts. Prissa insists that it is vastly indelicate, and that she has done with us. Hey day, what prudish notions are those, Priscilla? I banish prudery. Suppose we had sent our love to him, where had been the impropriety? For really he had a person that was love-inspiring, tho' I escaped, and may say, *Io triumphe*. I answer not for the other girls, but am apt to conclude that Cupid shot his arrows, and that maybe they had effect. A fine evening this. If wishes could avail, I would be in your garden with S. Jones, P. Fishbourn, and thyself. Thee has no objection to some of our North Wales swains—not the beau inhabitants of North Wales, but some of the transitory ones. But cruel reverse. Instead of having my wishes accomplished, I must confine myself to the narrow limit of this farm. Liddy calls: "Sally, will thee walk?" Yes, perhaps a walk will give a new turn to my ideas, and present something new to my vacant imagination.

June 8–10: No new occurrences to relate. Almost adventureless, except General Lacey's riding by, and his fierce horse disdaining to go without showing his airs, in expectation of drawing the attention of the mill girls, in order to glad his master's eyes. Ha, ha, ha. One would have imagined that vanity had been buried amidst the shades of N. Wales. Lacey is tolerable; but as ill luck would order it, I had been busy, and my auburn ringlets were much dishevelled; therefore I did not glad his eyes, and cannot set down on the list of honours received that of a bow from Brigadier-General Lacey.

June 18: Night—Rose at half past four this morning, ironed industriously till one o'clock, dined, went upstairs, threw myself on the bed, and fell asleep. About four, sister Hannah waked me, and said uncle and J. Foulke were downstairs; so I decorated myself, and went down. Felt quite lackadaisical. However, I jumped about a little, and the stupid fit went off. We have had strange reports of the British being about leaving Philadelphia. I can't believe it. Adieu.

Sarah Wister / 147

June 19: Morning—We have heard an astonishing piece of news; that the English have entirely left the city. It is almost impossible. Stay, I shall hear further. Evening—A light horseman has just confirmed the above intelligence! This is "charmante." They decamped yesterday. He (the horseman) was in Philadelphia. It is true; they have gone. Past a doubt. I can't forbear exclaiming to the girls "Now are you sure the news is true? Now are you sure they have gone?" "Yes, yes, yes!" they all cry, "and may they never, never return." Dr. Gould came here tonight. Our army are about six miles off, on their march to the Jerseys.

June 20: Morning—Owen Foulke arrived just now and related as followeth: The army began their march at six this morning by their house. Our worthy General Smallwood breakfasted at Uncle Caleb's. He asked how Mr. and Mrs. Wister and the young ladies were, and sent his respects to us. Our brave, our heroic General Washington was escorted by fifty of the Life Guard, with drawn swords. Each day he acquires an addition to his goodness. We have been very anxious to hear how the inhabitants of Philadelphia have fared. I understand that General [Benedict] Arnold, who bears a good character, has the command of the city, and that the soldiers conducted with great decorum. Smallwood says they had the strictest orders to behave well, and I dare say they obeyed the order. I now think of nothing but returning to Philadelphia. So I shall now conclude this journal, with humbly hoping that the great disposer of events, who has graciously vouchsafed to protect us to this day through many dangers, will still be pleased to continue his protection.

✻ Sally later added a footnote: "Since my writing the above, General Arnold has forfeited all right to a good character by the shameful desertion of his country's cause, joining the British, accepting a commission, and plundering and distressing the Americans."

When the Wisters returned to Philadelphia in late July Sally "bid adieu to the peaceful though solitary shades of North Wales." She found her city friends in good health and "tolerable spirits;" her "heart danced and eyes sparkled at the sight of my companions of my girlish days. Add to this the rattling of carriages over the streets—harsh music, though preferable to croaking frogs and screeching owls." She particularly cherished a reunion with her Quaker friend, Debby, though the latter had warned Sally not to speak of politics. "I entreat thee, by our friendship, not to enter on any political disquisitions with us; it is not our providence, and will only serve to create disagreeable sensations." She had, however, eagerly awaited Sally's return: "I long to see thee, and to assure thee of my love. Tell me in answer to this, that it will be but a short space of time before I shall enjoy this pleasure." But the idealistic, child-like sensitivity of one soon clashed with the conventional, society-minded interests of the other. On January 4, 1780, Sally privately wrote in her diary of a painful separation: "The friend to whom my journal was wrote to has violated a friendship which commenced at school and till about two weeks ago was productive of infinite satisfaction to both of us. But it is with pleasure that I can lay my hand on my heart and say I am entirely innocent of ever intentionally offending her. I vainly imagined that our intimacy was founded on an immovable basis. I was deceived; but it will teach me not to place too much dependence on the friendships and professions of this world." Debby Norris married Dr. George Logan the following year, and Philadelphia society responded by lauding her beauty, intelligence, and cultivated manners. The couple entertained lavishly such notables as Thomas Jefferson, Benjamin Franklin, George Washington, and John Dickinson. Sally's letter and journal were first shown Debby twenty-six years after Sally's death, by her nephew, Charles Wister. Deborah (Debby) Logan returned the manuscript, and requested that the letter be destroyed.

In 1780 Sally heard news of the officers who had been quartered at the Foulke farmhouse. General Smallwood and Colonel Wood were still in the army. Years later, Smallwood would be elected governor of Maryland (1785), and Wood governor of Virginia (1796). Colonel Line was in Virginia, Captain Furnival in Maryland. Stoddert—later appointed Secretary of the Navy in John Adams's administration (1798)—was "much indisposed at his home" in Maryland. "The mild Captain Smallwood, and amiable Lipscomb are no longer inhabitants of this terrestrial world—snatched in the bloom of youth by unrelenting death from all earthly connections. I experienced a good deal of pleasure in the transient acquaintance I had with these young men; but they are no more. I felt sorry when I heard of their deaths. Yet why lament a fate?

> By thousands envied, and by heaven approved.
> Rare is the boon to those of longer date.
> To live, to die, esteemed, admired, beloved.

Dandridge—the gay, the gallant roving Dandridge—is at last bound in Hymen's fetters. I hope the lady may possess prudence, and discretion sufficient to effect a reformation in his principles."

For a decade Sally lived alone in a house on Chestnut Street. The United States Bureau of Census in 1790 listed her under "Heads of Families" as a "general woman," without children or servants. When her father died, however, Sally moved to Germantown to live with the rest of the family.

In 1800 the nation heralded its first literary magazine. *The Port Folio,* founded in Philadelphia by Joseph Dennie, was patronized by the literary elite, and widely read in many states. Not only did the magazine editorialize the need for women's contributions— quite a few women's writings were printed—it also scoffed at the male attitude that women were inferior: "Women are certainly not at all inferior to men in resolution, and perhaps much less in courage than is generally imagined. The reason they appear so is because women affect to be more afraid than they really are, and men pretend to be less."

John Quincy Adams, whose verse was frequently found in *The Port Folio*'s pages, feared that his poetic flights of fantasy, if published alongside those of women, would raise the eyebrows of his political associates. He therefore insisted that his work be signed with any of the letters of "Columbus." Sally Wister's brother Charles followed suit by having his poem signed "Llewellyn." Yet women too used pseudonyms or single letters in the publication. Sally Wister signed hers "Laura," her sister Betsy used the name Elvira, in addition to "E" and "E.W."

Two deaths shattered the closely-knit family in 1804: Sally's mother died in February, Sally in April, at the age of forty-two. Until her mother's death Sally appeared to be in good health. Her nephew, Charles Wister, wrote in 1886 that his aunt in the last years of her life "became extremely serious, eschewing everything light and frivolous, and occupying her mind with religious subjects almost exclusively. She was eminently conspicious for her devotion to her mother—she being her chief interest and source of happiness. The severity of the blow, therefore, that deprived her of the object of so ardent an attachment, it is almost impossible to estimate." Lacking both the will to live and the will to resist illness, she followed her mother by two months, perhaps of the same sickness. The family's physician, Dr. Benjamin Rush, wrote an obituary for the April 25th edition of the *Philadelphia Gazette:* "Died, on Wednesday last, Miss Sarah Wister. The distress occasioned by the death of this highly accomplished and valuable lady is greatly heightened by recently succeeding that of her excellent mother. Few families have ever furnished two such shining examples of prudence, virtue, piety, and eminent acquirements; and as few people have ever produced by their deaths more heartfelt grief to a numerous circle of relations and friends." ✳

Elizabeth Sandwith Drinker

✳ As a member of the Society of Friends in Wexford County, Ireland, William Sandwith was snubbed by the Irish for being an eccentric nonconformist. Quakers were Protestant dissenters. In 1727 he left this difficult environment, choosing a more productive life among Friends in Philadelphia, Pennsylvania. He prospered as a merchant and ship owner, and married Sarah Jervis, a shopkeeper's daughter, in 1731. Elizabeth was born four years later in the shopkeeper's home.

By the middle of the eighteenth century, Philadelphia flourished as the greatest commercial city in the colonies. This was a lucrative environment for Henry Drinker, an ambitious merchant and co-owner, with Abel James, of one of Philadelphia's leading export-import firms. After the death of Henry's first wife, he and Elizabeth Sandwith "declared their intentions of marriage with each other before several monthly meetings of the people called Quakers at Philadelphia" and were married by the customary Friends' ceremony January 13, 1761.

Ten years later, having tired of their Water Street house, the Drinkers purchased an expansive, elegant, three-story brick mansion overlooking the Delaware River, on Front Street and Drinker's Alley. From a garret window Elizabeth Drinker watched approaching sailing vessels, particularly those destined to unload at her husband's wharf. On dense, foggy days she listened to the clanging of wharf bells, rung to guide incoming market boats. The house's front steps lowered to the street walk; but behind the mansion was a large yard where, each spring, Elizabeth saw an effusion of "trees in full bloom, the red and white blossoms intermixed with the green leaves, which are just putting out flowers of several sorts blown in our little garden." The family stable sheltered a potpourri of horses, cows, and chickens. Eighteenth-century homes lacked plumbing; water was hoisted from a backyard well in the wash house. Near the wash house was the family privy. Colonists called them "necessaries," "bog houses," and "Commons," in reference to the British House of Commons. A large cesspool had been dug to groundwater level beneath the Drinker's "necessary." There was always the possibility of waste seeping into the well. Moreover, this was not a permanent method of waste disposal; there were times when the cesspool required cleaning out. On March 5, 1779, Elizabeth wrote: "five men with two carts, etc. are about a dirty job in our yard tonight. They are removing the offerings from the temple of cloaca, which have been forty-four years depositing."

Cats, dogs, chickens, and numerous children frolicked over the backyard. Elizabeth gave birth to nine infants, four of whom died before the age of five, and acquired twenty-five grandchildren from those who survived. After a wintery snowfall these small creatures scrunched over the yard like penguins.

The American Revolution caused serious disturbances to the Drinker family. Their troubles began in 1773 when the British Parliament granted a tea monopoly to the East India Company. This act so enraged the colonists they refused to buy tea. Bostonians violated three ships anchored in the harbor and smashed open 342 tea chests, dumping the tea overboard. John Adams—lawyer, politician, and future President—wrote from Boston: "Many persons wish that as many dead carcasses were floating in the harbour as there were chests of tea: a much less number of lives, however, would remove the causes of all our calamities." Abel James and Henry Drinker, East India Company's Philadelphia agents, were confronted by hostile mobs. The ship *Polly,* sailing on the high seas from England and loaded with tea cargo, was destined for Philadelphia. The two men were prepared to handle the cargo's receipt and sale, but public pressure against them mounted. To prevent an armed revolt the firm issued a written statement "that it is the general opinion of the people that they should not act under their appointment as agents, and do therefore decline under said appointment." When the *Polly* cruised into the Delaware Bay late in December, pilots refused to bring her into port. At the request of Charles Thompson,

Secretary of Congress, the ship's captain did not proceed to Philadelphia's Custom House. Instead, the vessel anchored off Gloucester. The following morning, while eight thousand people gathered to protest the ship's entry, its captain was informed that his boat had to sail back to England with the next tide. After being refitted at Chester, *Polly's* sails were billowed and she made course toward England, with all of her tea still onboard.

In 1775 few people doubted that a fuse had been lit for a bloodbath. Wealthy Philadelphians chose sides and became more rigid in their political views. However, most Quakers, including the Drinkers, refused to be actively involved in this militant clash of powers. The Drinker family was damned by Patriots because of their continued friendship with Loyalists accused of treason. The families of Samuel Shoemaker and Joseph Galloway had been friends of the Drinkers for many years. Both men, as distinguished political figures, rejected American independence from England, and chose to aid the British. When in 1778 the British army left Philadelphia, Shoemaker fled to New York City, Galloway and his daughter to England. Samuel Shoemaker's step-daughter, Anna Rawle (Clifford diary, page 283) remained in Philadelphia, as did Joseph Galloway's wife, Grace (Galloway diary, page 185). When Grace Galloway died in 1782 Elizabeth Drinker stood by her grave when she was buried. Two other Loyalists, also persecuted by the Patriots and mentioned in Elizabeth's diary, were Abraham Carlisle, a carpenter and builder, and John Roberts, a miller. Both men helped the British; both were executed.

Conservative people who denounced radicalism were oppressed by Congress. As a merchant Henry Drinker refused to take inflated continental money—currency essential to the revolution's success. Instead, he continued to transact commodities in scarce coin, and was therefore accused of contributing to the scarcity and high costs of products. Because of this, and his nonviolent stand as a Quaker, a committee to the Continental Congress gave the following report on August 28, 1777:

That the several testimonies which have been published since the commencement of the present contest betwixt Great Britain and America, and the uniform tenor of the conduct, and conversation of a number of persons of considerable wealth, who profess themselves to belong to the society of people commonly called Quakers, render it certain and notorious, that those persons are, with much rancour and bitterness, disaffected to the American cause; that, as these persons will have it in their power, so there is no doubt it will be their inclination, to communicate intelligence to the enemy, and, in various other ways, to injure the councils and arms of America: That when the enemy, in the month of December, 1776, were bending their progress towards the city of Philadelphia, a certain seditious publication, addressed "To our friends and brethren in religious profession in these and the adjacent provinces," signed "John Pemberton, in and on behalf of the meeting of sufferings held at Philadelphia for Pennsylvania and New Jersey, the 20th of the 12th month, 1776," was published, and, as your committee is credibly informed, circulated amongst many members of the society called Quakers, throughout the different states.

The committee then recommended that the executive council of Pennsylvania arrest eleven Quakers, including Henry Drinker. The "seditious" Quaker publication referred to in the Congressional report began with two quotes from the bible, and one from George Fox's 1685 epistle. It concluded:

Thus we may, with Christian fortitude and firmness, withstand and refuse to submit to the arbitrary injunctions and ordinances of men, who assure to themselves the power of compelling others, either in person or by other assistance, to join in carrying on war, and in prescribing modes of determining concerning our religious principles, by imposing tests not warranted by the precepts of Christ, or the laws of the happy Constitution under which we and others long enjoyed tranquillity and peace.

On September 4, 1777, upon orders from Pennsylvania's Supreme Executive Council, Colonel William Bradford of the militia arrested Henry Drinker and nineteen other Quakers. These men were exiled to Winchester, Virginia, without benefit of trial, even though Pennsylvania's Chief Justice granted them that right. The Pennsylvania government harassed newspaper editors who printed material supporting the integrity of those arrested, and made every endeavor to excite prejudices against the prisoners in the minds of the people. Thomas Gilpin and John Hunt died while in exile; a third, Israel Pemberton, died shortly after their release the following spring. *

September 2, 1777: H.D. having been and continuing to be unwell, stayed from meeting this morning. He went towards noon into the front parlor to copy the monthly meeting minutes. The book was on the desk and the desk unlocked when William Bradford, Blewer and Ervin entered, offering a parole for him to sign. This was refused. They then seized the book and took several papers out of the desk, and carried them off, intimating their design of calling the next morning at 9 o'clock, and desiring H.D. to stay at home for that time. As he was unwell, it was necessary. They accordingly called the 4th in the morning and took my Henry to the Mason's Lodge—in an illegal, unprecedented manner—where there were several other Friends made prisoners. I went this evening to see my H.D., where I met with the wives and children of our dear Friends, and with other visitors in great numbers. Upwards of twenty of our Friends called to see us this day.

Sept. 11: The sending off of our Friends is put off until 3 o'clock this afternoon; they find it difficult to procure waggons and men. My Henry breakfasted with us, then went to the Lodge. I went there about 10 o'clock. The town is in great confusion at present; a great firing heard below. It is supposed the armies are engaged. 'Tis also reported that several men-of-war are coming up the river. Sometime after dinner Harry came in in a hurry for his master's horse for a servant to ride, informing me that the waggons were waiting at the Lodge to take our dear Friends away. I quickly went there, and as quickly came away—finding a great number of people there, but few women. I bid my husband farewell and went in great distress to James Pemberton's. Sally with me. The waggons drove off about 6 o'clock, and I came home at dusk.

Sept. 12: A part of Washington's army has been routed. They have been seen coming into the town in great numbers. The particulars of the battle [Brandywine] I have not attended to; the slain is said to be very numerous. Hundreds of their muskets lay in the road, which those that made off have thrown down.

Sept. 15: I have heard no news from abroad this morning; but carriages are constantly passing, and the inhabitants are going away. Last night I heard of several friends having lost their horses —taken from the stables—for which reason I ordered our horse and cow to be put into the wash house, where they at present remain.

Sept. 19: Jenny awoke me this morning about 7 o'clock with the news that the English were near. We find that most of our neighbours and almost all the town have been up since one o'clock in the morning. Congress, Council, etc. are flown; boats, carriages and footpads going off all night. The town is in great confusion.

Sept. 20: The town has been very quiet all this day. It is said that Washington's army has crossed the Ford and are at present on this side. Some expect a battle hourly, as the English are on the opposite side. All the boats, ferry boats excepted, are put away, and the shipping all ordered up the river the next tide—on pain of being burnt, should Howe's vessels approach. The inhabitants continue going out. Some are returning.

Sept. 24: Joshua Fisher's goods taken from him by order of Gen. Washington. They continue pressing horses. Sister and H.D. Jr. sat up last night till 2 o'clock, as did many others in the city. Cannon placed in some of the streets. The report continues of the English approaching us, but I know not what to believe. The sign (over the way) of Gen. Washington was taken down this afternoon. There is talk of the city being set on fire.

Sept. 25: This has been, so far, a day of great confusion in the city, though in respect to ourselves we have experienced no injury, and but little fright. Enoch Story was the first who informed us this morning that the English were within four or five miles of us. We have since heard they were by John Dickinson's place. They are expected by some this evening in the city. Most of our warm people [Rebels] have gone off, though there are many who continue here that I should not have expected. Things seem very quiet and still. Should any be so wicked as to attempt firing the town, rain, which seems to be coming on, may Providentially prevent it. A great number of the lower sort of people are gone out to them. G. Napper went. I hear he brings word that he spoke to Galloway, who told him that the inhabitants must take care of the town tonight. They would be in in the morning. As it rained, they fixed their camp within two miles of the city for the night. It is now near 11 o'clock. It has been raining for several hours, which I look upon as a remarkable favor, as it's said that tarred faggots are laid in several outhouses in different parts, with mischievous intent. Numbers met at the State House since 9 o'clock to form themselves into different companies to watch the city. All things appear peaceable at present. The watchmen crying the hour without molestation.

Sept. 26: Well! Here are the English in earnest. About 2 or 3000 came in through Second Street without opposition or interruption—no plundering on the one side or the other. What a satisfaction would it be to our dear absent Friends, could they but be informed of it. It is recommended to the inhabitants to continue to assist in guarding the town each night for some time yet. Cornwallis came with those troops today. Gen. Howe is not yet come in.

Sept. 27: About 9 o'clock this morning the *Province* and *Delaware* frigates, with several gondollas, came up the river with a desire to fire on the town. They were attacked by a battery which the English have erected at the lower end of the town. The engagement lasted half an hour, when many shots were exchanged. Nobody that I have heard of hurt on shore, but the people in general, especially downwards, exceedingly alarmed. The cook on board the *Delaware,* 'tis said, had his head shot off. Another of the men was wounded. She ran aground and by some means took fire, which occasioned her to strike her colours. The English immediately boarded her; the others drew off. They took Admiral Alexander and his men prisoners. It seems he declared that their intentions were to destroy the town. Part of this scene we were spectators of, from the little window in our loft.

Sept. 29: Some officers are going about this day numbering the houses with chalk on the doors. A number of citizens taken up and imprisoned.

October 1: Several fire rafts, sent down the river to annoy the [British] fleet, ran ashore and were burnt.

Oct. 4: I wrote this morning to my Henry. While I was writing I heard cannon fire. Indeed, I heard them before I was up. I understood, upon inquiry, that a party of Washington's army had attacked the English picket guards near Chestnut Hill. This has been a sorrowful day in Philadelphia, and much more so at Germantown and thereabouts. It was reported in the forenoon that 1000 of the English were slain; but Chalkley James tells us that he has been today as far as Benjamin Chew's place, and could not learn of more than 30 of the English being killed, though a great number were wounded and brought into the city. He counted 18 of the Americans lying dead in the lane from the road to Chew's house. The house is very much damaged, as a few of the English troops had taken shelter there, and were fired upon from the road. The last accounts towards evening was that the English were pursuing Washington's troops, who are very numerous, and that they were flying before them. The Americans are divided into three divisions—one over the Schuylkill, another near Germantown, and the third I know not where; so that the army that was with us are chiefly called off, and a double guard this night thought necessary. Washington is said to be wounded in the thigh. Friends, and others in Jersey—and indeed almost all around the country—are suffering deeply. 'Tis now past 12 o'clock, and all in the house except myself are, I believe,

asleep. The watchman has cried the hour, and all seems quiet.
Fine starlight.

Oct. 6: The heaviest firing I think I ever heard was this evening
for upwards of two hours. It is thought to be the English troops
engaged with Mud Island battery. An officer called this afternoon to ask if we could take in a sick or wounded captain. I put
him off by saying that as my husband was from me, I should be
pleased if he could obtain some other convenient place. Two of
the Presbyterian meeting houses are made hospitals of for the
wounded soldiers, of which there are great numbers.

Oct. 8: Went to the playhouse, the State House, and one of the
Presbyterian meeting houses, to see the wounded soldiers.

Oct. 9: Firing last night, and heavy firing this morning from 5
o'clock 'till between 6 and 7. It was the frigate and the gondollas
playing upon the English, who were erecting a battery on or near
the banks of the Schuylkill. One Englishman was slain and two
wounded; two horses killed.

Oct. 10: Jenny and Harry went to the State House with coffee and
whey for the wounded Americans.

Oct. 11: Jenny and Harry visited the wounded again today, with
a double portion. The battery on Province Island was taken this
morning from the English, and retaken in half an hour. We hear
cannon firing almost every day.

Oct. 14: Much talk of Washington endeavoring to enter the city.
A number of people greatly alarmed on that account.

Oct. 18: The troops at Germantown are coming within two or
three miles of this city to encamp. Provisions are so scarce with
us now. The people round the country dare not come near us
with anything. The fleet not yet up, nor likely to be soon, I fear.

Oct. 20: There has been a skirmish this morning between Germantown and Philadelphia. There was very heavy firing a great
part of the afternoon. Last night about sixteen or eighteen flat
boats came up and got safely by the gondollas and battery, but
were fired upon by some of the English, who did not know them.
One man was killed. Tom Prior taken up today on suspicion of
sending intelligence to Washington's army.

Oct. 21: 2000 of the Hessians were landed in Jersey this day. 'Tis supposed their intentions are against the Mud Island battery. We saw a number of them crossing in the flat bottomed boats from our garret window.

Oct. 23: This day will be remembered by many. The 2500 Hessians who crossed the river on the 21st were last night driven back two or three times in endeavoring to storm the fort on Red Bank. 200 were slain and great numbers wounded. The firing this morning seemed to be incessant from the battery, the gondollas and the *Augusta* man-of-war, of 64 guns. The *Augusta* took fire and, after burning nearly two hours, blew up. The loss of this fine vessel is accounted for in different ways. Some say she took fire by accident; others that it was occasioned by red hot fire from Mud Island battery. Another English vessel, somewhat smaller, was also burnt. Many of the inhabitants of this city are very much affected by the present situation and appearance of things, while those on the other side of the question are flushed and in spirits. It was near noon when the *Augusta* blew up. Many were not sensible of any shock. Others were. It was very plain to those who were at the meeting, and appeared to some like an earthquake. The Hessians and British troops are encamped in Jersey this night; we can see their fires for a considerable distance.

Oct. 25: An officer called today to know if General Grant could have quarters with us. I told him that my husband was from me and a number of young children around me; that I should be glad to be excused. He replied as I desired it. It should be so. Tom Kite tells us that neighbour Stiles' house near Frankford was broken open the night before last by the Americans, and much plundered.

November 1: A poor soldier was hung this afternoon on the commons for striking his officer. The Hessians go on plundering at a great rate such things as wood, potatoes, turnips, etc. Provisions are scarce among us.

Nov. 5: A soldier came to demand blankets, which I did not in any wise agree to. Notwithstanding my refusal, he went upstairs and took one, and with seeming good nature begged I would excuse his borrowing it, as it was by Gen. Howe's orders. We have not bought a pound of butter for three or four weeks. All we get is from our cow, about two pounds a week. Very few of the citizens have any.

Nov. 15: The firing today has been like thunder, comparatively speaking, from the *Vigilant* and *Somerset* men-of-war upon the formidable Mud Island battery.

Nov. 16: The Mud Island battery is at last taken. The Americans left it about midnight last night when, it is supposed, the English were about to storm it.

Nov. 19: Gen. Cornwallis left this city the day before yesterday at 2 o'clock in the morning with 3000 men. A number of Americans were seen this afternoon in Jersey, opposite the city, and in other parts.

Nov. 21: I was awakened this morning before 5 o'clock by the loud firing of cannon, my head aching very badly. All our family were up but little Molly, and a fire made in the parlour more than an hour before day. All our neighbours were also up and, I believe, most in town. The Americans had set their whole fleet on fire, except one small vessel and some of the gondollas, which passed by the city in the night. The firing was from the *Delaware* vessel that lay at Cooper's Point, upon the gondollas. Billy counted eight different vessels on fire at once. One lay near the Jersey shore, opposite our house. We heard the explosion of four of them when they blew up, which shook our windows greatly. We had a fair sight of the blazing fleet from our upper windows.

Nov. 22: Firing again this morning—cannon and small arms. An American schooner was burnt in our river this morning by the English, nearly opposite our house. An earthquake was felt this morning by a great number of inhabitants. There has been skirmishing several times today between the Americans and the picket guards. 'Tis said seven or eight have lost their lives. One thousand men attacked the picket guards this morning, about 11 o'clock. They drove them off, when some took shelter in John Dickinson's house, and other houses thereabouts. The English immediately set fire to those houses and burned them to the ground. The burning of those houses is said to be a premeditated thing, as they serve for skulking places and much annoyed the guards. They talk of burning all the houses within four miles of the city without the lines. John Dickinson's house, that in which C. Thomson lived, Jonathan Mifflin's, the widow Taylor's, and many others were burned this afternoon.

Nov. 24: It is an agreeable sight to see the wharves lined with shipping. A number have come up today. The poor people have been allowed for some time past to go to Frankford Mill and other mills out that way for flour. Abraham Carlisle, who gives them passes, has his door very much crowded every morning.

Nov. 25: We were very much affrighted this evening before 9 o'clock. Jenny happened to go into the yard, where she saw a man with Ann, [an indentured servant, whose passage to America had been paid by the Drinkers]. She came in and whispered to sister, who immediately went out and discovered a young officer with Ann, coming out from the little house. Sister held the candle up to his face and asked him who he was. His answer was "What's that to you?" The gate was locked, so he followed Ann and sister into the kitchen. He swore he had mistaken the house; but we could not get him out. Chalkley James, who happened to be here, came into the kitchen and asked him what business he had there. He damned him and said "What's that to you?" He shook his sword, which he held in his hand, and seemed to threaten. Chalkley, with great resolution, twisted it out of his hands and collared him. Sister took the sword from Chalkley and locked it up in a drawer in the parlour. All this outcry was for his sword. He swore he would not stir a foot until he had it. I then sent for Joshua Howell, when the officer declared that he knew we were peaceable people; that he gave up his sword on that account, out of a pure, good nature. He told Chalkley in the kitchen that he would be the death of him tomorrow. Joshua got him to the door and gave him his sword, expecting that he would go. But he continued swearing there. Joshua left him and went to call Abel James. In the meantime, the impudent fellow came in again swearing in the entry with the sword in his hand. Sister had locked Chalkley up in the middle room, and we shut ourselves in the parlour, where he knocked and swore, desiring entrance. Our poor dear children were never so frightened, to have an enraged, drunken man, as I believe he was, with a sword in his hand, swearing about the house. After going two or three times up and down the entry, desiring we would let him in to drink a glass of wine with us, he went to the end of the Alley. When Harry locked the front door on him, he knocked and desired to come in. When J. Howell and A. James, whom Joshua had gone for, came they had some talk with him. He went off, or so I supposed. I had all the back doors bolted, and the gate and front door locked. About ten minutes after, Harry came out of the kitchen and told us he was there. I then locked the parlour door, and would not let Chalkley go out. Harry ran into Howell's for Joshua, who did not come 'till some time after the fellow had gone—Ann with him. He came over the fence. They went out the same way. 'Tis now near one in the morning, and I have not yet recovered from the fright. Ann called him Capt. Tape, or John Tape.

December 1: There is talk today, as if a great part of the English army were making ready to depart on some secret expedition.

Dec. 2: A young man of the name of McMickle called this morning. His business was to seize horses, but understanding to whom ours belong, said not one of them should be touched. Our saucy Ann came while I was at meeting, desiring to know what I would take for her time, and she would bring the money in a minute. Sister told her she did not know, but that she heard me talk of putting her in the workhouse. She replied "If you talk so, you shall neither have me nor the money." Sister then ordered her to come again at 12 o'clock, but she has not been since.

Dec. 7: We have but nine persons in our family this winter. We have not had less than thirteen or fourteen for many years past.

Dec. 11: These are sad times for thieving and plundering. It's hardly safe to leave the door open a minute.

Dec. 18: An officer who calls himself Major Cramond called this afternoon to look for quarters for some officer of distinction. I plead off; but he tried to persuade me that it was a necessary protection at these times to have one in the house. He said that I must consider it, and that he would call in a day or two. He behaved with much politeness, which has not been the case at many other places.

Dec. 19: Major Cramond came to know if I had consulted any of my friends upon the matter. I told him that my sister was out on that business; that I expected that we, who were at present lone women, would be excused. He said he feared not, for though I might put him off (as it was for himself he applied), yet, as a great number of foreign troops were to be quartered in this neighbourhood, he believed they might be troublesome. We are told this evening that Owen Jones's family has been ill-used indeed, by an officer who wanted to quarter himself, with many others, upon them. He drew his sword, used very abusive language, and had the front door split in pieces. Mary Eddy has some with her who, they say, will not suffer her to use her own front door, but oblige her and her family to go up and down the alley. Molly Foulke has been affronted, and so have many others. Lord Cornwallis has embarked for England, which occasions various conjectures. Lord Howe [General William Howe] is going to New York. Gen. Howe, it is said, intends to winter with us. I hope he is a better man than some people think him to be.

Dec. 20: Cramond called a third time with the same story over again. I put him off as before; he said he would call again tomorrow.

Dec. 27: A certain something, a piece of clockwork, a barrel with gunpowder in it, was found in our river. It blew up near the *Roebuck* man-of-war and destroyed a boat near it. Several others they say are found, which are thought to be the contrivance of some designing, evil-minded person or persons, against the shipping.

Dec. 29: Cramond was here this morning. We have at last agreed on his coming to take up his abode with us.

Dec. 30: Major Cramond took up his abode with us today. One servant is to be with him here; two others he has boarded at our neighbour Wells's in the Alley. He has two horses and cows which are to be put in our stable.

Dec. 31: J. Cramond, who has now become one of our family, appears to be a thoughtful, sober young man.

January 1, 1778: Crammond has three horses, three cows, two sheep, and two turkeys, with several fowls, in our stable. He has also three servants—two white men and one negro called Damon. The servants are here all day, but away at night. He has three Hessians who take turns to wait on him as messengers, or orderly men, as they called them; so that we have enough of such sort of company.

Jan. 5: J.C. had eleven or twelve officers to dine with him today. They made very little noise and went away timeously. Most of our acquaintances seem to be much taken with our major. I hope he will continue to deserve their good opinion. He tells us this evening that a cessation of arms is concluded upon; that Gen. [Charles] Lee is out on his parole. Everything that I hear (as it makes for the continued confinement or deliverance of my dearest Henry) has its effect upon my spirits. A number of those floating barrels of gunpowder continue coming down the river. They have been frequently firing at them today. The weather is much moderated, so that most of the ice is out of the river. Some vessels came up today.

Jan. 19: This morning our officer moved his lodgings from the blue chamber to the little front parlor, so that he now has the two front parlors, a chamber up two pair of stairs for his baggage, and the stable wholly to himself, besides the use of the kitchen.

Jan. 20: The playhouse was opened last night for the first time. Our major attended.

Jan. 27: The troops have been out these two days foraging. It is amazing to see the great quantity of hay they have brought in— seventy odd loads I am told they have taken from Abel James. What will they do when the present supply is gone. Large as it seems, I am told it will last but a little time. They use, 'tis said, twenty-four tons per day.

February 14: I am out of all patience with our major. He stays out so late almost every night.

Feb. 17: Our major had eight or ten to dine with him. They broke up in good time; but he's gone off with them, and when he'll return I know not. I gave him some hints two or three days ago. He has behaved better since. Part of the army went out last night; they have sent in great quantities of wood and hay.

Feb. 19: The army has brought in a great quantity of hay, with Joseph Galloway's wife, goods, and chattels.

Feb. 26: We had the reading today of a paper drawn up by Alexander White, which he presented to Congress with reasons why our Friends should be set at liberty, on the score of humanity, justice and good policy; but all in vain. Those are things they seem to be unacquainted with.

March 31: Molly Pleasants sent for me before dinner. I went. She showed me a paper she had drawn up, to take or send to Congress. In the afternoon Owen Jones came to desire I could meet with the rest of the women concerned at 5 o'clock, at Mary Pemberton's, which I did. Nicholas read the address and all the women signed it. It is partly concluded that Susan Jones, P. Pemberton, M. Pleasants and E. Drinker are to take it. A person has set off, I believe, to Gen. Washington for permission for a waggon to pass with stores for our dear Friends. Dr. Park has undertaken to supply the medicines.

April 4: Our address to Congress is to be written over the third time, as it was altered on account of the death of our Friend, John Hunt. We are setting off tomorrow. May the Almighty favour our undertaking.

April 5: I left home after dinner and went to Molly Pleasants, where were a great number of our Friends met to take leave of us. S. Jones, Phebe Pemberton, M. Pleasants and myself took coach about 2 o'clock, with four horses, and two negroes who rode postillion. Owen Jones accompanied us to the ferry, over which we passed without difficulty or interruption. We went no further than John Roberts's mill, about ten miles from home. We did not meet with above two or three persons on the road. We were kindly entertained by the woman of the house and her daughters—the owner at this time being a refugee in town. In the evening came a scouting party of near one hundred men. Two of their officers came into the house, saying that they had heard there were ladies from Philadelphia here; asked how many miles it was thither. They were strangers who had lately come from New England.

April 6: Left Roberts's after breakfast, and proceeded to the American picket guard, who, upon hearing that we were going to headquarters, sent two or three to guard us further on to another guard, where Col. Smith gave us a pass for headquarters [at Valley Forge]. We arrived there at about half-past one o'clock. We requested an audience with the general [George Washington] and sat with his wife (a sociable, pretty kind of woman) until he came in. A number of officers were there who were very complaisant. It was not long before G.W. came and discoursed with us freely, but not so long as we could have wished, as dinner was served, to which he had invited us. There were fifteen officers, besides the general and his wife, Gen. [Nathanael] Greene, and Gen. Lee. We had an elegant dinner, which was soon over. We went out with the general's wife, up to her chamber, and saw no more of him. He told us he could do nothing in our business further than granting us a pass to Lancaster, which he did. He gave a letter to Israel Morris for Thomas Wharton. We came altogether to James Vaux's, who came over to invite us. We crossed the large bridge over the Schuylkill just by his house. We drank tea and lodged there.

April 7: Left James Vaux's after breakfast and changed one of our horses for C. Logan's. We found the roads exceedingly bad. Some of us were frequently in and out of the carriage. We dined at a kind Friend's named Randal Mellon, and left his house about 3 o'clock. Went on through deep ruts and mud to Robert Valentine's, where we drank tea and lodged. Our friends are very kind to us, making fires in our bedrooms, which is very comfortable, as we are but weakly, the season rather early for travelling.

April 8: Left R. Valentine's after breakfast. Jacob Parke escorted us eight or nine miles through the worst roads we have yet met with, to one Thomas Truman's, where we dined on the usual fare —bacon and eggs. We left them after dinner and journeyed on to James Moore's in Sadsbury, Lancaster County, where we drank tea, supped and lodged.

April 9: We set off on our journey 'till we arrived at James Gibbon's, where we dined. While we were there, J.G. and several other Friends came there from meeting. James Webb and wife among them, with whom we went home and took up our abode for a short season. Here we understood that our Friends were, by order of the Council, to be brought to Shippensburg, and there discharged. This day we forded three large waters, the Conestoga the last, which came into the carriage and wet our feet and frightened more than one of us. It was near 5 o'clock when we came here. As soon as we had dined ourselves, and wiped out the coach, we set off for Lancaster, one and a half miles, and drove directly to Thomas Wharton's door. We were admitted to him and a number of others; but we desired to speak to him by himself. We had about half an hour's conversation with him, which was not very satisfactory, as they were going to coffee. We drank a dish with his wife and the rest of the company, then came back to J. Webb's by moonlight, where we drank tea and lodged.

April 10: We arose this morning, dressed ourselves, and after breakfast went to Lancaster. We were this day waited upon by Timothy Matlack, who undertook to advise us—perhaps with sincerity. We paid a visit to three councillors. After the Council had sat some time, Timothy came for our address, which was signed by all the women concerned. He said he would come for us when it was proper; but after waiting above an hour, he informed us that our presence was not necessary, and put us off in that way.

April 14: We went to town before breakfast to look for Joseph Reed, who we met, along with Thomas McLean and two others. He confirmed the death of John Hunt. We discoursed with them for some time. They appeared kind; but I fear it is from the teeth outwards.

April 20: John Musser returned from Winchester with letters from our husbands, giving us expectation that they would be with us here the latter end of this week.

April 24: We went to town after breakfast and drove directly to the Court House. We presented our second address (requesting a pass for our Friends), as the first was not answered to our minds. George Bryan said that all was granted that could be. He would not feed us with false hopes. We desired they would reconsider the matter, which he did not refuse. While we were at dinner, Timothy Matlack came from Council, saying he was sorry to tell us nothing further could be done towards granting our request.

April 25: About one o'clock my Henry arrived at J. Webb's, just in time to dine with us. All the rest of our Friends came this day to Lancaster. H.D. is much heartier than I expected; he looks fat and well.

April 27: Our Friends applied to the Council this morning for a paper of discharge, which was not complied with. Permission to pass to Pottsgrove in the county of Philadelphia was all they would grant.

April 28: About 8 o'clock we took leave of the family, and turned our faces homeward.

April 29: We left Downington about 10 o'clock and proceeded on to Robert Jones's, about seventeen miles, where we dined. Here, I. Morris came to us from Washington's headquarters, and brought a pass for all our company, horses, etc. After dinner we went on to J. Roberts', being frequently stopped by guards at different places on the road.

April 30: After breakfast we had a sitting at John Roberts'. John Pemberton spoke to the Family. We set off after 8 o'clock, travelled on without interruption, and were welcomed by many before, and upon, our entrance into the city, where we arrived about 11 o'clock, and found our dear families all well.

May 13: Major Cramond had a concert this afternoon; seven or eight officers were with him. Doctor Knowles, one of them, came into our parlour and had some talk with Henry. There is some movement in the army which we do not understand—the heavy cannon are ordered on board the ships, and some other things look mysterious.

May 16: Some of the officers have orders to pack up their baggage.

May 18: This day may be remembered by many from the scenes of folly and vanity, promoted by the officers of the army under pretence of showing respect to Gen. Howe, now about to leave them. The parade of coaches and other carriages, with many horsemen, through the streets towards the Northern Liberties, where great numbers of the officers and some women embarked in three galleys and a number of boats, and passed down the river before the city, with colors displayed, a large band of music, and the ships in the harbour decorated with colours, which were saluted by the cannon of some of them. It is said they landed in Southwark and proceeded from the waterside to Joseph Wharton's late dwelling, which has been decorated and fitted up for this occasion in an expensive way for this company to feast, dance and revel in. On the river sky rockets and other fireworks were exhibited after night. How insensible do these people appear, while our land is so greatly desolated, and death and sore destruction has overtaken and impends over so many.

May 19: A large number of the British troops marched out this evening,—the light-horse and cannon also. Whether they expect an attack from Washington, or whether they are going after him, remains unknown.

May 20: The large body of troops that went out last night returned today at about 2 o'clock, having done nothing to any purpose.

May 21: Spent the afternoon at Owen Jones's. Grace Galloway was there.

May 22: The officers have orders to put their baggage on board the vessels. Our major packed up his matters today for that purpose.

May 23: The army, 'tis thought, is going in reality to leave us, to evacuate the city. Some hope 'tis not the case, though things

Elizabeth Sandwith Drinker / 171

look like it. Many of the inhabitants are preparing to go with them.

May 24: The officers' baggage going on board the vessels all day. The people talk confidently now of their leaving us.

May 25: A number of the citizens are in great distress on account of this movement of the British army.

May 30: 'Tis reported that the British are giving the remainder of their stores of wood and hay to the poor, which seems to prove they intend ere long to leave us.

June 6: The Commissioners from England arrived today. Lord Cornwallis, also. A visit from Gen. Washington is not so soon expected as it was a day or two past. Nor does it look so likely that the British troops will soon leave us.

June 8: Orders given this day for the two regiments of Anspachers to embark. Our major goes with them. The troops appear to be all in motion. There is talk again of their leaving us entirely. J. Cramond supped with us. He is now going to bed, to be called at one o'clock to go off with his company. I intend to sit up until he goes.

June 9: The major left us at a little past one this morning. He was very dull at taking leave. Sister and self stayed at the door until the two regiments (which were quartered up town) had passed. J.C. bid us adieu as they went by. A fine moonlight morning.

June 15: Three regiments of Hessians passed our door, to take a boat up town.

June 16: Enoch Story took leave of us. He and his family are going with the fleet.

June 17: Troops still crossing the river. Vast numbers are gone over, and many continue with us yet. Capt. Ford and Richard Waln took leave of us today, as did also our John Burket. Sammy Shoemaker and Daniel Cox have gone on board one of the vessels, as have also many other of the inhabitants.

June 18: Last night it was said there was 9000 of the British troops left in town, 11,000 in Jersey. This morning when we arose there was not one redcoat to be seen in town. The encampment in Jersey also vanished. Col. Gordon and some others had not been gone a quarter of an hour before the American light-horse entered the city—not many of them, but they were in and out all day. A bellman went about this evening, by order of Col. Morgan, to desire the inhabitants to stay within doors after night; that if any were found in the streets by the patrol they would be punished. The few that came in today had drawn swords in their hands. They galloped about the streets in a great hurry. Many were much frightened at their appearance.

June 19: The English have in reality left us, and the other party took possession. They have been coming in all day—and the old inhabitants, part of the artillery, some soldiers, etc. Washington and his army have not come. 'Tis said they have gone otherways.

June 22: The stores and storekeepers ordered to shut up, and to render an account of their goods.

June 24: The dealers are forbidden to sell their goods, so that it is almost impossible to get anything. We had this morning a very plentiful market, but as the country people could not get goods for their produce, 'tis to be feared it will not be the case much longer.

June 30: A young soldier who is disordered in his senses went up our stairs this afternoon. We had no man in the house. Isaac Catheral came in and went up after him. He found him in the entry up two pair of stairs, saying his prayers. He readily came down with him.

July 2: The Congress came in today—firing of cannon on the occasion.

July 4: A great fuss this evening, it being the anniversary of Independence—firing of guns, sky rockets, etc. Candles were too scarce and expensive to have an illumination, which perhaps saved some of our windows. [The illumination of candles in windows signified support for the Revolution.] A very high head-dress was exhibited through the streets this afternoon on a very dirty woman, with a mob after her with drums, etc., by way of ridiculing that very foolish fashion.

July 23: They have taken account yesterday, or the day before, of Sammy Shoemaker's and Joseph Galloway's property, with design to confiscate.

August 1: Our neighbour, Abraham Carlisle, was yesterday taken up and put into jail.

August 12: They are pressing waggons today—for what purpose I know not. The lamps have not been lighted for some time past, nor does the watchman call the hour as usual.

Aug. 14: One George Spangler was executed today for some assistance he had given to the British army. He has left a wife and several children.

Aug. 20: Grace Galloway was turned out of her house this forenoon and Spanish officers put in.

Aug. 21: Becky Shoemaker was again ordered out of her house last night. Nobody is allowed to go to New York without a pass from Congress.

September 10: We are reduced from five servants to one, which won't do for long. It is the case with many at present. Good servants are hard to be had. Such a time was never known here, I believe, in that respect.

Sept. 25: Abraham Carlisle's trial came on today and is not yet concluded. We are at a loss how it will go with him.

Sept. 26: I went this afternoon to visit our distressed neighbour Carlisle, whose husband they have brought in guilty of high treason; though it is hoped by many he will not suffer what some others fear he will.

Sept. 30: John Roberts' trial came on today.

October 2: John Roberts is brought in guilty.

Oct. 17: John Roberts condemned to die—shocking doings!

Oct. 24: John Roberts' and Abraham Carlisle's death warrants were signed today and read to them.

Oct. 28: That New York is evacuated proves a mistake; as also, that France and Great Britain have settled matters; at least we have no proof of it. Jane Roberts, wife of John Roberts, Owen Jones and wife, and James Thornton were here this morning. H.D. and self went with them to visit our neighbour, Ann Carlisle. James had something to say to the afflicted women, by way of Testimony, which I thought encouraging. The time for the execution of their husbands is fixed for the 4th of next month. The distressed wives have been with the men in power, and several petitions are being signed by different people to send in to the Council or Assembly. 'Tis hoped and believed that their lives will be spared. It would be terrible indeed should it happen otherwise.

November 3: Preparations are being made for the executions of our poor friends tomorrow morning. Not withstanding the many petitions that have been sent in, and the personal appearance of the distressed wives and children before the Council, I am still of the mind they will not be permitted to carry their matter to the last extremity.

Nov. 4: They have actually put to death—hanged on the commons—John Roberts and Abraham Carlisle this morning, or about noon. An awful, solemn day it has been. I went this evening with my H.D. to neighbour Carlisle's. The body is brought home and laid out—looks placid and serene, no marks of agony or distortion. The poor, afflicted widows are wonderfully upheld and supported under their very great trial. They have many sympathizing Friends.

February 11, 1779: Stepped into neighbour Carlisle's. She is very much agitated by the visit of Smith and Wills, who came here this morning to take an account of Abraham's effects.

Feb. 24: Spent the afternoon, Nancy with me, at Grace Galloway's. She lives with Debby Morris. A good deal of company there.

Feb. 26: Our great men, or the men in power, are quarreling very much among themselves.

May 25: A great concourse of people assembled at the State House by appointment at 5 o'clock this afternoon. Men with clubs have been to several stores, obliging the people to lower their prices. Tommy Redman, the doctor's apprentice, put in prison this afternoon for laughing as the regulators passed by.

May 28: George Shlosser and a young man with him came to inquire what stores we have. They looked into the middle room and cellar. Their authority: the populace. I went this morning to Sally Emlen's, who has been frightened by a mob that surrounded the house at past one in the morning, the day before yesterday. After making a noise for some time, they went away. The Inspectors, I find, have been at most houses today taking account of stores and provisions.

June 6: John Drinker yesterday was taken before the Committee for refusing to show what provisions he had.

June 14: George Pickering came this afternoon for the nonassociation fine, which came to thirteen pounds. He took a looking glass, six new-fashioned pewter plates, and a three quart pewter basin.

June 26: The bellman went about the city at near ten this night, desiring the people to arm themselves with guns or clubs, and to make a search for such as had sent any flour, gunpowder, etc. out of town—with great threats to the Tories. Said it was by order of a Committee.

September 14: This morning in meeting time (myself at home) Jacob Franks and a son of Cling, the vendue master, came to seize for the Continental Tax. They took from us one walnut dining table, one mahogany tea-table, six handsome walnut chairs— with open backs, crow feet, and a shell on the back and on each knee—a mahogany framed, sconce looking-glass, and two large pewter dishes. They carried them off from the door in a cart to Cling's.

Sept. 26: Our neighbour Franks, the baker, died this morning of a fever which, at present, prevails much in the city and country. Many have died.

Sept. 30: A great number of people ill of a fever—many dead. Scarcely a house but some one or more are indisposed.

October 4: Johnny Drinker was taken up today by a mob (part of the militia) as he came out of meeting, where he had been sitting six hours. They allowed him to go home to eat his dinner, and after took him, with Buckridge Sims and Tommy Story. They led them around the streets with the drum after them beating the Rogues March. They then stopped at the door of Wilson, the lawyer, who they intended to take, but met with opposition. Joseph Reed at the head of many light-horse came up and a battle ensued. Two or three lost their lives and many were wounded. They rescued the prisoners, but thought proper to send them to prison, where they are this night. It seems the intent was, or is, to take up a number of the inhabitants who they call disaffected and send them off to some other part, perhaps New York. A guard is set at the prison and the light-horse are patrolling the streets.

May 1, 1780: Jeremiah Baker took a mahogany folding or card-table from us this morning for a Northern Liberty Tax.

June 10: James Pickering, a captain, and six or eight others with bayonets fixed came and demanded our horses. After some talk they went and broke open the stable and took a fine horse bought some time ago, and a mare belonging to J. Drinker. They took horses from many others. They now act under a martial law, lately proclaimed.

June 25: A Friend from the country by the name of Robertson, in publick testimony this morning at the Bank House said that Pennsylvania, once the flower of America, was now a den of thieves.

July 7: On the third day last, Adam Lapp seized for tax the dining-room table, six walnut chairs, tea table, a pair of brass andirons, and two brass kettles.

October 2: This afternoon was buried Anthony Morris Sr. and Patty Hudson. Some day last week was buried our little neighbour John Folwell, and David Frank's wife, and many others—a very sickly time.

Oct. 4: This afternoon David Sands, Sammy Emlen, Edward Hallock, and John Parish drank tea with us. Towards evening we had a sitting, when each of them had something to communicate. A scene of the blackest villainy had just been disclosed: that Arnold had gone off to the enemy; that Col. André (Gen. Clinton's aid and confidant) was apprehended in disguise in the camp; that West Point (where Arnold commanded) was to be the sacrifice; and that all the dispositions were made for delivering it up last monday, the 25th, at night. It is further said that Gen. Washington arrived at West Point just after the plot was discovered. He lodged there that night, and was to have been given up with the fort. Gen. Arnold was, by his orders, pursued, but without effect. Col. André, 'tis also said, is condemned to be hanged. On Seventh day last, the 30th, was exhibited and paraded through the streets of this city a ridiculous figure of Gen. Arnold with two faces, and the devil standing behind him pushing him with a pitch fork. At the front of the cart was a very large lanthorn of green paper with a number of inscriptions, setting forth his crime. Several hundred men and boys with candles in their hands—all in ranks; many officers, the infantry, men with guns and bayonets. Somewhere near the coffee house they burnt the effigy (instead of the body, as was said in the papers).

October 19, 1781: The 17th of this month Gen. Cornwallis was taken, for which we grievously suffered on the 24th by way of [others] rejoicing. A mob assembled about 7 o'clock or before, and continued their insults until near 10, to those whose houses were not yet illuminated. Scarcely one Friend's house escaped. We had nearly seventy panes of glass broken. The sash lights and two panels of the front parlor broke in pieces. The door cracked and violently burst open when they threw stones into the house for some time; but they did not enter. Some fared better and some worse. Some houses, after breaking the door, they entered, and destroyed the furniture, etc. Many women and children were frightened into fits, and 'tis a mercy no lives were lost.

December 31: I have been but four or five times out of the house for upwards of four months. On the 22nd one Johnson, an under-sheriff, and one Brown or Ritchie, who did not seem free to tell his name, came as they said with an order to search our house for British goods; which they accordingly did, examining drawers, trunks, closets, presses, etc. They had nearly finished their search, being in the garret, when H.D. came home and ordered them out of the house. They produced their order, signed by J.B. Smith. John Drinker's son Henry was the person meant by the order, and John Thomas, so that our house was rummaged by the mistake of the Sheriff. Henry Drinker, jr., hearing that they were at our house, had time to hide his goods, if he had any. They did not go to look after them, being as I suppose ashamed of the mistake they had made, as well they might, and afraid too. While they were in our entry up two pair of stairs Billy Sansom came up and said something provoking to this Ritchie, who immediately took two pistols in his hands and offered one to Billy. Billy did not take it. Ritchie put them in his pockets again. 'Tis a bad government under which we are liable to have our houses searched and everything laid open to ignorant fellows, perhaps thieves. H.D., had he been so disposed, could have made them pay dearly for their mistake.

✳ Philadelphians suffered far more from yellow fever epidemics after the Revolution than they did from hardships during the war. These epidemics reached their peak during August, when vast swamp-lands nearby bred a multitude of mosquitoes, yellow fever carriers. The Drinker family extricated themselves from this dangerous environment by fleeing to their country estate in Germantown. Henry had to commute to the city for business; Elizabeth, therefore, was kept informed of the hideous disease. She jotted down in her diary on August 23, 1793, that "a fever prevails in the city, particularly in Water Street, between Race and Arch Streets, one of the malignant kind. Numbers have died of it. Some say it was occasioned by damaged coffee and fish; others say it was imported in a vessel from Cape Francois which lay at our wharf, or at the wharf back of our store. Doctor Hutchinson was ordered by the Governor to inquire into the report. He found, as it's said, upwards of seventy persons sick in that square of different disorders, several of this putrid or bilious fever. Some are ill in Water Street and some in Race Street. It's really an alarming and serious time." August 27: "The yellow fever spreads in the city. Many are taken of it, and many of other disorders. They have burned tar in the streets and taken many other precautions. Many families have left the city." August 28: "Henry Drinker left us at about six this morning. I gave him a

Elizabeth Sandwith Drinker / 179

William Birch's engraving, "Arch Street Ferry, Philadelphia," shows the wharf area seen by Elizabeth Drinker from the dormer windows of her home, a short distance from the left. This is probably where the 1793 yellow fever epidemic began. The roof of the James & Drinker warehouse is shown in the distance, to the left of the vessel.

small spoonful of Daffy's Elixir and vinegar in a sponge, and a sprig of wormwood. The inhabitants are leaving the city in great numbers." September 3: "The physicians have given their opinion that the disorder spreads in the city. The Assembly, who have lately met, talk of breaking up. The square opposite us in Water Street appears to be depopulated by deaths and flight." September 4: "A man here this afternoon informs us of the death of one Stevens in Chestnut Street who buried 5 of his family. He was a sadler. It is said that many are buried at night and taken in carts to their graves. 'Tis thought by some that the present tremendous disorder is a degree of the pestilence. May we be humble and thankful for favours received. We were told a sad story indeed, today, if it be true. It was repeated by different persons and, everything considered, it seems not unlikely, of a young woman who had nursed one or more in Water Street, who died of the disease. She being unwell, the neighbours advised her to go somewhere else, as none of them would choose to take her in. She went out somewhere—I did not hear in what part of the town it was—and lay down ill at a door. A magistrate in the ward had her sent in a cart to the hospital, where she was refused admittance, and was near that place found dead in the cart the next morning."

The Drinkers kept away from the city these hot months, until cold weather killed the mosquitoes. They were not spared the ravages of bacillary dysentery, "putrid sore throat" (usually diptheria), tuberculosis, measles, and malaria. To ward off smallpox Elizabeth had everyone inoculated, when a lancet dipped in fresh smallpox germs pierced each family member's skin. This was quite dangerous, for there was always the chance one or more would then get the disease. Years later, Elizabeth's grandchildren were spared this hazard by being vaccinated. Edward Jenner's substitution of cowpox was used.

A tragic illness was endured for many years by her daughter, Molly Rhoads, who suffered severe abdominal pains during the late stage of pregnancy. Compassionately concerned, Elizabeth wrote in her diary: "Though I dreaded how things might end, yet I did not suspect how it was with her at that time, but judged it to be a lingering labour. In the afternoon Sally Lampley came, who is to nurse Molly. Her pains, though not much stronger, were improved by her efforts. From many things that occurred I was led to conclude that all was not right, by the difficulty and tediousness, etc. And so it proved. The birth presented, and the child came into the world for some time double wedged, and the poor mother benumbed. No regular labour pains. The doctor got down the feet and legs. It was long afterwards that it was wholly delivered. I did not know her situation 'till after all was over. It had frequently evacuated before birth, being, as I afterwards supposed, in the agony of death at that time. It was stillborn between 5 and 6 o'clock, a very pretty well made boy, resembling both father and mother. A middle sized child, rather tall. The loss gives me great concern, not only being deprived of a sweet little grandson, but the suffering of my poor child, who lost what may be called the reward of her labour, and promising a good breast of milk. She may pass through, if she lives, the same excruciating trouble a year the sooner for this loss. Doctor Way said her labour was very severe indeed, that he never knew a young woman to pass through so much, with equal fortitude and patience. She was got to bed in a very low state, but nothing like dismay. I gave Molly an injection [douche] but perceived that it run off in a way that occasioned great alarm to me. It was again repeated and the same effect followed. I am greatly apprehensive on this account. She is undoubtedly much hurt, but the doctor says all will be well again. I wish it may, but have distressing doubts about it." Elizabeth sensed the truth; the doctor had failed to discover the source of her daughter's illness. Though she lived eighty-two years, Molly had to endure a fistula, or opening, between her rectum and vagina, through which flowed a seepage of feces. A surgical cure was then unknown.

For particular disorders requiring bloodletting—such as rheumatism, pleurisy, skin sores and inflammations, and various fevers—a doctor was called in. A vein was opened and a quantity of blood withdrawn. "My veins are small," wrote Elizabeth, "and the largest lays over an artery, which makes it difficult for me to be bled, tho' I have been bled maybe fifty times in my life, or near to it."

Elizabeth treated, with warm compassion, her children's unpredictable accidents. Her ten year old son Henry "fell into the river this afternoon, and after a quarter of an hour remaining in his wet cloaths, came home very cold and coughing. We stript him, and after rubbing him well with a coarse towel, put on warm dry cloaths, gave him some rum and water to drink, and made him jump a rope till he sweated." Eliza, her young granddaughter, "put a piece of a nut shell up her nose. The doctor has made an attempt to take it out with an instrument but without success; they bound her eyes and held her down fast; she cried so that nothing could be done." Dr. Kuhn ordered her nose syringed with warm water and swabbed with oil, but the child was so terrified, no one could approach her. Two days later, "Dr. Shippen, who Kuhn called in, tried with an instrument to take the nut shell out of the poor dear child's nose, but could not effect it." She later fought off Kuhn's second attempt to remove it. Failing, he shrugged off responsibility, concluding that perhaps it might rot away. Rot it did, so much so that whenever the child hugged her grandmother, Elizabeth breathed in an offensive odor. The child's father finally pulled the shell out with a hooked instrument, but only while three people held her down as she howled.

Despite the fact that Elizabeth spent much of her time tending to the needs of her children and grandchildren, she managed to do a voracious amount of reading, often jotting down in her diary opinions of various books. January 7, 1796: "It may appear strange to some that an infirm old woman should begin the year reading romances—'tis a practice I by no means highly approve; yet I trust I have not sinned, as I read a little of most things." April 19, 1796: "I have read a large octavo volume entitled *The Rights of Women* by Mary Wollstonecraft. In very many of her sentiments she, as some of our friends say, 'speaks my mind.' In some others, I do not altogether coincide with her. I am not for quite so much independence." August 9, 1800: "I sent Paul to the library for the works of Rabelais, a French author. I expected something very sensible and clever, but on looking over the books, found them filled with such obscene, dirty matter that I was ashamed I had sent for them."

Elizabeth Drinker died on November 24, 1807, at the age of seventy-three—two months after the death of her forty-six year old daughter, Sally Downing, and two years before Henry Drinker's death at the age of seventy-six. According to the Friends' Monthly Meeting Burial Book, Elizabeth's leave-taking was caused by "lethargy," Henry's by pneumonia.✱

Grace Growdon Galloway

٭ Had Joseph Galloway not had legal control over his wife Grace's inherited property she would not have had to endure years of torment and anguish. Mrs. Galloway was the victim of a revolution she quietly opposed, of a husband who used her inheritance for his own interests, and of a stepmother who had Pennsylvania's new government give to her the choice land tracts belonging to Grace and her sister Elizabeth.

Grace's Quaker father, Lawrence Growdon, was born March 14, 1694, in his family's mansion (Trevose) at Bensalem Township, Bucks County. As a young, adventurous man he sailed to Bristol, England, where he became a wealthy merchant, married, and fathered two daughters. Following his return to Philadelphia in 1733, Lawrence was elected to the Pennsylvania Assembly. Six years later, after his wife's death, he married Sarah Biles. He was soon commissioned a Justice of Bucks County and, in 1750, became Second Justice of Pennsylvania's Supreme Court, a position he held for fifteen years even though he was appointed a member of the Provincial Council in 1758. When he died in 1770 his property wealth amounted to more than 13,000 land acres, valued at 113,478 pounds sterling. The most valuable property was Trevose (444 acres), Belmont (574 acres), King's Place (297 acres), Richland (10,160 acres), and large tracts of the Durham Iron Company, including the blast furnace, mines, forges, waterpower, and quarries.

On October 18, 1753, Grace Growdon married Joseph Galloway, a prominent lawyer, in Philadelphia's Christ Church. Both were strong-willed, and their marriage was a turbulent one. Of five children born to them only Elizabeth (Betsey) survived infancy.

When Lawrence Growdon's will was probated his wife Sarah was bequeathed "an annuity of two-hundred pounds per annum during her natural life." The remainder of the estate was be-

The portrait of Grace Growdon was painted from a drawing shortly before her marriage to Joseph Galloway. The painting was shipped to England in 1829, probably at the request of Grace's granddaughter, Ann Grace Roberts Burton.

queathed to his daughters, Grace and Elizabeth (living in England and married to Thomas Nickleson), in order to assure future inheritance through the family line. As required by law, the entire property was placed under Joseph Galloway's control during his life, after which it would revert back to his wife or her heirs. In addition, Joseph had the responsibility of handling Sarah Growdon's annuity.

Joseph Galloway was chosen to the Pennsylvania Assembly in 1757, its speaker from 1766 to 1774. His prestige was such that when Benjamin Franklin left for England in 1764 he placed his papers and letterbooks with Joseph for safekeeping. After being appointed by the Assembly to the Continental Congress in 1774, Galloway tried to dissuade radical members from stirring up a revolution. Convinced that a revolt was in violation of the British constitution, disgusted with the radical wing's need for violence, Galloway left Congress, taking refuge in the peaceful environment of Trevose. There, Benjamin Franklin urged his friend to join the struggle for independence. Instead of complying, Joseph joined General Howe's British forces in December 1776 as a civilian advisor. Grace remained at Trevose. In 1777 she lodged a complaint with the Supreme Executive Council, fearing that she would be assaulted by radical thugs. The Council asked the sheriffs and magistrates of Bucks County "to prevent so far as in your power, any insult being offered to Mrs. Galloway, and the publick may rest assured that due notice will be taken of all offenders against the peace and welfare of this state." The Council's benevolence, however, was not long-lived. The large influx of Loyalist refugees into Philadelphia from other colonies, who were hopeful of a peaceful occupation of the city by British soldiers, so alarmed the radical wings of the Continental Congress and Pennsylvania Assembly they encouraged the harassment and arrest of those who disagreed with their cause. When the Test Act was passed, requiring allegiance to the new, revolutionary government, citizens refusing to take oath were denied political office and the vote.

At eleven o'clock on the morning of September 26, 1777,

General Howe and three thousand British troops marched into Philadelphia, along with a group of Loyalists, including Joseph Galloway. Citizens crowded sidewalks, cheering the soldiers' arrival. Galloway was appointed superintendant of police. His wife joined him the following year.

In Lancaster—where the Continental Congress, Pennsylvania Supreme Executive Council, and Pennsylvania Assembly had fled—the Assembly passed a law for the attainder of a list of persons suspected of committing treason. High on the list was Joseph Galloway. Those listed who failed to surrender before April 20, 1778, would be judged guilty, their property forfeited to the state, to be either sold or rented at the state's discretion. On the 6th of May the Assembly appointed five men Commissioners of Forfeited Estates—Charles Willson Peale (militia officer, artist), William Will (militia officer), Robert Smith, Samuel Massey, and Jacob Schreiner—whose duties were to ferret out accused traitors, arrest them, and seize their property. In payment, the commissioners were assured five percent of the amount gained after the property was sold or leased. Peale, blindly obedient to those who would be influential to him in the future, so disliked Loyalists that he thought their houses should be painted black, much like "the Turks use to designate the residences of liars." He did not have long to wait to vent his hostility.

In the middle of June, British and Hessian troops evacuated Philadelphia for New York. A number of these soldiers, furious over their orders, destroyed citizens' property. When commanded to burn deserted Rebel ships, soldiers allowed two nearby horse stables to be consumed by fire. Joseph Galloway and Elizabeth (Betsey), then nearing twenty, sailed from the port with Lord Howe the night of the 18th. Grace remained in Philadelphia to keep her inherited property and home from being seized. The day after the British evacuation Peale rapped upon the front door and told Grace she would have to leave.

Philadelphia, possibly the cleanest city in the colonies before the Revolution, was now found by returning Patriots to be in a shocking state of filth and disrepair. The State House, according to a New Hampshire delegate to Congress, "was left in a most filthy and sordid condition, as were many of the public and private buildings in the city. Some of the genteel houses were used for stables, and holes cut in the parlour floors" served for the disposal of horse manure. The burying ground for the poor was piled high with fresh soil, covering the bodies of executed American soldiers and those who had starved to death in prison.

One returning citizen, according to a report in Boston's *Continental Journal and Weekly Advertiser,* was shocked by what he considered to be a lack of morality among women in Philadelphia. Those who had copied British tastes in fashion, he believed, were "absurd, ridiculous, and preposterous." He strongly suspected that the rage for padding at the back, called the "cul de Paris" outside France, was conveniently used by some "to counterbalance extraordinary natural weight which some of the ladies carry before them. You will probably be surprised at this, but you may rely on it as a fact: indeed many people do not hesitate in supposing that most of the young ladies who were in the city with the enemy and wear the present fashionable dresses have purchased them at the expense of their virtue. It is agreed on all hands that the British officers played the devil with the girls."

Under the new American regime mass arrests were made against citizens who had aided the British during the occupation. A few were executed. "Patriotic" men prospering from wartime contracts sought prestige by buying fashionable mansions. An elegant carriage was essential if one wished to acquire status, and the rush was on to purchase those confiscated from wealthy Loyalists. Among a number of these newly prominent citizens the lust for wealth had replaced the idealistic crusade for national freedom. The exorbitant charge for articles needed by Washington's army, the vacillation of members of the Continental Congress in supplying the army adaquately with food, clothing, and medical supplies, and the depreciation of American currency resulted in most of the deaths of an estimated 2,500 American soldiers who died of disease, malnutrition, and freezing weather during the winter of 1777–1778 at Valley Forge. Washington complained bitterly of ineptitude and corruption. While in Philadelphia he told Congress that "speculation, peculation, and an insatiable thirst for riches seem to have got the better of every other consideration and almost every order of men."

In the fall of 1778 the Chief Justice of the Supreme Court (Thomas McKean) ordered the seizure of Joseph Galloway's estate. Grace's stepmother, Sarah Growdon, was afraid that Grace would lose everything and that she herself, thereby, would no longer have an income. Through her attorney, Andrew Robeson, Sarah took legal action to retain her annuity—which had accumulated to 650 pounds—by acquiring ownership of three of her stepdaughter's tracts: Belmont, Richlieu, and King's Place. Grace's sister, Elizabeth Nickleson, as an Englishwoman living abroad, had no legal rights in American property according to the Pennsylvania government.

The confiscation of her property, and separation from her family caused considerable anguish to Grace, whose health deteriorated to the brink of madness. Letters to and from her family were smuggled, often concealed in quills. Many were small, and tightly written.*

July 9, 1778: Israel Pemberton advised me to see lawyers, as men were nominated to seize our estate. I sent for Lewis [William Lewis, lawyer] and gave him ten guineas. He promised to consult Abel James and Mr. Chew [Benjamin Chew, lawyer] to see if I could have dower.

July 10: Jones girls here in the afternoon and told me twelve French ships of the line was gone for New York. I was quite mad with [Sir William] Howe for betraying us to the provincials, as it was in his power to have settled the affair.

July 12: I was very unwell in the morning. The French Ambassador came this day. I looked out and saw the cannon and soldiers and I thought it was like the execution of my husband and hurried away, determined to see no more of it; but Nancy Clifton came and I went down to her. She told me the *Roebuck* [British ship] was not taken, which raised my spirits. I looked out and saw a contemptible sight. There was eighty-two men drawn up before the general's and our house on the opposite side of the street, under arms. Gen. Cadwalader and Mr. Morris, with some of the aides-de-camp, came with them. There was one coach and three chariots, and the French count and his legion of horse, which consisted of no more than eight, beside an officer or two. He and his legion rode before, and when they alighted at the general's there was thirteen cannon fired.

July 18: Israel Pemberton told me he heard I could not recover dower. He altered his discourse entirely. Bill Turner and his wife heard J.G. [Joseph Galloway] and my child is well. The French fleet blocks up New York.

July 21: About 2 o'clock they came—one Smith (a hatter), Col. Will, one Schreiner, and a dutchman (I know not his name). They took an inventory of everything, even to broken china and empty bottles. I left nurse with them, called Sidney Howell, and sat at the door with her. Mrs. Erwin and Mrs. Jones went about with them. I had such spirits that I appeared not uneasy. They told me they must advertise the house. I told them they may do as they pleased, but 'till it was decided by a court I would not go out unless by the force of a bayonet. When I knew who had a right to it I should know how to act. I sent three times for Lewis, but he did not come. I sent for Ben Chew. He came but thought I talked too high to those men, 'tho he himself had advised me to say all I did say, except that of the force of a bayonet. In short, he acted far from a friend and I see plainly he is rather cold and cares little where we are brought to beggary so he is out of the scrape. He tells me I can't stay in the house. Yet on my saying "Where should I go?" never offered to take me in; nor did Molly Craig, who was here, and Peggy Johns. Not one has offered me a house to shelter me; but Betsy Jones behaves the best of all. Oh God, what shall I do? There is no dependence on the arm of flesh; nor have I one hope in this world nor anything to rely on. I am afraid how my child and husband came out of New York. All hope is over.

Grace Growdon Galloway / 191

July 22: I was ill in the morning. Israel Pemberton here but could not see him. Lewis here. He gives me no hope of saving anything and behaves so exceedingly cold and disrespectful that I find my ten guineas thrown away. Nor does he seem to try to do anything for it. I sent for Mr. Dickinson last night and he told me he would look over the law to see if I could recover my own estate. This evening he came and told me I could not recover my dower and he feared my income in my estate was forfeited likewise; yet no trial would be of service. He advised me to draw up a petition to Chief Justice McKean for the recovery of my estate. He refused a fee in the politest manner, but begged I would look on him as my sincere friend and told me he would do me any service to the utmost of his power. I think he behaves much better than Chew. So I find I am a beggar indeed. I expect every hour to be turned out of doors, and where to go I know not. No one will take me in, and all the men keep away from me. Was I assured that my husband and child was happy nothing could make me very wretched; but I am fled from as a pestilence.

July 23: Owen Jones very calmly told me he presumed I would not go from my house unless I was carried out. I told him I would, for there was not a man but would sneak and fly from me in time of trouble.

July 28: Owen Jones and his wife invited me to come to their house if I was turned out. Peale [Charles Willson Peale] came to tell me I must give three-hundred a year or move out of my house. I told him I would go out. Sent for Lewis; he and Mr. Chew concluded I should claim my own estate. I am in better spirits.

August 1: I was pretty cheerful. In the afternoon Mrs. Wharton sent to know if I would take a ride. She called on me just before sunset. She seemed very reserved, but when she found I was not like to trouble them she cleared up. We went all the back ways of the town and rode three miles round. Just as we came to Second Street she ordered the man to go to our house. I then said I was in hopes I should have seen friend [Thomas] Wharton, as I wanted to speak to him and had no way of coming. She said

"I tell thee, friend Galloway, thee can't go now, as it is like to be a gust." I said there was no prospect of a gust. She then said "I left Rachel and Suky Hudson at our house and promised to take them home." I then said I was sorry I should take her from her company, but I wanted to see her husband if it was but for five minutes, as I had no other opportunity of seeing him. She then told me she did not know of Hudsons coming when she sent to me, and thought I wanted to ride. I replied the only inducement I had for coming today was to see her husband, but since it was so disagreeable, my going to her house, I wished he would call on me and, if I had known I could not see him I would not have come. She replied "Why was thee not glad of the ride. I thought thee would be glad to ride out." I told her that such rides as this I would not give a pin for, and the exercise of riding three miles and being out half an hour would contribute but little to my health; but my affairs would soon be settled and, if they allowed me my estate, I should be able to keep a carriage of my own and not be beholden to anyone. If they did not let me have my own I should not be here. She then repented: "Not here? Why, where will thee go?" I said to my husband, and that nobody had need to fear that I should trouble them, for I would live on bread and water before I would accept a favour that I could not repay. She then said she was glad I kept the house. I told her if I had not I would not have troubled my friends but for a few days 'till I could look about me, for I knew the Philadelphians too well to expect any favours. I could feel and had been hurt by the slights that I had received from some that called themselves friends. But I would have nothing but what I could pay for. She then made an excuse that their horses would not stand, but I know they had stood when she choose to go. Therefore I treated it with contempt. As she saw I was vexed she pressed me to send for her carriage, which I refused. I told her I may now never see her husband. She said "I will send for thee some other time." When we came to our door I desired her to give my love to her husband and tell him I wanted to speak to him much, but had no way of coming; therefore I begged he would call on me when they rode out. Sam Rhodes helped me out of the carriage. I went in without thanking this little, great woman for the ride. I was not gone more than three quarters of an hour before my heart was ready to burst at the mean figure I must have cut in begging to go to another person's house and be told I could not.

Aug. 3: I received a letter from the president [Council's acting-president, George Bryan] informing me that my estate was confiscated during the life of Mr. Galloway. I sent for Ben Chew. He desired me to send for the president and ask him some questions; but he gave me no comfort.

Aug. 5: President Bryan was here in the morning. He said he was no lawyer but the law was in his letter:

> When a lady marries, (unless by a special reserve of her lands in the hands of Trustees, made before the contract,) the use and profits of the real estate belonging to her rests in her husband for and during their joint lives, and if children be born then for his life. This estate, so acquired by wedlock, the gentleman can sell. It may be seized by creditors and applied to their relief; And it may be lost by attaint, and then it devolves to the publick as a forfeiture. But the moment the husband dies it returns to the widow, or if she be deceased to her children or other heirs. . . . in every case of attaint for treason, support for the wife and children shall be awarded by the Judges of the Supreme Court, out of the estate of the husband.

Just after he went I heard from Mr. G., which raised my spirits. Peale and Smith came to tell me I must go out of my house. I told Peale I had taken it of him. He answered another gentleman had let it before to the Spanish ambassador and I must go out. I told him I would take the advice of my friends. They said out I must go, but agreed to call tomorrow about the house and goods. I sent for Owen Jones and Israel Pemberton. Owen told me he would not have me go out, but consult my friends. In the afternoon the fellows came and appraised the goods, but the French consul was here to take the house and I told him as I found they would not let me stay in it he had my voice in preference to the Spaniard. I talked to the men about it, but they confessed the house was not let at all, yet said I must go out. I went to Debby Morris's and was in high spirits, as I had another note from J.G. Debby told me she would not leave the house unless carried out. Sidney Howell and Mrs. Erwin with the men were appraising the goods when I came home. My spirits began to flag. I spoke to the men about the Frenchman, but they would give me no answer. Israel Pemberton and Owen Jones were here. Israel blamed me for consenting to let the Frenchman have it, and he said I would not take his advice. Becky Shoemaker [wife of accused traitor Samuel Shoemaker] would be advised to stay in her house. He told me not to go 'till forced, for they had no right to turn me out.

Aug. 8: Peale and Will came to let me know that I must go out Monday morning, for they would give the Spaniard possession.

Aug. 9: I sat writing in the morning and am very much distressed. I think I must go to New York. I am very low spirited and uneasy about the fire at New York, but Mr. Jewel told me they was out of the way of the fire. Sally Cox, Becky Redman, and Molly Craig drank tea here. Lewis promised to go to the president in the morning, and hoped to give me a good account tomorrow, and prevent their coming. I am in better spirits. I asked Molly Craig to let me come to her house, and Mr. Craig consented. They use me very kindly. I am in tolerable spirits. Mrs. Redman and Mrs. Boudinot think I shall be turned out tomorrow.

Aug. 10: Peggy Johns and Becky Redman came in the morning. Lewis sent me word Smith had gave his honour not to molest me 'till the opinion of the Executive Council was known. But in a short time after came Peale, Will, and Schreiner with a Spanish merchant and his attendants, and took possession of my house. I was taken very ill and obliged to lay down. I sent them word I could not see them. They went everywhere below stairs, and the Spaniard offered to let me choose my own bed chamber. I sent them no message, but was very ill upstairs. Between 2 and 3 o'clock the last went away. Peale told nurse now that they had given the Spanish gentleman possession they had nothing more to do with it; but they took the key out of the front parlour door and locked me out, and left the windows open. J. Mathers brought me some news from my dearest child, and told me Mr. G. fell from Mr. Low's house at the fire and hurt himself, but not dangerously, and that if an act of oblivian would take place he would come home, if not go to England. This sinks my spirits very much. I sent for Israel Pemberton and told him they had taken forcible possession of my house. He advised me to stay in the house and take the lock off the door. I sent for Tim Matlack [secretary of the Council]. At night he came and said I must go out of my house. Molly Craig told him she had a mind to get in at the window and take the lock off the door, and to fasten the window. He told her if she had she would be hung. At last I coaxed him, and he seemed as if he was desirous I should have my estate, but was violent in respect to their laws. He told me the lawyers flattered me, for I must give up possession or I could have no maintenance. I was frightened and would not have the lock taken off, but went to Gen. Arnold [Benedict Arnold, commandant of Philadelphia] and told him how exposed my house was, and he kindly sent a guard. Mrs. Craig went with me. He treated me with great politeness, and I went to bed in better spirits. John Roberts [Quaker convicted of treason] sent to gaol.

Aug. 11: It rained all day and I was very heavy and low spirited. I sent for Sidney Howell and she spent a dull day with me. Sent for Mr. Chew. He came in the evening and made me copy some questions for Boudinot [Elias Boudinot, lawyer, delegate to the Continental Congress]. He stayed and supped with me and was very friendly. He told me to have the lock taken off the parlour door; but I am afraid. He gave me good spirits; but I am afraid of tomorrow if they should come to turn me out. I am fearful all is not well at New York. What a miserable situation am I in. No good prospect before me, but must hope.

Aug. 12: Peggy Johns dined with me. I was very low and just after dinner Peale came and asked me what rooms I intended to let the Spanish gentleman have. I told him none. Nor would I give up possession of my house, that I had been very ill used in having my parlour shut up and the key taken away, and that the house was thereby exposed to be broken into. He told me if I intended to dispute with the Executive Council of the state he had nothing more to say. I told him not to mistake me, for I would not contend with the Executive Council: "But I contend with you, sir, and this Spanish gentleman, and will not go out of my house 'till I know the opinion of the Council." He told me I must. I replied "I would not, and if I did go they must turn me out." He replied "Then we must turn you out." I said "Very well." He said my servants had affronted the Spanish gentleman's servants by saying this house is Mrs. Galloway's and they had no business there. I told him it was a lie; I had no servant that had anything to say to them. He replied "Then it was your visitors." I saw that the fellow would say anything, and treated him with the contempt he deserved. Sally Pennington came after he went, but I was so disturbed at every knock at the door that I was quite miserable. Mr. Boudinot came. I gave him the paper and he told me to keep in my house and if they made a forcible entry he would bring an action against them. Lewis came afterwards and said he and Mr. Boudinot would go to the Council tomorrow and settle the matter. Ben Chew came, after them, but was not so clever as last time. He told me not to stir out of my house. Mr. and Mrs. Craig and Peggy Johns went away about 10 o'clock. I am in better spirits but dread tomorrow.

Aug. 13: A rainy day. Very unwell when I got up. Mrs. Erwin here; begged her ask her husband and Billy Gray to be security for me if they will let me have the house. Mr. Erwin called afterwards and said they will. Peggy Johns here but I was taken ill and was on the bed 'till night. These villains will kill me. Owen Jones and Lewis here in the evening and Lewis says he will take care they shall not trouble me tomorrow. I am very ill and low. After they went I sat down and wrote. My hopes and spirits are quite gone. They will kill me if I am harassed much more.

Grace Growdon Galloway /197

Aug. 14: Molly Craig and Peggy Johns drank tea with me. Debby Morris here. Mr. Craig came and supped with me. Mr. Boudinot sent me his opinion that I may stay in the house 'till the affair is determined by the Council. Spangler was hanged today. Very low and unwell. All is dark and gloomy.

Aug. 15: Billy Gray stopped in the evening and said he would be security for me if I took the house. Lewis came and read a petition to be presented to the Executive Council on Monday. I signed it but could not have time to understand what I signed, for Mrs. Straker came with her husband and Mrs. Wilson to desire me to send news by her to New York, and pressed me so much to let me know where I was going that at last I told them to Mr. Craig's. I am vexed at their impertinent interruption. Mrs. Cox, Willy Bond and all the Chews here. They always come in an evening, tho' they know that is the only time my friends come on business. I am provoked that I did not read the petition. Sidney Howell here, I am quite worn out with such heaps of company.

Aug. 16: I find Shoemakers had been before me. The Quakers all assist her but they would let me fall. I sent twice to Lewis for a sight of the petition, but he would not let me see it, and as I have no friends they treat me as they please. So much for Mr. G.'s great friends. He has not one who will go out of the way to serve him. I am in hopes they will let me have my estate, but that will be on my own account. No favour shown to J.G. or his child. Nor has he a friend that will say one word in his favour. I am tired with sending after a set of men that always keep from me when I most need them. I am vexed.

Aug. 17: Lewis came and informed me the Council had put off the sale of the goods, and I should now remain quiet, as the proceedings of those men were illegal. I was in good spirits.

Aug. 18: Sent for Mr. Boudinot. He came in the evening. I gave him ten guineas. He told me he thought my estate was not forfeited, and by staying in the house I may perhaps get it for a maintenance out of Mr. G.'s estate.

Aug. 19: I went to see Mrs. Potts. She told me Betsey [Galloway] went but little out and, by what she said, I fear is not taken notice of. I could wish she was with me but a few minutes. The letter she brought was in no way satisfactory:

My dear, I cannot express the pain we suffer at our separation. I have as yet heard nothing certain from you. What are you likely to effect? Is your staying from us likely to be of any service. If not, make all the expedition to us possible, tho' I must in that case proceed to England. Betsey will stay here until you come, or if you stay where you are she will come to you. Have you any and what Friends? Will they exert themselves in your behalf. Your own estate they can forfeit only during my life—get some friend to purchase that for you; leave him a power or instructions for that purpose if you come. Do let me hear from you as soon as possible.

14 Aug. 1778 [*Joseph Galloway*]

Mrs. Craig and Mrs. Cox sent for me to come home. I heard Peale had been there to inform me I must go out of my house tomorrow at 10 o'clock. I was much shocked, as I expected the Council had put a stop to it. I sent for Mr. Chew and Lewis. They seemed surprised. Lewis concluded to go to the president in the morning to know the meaning of it.

Aug. 20: Lewis sent me word that I must shut my doors and windows and, if they would come, to let them make a forcible entry. Accordingly, I did so, and a little after 10 o'clock they knocked violently at the door three times. The third time I sent nurse, and I called out to tell them I was in possession of my own house and would keep so, and that they should gain no admittance. Here upon which they went round in the yard and tried every door, but could none open. Then they went to the kitchen door and with a scrubbing brush, which they broke to pieces, they forced that open—we women standing in the entry in the dark. They made repeated strokes at the door, and I think it was eight or ten minutes before they got it open. When they came in I had the windows open. They looked very mad. There was

Peale, Smith, and a Col. Will. I spoke first and told them I was used ill, and I showed them the opinion of the lawyers. Peale read it; but they all despised it, and Peale said he had studied the law and knew they did right. I told them nothing but force should get me out of my house. Smith said they knew how to manage that, and that they would throw my clothes in the street. He told me that Mrs. Simpson and forty other [Patriots] were put out of the line in one day. I said they had their furniture to take with them. He said that was owing to the generosity of the British officers, but the police would let no favour be shown. I told him I knew that was not true. He told me he knew better and hinted that Mr. G. had treated people cruelly. I found the villain would say anything so I stopped after hearing several insulting things. Mrs. Irwin and Smith sat and talked of the English cruelty, and Sidney Howell whined out her half assent to the same. Meanwhile, Peale and Will went over the house to see nothing was embezzled, locking up the things. Mrs. Irwin sat talking in the kitchen as they took my things to her house. Peale went to the general's [General Cadwalader] and asked for his chariot, and then returned and told me the general was so kind as to let me have it. Mr. Peale was willing to accommodate me as well as he could. I told him he need not give himself the trouble, for if I wanted the chariot I could send to the general myself. Just after, the general sent in his housekeeper with his compliments and let me know that I was welcome to his chariot, and he would have it ready any hour I pleased. I then accepted of it and told her I would send for it after every mortifying treatment. I was tired and wanted to be turned out. Peale went upstairs and brought down my work bag and two bonnets and put them on the side table. At last we went in the entry to sit and I asked the two Grays if they would witness for me, but they both went away. Two of the men went out and after staying some time returned and said they had been with the Council and that they had done right and must proceed. I did not hear this myself, but the rest of the women did. Mrs. Craig asked for my bed, but they would let me have nothing and, as I told them, acted entirely from malice. After we had been in the entry some time, Smith and Will went away. Peale said the chariot was ready but he would not hasten me. I told him I was at home and in my own house and nothing but force should drive me out of it. He said it was not the first time he had taken a lady by the hand. An insolent wretch; this speech was made some time in the room. At last he beckoned for the chariot, for the general would not let it come till I wanted it. As the chariot drew up Peale fetched my bonnets and gave one to me, the other to Mrs. Craig. Then with the greatest air, said, "Come, Mrs. Galloway. Give me your hand." I answered, "Indeed I will not; nor will I go out of my house but by force." He then took hold of my arm. I rose and he took me to the door. I then took hold on one side, looked round, and said, "Pray take notice. I do not leave my house of my own accord, or with my own inclination, but by force. And nothing but force should have made me give up possession." Peale said, with a sneer, "Very well, madam." When he led me down the step I said, "Now, Mr. Peale, let go my arm. I want not your assistance." He said he could help me to the carriage. I told him I could go without, and "you, Mr. Peale, are the last man on earth I would wish to be obliged to." Mrs. Craig then stepped into the carriage and we drove to her house, where we dined. It was near 2 o'clock. I did not seem to be much concerned, but went to Dr. Redman's after dinner. The women behaved very well, but the doctor took little notice of me. Drank tea at Mr. Craig's. Neighbour Eddy came to see me, as did Sidney Howell, Debby Morris and Mrs. Redman. I was much distressed in the afternoon when I reflected on the occurrences of the day, and that I was drove out of my house destitute, without any maintenance. In the evening a fire broke out at a malt house just behind our house and I was much alarmed and stood in Mr. Redman's garden, where we could see the fire plainly. So many things made my head light, and I appeared to be in good spirits, tho' I have no expectation of having anything. I sent for Mr. Chew. He came and told me I must sue them for a forcible entry. I am just distracted, but glad it is over.

Grace Growdon Galloway /201

Aug. 22: I hear Becky Shoemaker has agreed to go out of her house quietly. The Quakers take care of her, but I may shift for myself. I am very vexed and told Johnny Lawrence that I would not sue the agents Peale, Will, Smith, etc., as no one would join me. Shoemaker's wife will not let me be looked on as her friend, and all the Quakers are for her. I belong to nobody. I had a letter from J.G. this evening dated the 19th:

> My dear. I have wrote to you several times to inform you of our health. This will be some satisfaction to you amidst your difficulties. I hear you have been kindly treated by Gen. Arnold and Mr. D., and I thank them for it. But since, I am told your goods have been inventoried, and yourself threatened to be turned out of your house. Your friends fear fate of seeing you. If this be true, let me entreat you to fall on means to come to us. I feel more infelicity on your account than I can express, but I rest assured that inhumanity can never prosper, and that the justice of a divine Providence will reward the authors of it in due time. Let me know the truth of the report I hear, and if you should not come to us soon. We pray God to bless and preserve you.

I am in good spirits.

Aug. 26: Nothing likely to turn up for my advantage. Nobody takes any notice but to come and hear what I have to say. The weather has been so hot ever since I came here, it being in the close part of the town, that I am much disordered.

Aug. 27: Mrs. Montgomery was here in the evening. She told me Mr. McKean said he could not come to see me, as it may give offence, but he should be glad to see me anywhere that it would not be known. I do not believe her. Lewis was here. I told him to stop the action, for I would not sue the men.

September 4: Nothing to raise my spirits. Mrs. Craig, I think, is tired, and what she does is really through charity. To be independent is to be happy. The weather is so cold I sat by the kitchen fire. He is a strong Whig, she a violent Tory. Many things has since intervened. I have neglected to set them down as they consisted of little more than slights and neglect from my pretended friends. As the people where I am are civil I thought it best to forget little slights and want of attention in those who I must lay under obligations to. But Chew's family has treated me with contempt, and he behaves no way like a friend; but as I can find nothing in my own heart that has in any shape been the occasion I look upon them with that contempt they deserve. I can say I now know the world, for I have not one friend to depend upon.

[Letter to Elizabeth Galloway, dated September 23, 1778:]

I was only reconciled to your going as the only means of your safety and preservation. The absence of my child has quite overcome me. The danger of voyage, joined to my want of her company, are almost too much for me. I cannot confess the trouble of my soul when first I received your letters; but what can I do. Should I leave this place they will not only take my income, but confiscate my estate, and then perhaps, my dearest child may become a beggar. Therefore, while I have the least shadow of saving something for her I will stay. This day of 23rd they sold all our furniture and chariot. I would have got some things but it was impossible for me to give the price . . . the few books my child left, with the baby tea chest and work basket . . . sold for fifteen pounds, so I could get nothing. Such troubles coming to me every day that my life is tiresome to me. How can I get them to decide my fate, shown no hope of my own estate. I think it best to petition rather than claim my right, for if they possess my estates as a maintenance I can but claim afterwards. . . . Let me hear from you before you go [to England]. My heart sinks at the thought of a winter voyage. Take care to have your things well aired before they are packed . . . and put on nothing damp. Forget not to take a Bible with you. I hope I may live to meet the only two people that are dear to me on earth.

Affectionate mother, G. Galloway

Grace Growdon Galloway /203

October 20th I received a letter from Mr. G. dated the 6th—fourteen days coming. Friday the 23rd I received three letters from my dearest child dated, the last dated the 9th:

> As we expect to sail in less than a week I embrace this opportunity to tell my dear Mama how sincerely I love her and that change of place and situation, if possible, increases my affection for you. We never know how much we value any thing till we are deprived of it. 'Tis true I have often felt the want of a mother since I came to New York, but I trust the almighty being will suffer me through the difficulties I may have to encounter, as well as those that are past. I am so fully convinced of the necessity of my going with Papa that I should be easy under it did I not leave you in the forlorn situation you are in. Yet when I suppose myself with you I must suppose your distress increased, for was my person safe (which in some of your letters you seem to doubt); yet the insults I should raise would be a constant source of uneasiness to you. Be assured, my dear Mama, I will endeavour to follow your advice, indeed I am no longer a slave to appearances, and am convinced that the man of fashion is seldom the man of sincerity. I could say much on this subject but will change it to one more interesting, which is giving you an account of our present affairs. Lord Howe was so kind as to offer us a passage with him in the Eagle, but Papa was obliged to decline that benevolent offer, as Howe went so soon that we could not have heard from you or informed you of my intention of going, before he sailed. Could we possibly have gone in the Eagle I should have been as happy as I possibly could be in this dreadful separation, for besides respecting Lord Howe as a great man, I love him as a friend. We now propose going in a transport, where I have the best stateroom. Let me my dear Mama entreat you if you do not find it best to stay in Philadelphia, to come to us. If we have bread for ourselves we can spare a little for you and nurse. Give my love to that good creature. I have a thousand reasons for loving her, but particularly I shall always remem-

ber her attention to me in my last sickness, and her affection for you, which she has shown me on every occasion. I wish to have it in my power to convince her I am not ungrateful. . . . I shall go first to London with Papa and will contrive as soon as possible to go to see Aunt Nickleson, agreeable to your desire. I shall write you once if not oftener before we sail; pray send your letters as Papa directed and they will be forwarded to us. Good night, my dear Mother, and believe me, your affectionate and ever dutiful daughter.

Elizabeth Galloway

I received a letter from Mr. G. and one from my dearest child dated the 15th of October, the last I expect to receive from New York. My dearest child sailed for England either the 17th or 18th of October. October the 25th at night I dreamed that the vessel in which Mr. G. and my child sailed in was sunk and they were all lost. Tommy Eddy told me it was not true, but that there was five or six men-of-war [British ships] taken or lost. I then thought the news true and awoke in a fright. I went to sleep again and dreamed that my dear child was going home with me to Trevose, that it rained and she was but poorly. By the coachman's not driving right we were obliged to walk to the carriage. The roads was full of water, she got wet in her feet, and I was greatly distressed. But a poor fellow took her up to carry her to the carriage. I was afraid she had taken her death. We was afterward plagued about the carriage and drove into a narrow place, and was in great danger. I awoke in great terror. I heard the next day of a letter being intercepted from Mr. G. to his sister, which they afterwards printed, but it did him no dishonour. What pain I feel to think my dearest child must be drove from her native country, and all she has taken from her, and I incapable of doing anything for her. No one can imagine but those who had the like trial. God grant them a speedy and a prosperous voyage.

November 4: This day John Roberts and Abraham Carlisle were executed. All things are gloomy. I went to neighbour Eddy's. She came home tonight, but I was called home to see Ben Chew.

Grace Growdon Galloway /205

His behavour was so cold, nay, disrespectful to me that I was quite shocked, and wished I had not seen him. He has altered ever since Mr. G. was going home. In short, he was scarce civil. I have no friends.

Nov. 5: I removed to Deborah Morris's. Craig and his wife came with me. Glad I am to have a room I can call my own.

Nov. 13: I went with nurse to Mr. Craig's. Major Franks overtook us and told me he heard I was in great trouble at a report that Mr. G. was taken and carried into Boston, but that it was false. I told him I had not heard of it before, but I did not believe it, as Mr. G. went under the care of a man-of-war. The man-of-war would be taken too. When I got to Craig's I was more uneasy. But they all assured me it was a lie. They had made inquiry into it. In the evening came on a storm and it rained very hard, but I would come home, and I leaned on Johnny Commins. He held an umbrella over me; but I was so wet in my feet and petticoats, as if I had been dipped in water; I was so frightened that we went into Owen Jones's. They told me to be easy, for Mr. G. was not taken. I came home from there in better spirits, and as I was walking in the rain my own chariot drove by. I own that I then thought it hard, but kept up pretty well; but when I turned into the alley my dear child came into my mind, and what she would say to see her mamma walking five squares in the rain at night like a common woman, and go to rooms in an alley for her home. I dare not think, and when I got in shifted all my clothes, for I was dripping wet. Debby and I supped together, and she tried to persuade me this report was a lie, but at night I was very uneasy and was determined should it be true to go to them, tho' I perish too. I slept very disturbed and uneasy. As to myself, I fear nothing; but when they are concerned, I am miserable indeed at the thought of danger.

Nov. 14: My spirits are low, and I thought of nothing but how I could get to Mr. G. and my dear child if they were taken, and how I could assist them.

Nov. 25: I supped by myself. I want to write to my dearest child but cannot. Have such dreadful thoughts of her being dead that

I have no peace, and am determined to go to her in the spring. As to myself, I am happy and the liberty of doing as I please makes even poverty more agreeable than any time I ever spent since I married. But my child is dearer to me than all nature, and if she is not happy, or anything should happen to her, I am lost. Indeed, I have no other wish in life than her welfare. Indeed I am concerned for her father; but his unkind treatment makes me easy, nay, happy not to be with him. If he is safe I want not to be kept so like a slave as he always made me, in preventing every wish of my heart.

Nov. 27: I wrote to my dearest child by way of Mrs. Potts. Ben Linthorn came in while I was writing and interrupted me. He brought me a small turkey and I thought it a present. After I had sent my letter he stayed and supped with me. I treated him kindly and told him how I was left. When he was going I asked him what he would have for his turkey. He modestly told me twenty shillings. I told him I could not afford it. He had got his supper for nothing, and meanly took the turkey back with him. I told Debby of it. She was surprised, but I was not. He never shall have another meal of me; am vexed and disappointed. Smith has not been here today. I think he is affronted, at which I am not sorry. If J.G.'s eyes are not yet opened to those he calls his friends he is then unworthy of my attention. But his baseness has pulled down me and my child with him. Every insolence I meet with from these low fellows makes me reflect on the treatment I have met with on their account and the little care he has taken to keep me from being insulted by them.

December 1: I went to Mr. Craig's with Debby. Saw my own chariot standing at my door for the use of others, while I am forced to walk. It hurts a little but not so as to mind it, for in a few moments I got over it. Craigs were glad to see me, and I was very merry. Mr. Craig came home with me and Debby and I supped alone. Reed is this day chosen president. Sent nurse for a bushel of salt to Tommy Wharton which he promised me in the summer. But, like all others he disappointed me, and would let me have but half a bushel. It is unkind to go from his word, but there is no dependence on man and I must bear it. Had the colic after I came home but am happy as I can be in the absence of my child. May God bless and restore her to me and I hope all will be right yet. I shall ride when these harpies walk, as they use to do before they plundered me and others.

Dec. 2: Jo Thornton came to bring me cider, and he told me Gill was to have my place Trevose. Notwithstanding, I have given up all. I found this stroke hurt me very much, as I always thought they would have let me rent my own as they have done others. But now I see they are cruel as the grave and never to be satisfied. My mind is more discomposed than usual. Went and talked to Debby. She went out and Molly and I went to see Sarah Zanes. I talked a great deal to her, and spent my time very agreeable; but my mind is greatly distressed. Debby supped with me. I was unwell and took an anodyne. Talked to nurse at night of J.G.'s improvident disposition and his leaving me so destitute, and letting all his tenants be out of my power by telling them he would never ask any rent of them, tho' he knew I was here.

Dec. 3: As everybody keeps me at a distance, so am I resolved not to make my house a place of resort. But I find people expect I should still entertain them tho' no one house in town have ever given me a meal, nor think of asking me. I am very uneasy but must be kept at home. Nobody wants me at their houses.

Dec. 9: Henry Symons came in the morning and brought me fowls and cider. I sent for him in my room; he sat with me some time. Went to see neighbour Eddy. She talked to me about keeping slaves, but tho' I opposed her—I am not convinced it is right—I dreamed of our negroes and could not get them out of my mind. I am uneasy about them. Supped at Craigs'. He came home with me. I am not quite well, and the slaves run in my mind. I took an anodyne but had no good rest.

Dec. 16: Mr. Craig and Tommy Story drank tea with me. A dark, rainy day. Kensay told me Mr. G. had four hundred pounds advanced on his rent. This unhappy man has ruined himself and

I find he conceals all he can from me. Was it not for my child I would never care anything about him, for his base conduct with me when present, and his taking no care of me in his absence has quite made me indifferent to him.

Dec. 23: The weather very cold and bleak. I fear my wood will not be got down. I am now quite overcome at being kept out of my estate, for I am like to want everything.

Dec. 25: It snowed and was extremely cold. This morning I had a flat load of wood come down: there was not another flat at the wharf, and in a few hours after, the river was fast. It looks like an act of providence to me. Sat by myself the whole afternoon and slept. Am so unwell can hardly keep up. Smith here for a few minutes but he would not stay to divert me. After supper Debby came in with her work. I am quite sick of seeing patching; her company this way is disagreeable. Spent a wretched Christmas indeed. Nothing diverting, and am ill.

January 1, 1779: I was taken so ill last night that no anodyne would ease me. I sent for Dr. Chevot, Dr. Cadwalader, and Dr. Redman; but before they came I was taken with a puking and found it was a true bilious colic. After the puking stopped I took a large anodyne. By the time the doctors came I got ease; but they all thought me in a dangerous way. Oh, my dear child, how did I then think of you. A sad New Year's day to me. I got up in the evening and was better, but continued ill for many days after and was very weak. Everybody thought me in a dangerous way. Mrs. Redman came in the evening but I was too ill to talk to her. Want of exercise is my bane. My mind is bewildered about my poor child, and I am afraid to die. God, I hope, will restore me to meet her.

March 7: Tommy sent me word that he heard J.G. and my dear child arrived in London. Drank tea by myself. In the evening Mrs. Shoemaker and her daughter came and told me her husband had wrote to her that my dearest child was well and that there is a letter for me at New York. I am very glad of this news but am impatient for my letter and fearful of what situation they are in. Mrs. Smith came in a little while; but they all went before supper, and Debby and I supped together. I think to go home [London] this spring.

March 10: Nancy Clifton said Mr. Morris had been to Joseph Reed to know why I had no maintenance allowed me, and that Reed told him I had a very handsome allowance, but if I was so proud as not to accept it, it was no fault of theirs. I was provoked, as I have none, nor can get one from them. Debby came after supper. I read her my verses. I am not pleased with them nor with myself. Know not how to act, whether to go to England or stay. Was it not for my child I would get into some business here; but can't be easy without her.

March 11: A Mrs. Turner, who brought the news from New York of our people's safe arrival [in England] came to pay me a visit; but as she knew nothing more, I did not know what to say to her. Here she sat, and I was so bad in the colic I could hardly converse. At last I told her I must lay down. She then took her leave and I was on the bed the great part of the day. I can't help thinking at the absurdity people fall into of wanting to see everything that comes from New York, as if those sort of people could give any information to be depended upon. I am convinced of the contrary and at a loss what questions to ask them, as I know they cannot inform me of anything I wish to know. Those visits to me are no way desirable or pleasing.

March 20: Sarah Zanes came in the afternoon with Thomas and Susanah Lightfoot [Quaker preacher]. They had sent me word that Susanah wanted to see me. When they came up they immediately fell into silence. My mind was roving 'till at last I thought that as those good people came in great love to see me, I ought to not only attend to what they had to say, but bring my mind into a right frame to attend their message. Susanah seemed much oppressed and, after some time in silence, she said that my situation had been often in her mind. She thought it her duty, drawn by love, to visit me in my affliction to beg that it might draw me nearer to that power who could alone relieve. For we had seen that the arm of flesh had failed in many instances, and there was no reliance thereon. She desired me patiently to desire assistance from Him who was always ready to help those that called on Him. She thought He was ready on His part if I did not do mine. She begged me not to neglect my duty, but pray to Him and He would help me. As it was uncertain how short a time we may have for the great change, she desired me to be prepared, the sooner the better, for it must be of service to me whether I lived or died. She hoped I should be able to say with David it is good for me to know affliction, as by that means God may call me nearer to himself, and wean me from the things of the world which she thought I may have been attached to. Her discourse made me feel a new heart and softened me more than I ever was before. Her discourse was so pertinent, kind, and friendly that it gave me a pleasure beyond expression. I should have been glad of their company, but they went as soon as she had done, and left me in a pleasing frame of mind not to be described. A fire in Spruce Street in the evening. Debby supped with me. I am sorry I had not more of the Friends' company. I think the evening the best I have known a great while. I feel a joy not to be described, and would gladly give up all outward show for this peace and serenity of mind. This Friend, Lightfoot, I feel a real love for her and, as I had never seen her before, I hope providence will send her to me again. I think myself quite calm and happy.

March 26: A fine day. Mrs. Redman and Mrs. Groves drank tea with me. I have now no friendship for Mrs. Groves, and spoke very freely of the present government. I said they robbed me and others to support a set of low people, to the disgrace of their state, and that I wanted to converse with no more Whigs. Money is now twelve for one. Two vessels lost by the English, and the men brought prisoners here today.

March 27: Ned Tilghman drank tea with me. He behaved very well. I told him I thought it ungenerous to endeavour to sink Mr. G. in order to support the proprietor's cause. I know they are all enemies to my family. I got my table from General Arnold, but lost several knives and forks. Supped by myself. Fine weather, but I am not well.

Grace Growdon Galloway / 211

March 30: Got the letters from my dear child and her father. I am glad to hear they are well, but I am in no way satisfied as to their way of life. I was ill in the colic when I got the letters.

I have so many things to say to my dear mamma that I am at a loss which to begin with. I was at first very adverse to going to England and had determined to stay at New York and take the chance of getting to you. But from some particular circumstances, which I would not choose to commit to paper, even in this way, but which I will tell you when we meet. I complied with the advice of the few friends we found, who all agreed that the most prudent thing I could do would be to go. . . . The treatment we met with at New York has convinced me that the child of affliction will ever be neglected by the vain. Dissipation is a foe to hospitality. London is more dissipated than New York. I now see the absurdity of entertaining strangers, many who are much your friends in your own house never wish to see you in theirs. Those who do not live as well as yourself are often prevented by pride from returning kindness received, and those who are in a style above you think the honour of their company is a sufficient recompense for the trouble and expense you are at in entertaining them; but what is to be said of our equals—nothing. . . . I have not seen Sir John Balfour or any of the great who knew me in Philadelphia; but Sir William Howe, whose lady waited on me, and rarely, I believe, have taken notice of me. Had I been permitted to receive her civilities, but parties run too high here that it was not thought prudent for us to begin any connections. Politicians may say I shall overestimate Lord Howe as a good man, and one to whom I am obliged, if it is only for the part he has appeared to take in the distresses of our family. . . . I dislike this town; the houses, I mean, so few are open to receive me. At the same time, I keep up my spirits, and despise the great because they are great and despise me for being little. But it is now the holidays, and all the fine folk are out of town. I have met with one who I hope to find an agreeable acquaintance on her return, if I can make myself agreeable to her. . . . I was much distressed at receiving no letters or accounts from you by the vessels that have arrived since us. I cannot reconcile myself to the idea of not seeing you soon. Why do we live if it is not to enjoy the society of those we most love.

Your affectionate daughter.
Jan. 4, 1779.

April 6: I awoke early in a fright. Dreamed I was going to be hanged. Dr. Cadwalader was here in the morning. The good, old man calls to see me often and I both love and revere him, tho' he is so great a Whig as to think the war is over.
April 14: Israel Pemberton is so ill they think him just going off. All our estates were put in the news today:
[*The Pennsylvania Gazette and Weekly Advertiser*, April 14, 1779: Thirty-seven people were listed.]

Philadelphia, April 10, 1779. The public are hereby advertised that the real estates late of Joseph Galloway . . . and others, situate, lying and being within divers counties of this State, forfeited to the use of the Commonwealth by the attainder of the said persons, and every of them, for high treason, will be speedily sold by public auction or vendue, to the best and highest bidders, exonerated and discharged of all former claims or demands made under any of the said traitors; the said real estates to be assured to the buyers by deeds or conveyances, under the Seal of the State, signed by the President or Vice-President in Council, upon payment of the purchase money. And all creditors and others are hereby informed, that by an Act of Assembly entitled can act for the attainder of divers traitors if they render not themselves by a certain day, and for vesting their estates in this Commonwealth, and for more effectually discovering the same, and for ascertaining the lawful debts and claims thereupon; three months are allowed to all creditors and others, having claims and demands on the personal estates late of the traitors aforesaid . . . and in six months for all claims on the real estate, late of the traitors aforesaid. . . .

Published by order of the Council
Timothy Matlack, Secretary, and Keeper
of the Register for forfeited estates.

April 15: I had my tea from New York. Young Foulke kept it several weeks in paper and made an excuse he was afraid to bring it. Daniel Mifflin brought me three hundred pounds [currency] for which I signed a note payable to Charles Mifflin. I supped by myself this evening on asparagus.

April 16: Mr. Boudinot was here in the evening. He told me my estate was not forfeited, even during Mr. G.'s life. But he thought it best to put off trying it 'till more moderate juries could be had. He said he would give his opinion in writing. He behaved very well.

April 17: This day is extremely cold. Mrs. Growdon [stepmother] came with Isaac Penington in a chair here to see me. She came to make her claim on my estate. She looked so mean and was so indifferent about me that I cared very little about her, tho' she said she would not go out of town without seeing me.

April 20: I went to Billy Turner's. The two Mrs. Bonds were there. I got my spirits at command and laughed at the whole Whig party. I told them I was the happiest woman in town, for I had been stripped and turned out of doors, yet I was still the same and must be J.G.'s wife and Lawrence Growdon's daughter, and that it was not in their power to humble me, for I should be Grace Growdon Galloway to the last, and as I had now suffered all that they can inflict upon me, I should now act as on a rock, to look on the wreck of others and see them tossed by the tempestuous billows, while I was safe ashore; that if my little fortune would be of service to them, they may keep it, for I had exchanged it for contentment; that a wooden waiter was as useful, tho' not so sightly, as a silver one. That I would never let these people pull me down, for while I had splendid shilling left

I would be happy in spite of them. My borrowed bed, I told them, was down and I could lay me down and sleep composedly on it without feeling one thorn, which was more than the creatures could do who had robbed me. But all that vexed me was that I should be so far humbled as to be ranked as a fellow creature with such brutes, for I could not think they could be called men. So I ran on and was happy, tho' Madam Bond seemed sometimes to wince.

May 2: I got up very unwell with a cold. Neighbour Smith came in and said many of the [British] army disliked Mr. G. I was very warm and provoked. He did so much for nothing, while people think he was so well paid. But a vain man will neglect his family for a name, and he might have been much respected if he had been well paid. But this woman is a fool. She went away and Mrs. Redman, Sukey Jones, and Nancy drank tea with me. I was so unwell that I could hardly hold up. They went about six o'clock, but Nancy returned with Polly Wharton in the evening. I was then very ill and they stayed but a little while. But Mrs. Redman still sat, tho' she saw I could not talk. I was so faint and my nerves so affected that I was ready to go wild. Why must I have people by dozens that will not get me to their houses, but let me dine at home; so that I can give them a dish of tea tis all they care. For the whole town are a mean pack and as such I despise them.

May 15: One of John Hughes' sons had claimed a prior right to Hog Island [part of Joseph Galloway's estate]. He took two-thirds of it and sold it to that wretch Col. Procter for thirty-thousand pounds—a fellow that but a few years ago was a footman to Capt. Hay. I was so ill both with fever and the colic that I did not rise 'till the afternoon. Young Ben Chew brought a Mr. Milligant to see me. He is going to England. I desired him to tell J.G. all we had was gone, and how his estate was taken away. I sent for Owen Jones. He came and drank tea with me and told me it was no matter how the estate went, for if J.G. returned he could recover all. I told him it was nothing to me, for I never would have any of J.G.'s estate and I gave him my reasons why, but reflected as little as possible on J.G.

Grace Growdon Galloway /215

May 17: I wrote to my child. Mrs. Montgomery was here. She told nurse that she had spoken to Mrs. Reed about my allowance. She answered her that she heard great talk of Mrs. Galloway's being ill and that she lacked the necessaries of life; but that there was some allowance made me and I must petition, that Mr. Reed had nothing to do in the affair. I was very angry, as I did not want Mrs. Montgomery to go to either the husband or wife.

May 24: A mob is raised in the town and they are taking up Tories. We were much alarmed. I sat up 'till after two. Went to Smith's. He is very reserved but, I find, is much frightened. We are quite alone.

May 25: The Germantown militia and our own are all in arms in order to lower the price of goods. Joseph Reed headed them. A town meeting was held in the State House yard, and Levy Hollandsworth, with many others, are threatened. Mrs. Redman drank tea with me. She told me many was sent to the gaol. I was much alarmed, as is the whole city. We put away our valuable things, thinking they will search the house for flour and stores. No man is safe. Isaac Morris slept here.

May 26: Many are released today from prison. But poor, unhappy Levy Hollandsworth they keep close, and say he shall be tried for his life. Another town meeting held today. They propose to send all the Tories out of the lines. Nothing but distress and distraction. I am still weak and low. Molly Craig and Peggy Johns drank tea with me.

May 28: I was very low and weak. I walked about by myself in the house. Sent for Sidney Howell in the evening. She came and we walked about half a square. The weather very hot and oppressive all week. Dr. Chovet drank tea here and Sidney supped with me. Men go about examining people's stores of flour, but did not come to our house. I am afraid to be sent away.

May 30: It is extremely hot and it rained a little in the afternoon. I am very low and uneasy about my dearest child. I have had uneasy, bad dreams about her. I supped by myself. Young Owen Jones was here. He told me Matlack would not let him have the returns of my estate, 'tho he told him if I had them not by the

25th it would not do. So the villain has now prevented me from claiming. I am so low about my child that I know not what to do. This has been a truly disagreeable day.

June 8: I cannot get Owen Jones to change my money. I am very uneasy about it. They talk of sending us all away to New York.

June 9: T'was a cold, windy day; but Tommy Morris brought his chair and took me three miles round. I met my own chariot with the old don and we was forced to break the road in a bad place. But I did not mind it. I was in good spirits, as I had a pleasant ride.

June 16: It began to rain about noon. Sat by myself all day. Mrs. J. Lawrence was here a little while in the evening. No news from South Carolina yet, but she says there has been no battle at Charleston. I hope it will prove a lie that the English are defeated. But if I was out of debt, I should care little about them —they seem all bewitched. Debby and I supped together. I am rather uneasy about my dear child and many other things, but yet not unhappy. Hope supports me. Yet this day twelvemonth I parted with my dearest child, and this night Don Juan had a dance, I think, by way of rejoicing.

June 17: I sat in my room 'till five o'clock reading "Arabian Nights" entertainment, but my whole heart was taken up with my child. I traced in my mind the whole of that dreadful day in which I last saw her. I was going out, but recollected this day twelvemonth, and would not go out. I am greatly distressed, as I see no more prospect of meeting them again than I did ten months past. I am very low spirited and fear that all is over with us. No good news, and hard money falls [in value] fast. Oh God, save my child and husband.

June 23: Mr. Swift and Dr. Smith drank tea here. They seemed as if they thought the English would do nothing. Smith told me they were valuing my estate and that Mrs. Growden had claimed and they have granted her dower. I am really shocked to hear of such fraud. I fear it is true, as Penington has been very shy and I know he is a sly chap. Swift invited me to his house. Smith said but little, but his fresh claim to my estate is a stab.

Grace Growdon Galloway / 217

June 24: I sent for John Thompson. He told me he had heard nothing of it, that he would inquire about it, but that the old laws were in force and Mrs. Growdon could not have the dower. I said that Mr. Galloway and Abel James had left that affair in so unsettled a state. He seemed to throw the blame on J.G., but I told him there were faults on both sides, and that everybody was partial to their own interests, and that Mr. G. had his foibles, but he was an honest man. Thompson seemed rather cold on the affair. He sent me pens yesterday and has been very obliging to me before; but I am not pleased with his visit. I wish I had not sent for him, as neither he nor James or Penington are friends to us. More company came in the evening. I have no time to speak to anyone; yet these good friends would let me perish before they would get me to their houses.

June 30: This day all my estate was advertised to be sold during the life of Mr. G. in Bradford's paper. I am just distracted and know not how to act. I talked to young Owen Jones and Billy Smith about buying it, but see so little advantage in that that I am bewildered and know not what to do. I sat down and summed up the conduct of those J.G. called friends and found he had not one friend in the place that would reach out a hand to keep us all from sinking. I am distracted about my child. I went to bed very distressed and unwell. I see nothing but misery before me. The English deserve not the name of Britains. I am very low-spirited and unwell, and resolved not to claim my estate for the following reasons—First, should I claim and they grant me the whole, I then would be subject to the state, and by owning their authority subject myself to all the penalties of their laws and thereby banish myself from my husband and child, or render myself liable to an attainder. Secondly, if they grant me only a maintainance I should then become their pensioner, liable to the same penalty. Should they be inclined to litigate, they draw me into a tedious and fruitless law suit, and involve me in great trouble. But any claim or petition, I think, would not be granted. The whole must be mine or I can have none. I fear that to purchase it will ruin me greatly in debt, and the taxes are so high

I could clear little by it. Even this would keep me here, for I have no friend to act for me; so I must leave it, as I am determined to go from this wicked place as soon as I can hear from J.G., and not by my own impatience put it out of my power to leave this Sodom. Could I be content to stay, I believe, I may nearly carry my point. But go I will, and I have no inclination to be tried for treason in attempting to get off. They may give me a passport on my promise not to return; but then should I be kept here, or tried for my life if I attempted to go, a writ of attainder would be brought against me, and my whole estate confiscated, for they would be glad of an excuse to do so. Therefore, I am determined to sit still, and should I not live to get to my dear child and Mr. Galloway, let this be shown them as my reason, for I am friendless and alone.

July 1: I was taken very ill at noon and obliged to lie down. I sent for neighbour Zanes and when she came I was so low and faint that I was ready to give out. I talked freely with her of my situation, and that I was afraid to die, that 'till I could be brought to forgive my enemies and rely in nothing but a divine being I could not be happy. She encouraged me and roused me from that dejection of spirit. I got up, ate some cake, and drank; after which I was better. It was a rainy afternoon and Owen Jones came to talk with me about my estate, as I had sent for him. I find he would not advise me to buy, as I may be drawn into many difficulties. He thought that nothing can be done but waiting, with patience. I have now come to a resolution of letting it go without dispute.

July 2: Mrs. Craig, Betsey Johns, Mrs. Cox and Nancy Redman drank tea with me. I was tolerably cheerful, but my dear child is never out of my mind. I am afraid things go wrong in England and that no troops will come in this year. Mr. Chew was here in the evening, and Isaac Morris. At last he went away, and Mr. Chew and I had a deal of talk. He told me if I did not intend to stay, laying a claim to my estate would be of no use, for by so doing I made myself a subject of the state, and they would not let me go away. This and other reasons made me lay aside all hope of redress. I find Chew has little hope of the English doing anything. I think of going to New York beginning of September. I am very uneasy about my child and J.G.

July 5: Nicholas Waln sent his carriage to take me out. It was violently hot, but Debby and I went to Frankford and came home. I think I never enjoyed a ride so much in my life. Everything looked so pleasant and the fresh air revived me. We saw Abel James on the road by his house. He looked rather grave but told me my stepmother had dower granted her, and that it was no matter to me, as they could not sell my land. He said he did not know how to advise me but thought my friends in England, as well as here, would be best pleased if I did not ask anything of these people.

July 10: I had a very bad night and was very unwell. Saw neighbour Zanes. There is something so honest and blunt in that plain woman that I prefer her company to most others. I think her good, and she has no cant, but is rough and open. Liddy Richee came in to see me, but she talked so loud and so much, and my spirit was very low, that I was glad when the visit was ended. Her mother wants me to come to their house; but I begged to be excused, for no change of circumstances will alter my opinion of people I think not good. I was taken ill with the colic and forced to take a physick, and was on the bed 'till noon. Dr. Chovet called in the evening. He advises me to be bled, which I intend to be tomorrow. I am in a poor state of health and never wanted to see my dear child and J.G. as much in my life. I hope providence will grant my prayer of a happy meeting with them. Debby supped with me.

July 18: Neighbour Jones and Becky drank tea with me. I spoke very freely of people's slighting behaviour to me, and said I was more hurt by the Tory's behaviour than the Whig's. I ennumerated the various insults I received. At last came in Chovet, and after him Craig. He behaved friendly; but 'tis dreadful to be kept in one's house for days. But I am to be humbly thankful that they deign to visit me, and I am not to expect they should send for me to see the insides of theirs. Craig supped with me and was very friendly. I am rather low. He wanted me to put in my claim. I went into Smith's and summed up the conduct of the English. I am fearful I talked too free; but they do nothing for our relief, and the [British] army, instead of protecting their friends, are courting their enemies. Nothing but pleasure is attended to by them.

July 27: Another town meeting. The Republican Society [Anti-Constitutionalists] got the day of the Constitutional Society. Nothing said of us women, to send us away. I think they are all alike. Mrs. Redman drank tea with me; indeed, she has acted the same part by me throughout the whole. I think she really loves me; but I am dull and uneasy that no fleet arrives. Neighbour Zanes was here after supper. I have more than common love for this good woman. She stills my passions and calms my soul. I have unity with her and love her more than almost any other. God grant me a sight of my husband and child. I am now out of debt.

July 30: I am in better health today, yet very much out of spirits, as they [British] do nothing, and the Continentals carry all before them. Becky Shoemaker was here in the evening. I told her we were sold; that the greatest rebels was in the King's army; that we was all ruined, and I gave all for lost. I am very uneasy and out of temper. I think that Col. Johnson deserves to be shot to let twelve hundred [American] men take the fort [Stony-Point, New York] with 600 men. It was a greater exploit than all the British army has ever done.

July 31: My spirits are very low. 380 English prisoners were brought to town this morning from the fort—no officers with them, and I hope they will be all broken. Mrs. Lawrence was here in the evening. They all think me out of heart, as I detest the English conduct and think all lost. From the English papers I find they out lie the Whigs, and do nothing but dream and build castles in the air. If I could but be with my child I should be easier. As I went down the alley first one of my garters came off, then the other. I am superstitious enough to fear it bodes me no good. Oh, that I could hear from my child and J.G. Oh Howe [Sir William Howe], how I detest thee. This month is now ended and I am as much at a loss whether to go or stay. My feet swell so I can hardly move them, and my nerves are so weak I fear I cannot now bear a voyage, and tho' I am declining for want of exercise, yet no one will take me out or give me a meal if I was perishing. All the notice taken of me is to come and pump me for news and talk me almost to death. Neighbour Zanes is the greatest consolation I have, in her plain, rough way. I find that honesty my soul pants after. She soothes my spirits and speaks peace to my soul. John Stapler supped with me, and I paid him for the loaf sugar, and I am in better spirits than I was. Oh that I may live to get to England to my dearest friends. But all is cloudy, and I am wrapped in impenetrable darkness; will it, can it ever be removed? Shall I once more belong to somebody, for now I am like a pelican in the desert.

August 2: I sat by myself all day. It was rainy, and my spirits are rather better from a newspaper from New York which gives hope that something will be done. It was dated the 26th of July, and I find that Mr. G. will be called as evidence on Sir William Howe's trial, so that I know not what to think of his coming over in the fleet; but I hope they will do something for him at home. I supped with Debby and six country friends. These honest, ignorant people are the happiest on earth. I am pleased to see their ways.

Aug. 8: I was alone 'till evening. Then Sidney Howell came and sat with me some time; but I do not like her much, as there is no dependence on her. After she was gone I went into Debby's room; she and I quarreled at her saying before Buckley that the English army recommend me to the King some of their generals. I told her I should not go to beg favours of the officers of the army; that I neither wanted nor asked no favours of anyone; that I could say I owed nobody in this city an obligation; and that I may want a morsel of bread before any of them would give me any. Therefore, I desired she would not represent me as an object of distress to such sort of people as neither cannot nor would not give me any relief. I had been treated meanly by the whole city, who was afraid to give me a meal; that I wanted nothing of them, and would pay everybody when I went away.

We had high words. I supped by myself and will not stay with her if I see any more such behaviour.

Aug. 10: Ezra Comfort brought me my dearest child's trunk of papers in the morning. This threw me into a low frame of mind; I was very much moved, and unwell the whole day. It was very hot and gusty. Neighbour Zanes and Isaac Morris were here a little in the evening as I was at supper. Peggy Rawle brought me a letter from Mr. G. and my dear child, but there was nothing in either of them to give me satisfaction. I think they are rather in obscure circumstances. I was so moved on my child's account that I could not forgive J.G. for not taking more care of his family. I am just distracted and see nothing but losses and distractions before us. My child, I fear, is unnoticed. I am wretched.

Aug. 16: Abraham came to buy my right in my estate, but I would not see him. Debby came upstairs and seemed much displeased that I would not sell my right to my estate. At last she got me to say that I would sell if I could have the full value of it in hard money [silver coin]. She was so eager that I was surprised at it. I was restless and out of humour. My mind was much discomposed while she seemed to be so important and so reserved. I knew not what to make of it. But in the evening Mr. Keen came to the door to see me. The weather was very hot and, as he is a man who has not been friendly to me, I was not pleased with his company, and spoke my mind very freely on the injustice of the state. He told me I ought to put in a claim. I said they knew they had no right to my estate and that I would not ask that as a favour, which I had a right to command, and that I never did or would acknowledge their authority, as I was an Englishwoman and could not be a traitor to their state. If they were men, not to say gentlemen, they would blush at the illiberal treatment they had given me. He was going away when out ran Debby with "Can nothing be done for friend Galloway?" Down he sat again, and she, in a low voice, talked to him of my affairs. I found she was telling him all that we had talked in confidence before. I checked and pulled her many times, yet she would whine on. At last she told him I said the estate was worth thirty thousand pounds. On this I was vexed beyond measure, and said I did not tell her so. Keen found I was displeased at his being consulted and went away. I then asked her why she talked to him about it. Her answer was "Why, he is no Whig." I told her he was a man that I had no opinion of, that I was capable of judging for myself, and I wished she would not trouble herself about my business. The more I think of her impertinance the more I am provoked. She was very angry and went to bed before I supped. Smith and I had our quarrel last night, but we are now friends. He told me to do nothing in it, but let all go. I am very distressed to be treated so like a child. It hurts me.

Aug. 19: Ned Penington drank tea with me. He said they have stopped the sale of Richelieu, Belmont, and King's Place for his aunt [Grace's stepmother], and that she has both dower and annuity granted to her. We had much talk and I asked him if that was just, and if it did not look like taking advantage of the times. He said she was advised to claim the dower at first, but he dissuaded her from it, but now she could not live without it. I asked him how he thought I lived. He answered "Indeed, I don't know." But I told him I had no inclination to raise disputes, and I had rather she had it than others. I asked him if he thought I had better buy. He said that if it went off low he thought I had; but he could recommend nobody to buy for me. He went to Lewis to see if it could be prevented that those wretches may not destroy the wood. I am just distracted for there are numbers waiting to buy, and they openly declare they will destroy the wood. Some say they will not leave a stump on the land. I know it will go for a song, but if I buy it they will not let me leave the country, or they will, and confiscate the whole of my estate. Next, the taxes will eat up the whole income and I shall save nothing, and it will again throw me into their power to tax me as they please. Next, I have no friend to do any business for me and I am incapable of doing it myself. I should be as liable to have my wood injured by bad tenants if I was not here, likely to be imposed upon by artful men—few honest men to be found, and none disinterested. And, after all, I cannot stay without my dearest child, which I must do and make myself a prisoner if I purchased. On the other hand, I cannot bear that my child should

lose her whole inheritance and have the whole destroyed. Every-·
thing looks so dark that I have no hope from the English; nobody
will advise me how to act. I am just distracted and overcome with
trouble for fear my dear child should lose all. But as she is away,
I fear they would not let her inherit from me if I should die here.
On the whole, I think I must leave it and go home, as no friendly
hand is stretched out to cheer or help my benighted soul. To God
alone must I commit my cause. I have never been in so much
trouble before. This is the day twelvemonth I was turned out of
doors. My trouble is threefold greater now, as all is gone, and
we are ruined. Oh, my dearest, dearest child. My heart is ready
to break. Sarah Zanes tells me to leave it; but none of my pretended friends comes near me. Oh may I be directed to do right
in this great trial.

Aug. 20: I did not get up 'till late. I am yet undetermined how
to act. I think it best to leave it, but my child's interest argues for
buying. But can I give her up and not be with her? I am almost
out of my wits. Debby came not near me. I sat by myself, but in
the afternoon went to Smith's. I told her that what she told me
about Debby being a Whig was true and, indeed, her whole
conduct is extraordinary. Neddy Penington sent me a letter in
the morning and Lewis one at night that Vice President Bryan
had told him they would take every precaution against destruction or waste on the land. Billy Smith says it is a vague answer
and they will not, or cannot, help it.

Aug. 21: I was more composed today and have better spirits. Abel
James came, unsent for. He told me he had been with the attorney-general to see if they gave the purchasers leave to cut the
wood; but he could get no answer from him, but he spoke very
respectfully of me and my child. Abel advised me to purchase
Trevose and Vandergrift Place on account of the wood. Durham, he thought, would be but little injured, and he offered to
buy it for me in trust. I gladly accepted his offer and told him I
would be directed by him. Abel's kind and friendly behaviour
raised my spirits. As he went away he desired me to write in a
letter what I would have done, which I did, and sent it by Billy
Smith the next morning. Fisher was here in the evening, but so

drunk that he could say little more than express his friendly regard for me, and his readiness to save me. Two of the Jones' girls were here in the evening with Sidney Howell and Sally Fisher. My spirits are raised to find I have some friends. It was 2 o'clock before I finished my letter to Abel and I was so agitated that I slept not the whole night.

Aug. 23: Mr. Lewis left a note to let me know that the attorney-general's opinion was as I wished it—that they could not cut wood or make waste. This raised my spirits and made me thankful; but I was so unwell I did not leave my room until late in the afternoon. I went to neighbour Smith's. She told me the English were expected in a month, and thought I had better not buy. But I am of a different opinion, for I fear the English will never get footing here again. The Rebels have taken 150 men at Paulus Hook without firing a gun. As it is the French King's birthday there is great rejoicing and a scaffold erected across Market Street at our door, to play fireworks. I went to the end of the court, but when I saw it opposite my own house—and that in the possession of this president [Joseph Reed]—I could not stand long, to think that bad man has got our house and supplies, J.G.'s place, and this day my own fortune may all be out of my family, or I obliged to buy it. Yet, bad as appearances are at present, I am not low.

Aug. 24: The weather is very hot, oppressive, and showery. At night Bill Smith came home and said they bid too high for me to get any of my estate, but that no man of reputation [other than] my friends appeared in my behalf at the sale. He said not one man spoke against me, but that Young, the sadler's son, had bought the tract. No restriction against waste [timber destruction] was published. This made me very low. Sally and Peggy Chew came in, and I abused the English army and said they had ruined me. They would not stay, as my talk did not suit them. But after consulting Smith I grew more calm, and went to bed more composed.

Aug. 25: Sam Rhodes and Abel James were here in the morning. They would have me fee [James] Wilson and claim my estate.

Rhodes was to write for Boudinot's opinion and get the thing stated. I sent for Owen Jones and Abel and we drank tea here. Owen is for having me try to prevent waste, but not speak of the claim. We expect the British can do nothing, and the country is gone. Very hot and frequent showers.

Aug. 26: Smith went to Chew, who said he always thought that the law did not extend to my estate, but as it depended chiefly on Thomas McKean, he thought no law would be regarded; had McKean not been against me, they would not sell my estate. I am quite of the opinion the money will be thrown away; but I will try always for my dearest child. My spirits are very low. The weather is now fair, but very cool. I am more composed today.

Aug. 27: More resigned today, but think all lost. I had the deed for the 24th share of Durham and find it made in J.G.'s name only. Oh how this unhappy man has injured me and my child, for this deed cuts off all the water from my estate. He was so base as to take it out of my family. It seems that these people have not yet advertised it, but if they do we must buy it. Jesse Jones was here in the evening. I talked to her very freely and said we were all sold, and brought to beggary. I took a walk to the Turners with Sally Zanes. At our return I found Peggy and Betsey Johns here. I spoke in the same way to them and said I now hated both sides, and said we were all betrayed. Everybody is now near giving up. A large ship was taken and, coming up, one of the fleet. The English are beaten everywhere. I supped by myself. After supper Debby sat with me, and I was so low I could not help shedding tears. My dearest child, what can I do for thee? As to J.G., tho' I have some affection for him, yet I despise and abhor his vanity and baseness. I am now truly set against him, yet I do not tell anyone—this makes it worse to bear. But all his unkindness is in my mind, and all within is distress and confusion. I seem quite an outcast of mankind, and my soul is struck with a thousand daggers to find how this man has imposed upon me, as well as treated me unkindly. Was it not for my dearest child I would embrace poverty much sooner than live with a man who would grasp at all I have, and treat me worse than a slave. I fear my child will feel his ill humour. Everybody else does something for the support of their families.

Aug. 28: I got up before eleven to see Abel. The 24th part of Durham will be sold forever and, they say, there are two more lots that J.G. has sold. Now if this is true he has imposed upon me—the thought of which has quite upset me. I can bear from my enemies, but to be deceived by a husband is too much. However, he has ruined us all. My soul is all distracted. I know not what to do. Dined with Debby, but I was so unwell that I was forced to lay down very feverish and disturbed. When I rose Isaac Morris sat some time with me, but nothing can raise my spirits as I can't tell what hurts me. Friends can give me no comfort. They think 'tis only the taking of my estate, but my wound proceeds from the ungenerous conduct of J.G., and I blush for him. Debby supped with me. I am more composed, but distracted beyond expression. All my hopes and ambitions are crushed. Oh my dear child.

Aug. 30: I was very unwell all day. Mrs. Redman and John Thompson drank tea here. I talked freely to him in the back parlour. He thinks they want me to descend to abject treason for my estate, which I will not do. I told him the deed of J.G. had hurt me more than all the provincials had done. Everybody has given up the [British] cause but women and a few weak men.

Aug. 31: Polly Biles and Abel James dined with me on cold ham. Wilson has not yet given his opinion, but I told Abel that if nobody would join in with me I would not claim, for they would hardly give my estate to me, and it would be throwing money away. If I could keep the purchasers from making waste, it would be all I could expect. I see Abel is rather cool about it. Biles takes up their attention, but I will not play the piper for others. I am now more easy, as I will not sue alone. Abel was very friendly.

September 1: The weather very cold for many days past. My spirits are very low, as I find all is like to fall through about my claim. I can see no reason for throwing away five guineas to fee Wilson when I had the opinion of lawyers before and nothing is done. The wasting of my little stock makes me low-spirited, and I hear nothing from my dear child. The world has now left me with

nought but their pity. Supped by myself. I opened the third
bottle of spirits of those put in the back closet. I think it is weaker,
and the key is broken. I can keep no liquor locked.

Sept. 2: I went to Sukey Jones' wedding. She was married to John
Nancarrow, and though I was not at the meeting I signed the
certificate. They sent a chariot with Jonathan Jones to fetch me.
There was upward of forty at dinner. I supped there, but was
hurried home before ten. Debby returned in the chariot with
me. Nothing disagreeable happened, but I did not enjoy myself,
as I have not been used to the company of Friends [Quakers]
enough to fall into all their ways. The thought of the long separation from my dear child and the uncertain way of life she is in,
with the certainty of all our estate being lost here, and my in-
capacity of getting a maintanance, has almost broke me. Nothing
but melancholy and dismay reign in my soul. War is declared by
Spain against England.

Sept. 3: A rainy day. I got up late very unwell. A troublesome
night. Bad dreams. I was alone all day. Nobody now comes near
me; I am now fallen below their notice. Oh world, what is to be
coveted from thee when only prosperity is met with the smiles
of deceit, and frowns and contempt attend the unfortunates.
Imprudence and ignorance bear all before it; honesty and misfor-
tunes are fled from as contagion, and the insolent eyes of the low
and base now make modest merit sink beneath them. I went into
Smith's but he had company, and his wife can give no relief to
the mind. I came home and supped by myself. I have presages
of my cause going against me, and Abel and the others let time
slip away without doing anything for me. This and the danger
of my getting safe home [to England] if I attempt it, make me
very low. My child is always in my mind. Nurse does not act as
she ought to. I am without a friend; but my concern is for my
child.

Sept. 6: Abel James and Smith came and told me I must send to
warn the purchasers against making waste, and desired me to
send to John Chew and John Lawrence, which I did. The weather
is not so cold as it was. Sent for Mr. Wallace to get me coffee,

spirits, salt and sugar, as there is hardly any to be got in town. The committee has lowered the price, but the merchants will not sell at their price. Nor will they send for more goods. There is no flour to be got in town, and they take all the butter and things from the market people. Nor will they let anything be taken out of town without a permit. I supped by myself. I am very low and know not how I shall live. No news from my dear child.

Sept. 7: John Lawrence, Sam Rhodes and Isaac Morris drank tea here: Mr. Shea came afterwards, and I desired him to go with Johnny to warn the purchasers against cutting wood. I moved my wine and spirits downstairs in the closet. There are 18 bottles of wine, 15 bottles of spirits, 3 case bottles of spirits (1 half-full of raspberry brandy). The Whigs are in high spirits. Independency is offered.

Sept. 8: A hot day. Billy Redman came just as it was dark and saddled herself 'till after ten. I am so tired of having people here at night that I know not what to do. I cannot eat my morsel alone, tho' nobody will have me to their houses. There is hardly any flour, salt, coffee, tea, sugar, spirits or wine to be got in the town owing to a regulation of the "mobbing committee." The country people will not bring butter, and they stop them on the road and take their marketing from them. In short, everything is so high that I know not what will become of us. Smith told me that Abel is, and always was, a Whig. Had I known this I would have been more cautious of throwing myself into their hands. I am just mad. No news from England. I know not how to act, whether to stay or go. Nor have I friends that can advise me—I mistrust all mankind.

Sept. 9: I had a bad night and was very unwell all day. I had a letter from Johnny Lawrence informing me that Young said he certainly would cut the wood. I am at a loss what to do. Abel came here and said Wilson was to give his opinion tomorrow, and he took Johnny's letter with him. Everybody thinks the English have lost America. All we have is gone. I am so low that it seems as if all was over with us. I have not spirits to keep about, but I force myself, for we have lost everything. How I shall live this winter I know not. I am determined to throw a remonstrance in to McKean. I hear nothing from my dearest child. Nothing ever was so dark before—everybody out of heart. No hope remains for the friends of government. I supped by myself.

Sept. 10: Abel was here in the morning. He told me he had been with the president [Reed] and had talked with McKean about their making waste; that he was quite in a passion and said they had no right and it should not be done. But Abel confessed he spoke generally and did not mention my name. McKean could not grant me any of my estate—it was too late. He was inclined to favour the people as much as possible. But I find that Abel undertakes for all, of which I am the least part. I can get no opinion from Wilson; but, as I paid for it, I will have it from under his own hand, as I am suspicious that those questions are not about my affairs. There are but two: if I can have a right to my own estate or whether it comes under the forfeiture of their law during Mr. G.'s lifetime; and whether I can sue in my own name. The latter was answered a year ago. Therefore, my money was thrown away if that is all the satisfaction I can get. I think I am trifled with, and my money is to pay for other people, as they say they put a number of questions which, in my case, can be but few. I was better today both in health and spirits than I have been a great while. I dined with Debby. Becky Shoemaker was here in the evening. She says she will do nothing. I wish I had been wise enough not to be drawn in. All looks black for the poor Tories.

Sept. 11: I was very sick in the morning, and continued in pain all day. Augustine Willet came after dinner. He wants to stay longer on Trevose. It seems Gill took the place and Willet rents from him. I was very plain with him and kept my temper, but I would enter into no bargains with him, for I find they are a set of rogues all together. I went to Smith's. I sat a little while, and John Lawrence drank tea with me. He is sure I can recover great damages if they cut the wood. Mr. Chew came in the evening and, 'tho I was called from his house, Smith came in and prevented us from talking. Smith says Abel is now courting the people in power and worshipping the rising sun. After he went, Chew said he was trimming and that he was unbearable. I asked him if he had been long acquainted with him. He told me he had never spoken to him in his life 'till the winter since I came here, and that he would not like to associate himself with a man of his character—this I know—but Smith told me he had been in [touch] with him for many years, and that he used to go often to his house, which I told Chew. He said it was not so. This is one of the multitude of lies Smith has told me. Chew showed a contempt and dislike toward him. I joined in with him. I told him he was the vainest, boldest and most impertinent man I ever saw. Chew stayed 'till after ten. I went to supper while he was here. I told Smith that McKean ought to do justice without being petitioned; but Smith behaved like a trimming fellow, and Chew like a man of spirit and honour. I could love him dearly if he would be consistently my friend. Oh, how shall I act? I am caught in a trap. Help me God.

Sept. 12: Abraham Kinsey came to inform me they were cutting wood on Vandergrift tract. I wrote to Abel James about it but could get no horse or man to carry it. At last, nurse found Jody James, and he took it to his father. Smith returned at night and talked in so unfeeling a way that I was quite mad and I abused the chief-justice, attorney-general, president, and my own lawyer. I also said I may ruin myself and have no redress. Smith got mad and left me, and I was frightened and sent twice for him. At last he came and said he was not offended. My mind is so discomposed that I was just distracted. All my hopes are again cut off. I wish they had let me alone. I should have them sunk quietly. I took a large anodyne. My dear child is always before my mind. Oh my God, bless and restore her to me.

Sept. 13: In the afternoon Mrs. Lawrence, Mrs. Allen, Peggy Chew and John Thompson drank tea here. I told them all I would go to England. John Thompson sat after them and I told him of Smith's speeches of Abel. Just at dark, Abel and his son Chalkley came in. He seemed angry and treated me very roughly. I never felt more mortified but once in my life. He told me Chalkley had been up and that no wood had been cut, and that he would have me have notice given to the tenants, that if I went on talking at this rate nothing could be done, and as to my going to England I could not go this fall—I wanted to be on my own estate—that Becky Shoemaker had hurt herself by her tongue, but that I must conquer my passions and get Trevose if I can. He appeared angry, as if he thought I doubted him. I am delighted with the hope of going to Trevose, but uneasy about Abel's behaviour.

Sept. 14: Joe Penrose drank tea with me. I told him I was in hope of going to Trevose again and that I would not go to England. He advised me to sell my reversion of my estate, but I told him I would not, and that if I must fall it shall be nobly. He told me that according to the course of nature I could not live long. If he wants a bargain I have disappointed him. He was civil in his rough way. But he said nothing of the money coming to me. I shall trust no man for the future. If they act well I am obliged to them; if not, I will lay myself open. The weather is very cold. Debby is ill in her room. I supped alone.

Sept. 15: I was very unwell. Smith got me a notice for the purchasers of Richland. I am rather low, owing to my not hearing from my dearest child. Mrs. Smith, Willy, and her son Billy drank tea with me, but I had no pleasure in their company. I find by the paper that Lord Howe is very ill-natured and, indeed, unmanly to Mr. G., I despise them all from my heart. Neighbour Jones came in after tea, but nobody has any good news. The Tories are all down, America seems lost, and we are ruined. God preserve my ever dear child and make her good and happy. 'Tis all I wish and all I ask. I took a copy of the notice to the purchasers to Billy Smith to be sent to him, as I hope he will be my friend. Thomas Stapler was here in the afternoon and I find that Penington has been with him to get this year's rent for his aunt [Sarah Growdon]. They will get to the last farthing from me—ungenerous wretches. I find none to depend on, but I hope providence will support me as hitherto. The weather is very cold and I keep no fire, as I have but little wood. It is twenty-five pounds a cord for bad oak. How I shall live I know not. I sat a little at Zanes' and at Smith's in the evening. It's too cold and damp to walk. All is dark and uncertain that is to come, but my spirit is not so low as

Grace Growdon Galloway /233

sometimes. No letters for me, tho' others have got some. Oh my dear child, to know of thy welfare is still at my heart. I wish most affectionately for J.G.'s too, tho' his treatment of me has been wrong. That I may hear soon from my child is my prayer.

Sept. 18: I sat upstairs mending my carpet all day. Debby is worse. I just went to Smith's and Zanes'. Everybody is sick, and Joe Redman likely to die. Billy Smith told me this evening that I could now have no part of my estate, as it was sold. But I find that Abel went with Parrot's wife and was told she may have any part of her husband's estate she chose. Wilson has given no answer in my case, and I find Abel's attention is taken up so much with other women that he lets me fall a sacrifice, and cares nothing about my affairs. He foolishly joins with McKean that, as I did not claim, they can do nothing. But as an honest man how could he suffer my estate, which was not forfeited to be sold. For no other reason than because I did not pay him a compliment. He now says that had I claimed they would have given it to me. I believe it all false, but I am now uneasy that I did not do it, for I fear that I failed in my duty. So all with me is over and I am left, after I have had those fine hopes stuffed into my head, with the loss of two hundred pounds. I am made very uneasy. I wish they had let me alone. I was resigned 'till they raised my hopes, and now they leave me worse than they found me. Oh, man where is thy friendship? I am very uneasy and dissatisfied.

Sept. 19: Debby was very ill all day. Fine weather, but I had no company, nor nowhere to go that I liked. As I was eating supper Dan Clymer came in and supped with me. He professed the highest regard for me and, as he has behaved well not only to me but to the oppressed women in general, I could not help treating him as my friend. His behaviour was as it use to be— rather childish; but he seemed immoderately glad that I would let him come as a friend, and asked after my dear child. He said he always had a regard for her and me, and indeed I think him sincere. Forgive me, my only child, if I do ought that is not right, or ever take an enemy of yours as my friend; but indeed I think him not so, and I was glad to see him. I must now make friends. Poor Joseph Redman died this evening about seven o'clock. He had but few days illness. Almost every family has some sick. The town is very unhealthy, and many died lately. They are taken suddenly, and soon go off with marks of a putrid disorder. I am afraid to stir out.

Sept. 21: I received a letter from J.G. and my dearest child. They were old dates, the 28th of March and the 2nd of April, but they gave me a pleasing account of my relations, and I am overjoyed at it. I read them to Owen Jones' wife and daughter Sukey, and Debby. I am quite delighted. I went to see Becky Shoemaker, and read part to her. Drank tea there. Becky was very kind. The letters came through her.

Sept. 23: Abel James was here in the morning. I went down but was very bad in colic. He had nothing to say to me, but was very grave. I think Smith has told him tales. I am uneasy to be treated so by him, for if he had not sought me I would not have applied to him. As I am not conscious of doing anything to offend him —he is so solicitous for the other women—I wondered why he behaved so to me. Owen Jones was here in the evening, but he had nothing to say that would give me any comfort.

Sept. 24: I sat a little with Mr. Smith. He told me that nothing would be done for me without a petition. I told him I never would send one in. I think Abel leaves me out of the numbers he patronizes, but I told not Smith so. A number of Friends [Quakers] is come to the Yearly Meeting, but in a style such as I never was conversant with, and they are treated accordingly in the lowest style. I supped by myself.

Sept. 25: This is the birthday of my poor child. I sat in my room all day at work, with many melancholy reflections, as I know not what her situation is at present. I dined on bread, butter, cheese, and apple, and went down before five to send nurse out for things. She returned with a chilly fit, so I was obliged to sup with Debby. There was not less than fifteen or twenty people, and only a shoulder of bacon, a leg of veal, puddins, and an apple pie.

Sept. 27: I stepped to Sukey Nancarrow in the evening. I told them the Quakers were all Whigs. We had an argument on self defense. I came home and supped with Debby and her friends. The house is full and nurse is sick. I know not how to act. I am not well myself, but not quite unhappy. I want to hear from my child. No news.

Sept. 28: Polly Biles was here in the afternoon. She would have talked me to death, but I treated her very coolly and she went before tea. I stepped into Smith's, but was sent for by Thomas Stapler. He paid me two hard dollars for a tree they cut down and spoke as if he would do what he could to help me. After he went came Tommy Austin and he chatted away a little while, and then came Isaac Morris and he stayed 'till near two o'clock, and talked much, but I neither heard nor attended to what he said. Tho' he is very friendly, yet I can't but think myself unfortunate to be obliged to hear such stupid people talk. Mrs. Butler called for a few minutes in the afternoon. I am not well and am not happy. I know not how I shall do this winter.

＊The Pennsylvania Supreme Court decreed on October 1 that Sarah Growdon had legal rights to Belmont, Richlieu, and King's Place, "for and during the term of her natural life subject to the payment of taxes and all publick assessments," that arrears amounting to 650 pounds be granted her from the sale of Galloway's forfeited estate, and that Mrs. Growdon pay "one third part of the expenses of the commissioners in settling and making their report."

Late in 1779 Grace penned a letter to her daughter, expressing contempt for the immoral, unjust behavior of people: "War with its iron hand corrupts manners and invades the mind as much as it destroys the body, and all ranks of people are more or less affected by it . . . in short, America is not the same. The very climate seems changed." Philadelphia, before the war, was one of the most cultured cities in the colonies. Graceful manners and elegant tastes were once patterned after those of London society. One acquired good breeding from infancy, and it was so ingrained by adulthood that it appeared unaffected. However, by the late 1770s most of the numerous members of society who remained loyal to the Crown had fled. Their confiscated mansions were now largely occupied by people lacking good taste, unfamiliar with exquisitely carved Chippendale and Queen

Anne furniture, Delft fireplace tiles, and delicately designed Chinese wallpaper and porcelain. In one recorded instance the occupants of a mansion vulgarly abused the furniture. Moreau de St. Mèry, owner of a bookstore and printing business observed in the 1790s that men, having washed their meals down with cider, beer, and wine, continued to drink "right through desert, toward the end of which any women who are at the dinner leave the table and withdraw by themselves, leaving the men to drink as they please, because then bottles go the round continuously, each man pouring for himself. Toasts are drunk, cigars are lighted, and diners run to the corners of the room hunting night tables and vases which will enable them to hold a greater amount of liquor." St. Mèry was also astonished that Americans, "in spite of their pretended detestation of the English, really love them, even though they fear them. In spite of their conceit, they subconsciously feel themselves to be inferior to the English, and this leads them to treat them with adulation."

Throughout the spring and summer of 1780 "notices of deeds examined and sold" involving Galloway's estate appeared in *The Pennsylvania Gazette and Weekly Advertiser*. Much of the proceeds from sales and rentals were used to support the University of Pennsylvania, then under construction. Part of Joseph's estate, a hundred acre tract on Hog Island, was sold "subject to the yearly rent of 12½ bushels of merchantable wheat, payable to the Trustees of the University of this State." Trevose and Durham were sold in January 1781.

Such cancerous incursions of injustice eroded Grace's spirit and will. It became increasingly more difficult to find people who would smuggle out letters. She resigned herself to simply writing them in notebooks, hoping that one day they might be read by her husband and daughter. In 1781, a few months before Grace died, she wrote in the pages a letter to Elizabeth:

> I write but seldom, as little as possible. My whole heart is absorbed by you. Nor can I form a wish on earth beyond your welfare from time to eternity. I am yet in Philadelphia where I have neither been permitted to live in peace, and as I never

meddle with politics, I hope never to give any just reason of offense.

I have not been in a situation of walking abroad for more than a year past, and I sit in my room as ignorant of all the grand bustle of life as any recluse or pious person in this or former ages; my quilt and a few books when I am free from pain employs my time. I care little for the world, but all good people I love and by such only am I desirous to be esteemed. I petitioned the Council for a longer stay in Philadelphia, as I then was in too low a state of health to undertake a journey to New York, and with the interests of Mr. Thomas Barclay and Doctor Jones's affidavit they have let me remain till this time. Nor shall I remove of my own accord. At the time when I was going to be sent away I received a note importing that a letter of mine was of some ill consequence, and in what way I am at a loss to imagine. This, added to my *trouble,* embarrasses me, as my mind was at that time sinking under a want of health and spirits, and to be sent away without a friendly hand to help support me made it almost too hard. Cold comfort I received.

The letter I sent by Major West. He came in just as I was going to seal it; but, as I knew not how to direct it to you, he advised me to direct it to another person and told me he would seal and send it under cover to your pappa if he had not an opportunity of delivering it himself. I thought it best to remain silent for I know not how to guard every expression so artfully; ill minds may pervert it.

You ask me how I live. I cannot now answer that question, but only assure you that I neither borrow nor am dependent on anybody. Nor will the state allow me one farthing. If my furniture had not all been taken from me perhaps I may have been induced to keep house. But furniture is not to be got— kitchen utensils in particular—but at such excessive prices that no common people could afford it. Nor do I think things here will ever be low again. We have lost all.

I know not how you live—but from report. Your friends hope well, your enemies say otherwise. I am not even so well informed as to give any answers to questions often asked me. This gives me great pain on your account. They now say you dislike London. This carries an inference that wounds me deeply. It's easy to write so as to give me an idea without being particular.

It is now going on three years since I was left in this dreadful situation, and my health now so impaired that I never hope to have it in my power to see my relations or native country more. Want of health and to save your inheritance alone detains me. If by it I save my child all will be right.

I now know little that will entertain you. The young and gay are too much taken up to visit people in affliction, and I have nothing to recommend me to their attention. Indeed, my dear, I am not like the same person in any thing but my unbounded affection for you and my solicitude for your welfare.

Grace Galloway died at home shortly before sunset on February 6, 1782. Anna Rawle (Clifford diary, page 283) was told of her friend's death from an aunt, who wrote: "I was an hour the other evening with Sukey Nancarrow. She told me G.G., in the last week of her life, tho' extremely restless and at times flighty, yet at intervals was perfectly sensible of her situation and her danger, talked much of the alteration in the former, and prayed to be admitted to a greater change from the latter—Drs. Jones and Kuhn were often earnestly asked their real opinion by herself, but the first intimation *save the awful one her own feelings gave,* was told by Dr. Kuhn the day before she died. There was no one in the room but Sukey and he. Friend Galloway had been telling Sukey she knowed she was dying, and upon his sitting by them she repeated it and begged his opinion; he made no reply— Sukey softly said, 'T'was then too late for flattery.' Friend Galloway urged for his thoughts. The doctor then leaned to her and said, 'Madam, I have never seen you so weak as I see you now.' 'Then you think I *am* dying. Sukey, can you kiss a dying woman?' —My friend approached her, and a few silent moments passed. Dr. Kuhn went. Friend Galloway and Sukey had then some serious conversation." Grace died the following afternoon, "blessed with a silent, peaceful exit." George Dillwyn—Quaker preacher, Margaret Morris's brother-in-law—had been admitted into the room a quarter of an hour before. As George stood at the foot of her bed each had "their eyes fixed on the other, both seeming in fervent supplication for the same great purpose." A very large crowd gathered at the burial, though Anna Rawle believed that Grace had "been cruelly deserted by her gay acquaintances." One wonders what thoughts were in the mind of Chief-Justice Thomas McKean as he stood over the grave.

Her estate, though confiscated, she willed to her daughter. From London Elizabeth (Betsey) took legal action through her Philadelphia trustees. While John Adams and Benjamin Franklin, as peace commissioners in Paris, were opposing British demands for retribution to Loyalists, Elizabeth was pressing for action with the skill and perseverance of a lawyer. From Seaford, England, August 12, 1783:

You will attribute my having so long deferred acknowledging my obligations to you, to no other than the real cause my injuring you by a correspondence. . . . Whatever the debts are, left by my dear mother, it is my earnest wish that they may be discharged with all convenient speed; and to enable you to do it I entirely approve of your selling my moiety of one or both the houses in Arch Street. In these houses, as well as my moiety of Langhorn Park, my father informs me he never had nor can have any right, as the title did not vest in law in my dear mother during her life. But that one moiety of them falls to me in fee immediately on my grandmother's [Sarah Growdon] decease, and therefore they cannot be liable to confiscation under the law pressed against him. . . . So as to nurse Harrison's demand neither my father or self can form any conjecture respecting the amount. However, as she informs me by a letter just received, that she intends for England this autumn, has received her legacy, which my kind friends have advanced, and drawn on my father for twenty pounds, we think it will be best to leave the settlement of her account to us upon her arrival here. . . . I concur in opinion with you that if upon the death of my grandmother the government should dispose of my father's life estate in King's Place, Belmont and Richlieu, that it will be for my interest to purchase them if they can be had on any reasonable terms. And for this purpose as well as for the payment of debts, it is my desire that the monies arising from the sale of the houses in Arch Street should be applied.

Following the Peace Treaty of 1783 Congress made no effort to compensate for confiscated estates other than recommending that states allow Loyalists to return for one year "unmolested in their endeavours to obtain the restitution of their estates, rights, and property," that further confiscation of their property and real estate cease. Many states ignored the recommendations. Elizabeth wrote the trustees from London on January 4, 1784:

As to my return to Philadelphia, many reasons render it uncertain, unless you should think it absolutely necessary for the preservation of my interest . . . Upon considering what my friend Dr. De Normandie at the desire of my friend Abel James writes me, and what people from Philadelphia say respecting the increased value of property in, and near Philadelphia, and being desirous of deriving some immediate benefit from the remains of my shattered fortune, I think it best to dispose of the following estates: 1. All the several tracts of Durham marked in the partition between the owners, No. 1, 2, 3, 4, 9. 2. The tract of 508 acres in Richland Township. 3. The tract on Delaware, of 160 acres. 4. One moiety of Langhorn Park. 5. One moiety of both the city houses. Provided the sales may be made to advantage and for ready money in good bills payable to me in London. The Trevose tract including Trevose proper, Belmont, Richlieu, and King's Place containing 1723 acres I mean to reserve for the present, desiring if it can possibly be done at a reasonable price that the life estate of my father may be purchased in these tracts, in order to secure them in future from that waste by which they have

Grace Growdon Galloway /241

already suffered so much. The purchase money may be paid out of the sales of my other estates.

Writing from London on June 14, 1784:

I submit to your consideration, whether it may not be best to dispose of those tracts in the country which yield little or no annual profit. . . . I mean Richland and the river tract and Langhorn Park, leaving the Durham estate to the last. My reason for intimating this idea is I am informed that lands in the country are not in much demand owing to the scarcity of cash . . . My father informing me that the power given you by the will does not extend to the estate fallen to me by the late death of my Grandmother Growdon. I have sent a power of attorney authorizing you to act in all things where my interest is concerned. . . . I much approve your resolution to take every method to secure the tracts of Belmont, Richlieu and King's Place should the state not restore them to my father. I concur in opinion with my friend J. Thompson that they ought to be purchased at any rate as the value of the whole estate in Bensalem depends on the timber on them.

And again from London on January 15, 1785:

Should the state seize and sell the lands allotted to my Grandmother Growdon there can be no doubt but they will be rendered of little value by the destruction of the timber. But should the state permit you to take possession of them for me, I shall be obliged by the remittance of the residue after deducting what you think reasonable for your trouble. In my former letters I desired you would sell my unproductive property, and with the money purchase in the incumbrance of my father's life in such of my other estates as yielded an income. . . . I see myself entitled to a considerable estate sufficient to maintain me in decent affluence and yet I am receiving no manner of benefit from it. Destitute of the means of subsistance, I am sharing with my distressed parent his small allowance from the government, which with the strictest economy is scarcely sufficient to support us in a state far beneath what we have been used to. In this disagreeable situation I must remain unless my estate can be so managed by your kind offices as to relieve me from it. For these good reasons I was and still am very anxious that the best measures should be pursued to enable me to derive some immediate benefit from it. For I conclude you will not differ in opinion from me that it will be more to my advantage to receive soon three-fourths of my estate or less than the whole than when I am no longer capable of enjoying it. As to their being as much damage done to the several tracts I desired might be sold, as can well be done, it does not remove or in the least affect my principal motive for desiring you to sell them and to purchase my father's life in others. For this was, that you might by selling them procure the means of obtaining immediate possession of such others as yielded a considerable income, and that I might enjoy that income as the means of my present subsistance . . . the damage done cannot be refrained by a delay of the sale during my life, if ever.

After a long delay the Pennsylvania Council granted Elizabeth the right to purchase her property. She swiftly told her trustees to buy a few tracts, to delay purchasing others until the cost was reasonable, and to bring suit against those occupants who had cleared forested areas. The status of Belmont, Richlieu, and King's Place was resolved when the Court decreed that on the death of Sarah Growdon these estates reverted back to Grace Growdon's heirs. By the middle of 1787 Elizabeth had possession of all of her real estate property except Durham and Trevose. It was highly unlikely that these would be sold—the American economy was unstable, money was scarce, and property sales yielded little. Writing to the trustees from Bristol on June 3, 1787, Elizabeth resolved to sell all of her property:

I find from all accounts that real estates have greatly depreciated in value and must, from the state of the country, necessarily continue to do so for years to come. . . . I am decidedly of the opinion that it would be more appropriate to me to obtain now whatever may yield than to wait for it two or even five years. . . . For these reasons I request you will advertise in the several American papers every tract of land I possess in America describing them particularly, to be sold for ready money either in the whole or separately. The like to be made not before the money is paid or secured to be paid in London. My principal purpose is to transfer the value of my estate in Pennsylvania to this country, be what it may, and that without running the least possible risk. When I consider the state of America, the situation of my property, and my own interest, every rational consideration leads me to do it.

The trustees advised against it; the property remained largely unsold.

When Elizabeth married William Roberts, a barrister at law, in the 1790s the couple agreed to a postnuptial contract guaranteeing Elizabeth and her heirs sole ownership of her estate upon her father's death. The contract was invalid by English law, but legally sound in Pennsylvania. She and her husband separated shortly after the birth of their daughter, Ann Grace Roberts. Joseph Galloway died at Watford, County of Hertford, on August 29, 1803. His will and testament dictated that his wife's estate would hereafter be owned by his daughter, clear of any rights or claims of William Roberts. The trustees then brought ejectment proceedings in the Courts of Bucks County to dispossess the tenants of the Durham estate. When the case reached the Pennsylvania Supreme Court its judges declared that Joseph Galloway's attainder for treason vested no claim to the real estate of his wife, that it was freed from Galloway's tenancy by his wife's death, that the property rightfully belonged to Mrs. Galloway's heirs. This ruling also affected the occupants of Trevose. The Supreme Court had taken twenty-six years to rectify an injustice perpetuated by political revolutionaries.*

Mary Gould Almy

* Each March over Newport, Rhode Island, great flocks of
wild geese were observed flying northeast, followed by the Bob-
o-Lincoln that inhabitants said always made its first appearance on
May 12th. Their presence signaled the end of severe frosts, and
an awareness that Newport would soon be populated with the
bustling activities of the summer crowd. Wealthy families from
the West Indies and Carolinas, escaping sweltering heat, took
summer residence there, where a fine sea breeze brushed
through the town from about ten in the morning until sunset. Dr.
Benjamin Waterhouse told Thomas Jefferson that the healthy
climate and resources of the Redwood Library gave Newport
"both a literary and a genteel air; and rendered it the best bred
society in New England."

Before the Revolution, Newport was gay, aristocratic, and one
of the leading commercial centers in the colonies. Women frequently packed their silver tea service, climbed into carriages,
and rode over unpaved streets, past exquisite gardens and avenues of trees, to a cliff above the Narragansett Bay, where, sitting
in elegant, laced gowns, they gossiped over teacups. At mid-
afternoon social affairs, guests ate lavishly, while musicians
played strains of Vivaldi and Handel. Mrs. Berkeley, an Englishwoman, described the vanity of Newport society. She saw "men
in flaming scarlet coats and waistcoats, laced and fringed with
brightest glaring yellow. The sly Quakers, not venturing on
these charming coats and waistcoats, yet loving finery, figured a
way with plate on their sideboards." She mentioned one Quaker,
Ebenezer, who, on a recent trip to England, had ordered made
"a noble large teapot of solid gold." Ebenezer displayed it
proudly to his Newport friends, telling them he needed "something finer than anybody else. They say that the Queen has not
got one."

Anglicans, Jews, Congregationalists, Quakers, and members

Although the island had been stripped of trees, numerous buildings, and wharves when Samuel King engraved "A South-West View of Newport" in 1795, the town still retained much of its charm. The graceful spiral of Trinity Church (center) was visible above the variously colored wooden houses, and quaint windmills still had their rotating slats wafted by sea breeze.

of other religious sects lived together peacefully. They flocked to some of New England's finest churches. The town's Anglican "aristocracy," a number of whom remained loyal to the Crown during the Revolution, congregated at Trinity Church. This beautifully designed wooden structure, with its steeple consisting of a square tower, belfry, lantern, and delicate spire, was patterned after Sir Christopher Wren's London churches. Jewish families flocked to the Touro Synagogue, a brick structure on a foundation of freestone. Twelve interior Corinthian columns represented the twelve tribes of Israel, and a trap door gave access to an escape tunnel leading to Barney Street.

Nearly all of Newport's buildings were of wood—only six were brick. Eleven hundred dwellings existed, their exteriors painted in various shades of blue, red, white, yellow, or left unpainted to weather to a gray. Although most interior furnishings were simple and utilitarian, the homes were immaculate, with good ventilation. Many of the walls were covered with printed canvas or paper, or painted wooden panels. Most of the high-cost mansions faced the Bay on Thames Street. Their gardens, fashioned in English style, fronted these houses, being placed near the water and the families' wharves. A few houses were surrounded by gardens and enclosed with wrought-iron or wooden fences, or walls of brick or flat stones piled on top of each other.

Newport's streets were generally lined with rows of small homes, having front steps onto the streets and tiny gardens in back. A French lieutenant stationed in Newport during the Revolution wrote that these wooden houses were sometimes "constructed outside the town and when finished are brought in on rollers (or carts) to their final location." The carts were attached to one another, and were drawn by as many as thirty or forty oxen or horses.

Among the town's wealthiest citizens were numerous shipping merchants, who owned more than twenty wharves south of Long Wharf. The British Parliament slapped heavy duties on items imported by the colonies, and Newport's merchants cunningly evaded paying revenue officers. Tea chests were cleverly hidden between barrels of molasses; goods leaving Europe were labeled erroneously, and the British informed falsely that a cargo's destination would be the West Indies; and Spanish products were often hidden under layers of salt. This didn't always occur, but enough so that within sixteen years the Crown lost about a million pounds in duties. Rather than using violent tactics against British abuse, Newport merchants had found a peaceful way to rebel.

Wharves supported sail-maker and block-maker shops, and sail-drying lofts. Whaling ships brought in oil and spermaceti for lamps and candles; cargo ships brought sugar, molasses, and salt from the West Indies, and wood from Honduras. Carpenters

Mary Gould Almy /247

made barrels and casks for merchants, who shipped fish, molasses, flour, hemp, rice, whale products, and lumber to the colonies, England, and Spain. Unfortunately, many merchants became rich by converting large quantities of sugar and molasses from the West Indies into rum, then shipping the rum to Africa, where it was traded for slaves. A large number of these chained captives—men, women, and children—could not survive the grueling trans-Atlantic voyage. Those who did were sold to southern plantation owners, or to the West Indies for more sugar and molasses, at considerable profit.

Newport's fresh breezes wafted the odors and reverberated the sounds of silversmiths, blacksmiths, bakers, coopers, masons, artisans, cordage and sail makers. On the Mall, between the Colony House and Long Wharf, Ann Franklin's printing firm was usually busy filling orders. The Brick Market at the base of the Long Wharf bustled with the activities of grocers and butchers on the ground floor, and businesses on the upper two. Carts laden with farm produce—including corn ground in quaint windmills scattered around the town's outskirts—clattered along and cluttered surrounding streets. These carts were often packed with woolen articles from the island's fulling mills.

Mary Gould was born in 1735, fourth in a family of eight children. Her father, James, was a teacher who had inherited a substantial estate and married Mary Rathbone. They spent money so lavishly that large debts were attached to James's will when he died. Three of Mary's brothers perished at sea, another settled in the Bahama Islands. A sister, Katherine, never married and lived to the age of ninety; another, Patience, married a hot-headed Tory, Augustus Clarke; a third, Wait, married a Carr and is mentioned in Mary's diary. At the age of twenty-seven Mary Gould married Benjamin Almy in Trinity Church. She was a Quaker, he an Anglican.

Until the explosive 1775 battles in Massachusetts, Newporters remained largely unaffected by the heated controversies that so disturbed other colonies. In 1775, however, Patriots intimidated and harassed Loyalists, a number of whom were forced to flee, their estates then seized. As elsewhere in the colonies, loyalties were often split within a family. Mary Almy opposed the Revolution, yet her husband took up arms against the British. Her strong antiwar convictions did not hamper relationships with patriotic relatives. While French shells exploded in the town in 1778 Mary sought the aid of a Rebel cousin, a Mr. Coggeshall. Three years before, Coggeshall gained notoriety in colonial newspapers by vulgarly expressing patriotic sentiments to a British patrol vessel: "Coggeshall, being somewhat drunk or crazy, went on the Long Wharf and turned up his backside towards the bomb brig in this harbour, using some insulting words, upon which the brig fired two four-pound shot at him."

As British harassment occurred more frequently, opposition strengthened. In March 1776, Patriots formed a Volunteer Patrol Company; two months later, the citizens appointed William Ellery to the Continental Congress in Philadelphia; and in July the Declaration of Independence was read from the balcony of the brick Colony House, where the Rhode Island General Assembly met.

The Almy family acquired the confiscated mansion of a Loyalist, Jahleel Brenton. Brenton, a navy captain, had refused to shift sides in the war, even though offered a higher commission by Whig friends. Harshly persecuted, he fled to England with two of his sons, followed by the rest of his large family in 1780. The Brenton mansion on Thames Street, south of Mary Street, had the traditional two-and-a-half English stories, with a high gabled roof and dormer windows. Enormous trees flanked the front corners, and fashionable carriages were driven around the circular driveway. Built in 1720, it was one of the most beautifully constructed homes in Newport. To pay expenses Mary rented rooms to boarders. The house was conveniently near the Colony House, where, for a time, Benjamin was a member of the Council and House of Deputies.

On December 8, 1776, Sir Henry Clinton invaded Newport with 76 ships and 6,000 British and Hessian troops. The Colony House was seized immediately and converted into barracks.

Women whose husbands were being trained by the Continental Army were cut off from them. Loyalist women welcomed the British, for they felt that, with law and order, peace would be restored. British officers in scarlet coats and waistcoats laced with gold, white gloves, and impeccably powdered wigs were lavishly entertained; on Sundays they crowded Trinity Church. The British began to feel more at ease when Clinton ordered that all citizens relinquish their weapons and that all fishing boats, suspected of being used for clandestine activity, be seized. Such measures stirred up more anger among the people, particularly among the poor, who suffered intolerably from lack of fuel and provisions. Furthermore, all available lumber was confiscated for troop barracks, and farms were crowded with soldiers.

In February of 1778 France signed a treaty alliance with the colonies, and in July a French fleet of twelve ships and four frigates, commanded by Comte d'Estaing, appeared off the Delaware Capes. General Washington proposed a combined American-French attack on Newport. D'Estaing's ships were to fire upon British encampments and land four thousand French troops within British lines, while eight thousand American troops, commanded by General John Sullivan—a force that included a regiment of blacks and Indians—invaded Newport from the island's northern tip. The attack was set for August 10th.

Benjamin Almy, and hundreds of other volunteers, left their Rhode Island homes to join Sullivan's army. The Chevalier de Pontgibaud, a French officer accustomed to fashionable military dress, ridiculed them: "I have never seen a more laughable spectacle; all the tailors and apothecaries in the country must have been called out, I should think;—one could recognize them by their round wigs. They are mounted on bad nags, and looked like a flock of ducks in cross-belts."

Mary Almy's diary begins with the intrusion of the French fleet, July 29, 1778. Following the Battle of Rhode Island, she sealed the manuscript, and gave it to her friend Sukey with the warning that no one else was to see it except Wait Carr, Mary's sister.*

Newport, September the 2d, 1778: Once more my dear Mr. Almy, I am permitted to write you. Great has been your disappointment, and great has been my sorrow, grievious to bear because it came from my friends, but I beg not to dispute at so great a distance. By your desire and my own inclinations, I am to give you an account of what passes during the siege; but first let me tell you, it will be done with spirit, for my dislike to the nation that you call your friends, is the same as when you knew me, knowing there is no confidence to be placed in them, and I foresee that the whole will end, as this maneuver did, in taking this island, to the discredit of the Americans. You will not be surprised at my warmth when you will find how I suffered, nor wonder at my freedom when you find this comes sealed and wrote for your perusal alone. Now to be brief. On Wednesday the 29th of July, at nine in the morning a signal was made for a fleet in sight; at 10 o'clock was discovered the number to be eleven large ships, a fine breeze of wind, and very fair. Each spoke as they wished, it must be Lord Howe. One half hour more threw us into the greatest consternation, the word rang through the streets, it's the French fleet. All was confusion in a moment, no time for preparation, a lively emblem of the poor soul that is called out of the world of a sudden, the great work he came to do was not begun. Our fortifications to keep off shipping were to have been put in readiness this week. The merchant looks upon his full store as nothing worth. The shopkeeper with a distressed countenance locks and bars the shop, not knowing what is for the best. At 11 o'clock they all drop anchor off Brenton's Neck, as was supposed, there to wait until the people of your side of the water were ready to attack the lower part of the island. Heavens! with what spirit the army undertook the old batteries: with what amazing quickness did they throw up new ones; the night did not retard them, so earnest were they to give the Count a proper reception. With a distressed heart I endeavour to comfort my poor children by saying that they would not come in till morning, and then began to secure my papers and plate in the ground, which I effected by 2 o'clock, and then

Mary Gould Almy / 251

lay down to contrive what method to take next day.

Thursday, July 30: Nothing remarkable happened during the day; the fleet all at anchor, an amazing preparation on all the hills, the pavements almost all torn up with the swiftness of the light-horse that brought the momentary intelligence; every idle person that loved news, this was his day. As every ear was open to the marvelous, when night came my heart ached with the many falsehoods that my ear had paid attention to the day long; the fault of our sex in general, repent when it is too late.

Friday, July 31: By daylight up and upon the house; a thick fog prevented our sight; all in terror till it clears off, about 8, when we perceive the King Fisher [Kingfisher sloop] at Coddington's Cove, and the two galleys to be on fire [the British had ordered all three destroyed]; then new agitations took fast hold of us, trembling, crying, hiding, to take the true comfort of trouble that had no remedy. At 10 o'clock the fog being quite gone, two large French ships of the line were discovered up the Seconnet passage, which was the cause of our ships setting fire to themselves, and setting all the people ashore.

Saturday, August 1: All the fleet in motion; everything in consternation; the inhabitants much distressed; the batteries all spirited; all warlike preparation; the streets filled with carts and ordnance stores; every busy soul harnessing, tackling and load with combustible matter, to supply every deficiency that their former negligence had made necessary, and by night they were so ready, that the foolhardy part would wish for nothing more than a movement of the French fleet into the harbour. But I lay down, earnestly praying they would never come so near.

Sunday, August 2: The morning fine and clear. I was upon the house when the sun arose, and found the Lark, Juno, Orpheus, Cerberus, frigates all coming down the river. Then new perplexities arose, new fears stared us in the face, till we were informed that three large French ships of the line had gone up Conanicut passage, and as they were not strong enough to cope with them, took advantage of the dawning day and a fine breeze to run from them, who, if they had been half their strength, would never have let them tell an American their boastful tale, of four British frigates running from their stations. At sight of eleven sail of the line my heart bounded with fright, and then would recover with anger and disdain, a most excellent remedy for a woman; indeed, by turns, it was the saving of my life. The day passed on with stillness; every person conjectured the meaning of the ships going up the river was to cover the landing of the troops, which we could see had gathered.

Monday, August 3: Early was the sound of joy proclaimed; a small boat came express from New York; as soon as she was seen every ship in the French fleet had the honor of giving her a salute. A bold, daring Briton had the command. He ran her upon Sachuest beach; all lay flat about the bottom of the boat, and never a man was hurt. All in high spirits; Lord Howe hourly expected with a great force. All the frigates ordered to their old stations; to be made a sacrifice, I am afraid. The whole town in some great confusion, not knowing what they would be at, some moving their goods out to the lines, the officers all bringing their baggage into the town. Constant fatigue for men, and horses and oxen; no rest by day or by night; still intrenching, weariness and painful watching, the portion of the thinking person. The tedious day gave way for the more tedious night. Every man ordered to be in readiness, the [American] troops were landing at Howland's Ferry. Oh! what a sound! When I look over the list of my friends on both sides of the question, my heart shudders at the thought, what numbers must be slain, both so obstinate, so determined. Well may we say, what havoc does ambition make! Cursed Frenchman! they would not have come, had it not been for you.

Tuesday, August 4: In the morning all a perfect calm; the French ships before the harbour, the French ships up the river, all riding it out with colours flying. Insolence never known before, for them to reign Lords of the Sea. What a shocking aggravation to hundreds in this garrison; but everything waits the coming of Lord Howe. An order is given out this day, from the agent to have all the transports ranged in the harbour, after unloading them, with all preparations ready for sinking them the moment they discovered the French fleet in motion. The night coming on, the express was ordered by Commodore Griffiths to take advantage of the night, and go to New York with despatches. Tired of myself, I have said in my wrath, if I live till morning, I will take a part of Church's house in the Neck for my mother and children, to take off part of the heavy burden that is upon me.

Wednesday, August 5: The first news in the morning. The three large French ships up the river made sail, the others at the mouth of the harbour made signals of unmooring, which threw the British frigates into confusion. They ran as near the land as possible, and took to their boats, first setting fire to their ships; and they blew up immediately, without saving themselves a shirt. At night they ordered all the sailors into town, if possible to keep some order with them. Never was there a more curious sight. In spite of myself, I, who in the morning was almost distracted with apprehension of every kind, at this sight laughed most immoderately. Every sailor was equipt with a musket that could get one; he that could not, had a billet of wood, an old broom, or any club they could find. They all took care to save a bottle of spirits, which they call "kill grief"; some fiddling, some playing on jewsharps, all in high spirits, tho' they had not saved a second shirt. Damning their eyes, they had fun, John Frenchman. By dark the bottles were exhausted, and they so unruly that we were obliged to be safely housed that night.

Thursday, August 6: Exceeding foggy morning; all terrified with apprehension that when the weather cleared, our destiny would be known; all the shops still kept shut, no business of any kind done, only carting and fortifying; the sound of a cannon, most distressing to women and children; an order given out to drive all the stock within the lines. The wretched inhabitants, how are they hurt by every party! My heart aches for the worthy ones.

Friday, August 7: A solemn silence reigns; no one could tell you any news; the fog was very thick; the people all tired out; the fatigues of body and mind, with a thousand perplexities, that attend such an uncommon case, made them ready to meet their fate, let it be for life or death. As all the infernal combinations have, in these latter days, been left for Saturday night, so we begin to think tomorrow night would be the very crisis, and propose to go early to bed, to be able to stand the shock; but at 8 o'clock, in came some of my distressed relations into town, to get assistance to move their furniture inside the lines, as the order is given to burn all the houses, and every building within three miles of the town, the moment they see any force landing, to prevent their making barracks of them. Unhappy victims! they know not what to do; to come into town, they are undone; to go back, they are entirely ruined if they stay. Heavens! what a scene of wretchedness before this once happy and flourishing island! Cursed ought, and will be, the man who brought all this woe and desolation on a good people. Neither sleep to my eyes, nor slumber to my eyelids, this night; but judge you, what preparation could I make, had I been endowed with as much presence of mind as ever woman was; six children hanging around me, the little girls crying out, "Mamma, will they kill us!" The boys endeavour to put on an air of manliness, and strive to assist, but step up to the girls, in a whisper, "Who do you think will hurt you! Arn't your pappa coming with them?" Indeed this cut me to the soul. After three years a lost wanderer, and could not meet a welcome. But I was roused from my stupidity by a violent firing. I call out for my children to run; we sally forth in the street; there was a scene, men, women and children, all in as great a consternation as myself, which sight brought me to myself. I directly order my little ones to make the best of their way along, each with a large bundle, while I step in to know what my mother would do. She told me to follow my children, that sister Carr and Sukey would lead her along. I then ran with as great violence as a creature could, till I overtook them. By this time, the ships fired continually, the women shrieking, the children falling down, crying. Gracious Heavens! It will ever be in my remembrance. I told you before, I had taken part of Church's house, and we were making the best of our way there. Everybody told us we were wrong, but I thought best to go where we had beds, and provisions were prepared, but as the ships came round the Point, we had every shot whistling over our own heads; and we passed two [sand] bars that were more dangerous. The boys had Billy in their arms; the others had such heavy bundles, my heart ached for them. I seldom spoke unless to encourage or to scold them, according as I saw it most necessary, till the largest ship came round, and gave such a broadside, as I really thought would have sent us all to another world. There we all lay, flat in the hollow, just before we came to Jemmy Cogge-shall, till that ship passed, and then jump up and run again. Cousin Coggeshall, seeing our movements for a long way, ventured to come to our assistance, being firm in the faith that every shot has its direction from the Almighty, and I am almost of his opinion, for if the Devil had the ordering of the shot, as he had of sending them here, there would not have been a soul left to tell the tale.

Saturday, August 8: Long before the appearance of day, was I in readiness to rise, nothing but frightful dreams and broken slumbers, listening to the noise of a fly, or mosquito, as they hummed around the candle; in this horrid way did I spend the night. The morning gun of the French Admiral had like to have frighted me to death. The first news that was told was, twenty thousand men, all landed without interruption. The king's troops all ordered within the lines, and to leave the lower part of the island. About 12 o'clock they [the British] set sixteen buildings on fire, which to me, ever will appear like cruelty and wantonness, as it answers no end. We endeavour to have dinner as soon as possible, knowing that every calamity can be easier borne with, that takes us on a full stomach. At one o'clock, signals for unmooring throughout the French fleet, a brisk gale blew, and entirely fair. One hour, the longest time that could be thought, then we should all be prisoners. Heavens! what distress! what consternation seized me! where to fly for shelter! The cellar was determined on; then should they burn the town! I dare not attempt it. While I was pausing, he was preparing to kindly shelter us under his large rock, where all his family had fled for safety. Then that precious comforter to the female came to my relief, a silent shower of tears behind the haystack, for my poor friends in town, who never were in half the danger as myself. Cousin Coggeshall's cherry rum being brought, I grew more and more enabled to bear my sorrows. In a few minutes a chaise brought my mother, sister and Sukey. They took the care of all the brood, and proceeded to the house I had taken. This charge being off me, I became myself. The French ships had all gone by the batteries without silencing one, and dropped anchor at the north end of Conanicut. Then came on a most horrible sight: all the British ships that were not sunk were set fire to, and the wind being high, the town was in the greatest danger. I then set out with as much eagerness for home, as I had left it, and got safe to my own house, fatigued and tired beyond all conception. To attempt to describe the horrors of that night would pronounce me a fool, for no language could put it in its proper colours. Fire and sword had come amongst us, and famine was not afar off, for the want of bread was great. About 12 at night the fire was deadened; all was still, only the sentries answering the few vessels that were left, they in town, to the guard boat's "all's well." As to me, from a large family I am reduced to none. All the gentlemen [her boarders] took refuge under cover of the troops. Ben is in New York, Jacob at Long Island getting wood,—my children in the Neck; what an agony was I in, when I had time to recollect my scattered thoughts. Heaven that ever has been kind to me, sent the captains of the transports to see me. They pitied and sympathized with me, and sent me two truly valuable sailors for my safeguards, whose kind care I hope I never shall forget. The night was spent in watching the fire, and at day I lay down to recruit my wornout feet, and indeed my whole frame. Thus ended the tedious Saturday.

Sunday, August 9: Early in the morning, our gentlemen came home to know how it had been with us; my trusty, careful William brought us all the news, took care of the cows and hogs, and carried messages to the children, whom he was very fond of, a long time before. He was very unhappy, that he could not make me believe, that we should never fall a sacrifice to a Frenchman, and all his stories savoured much of the strength of the lines, that it was impossible for the Americans to force them. About 10 o'clock he came to tell me a fleet in sight; it must be Lord Howe. A strange revolution, such a turn in affairs in a few hours. The officers of the navy, who a few hours before looked disconsolate and wretched, now mounted any horse they could catch, and rode with all speed to see those ships, that three days sooner would have saved theirs. The officers of the army that could be spared from duty a quarter of an hour, came with great speed, to say to their friends that Lord Howe was come. Nothing transpired more during the day, only great numbers went aboard; every soul in high spirits. The sailors' joy was so great as to tear all their tents, and play fury with everything in their reach. Towards evening, they carried great numbers of sailors to man the fleet. Nobody knew what they intended. Various conjectures, everybody turns politician forming and planning schemes for Lord Howe, to make this naughty French Count repent his having joined the subject to rebel against the true and lawful Sovereign. Night came, we went quietly to bed, and slept like tops.

Monday, August 10: All hands up early, great expectations from this day. About 8 o'clock, the French fleet all drew up in a line of battle. Lord Howe made every preparation for unmooring, the hours then seemed to creep, so anxious were we for retaliation. At 9 o'clock the English fleet were seen to stand out; it surprised us; but still it was thought it was only done to have sea room enough. What Count D'Estaing thought, Heavens knows, for his haste was great. He cut all his cables, and came firing through the harbour, as if the very Devil was in him, and our batteries returned his favours with a vengeance. One half the town went in the Neck to see a grand sea fight, but returned exceedingly disappointed, in a few hours. Then it was told, Lord Howe's strength was not sufficient to cope with such a fleet. At night, there was no appearance of either of the fleets, but happy were we, to get clear of Monsieur. For my part, I had grown so bold, as not to quit my house, on the second firing; for *my* young men had insisted on my going down cellar, that I should be very safe; and I was so exceedingly lame, occasioned by my Saturday flight, that to have gained a kingdom, I could not have run half the distance; and the great and heavy burden of a troop of children being taken off, I contented myself down cellar, behind an ashes hogshead, till the heaviest firing was over. But what was very remarkable, by all the hundreds of shot that came into the town, not a soul was killed or wounded.

Tuesday, August 11: This morning a violent storm (called the continental storm) came on, before day, and continued thundering and lightning most terribly all day. The wind blew a perfect hurricane, and it never rained harder since the flood. The tents were all blown to pieces, the soldiers and sailors were all like drowned rats. They were ordered into town to recruit a little, a few in a party, and to be ready in a moment. I ordered a good fire in the kitchen and something good to eat and drink, to comfort the poor souls that had comforted me formerly, with their cash in the shop. After a word of thanks and many blessings, they went to take the remainder of the storm. Night came on, and we repaired to bed, not afraid of any movements that night.

Wednesday, August 12: The storm still continues and with as much violence, as though it had just begun. My children are still in the Neck, the house really looks melancholy. No business going forward; all the shops still kept shut; nothing is to be seen in the streets, but carts and horses and some old worn-out drivers, who care not who was king, or who rebelled against him. It was enough for them to know, if somebody did not conquer soon, they and their horses must soon die, and as the men were the heads of large families, so the horses were of equal consequence, their labour was to support the whole; and let who would reign, their services must be paid for. Indeed the man and the brute both claim our pity. The night looks gloomy and very dark.

Thursday, August 13: The rain has a little subsided. The fog has entirely cleared away, by which we soon discover that your people [Rebel troops] had entrenched themselves much nearer.

Mary Gould Almy /259

A vast number of people are at work. The town much distressed for bread; but rice being plenty, nobody could suffer. There is great looking out for one fleet or the other. Altho' I am brought as low as death, believe me, my dear Mr. Almy, I am not like the driver I mentioned yesterday, who, if he could be quiet, cared not who governed. I am for English government, and an English fleet. I care not who takes the Frenchman.

Friday, August 14: This morning, three prisoners were taken, all gentlemen volunteers from New Hampshire who were reconnoitering the ground; unluckily for them, too near the lines; they were carried to the Provost, but treated well. The day was fine and clear, exceedingly hot. Nothing remarkable happened; the prisoners afforded conversation for the day, as human nature is ever pleased with everything that happens a little marvelous. No tidings of the fleet, no business going forward. My mother and children still in the Neck, and there I intend to keep them till things are altered. Tedious days, melancholy nights. I wonder what keeps me alive.

Saturday, August 15: I am awake early, but all things look quiet; scarcely a soul is to be seen from one end of the street to the other. When chance or inclination brought any of my friends, the anxious look, the distressed countenance, the melancholy tale, which every poor soul had to tell, made me more unhappy than when I sat brooding over my own peculiar situation. For I will acknowledge that sometimes I saw a gleam of comfort, speaking in the still small voice, you will once more be happy. Then with what spirit would I go through fatigues and difficulties, which at another time, I should have looked upon as an impossibility, and having the gentlemen that boarded with me, at home, I was as easy as a person in my situation could be. For indeed there never were better men than our roof covered. Mr. Amory, of Boston, was one, whose kindness I never must or shall forget. I am almost ashamed that I have never mentioned him before, in the many sheets this letter contains.

Sunday, August 16: No church, no appearance of the day kept up. Still carting, still fortifying. Your people encroaching nearer, throwing up new works every night. Our people beholding it every morning, with wonder and astonishment. And really, Mr. Almy, my curiosity was so great, as to wish to behold the entrenchment that I supposed you were behind; and a good young man by the name of Dr. Hussillon took me in a chaise to the hospital, which was formerly owned by Mr. Cozzens. There we had an excellent view of Vars' Orchard, and all the encampments around it. Believe me, my dear friend, never was a poor soul more to be pitied, such different agitations as by turns took hold upon me. Wishing most ardently to call home my wanderer, at the same time filled with resentment against those he calls his friends, so that I returned home more distressed, my spirits more sunk than when I went out. Great enquiry was made at my return, to know the reason of my distressed countenance; but others who knew I had my share of sensibility, let me enjoy my sorrow that had no remedy. Till night came on, I hid myself from the world.

Monday, August 17: Nothing happened worth notice; every moment expecting the French fleet [Because of the storm, the French fleet sailed to Providence for repairs, the British fleet to New York.]; everybody tired out with fatigues of every kind, and the apprehension of what was to come rendered us truly unhappy. About 12 they opened a new battery upon us, and the day was spent in exchanging shots; in the evening they entertained us with throwing shells. It would have been an agreeable sight, had we not been sure it was meant to carry death along with it. I sat upon the top of the house till 12, beholding and admiring the wonderful contrivances of mankind to destroy one another.

Tuesday, August 18: Awake early; the night one continual dreading, you ever the subject. Sometimes you were before me all pleasantness, your countenance like yourself when happy; then again, all was distress; fighting, firing and every horror that my heart foreboded, when awake. Oh! that it was at an end! that I knew the worst! At 8 o'clock the word was, that Col. Bruce of the 55th with a party, had brought in the picket guard at Southwest Beach, an ensign, a sergeant and twelve men; they were taken upon surprise. Never was more amiable conduct than the colonel showed. When he delivered up his prisoners, to go to the Provost, he very politely asked the young ensign if he would accept of 10 guineas, as he supposed he had no money that would pass. Oh! Mr. Almy! you must allow it was a noble deed. Were all prisoners treated like these, there would not be such a general murmuring. The day passed on without anything more which afforded conversation for the publick. They keep up an incessant firing from their batteries, this afternoon. In the evening, dull, melancholy and almost alone, I soon went to bed, to contemplate on what had passed during the day.

Wednesday, August 19: Little or no sleep, my mind exceedingly agitated, distressed for my friends, that I soon thought would be prisoners; forming a thousand different plans, to extricate them from their unhappy prospects, but all in vain. The morning came, and I had to drag on another day. Nothing remarkable happened during it. Every one's expectation is high, looking for the return of the French fleet, with English colours, which we imagine, would soon procure us a happy and lasting peace. Heavens! with what joy would I receive the glad tidings, what welcomes, ten thousand welcomes, to the long lost wanderers! Parents receiving their children from loathsome prisons, wives their partners, long banished from all they held dear. Brothers and sisters kindly meeting, after a tedious absence. The idea of which must remind us of the joys of Heaven.

Thursday, August 20: Early up; my family small; the children still in the Neck; my careful William, seeking every little piece of intelligence to raise my depressed spirits. About 7 o'clock he came to tell me there was a fleet in sight, and he hoped Lord Howe had given them a quieting dose; but my heart forboded something worse. All the horrors that had seized me at their last firing, now returned with double violence. But in the midst of all this confusion of thought I boldly determined to keep possession of my own house. And now I await the impending blow with as much fortitude as in my power. Looking back on my former conduct in life, and my own heart justifying me with this truth, I have ever done to others as I wish they may do to me. This thought comforted me, and I heard it was a French fleet, without such visible emotion as I had shown. They all came to anchor in the old place, down the Neck. It was very soon discovered that they were in a shattered condition, had lost their topmasts, and had one ship less than when they went out. The boats were continually flying from every shore around. All were in some agitation that we knew not our destiny, it was approaching very fast. Our apprehensions tortured us. The ten thousand lies which we heard rendered us incapable to stand the shock. We were worn out with the fatigues of this dreadful day, but dared not take any rest, for fear we should be caught asleep; never did I so dread the night, and yet so grieve to see the morning light. But as soon as we could see the Neck I was determined to be upon the house.

Friday, August 21: To my great astonishment, I went upon the house and no ships were to be found. Where they could be gone was a matter of wonder. Soon, very soon, it was reported through the town that they had quitted. There were various conjectures. The wise ones stood astonished. The people on the island still at work. Every thing wore the face of some perplexity. The poor soldiers were worn out with constant duty, and the great and mighty men just ready to sink under their burdens. But this news gave a new face, every thing wore a different aspect. Not, let me tell you, were they afraid of a Frenchman. But that fleet of ships they knew must surrender. The day passed on with swiftness, and at night I was forced to call to my assistance my poor scattered reason, and endeavour to compose myself to sleep.

Saturday, August 29: All is peace and quietness in the town. The first news was, the provincials [Rebels] had moved their encampment, carried off all their artillery, stores and provisions, and gone to the lower part of the island to secure their retreat. General Pigot gave orders for the [British] 43d and 22d regiments, and the Hessians and Anspachers to pursue them by daylight. In a few hours, a heavy firing was heard; he then gave orders for Fanning's regiment to go to their assistance and two hours after gave orders for the 38th to march directly and for Fanning's to return within the lines, and at 11 o'clock sent a light horseman to call the 38th back. All was horror and confusion. The Hessians overtook a party in the West road, near the Redwood farm; they pursued with violence, the others retreated with prudence, leaving the roads strewn with dead bodies. The East road was a scene of blood and slaughter, from cousin Almy's down to the foot of Quaker hill. All the crossroads were filled with them, and they kept up a smart firing till 2 o'clock, and then they began to bury the dead and bring in the wounded. Oh! How many wretched families were made that day. It would have softened the most callous heart to see the cart loads of wretched men brought in, their wives screaming at the foot of the cart, in concert with their groans. Fine youths with their arms taken off in a moment. In short it's too far beyond my power of description. The horrors of that day will never be quite out of my remembrance. I quitted company and hid myself to mourn in silence, for the wickedness of my country. Never was a heart more differently agitated than mine. Some of my good friends in the front of the battle here; and Heaven only knows how many of the other side. Instead of enquiring the news, or asking after a soul, a stupidity took hold of me. At last I shut myself from the family, to implore Heaven to protect you, and keep you from imprisonment and death. Every dejected look, and every melancholy countenance I saw, I trembled for fear they would say, your husband lies among the slain, or that he is wounded and a prisoner. Think you what a life I live, knowing your proneness to get into danger.

Sunday, August 30: The provincials are encamped on Windmill hill; there is little or no firing from either party. More regiments are ordered out. Something great is intended, if you should not slip away too soon. Constant riding from Quaker hill. Every hour we are expecting a general battle. My whole heart is sick with melancholy stories. Every hospital is crowded with wounded men. No church. No appearance of anything but horror and distress. The country people all plundered. In the midst of all the confusion, some were going into eternity, while others were robbing the innocent farmers' houses; death and destruction were before their eyes from every quarter, until the officers heard of their doings; they directly ordered guards to every house, whose kind protection was the saving of them. And to do justice to the British, their humanity and lenity were beyond all conception to the wounded prisoners. There was a hospital on purpose for them. Nurses were chosen amongst the inhabitants, that they might have every indulgence that their unhappy situation needed. Doctors, whose goodness, understanding and compassion ought never to be forgotten. And whenever justice is done at the end of the war, I hope this instance will be in your records. Night coming on, every thing as I suppose will be left for daylight.

Monday, August 31: By daylight the trampling of horses, the different sound of voices, brought to her thoughts a poor creature, who had scarcely had sleep enough to compose her distracted brain, but had brought herself willing to hear the worst. At 7 o'clock a light horseman with news; they [Rebels] are retreated, quite gone over Howland's Ferry. At 8 o'clock, a messenger. They began to decamp early in the evening, and before day their artillery, baggage, wounded men, and part of the army were over. At 10 o'clock Thomas Hill came in and told me he saw you on Friday and that you desired him to let me know by daylight on Monday morning, you should be at home at breakfast, with a number of gentlemen. Oh! Mr. Almy, what a shocking disappointment to you. Can you keep up your spirits! Heaven, I hope, will support you, so positive, so assured of success. Remember, in all your difficulties and trials of life, that when the All-wise disposer of human events thinks we have been sufficiently tried, then our patience in waiting will be amply repaid by a joyful meeting.

Mary Gould Almy / 265

* Ravaged by the British, damaged by French shelling, Newport in the winter of 1778 faced the bitterest weather its inhabitants had suffered through in many years. Harsh gales and biting snowstorms slashed across people's faces like iced needles, and caused the death of five British soldiers. The harbor smoked from the cold; wine and preserves froze in the bottles indoors. Boats continued to bring in cordwood from Block and Long Islands; coal deposits, particularly on Capt. Benjamin Almy's (Mary's "cousin Almy") land on Quaker Hill, supplied some coal for grates. But it was not enough. During the entire British occupation, several wharves and 480 homes, farms, and commercial buildings were demolished for firewood. All of the island's trees, except those bearing fruit, had been hacked down. The shipping trade was in shambles, and five thousand inhabitants had fled. Finely boxed pews and an altar had been ripped from the interiors of the Congregational Churches so that British soldiers quartered within them might keep warm. The Colony House was so damaged that, following the British evacuation of Newport in October 1779, the building had to be boarded up, and the Rhode Island Assembly and Supreme Court held meetings in the Touro Synagogue. Wood was so scarce that a cord of it sold for five times the cost of a bushel of corn, and ten times that of a bushel of potatoes.

Having raped the island, Sir Henry Clinton's army left Newport in October for an aggressive campaign in the South. The following summer, the French began to use the town as a harbor for their fleet, and an embarkation point for Marshal Comte de Rochambeau's army. On July 10, 1780, twelve French men-of-war ships and thirty-two transport vessels—carrying six thousand colorful troops of the Bourbonnais, Royal Deux-Ponts, Soissonais, and Saintonge regiments—weighed anchor in Newport Harbor. Newporters remembered well the French shellings, and were, for the most part, suspicious of French intervention. According to the Comte de Clermont-Crèvecoeur, when Rochambeau "reached the town he was astonished to find hardly a soul. The shops were closed, and the local people, little disposed in our favour, would have preferred at that moment, I think, to see their enemies arrive rather than their allies."

The next morning, Newport's citizens held a town meeting to resolve how to behave toward the French. Many of the inhabitants, siding with "His Most Christian Majesty's" (Louis XVI) fleet and army, argued that the French could lend them firearms and accoutrements for the militia. After a lengthy debate, the group announced that "the inhabitants and citizens of this town are called upon from the duty and regard they owe our country, and the gratitude and respect which is due from every citizen to the illustrious ally of these States, as well as to afford them the utmost aid and assistance, also to manifest every mark of respect and esteem upon their arrival; Wherefore, resolved, that all houses in the streets hereafter named be illuminated tomorrow evening, to-wit: Thames Street, Congress (heretofore called Queen Street), Lewis Street (heretofore called King's Street), Broad Street, leading out of town, the street leading over the Point Bridge, and the street leading from the Long Wharf to the point battery, and such other houses in this town as the abilities of the occupants thereof will admit, and that the lights be continued to 10 o'clock in the evening." Ten citizens, including Benjamin Almy, were appointed as "a committee to patrol the streets to prevent any damage arising from fire, and to preserve the peace of the town." It was then ordered "that this resolution be published and made known to the inhabitants of this town by beat of drum." Residents unable to illuminate their windows were supplied with candles paid for by the treasury. The following day, thirteen rockets were fired in front of the State House, and thousands of candles flickered from citizens' windows. Ezra Stiles wrote that "the Whigs put 13 lights in the windows, the Tories or doubtfuls 4 or 6; the Quakers did not chuse their lights should shine before men, and their windows were broken."

Despite the friendly welcome, Crèvecoeur remained critical. "The character of this nation is little adapted to society. The men are very cold, rather stiff, and reticent." He believed the women fell short "in one very noticible respect and that is their frigid manner." To him, Newport's women showed "little vivacity or gaiety in your company. If you do not wish to be bored, you must assume the burden of conversation, animating it with your French gaiety, or all will be lost." The Count was accustomed to women at the French court, who were highly flirtatous, and who entertained men with intellectual gatherings in salons. Crèvecoeur was further disdainful of women's attitudes during lavish dances given by French officers in Newport. He "always noticed that a Whig woman would not dance in the same room with a Tory woman, and vice versa." He found American men to be prudent, "but the women in this country do not know the meaning of diplomacy. They carried things to such a point that, when we first gave balls, the Whigs refused to come to a house to which Tories had been invited." Furthermore, several officers found it peculiar that women were expected to retire from a dinner table, while men remained to drink and smoke. In France both sexes left the table to enjoy drinking and conversing together in a salon.

Alexandre Berthier felt that even though he had found most of the town's inhabitants to be Tories, they shortly became quite friendly with the French. "All of the women are pretty and youthful, a fact which they owe to their customs, to the regularity and sobriety of their lives, and to the climate, which is very healthy . . . all the women had the same freedom towards us, something which we couldn't help but attribute to our amiability. And, charmed in finding a route which seemed to us so simple, we were very embarrassed and felt cheated to find, all of a sudden, an insurmountable barrier. And if a few of us did cross it, it was only by the base means of false promises, a type of seduction unknown before our arrival. As to married women there are no instances of seduction."

On March 6, 1781, the islanders wildly welcomed the arrival of General Washington. The *Newport Mercury* reported: "the town and fleet in the harbour were beautifully illuminated. The procession was led by thirty boys, bearing candles fixed on staffs, followed by General Washington, Count Rochambeau and the other officers, their aides, and the procession of citizens. The night was clear, and there was not a breath to fan the torches. The brilliant procession marched through the principal streets," avenues lined with three rows of French troops.

The French Army left Newport three months later, sailing southward for a rendezvous with the British at Yorktown. With the Yorktown victory, and delayed signing of a peace treaty, the war was over. Its ravaging rapacity, however, had so impoverished Newport that the town never regained the commercial prestige or visual beauty it possessed before the Revolution. In 1788 a visiting Frenchman wrote: "Since the peace everything is changed, the reign of solitude is only interrupted by groups of idle men standing with folded arms at the corners of the streets, houses falling to ruin, miserable shops which present nothing but a few coarse stuffs or baskets of apples, and other articles of little value; grass growing in the public square in front of the court of justice, rags stuffed in the windows."

Such was Newport's condition when, on August 17, 1790, President Washington, accompanied by Secretary of State Thomas Jefferson and other prominent dignitaries, arrived in the harbor by packet boat. As the vessel came to its mooring, church bells clanged, thirteen cannons boomed, ships displayed their colors, and hundreds of cheering citizens thronged the wharf. The young nation's political figures were graciously welcomed by a town committee that included Benjamin Almy. Washington was then escorted to the Almy home, where he boarded for the night, preferring a place where he could pay for his own accommodations, rather than stir up political controversy by residing in a private home.

The *Newport Herald* reported that "at 4 o'clock P.M. the committee waited upon the President, and escorted him to the State House, where he was received by the manager of the ceremony, who conducted him to the Council Chamber, where the clergy and other citizens were convened. At 5 o'clock they were ushered into the Representative's Chamber, where he was provided a very elegant dinner." The banquet ended with thirteen toasts,

Mary Gould Almy / 269

one for each state. Washington then rose, bowed, and proposed a toast to the town of Newport.

The State House (the old Colony House) had to turn down a number of requests to the dinner because of lack of space. A group of men holding a feast of their own in a nearby house toasted proslavery sentiments, "May the Rhode Island African Fleet Flourish!" "Disappointment to the Abolition Society!" An outraged citizen wrote the *Newport Herald* that it was "amazingly inconsistent that gentlemen at a banquet of wine should toast reprobation to tyranny and oppression, and in a breath or two more swallow down disappointment to one of the respectable societies on earth," signing the letter "Abolition Man." The following issue contained a letter in reply, whose author insisted that the African slave trade "prolongs the existence of this declining town, and, in fact, that Newport gets more out of African captains than it does out of abolition men!"

Mary Gould Almy died in March 1808 at the age of seventy-three; the burial service was held in Trinity Church. The *Newport Mercury* informed its readers that "she is deeply lamented by her husband, whose 'heart safely trusted in her,' and who, in being deprived in an advanced age of so valuable an associate, with whom he had lived almost fifty years, is overwhelmed with sorrow." His children had made their homes elsewhere, and so Benjamin moved out of the mansion. In the middle of the nineteenth century the house became known as the Female Seminary, at the turn of the next century the Coe building, and in the early 1920s this once elegant mansion, crammed behind the Colonial Theatre, was in such poor condition that, rather than seek funds to have it restored, ambitious profit seekers had it razed. Much of the ground is now a parking lot. ✻

Jane Young Ferguson

*Jane Young Ferguson, a hardy Irishwoman who lived to be ninety-seven, spent much of her life in the rustic woodlands and primitive villages along the Mohawk Valley in New York. She survived the bloody 1778 massacre at Cherry Valley by Indians and Tories. The northwestern region of Cherry Valley, in which she lived, was incorporated into the township of Springfield in the late eighteenth century.

The first person to inhabit this part of the wilderness, filled with wild animals, including prowling wolves, was a Scotchman named John Lindsay. Several decades before, a few German families had settled the more western regions. In 1740 Lindsay purchased a large tract, strapped down wagonloads of kitchen utensils, carpentry tools, bedding, clothing, and food barrels, and set out from New York City. He named the land Cherry Valley because of the profusion of cherry trees, and slashed tree trunks as boundary markers. Within a year thirty settlers had joined him, calling themselves the Scotch-Irish. They made crude paths through forested areas to settlements along the Mohawk and Schoharie rivers. Friendly Indians taught them survival and agricultural methods.

The families of John Kelly, James Young, and Richard Ferguson settled the northwestern area in the 1760s, when Jane was a small youngster. They felled trees for cabins of unhewn logs and cleared fields for food crops. Prior to 1778 the Mohawk Valley watershed was one of the major suppliers of wheat in the colonies. Wheat was threshed with the flail or by driving horses over it. After being winnowed the grain was taken on a two or three day journey in crude wagons to Albany, or to the Mohawk River and from there shipped to Schenectady, where it was carted to Albany. Schenectady, less primitive than the interior settlements, had taverns, stores, and a brisk river traffic. Its stone or brick dwellings were largely of Dutch architectural style.

This view of the Mohawk River, with the Hudson River in the background, was sketched in the late eighteenth century. The Mohawk Indians—a few are shown here paddling canoes past a rustic white settlement—were part of the Confederacy known as the Five Nations.

Houses were spotlessly clean, and backyards sprouted an abundance of vegetable and flowering plants. Each family's milk was squirted from a cow's udder at the back door. At sunrise the animal was led through the town's grassy streets to a common pasture at the outskirts; at sunset families heard the tinkling of cowbells as cows found their own way home.

In Cherry Valley, and elsewhere in the Mohawk Valley, life was largely self-sustaining. One simply adapted to the natural environment. Sap was procured from maple trees for syrup and sugar, a practice learned from Indians. Lacking tea, settlers made a brew from mashed dried peas, sweetened with maple sugar. Settlers spun, wove, and tailored their own clothes, relying upon itinerant cobblers for shoes. Yet these newcomers to the wilderness were not cut off from news of seaport towns. Post riders brought mail and newspapers that soon became dog-eared from being passed from house to house.

Within a month after the explosive battles at Lexington and Concord virtually every county district had formed a Committee of Safety. Meeting at Fort Plain in Canajoharie, district committees adopted resolutions of united action against British intrusion. Representing Cherry Valley were John Moore—soon to be selected as a delegate to the Continental Congress—and Samuel Campbell, a militia colonel. Patriotism rippled through the Mohawk Valley, though many inhabitants remained loyal to the Crown. Mobs, usually organized by committeemen, terrorized Loyalists, forcing many to flee to Canada, where they joined the British and recruited the support of many Indians.

During the British campaign of 1777–1778 the Mohawk Valley was the prime target of Colonel Barry St. Leger. He enlisted the aid of Sir John Johnson's Loyalist regiment—American exiles in Montreal—Captain Walter Butler's Loyalist rangers, and Captain Joseph Brant's Indians. The Indians were particularly anxious to avenge brothers slaughtered at the Battle of Oriskany (1777).

Fear soon gripped Cherry Valley's settlers, whose sole protection was a crude earthwork and palisade surrounding Campbell's house. The Marquis de Lafayette, after visiting Cherry Valley, asked military authorities for funds and troops. The inhabitants were then able to build a simple fort, one that enclosed the church and burying ground. In July 1778 a detachment of the 7th Massachusetts Regiment arrived with roughly two-hundred soldiers. The stockade was named Fort Alden in honor of its commander, Colonel Ichabod Alden. Alden and most of the officers quartered themselves among the populace. Captain Benjamin Warren wrote that "the inhabitants received us with the greatest tokens of joy and respect; it was like a gaol delivery; they began to take the fresh air and moved into the nearest houses, from their six weeks confinement" in the fort. When, on August 10, Alden received intelligence that Joseph Brant was planning an attack he sent sixty soldiers on a reconnaisance. They seized fourteen of Brant's men at Butternut Creek.

In late October, Indians of the Six Nations held a council of war, in which it was determined to destroy Cherry Valley, which they called "Karitongeh" (place of the oaks). On the 28th, five-hundred of these warriors left British Fort Niagara on Lake

Ontario. They were shortly joined by Captain Colvill's fifty British soldiers and Captain Butler's two hundred Loyalist rangers. An Oneida Indian, present at the Council, warned Americans at Fort Stanwix of the plan of attack.

General Edward Hand, commander of the American army's Northern Department, arrived at Fort Alden to determine the expediency of quartering more troops there. When word reached Hand of the imminent attack he dispatched Colonel Klock for reinforcements. It was too late. On November 8 a scout rushed into the fort shouting that the enemy was close by. When settlers swarmed against the fort's gate and demanded safety within, Alden refused to allow them in. He told them it was unnecessary, that a warning would be sounded when the enemy approached. Scouts were then ordered out to investigate.

The night of the 9th a group of scouts extinguished their campfire along the east bank of the Susquehanna River and slept. Before the sun's faint rays broke through the trees, Loyalists and Indians crept through the brush and ambushed the men. By nightful the enemy was encamped in a thickly forested area about a mile southwest of Fort Alden. Heavy snow began to fall; on the 11th it thickly blanketed the earth. The air was musky and thick, and a sprinkling of rain developed into a downpour. The enemy crept over a slushy path, passed two houses, and crouched in a swamp area not far from Robert Well's house, used by the Patriots as headquarters.

Hand's reinforcements, long overdue, had not arrived. At noon the enemy, numbering 650, began their carnage. Colonel Alden was cut down as he tried to reach the fort. Robert Wells, his wife, their four children, his mother, a brother, sister, and three servants had gathered in the Wells house for religious prayer. All were swiftly murdered except a daughter who fled to a woodpile, only to be found by an Indian and hacked to death.

Hugh Mitchell was absent from his house when the Loyalists and Indians struck, though he soon heard of it and rushed back to try to save his family. He saw his house on fire and found the mangled bodies of his wife and children. Mitchell suppressed the flames, then noticed a child still moving. He carried his eleven year old daughter through the door, and as he lay her on the ground he heard enemy movement. Throwing himself behind a fence, he watched with horror as a Loyalist named Newbury buried a hatchet in the child's skull. Captain Warren later saw the blood-spattered remnants of Mitchell's family: "Such a shocking sight my eyes never beheld before of savage and brutal barbarity; to see a husband mourning over his dead wife with four children lying by her side, mangled, scalped, and some of their heads, some of their legs and arms cut off."

Not far from the home of Jane Young, then thirteen, the enemy surrounded Reverend Samuel Dunlop's house. Through the intercession of a Mohawk chief the minister's life was spared, but being tightly bound he was prevented from going to his wife who was being mutilated.

Elizabeth Dickson's family lived on a southern hilly area. Hearing shrieks near the fort, she gathered her children and flattened them against the soil in the woods. When all was quiet, Elizabeth returned home for provisions and was killed by an Indian. The rest of the day and chilly night, her children remained hidden among trees. At daybreak the eldest child, finding the house empty, moved through a thicket at the foot of the hill. There she saw, at a distance, Indians sitting near a pole, on which were hung several scalps. She knew the red hair was part of her mother. Not long after, scouts from the fort found the children and hastened them to safety.

Thirteen soldiers and thirty-two inhabitants—nearly all were women and children—had been slain during the attack that lasted two days. All buildings except those belonging to Loyalists were reduced to smoldering ash. Many of the cattle had been killed, others were suffering because their tongues had been cut out. Fire had swept through stored food supplies. A man from another village, whose sister and niece had been taken prisoner, came to help bury the dead. He wrote to the *Boston Gazette* that "of the wretched surviving inhabitants, there are 182 who have neither house nor home, nor a morsel of bread; are almost naked, and a great part of them without a penny to purchase any of the necessaries of life. And in all this massacre there were but three men of the place killed, all the rest being helpless women and children. . . . We have now not one settlement left in this county at any distance from the south side of the Mohawk River, and have the greatest reason to fear, that in a very short time we shall not have one on it, unless very speedy and effectual measures are taken to check the savages and worse than savages, Tories.''

Many families had managed to hide in the woods or stockade, but many others were held captive and forced to walk in a cold rain to a secluded area two miles below the fort. There, without shelter and proper clothing, they huddled the night of the 11th, resuming their forced march at daybreak. Among them were Colonel Campbell's wife and children. Mrs. Campbell's mother could not keep pace with the others, though helped by them, and was brutally bludgeoned. Also murdered was Eleanor McKinney Cannon, who was sixty-one years of age. The following day all women and children, except the families of John Moore and Colonel Campbell were allowed to return to Cherry Valley. The children of the two women, except an infant, were given to various Indian families along the way to Fort Niagara. Their mothers remained in captivity until they were freed in a prisoner exchange.

Late in 1779 General John Sullivan's force broke the back of the Six Nations' organization, and two years later Captain Butler was killed by an Oneida Indian. Although Jane Ferguson refers to Butler as a colonel, papers found on his body certified him as a captain.

Not long before Jane Ferguson's death in 1862 she dictated the following journal to a granddaughter, Eliza Ferguson, a teacher in Springfield.*

My mother had six sisters and one brother. Their names were Mollie, Margaret, Nancy, Eleanor, Sarah, Rosa and Jane, and John. Their surname was Kelly. My mother's name was Nancy.

They were born in the north of Ireland. I have forgotten the name of the place in sight of the Giant's Causeway.

My father [James Young] had no brothers, he had two sisters. His mother died and one sister. The other one married in Ireland. None of his family came to America.

Mollie died in Ireland. Margaret married Archibald McKillip. They were married in Ireland. Had three children, all born in Ireland, Archie, John, and Daniel. Eleanor married James McDermid in this country. Had no children. Their eldest son and daughter came to America. Their uncle John Kelly promised to pay their passage if they would come, but when they got to Philadelphia their uncle John was out here [Springfield], and they had to be sold [as servants] for their passage. A merchant bought the boy for four years. The girl I do not remember about. The boy was a good scholar, his father was a school teacher. The merchant liked him, and gave him a chance to make some bargains for himself. He got money enough to buy a hogshead of flax-seed and send it to Ireland. They did not save any seed there; they pulled it before it was ripe. He received enough for his seed to bring over the rest of the family. The daughter married and went to New Jersey. The rest of the family settled in Philadelphia. They became wealthy. One daughter, Jane, married James McNiel. They had one child, and they ran away from Philadelphia and came here. He was a weaver by trade; they lived in an old house down by Mr. Oliver's. They had ten children. He went off and left her. Their uncle Archie carried her to Albany and paid her passage to where her sister lived in New Jersey.

Jane married soon after she came over to a man she became acquainted with on board ship. They were married at uncle Archie McKillip's; his name was McLelland. They owned the farm that George Clark owned this side of Cherry Valley. They had five children, four boys and one girl. They lived there until Cherry Valley was burned [Cherry Valley Massacre], when he was taken prisoner and two of his boys, about 10 and 12 years old. They were taken to Canada. His wife and the three younger children remained in the house. The Indians and Tories told her that if she would stay till morning they would come for her. When they were gone she took some of her things and fled. After he got to Canada he enlisted to get his two sons from the Indians, and his wife went to Canada. When the exchange of prisoners was made, one of the sons, Martin, came here to see if he could get some property, but he returned soon. He was killed in the next war [War of 1812].

John Kelly was married before he came to America. They had one child when they came from Ireland. I think they had eight children in all. They bought the farm where Thornton [Jane Ferguson's son] now lives. They lived there a number of years, and then went to Kentucky or some other western state. There we lost track of them.

Uncle Archie and his wife came over with Matthew Cannon and his wife [who was murdered by the Indians in the 1778 massacre]. Uncle settled on what is now the old McKillip place. Cannon settled in Middlefield, a few miles southwest. He was James's wife's grandfather.

Uncle John Kelly and wife, his father and mother and two sisters came later—his father and mother died as soon as they landed. Eleanor and Sarah were the girls that came with him. Sarah never married; she died at Ellen's.

My mother came next after Archie,—my father and mother; Aunt Jane; and Fannie, Mary, Robert, John and Jane [Jane Ferguson was three years old], their children, in the year 1768. We came to the place where Robert Young now lives. My father lived four years after he came there. James was born about two years before father died. He died June, 1772. The first winter we lived in an old house on John Young's farm—up by the spring, just back of the Cobble hill. We kept a cow, but no one could milk it but my mother. At that time there was no road through the woods. The only way to make a path was to cut the bark of the trees. Father went to the Corners one day for some hay for the cow, and when he started for home he missed the path and wandered on until he was tired, and then threw down the hay, but still kept on. Uncle Archie came over that day to see how we got along, and we told him that father had gone for hay. and had not come back yet. He went to the Corners and was told that he had started for home. He came back, and stayed with us that night, and in the morning the neighbours went out to look for him. They blew their horns, and at length he heard them and answered. He was in the hills in Middlefield at the head of the lake.

The next spring he built his house just where he laid down his hay, where Robert Young now lives. He bought his farm there —what they sold for 200 acres, when they came to measure it they had 600 acres. When we had lived there four years father and mother went to pay for their land. Mr. Lawyer, of Schoharie, was the owner.

When they were returning he went down into Bowman's creek to water his horse, and he felt a severe pain in his side; but they rode on. They turned up at the Drake place, and when they were on top of the hill he complained that he could not ride any longer. So she sat down and held the horses, and he laid his head in her lap and went to sleep. But the horses were hungry, and she could not hold them any longer, and she was afraid he would die before he could get home. She screamed, and he awoke, and asked, "What made you wake me? I was so happy." She helped him on his horse, and held him on, and led the horses home. He only lived two or three days after. There was no doctor nearer than Johnstown.

We lived there—that is, mother and six children of us—until spring; then we went to live on the Strickland lot, near Uncle Archie's. We lived there until our friends in Ireland heard of father's death, when they came. Uncle John Kelly lived with us, in our house, until he built himself one.

Soon after this the war commenced. We continued on the farm until Cherry Valley was burned. They had heard of the depredations of the Indians, and had been in the fort several times; during the summer they kept a scout out to apprise the people of the fort, and they were to fire an alarm gun for the people out around, and they were to rush for the fort. But in the fall, when they were not looking for the enemy, and nearly all of the people were out of the fort, the Indians came, and took the scouts prisoner, and came on to Cherry Valley early in the morning. They killed twelve in the house of Mr. Wells; some were his family, and some were officers. They lived where Phelons lie now. Mrs. Dunlop was killed while standing in the door; her daughter carried her out and laid her on the cider press, and covered her with her apron. Mr. Dunlop and daughter were taken prisoners. Mrs. Robert Wells was a daughter of Mr. Dunlop. He had another daughter married to Dr. Bullard, living near New York.

We stayed home until the next spring, when all the people were going to Schenectady. We buried all our iron, and took our other things with us. Uncle John's folks had a wagon that we carried them in. We drove several cows and four calves as far as Cherry Valley, as there was no grass yet. I suppose they starved. We walked down to the river [the Mohawk River, at Canajoharie] that day, and slept in an old house; and in the morning we went down and got up a boat and went down to Schenectady. We went into a small house there made of logs; but it was not comfortable for winter. Most of the people of Schenectady had farms around, and had houses on them where they went in summer to eat, or where their negroes lived whilst they were at work on the farms. We went into one of these in the fall. It was all boarded up, and a big Dutch chimney in it. They told us we might pick up the pine knots of the farm. We had one cow. That first summer we were there, a farmer over the river told us there was a piece of land he did not want to use; we might plant it, and we did, with potatoes and corn. In the fall the farmer wanted the land to sow winter grain on, and so we had to gather our grain before it was ripe. James and me rowed the boat across the river and carried it home, and boiled it and shelled it, and we had some beef; that was our living that winter, for our potatoes got froze. The next spring we moved over the river in a house that belonged to a Mr. Van Antwerp. We lived there whilst we stayed in Schenectady.

I was in Schenectady until peace was declared. I remember well the day the news was brought that Colonel Butler was killed. The Whigs all had their houses illuminated. The Tories would not light their's until they were threatened to be mobbed; and when the peace was declared they made a large bonfire of pine knots on the hill above Schenectady with an effigy of Arnold on top of it.

While we remained in Schenectady we were four miles from the town, and there were no schools or church nearer than the village. I never heard a sermon until I was seventeen, and that was in Cherry Valley. We had planted a piece of corn down there. In the summer we came up here [Springfield] to mother's farm, John and Archie McKillip, and brothers Robert and John, and me. They ploughed a large piece of land, and sowed it to wheat, and then returned to Schenectady, and stayed there until December 31st, when we started to come back here to prepare for moving up in the spring. The first day we came to Fort Hunter's creek. We stayed there all night, and New Year's day we came up to Bowman's creek. We had four cows and a colt to drive. Stayed all night there, and the next reached the house next to Uncle Archie's. We had cut hay there the summer before, but it had snowed all day, and the house was full of snow. I had to go in and clear up the snow, while Robert went to Mr. Wilson's after fire [live coals]. They made a shed of rails and put hay on, for the horses. We ate something that we had brought with us, and then laid down on a bunch of hay and slept.

They cut and drawed some wood, and then John returned to Schenectady for the rest of the family, and it stormed for four weeks so that he could not return. We were left alone, and none of the stoutest hearted.

In the meantime Uncle John Kelly had started, but the storm prevented them from travelling more than a mile or two in a day; and when I saw them coming down the hill, I was glad to see some one.

Before our folks came William Ferguson came, and his family. They had a babe six weeks old, and at one time there were

Jane Young Ferguson /281

twenty-two of us living in that house. We moved down to our house, which was a very poor one. Before we went to Schenectady we had prepared timber for a house, and when we were leaving we piled it all up in the old house; and, that summer we came up, the boys were burning logs near, and the grass took fire and conveyed the flames to the house, and it was burnt and all the timber. Then they went to work and built one of logs, but it was very uncomfortable, and all the summer the boys made shingles, and covered it in the fall; and we felt indeed quite happy that we had reached home again, and had a comfortable house; though the wheat we had sowed was winter-killed, and in the spring we had planted it with corn which the worms had eaten off. Yet we thought we had cause to be grateful.

Anna Rawle Clifford

* Laurel Hill, the Rawle's Pennsylvania country estate, stood imposingly above the east bank of the Schuylkill River, near Fairmount. The thirty-six acre landscape was lush with apple, peach, and cherry trees. In 1761, when Anna was age four, she frantically pressed against a windowpane, aware that her father —being carried in from the hills and rushed to Philadelphia— was fighting for his life. Spattered with cartridge powder and riddled with buckshot, Francis Rawle suffered an agonizing death after his hunting musket accidently discharged. His two younger children, William and Peggy, could not grasp the meaning of their father's absence.

Six years later, Anna's mother, Rebecca (Becky), married Samuel (Sammy) Shoemaker in a Quaker ceremony, and moved her children to Mulberry Street, later renamed Arch Street, in Philadelphia. Safely bundled in her bed at night, Anna could hear the city's watchmen as they vigilantly patrolled the streets, crying out the hour and what the weather was like. Occasionally their heavy footsteps and shouts warned of fires or of fleeing thieves. She felt safe knowing these watchmen were checking doors to assure their being locked.

Samuel Shoemaker, well launched on a political career, was quite wealthy. His real estate assets included: the Mulberry Street house between Front and Second streets; a wharf, office building, horse stable, and carriage house on the Delaware River waterfront; buildings on both Second and Fourth streets, which he rented; and a spacious mansion in Northern Liberties, north of the city. He had been a member of the Common Council for eleven years, before being chosen a Member of the Board of Aldermen. In addition, Shoemaker was commissioned a Justice of the Peace, served two terms as Mayor of the city, and was selected as a member of Pennsylvania's General Assembly. Yet he refused to take an active involvement in the struggle of the revolutionaries. He thought they would fail and held the Loyalist view that those who argued for independence had little property to lose by it, whereas the citizens who owned substantial real estate would suffer immeasurably.

When the British occupied Philadelphia in 1777, Shoemaker was appointed a Justice of the Peace. Because of this he was accused of high treason by the Pennsylvania Assembly in Lancaster, a body that authorized the confiscation of his estate by an act of March 6, 1778. In June, shortly before the evacuation of Philadelphia by British troops, Samuel and his stepson, William Rawle, escaped to New York with the British fleet.

A loud pounding reverberated through the Shoemaker home the morning of July 20 as the Commissioners of Forfeited Estates —Charles Willson Peale and his sidekicks—demanded entry. These agents listed every object in the house methodically and informed the family they would have to leave. When the Shoemaker's household possessions were removed and sold by the state, the three women moved across the street to the home of Rebecca's mother, Mrs. Edward Warner. Five percent of the proceeds went to the commissioners, the greater portion to the state treasury. The following year the state sold the mansion to Isaac Haines for £39,100, the wharf complex to Lacaze and Mallet for £149,000. Rebecca believed it futile to take legal action.

During May of 1779, Mrs. Shoemaker applied to the Supreme Executive Council for permission to go to New York. Her request was denied. In the spring of 1780, however, the Council was greatly alarmed over the contents of her dairy, which they had acquired. It was reported in Council that "Mrs. Shoemaker, wife of Samuel Shoemaker, has by letters of recommendation, and otherwise, assisted prisoners and others, enemies to this government, and to the United States, to pass clandestinely to New York." The Council resolved in session "that General Lacey, Doctor Gardner, and Mr. Whitehill, be a committee to meet tomorrow at eleven o'clock in the library room of the State house, and that Mrs. Shoemaker be notified thereof, that she may

attend the said committee, before farther proceedings are had."
At the conclusion of this investigation Mrs. Shoemaker was
granted a pass to New York, providing that she did not return
without obtaining permission from the Council. Anna and Peggy
remained with their grandmother.

The civilian government in New York had been abolished by
the British and replaced by a military faction. The British not
only confiscated unoccupied Patriot homes, but those belonging
to Loyalists as well, giving the owners little or no compensation.
Many of the city's families were forced to quarter officers. New
York was only about a square mile in size and, with thousands
of Loyalist refugees, the population had soared to 25,000. There
were far fewer dwellings than before the war: a quarter of the
city had been destroyed by fire in 1776, and sixty-four houses
had been leveled by another that broke out in 1778. Landlords
took advantage of the shortage by raising rents 400 percent over
prewar years. As a result, many of the poor were homeless, and
most of the middle and upper classes lived under crowded conditions.

The city's police force was so understaffed and inefficient that
citizens were afraid to walk the streets at night or mingle in
crowds by day. Thousands of idle British troops accounted for
an alarming rise in crime; accusations of robbery, drunkenness,
rape, and murder were frequently made at headquarters against
soldiers. Ewald Gustav Schaukirk, a Moravian pastor, wrote in
his diary that idle soldiers spread disease, resulting in the death
of citizens. Schaukirk found that soldiers' frustrations largely
stemmed from the belief "that the war might and would have
been ended before now, if it was not for the great men, who only
want to fill their purses; and indeed," the pastor reasoned, "it is
too apparent that this has been and is the ruling principle in all
departments, only to seek their private interest, and to make hay
while the sun shineth, and when they have got enough then to
retreat or go home—let become of America what will!"

Arriving in New York on June 20th, Becky Shoemaker's carriage took her past diversified stores, inns, churches, and fashion-

able homes lining Broad Way, to 18 Wall Street, where Sammy had rented a house. "Our rooms are good winter apartments," Becky wrote her children, "but being in a narrow street, and very low ceilings, they are extremely hot." Some relief from the scorching summer heat could be had by escaping to the cool breezes on Long Island or the upper part of Manhattan. New Yorkers were prohibited from traveling further. Along Manhattan's East River the Shoemakers could wade into cool water at low tide, where, in the fall, succulent oysters were found; along the North River (Hudson) they could bathe at a watering place established by British officers. On different days the sexes immersed themselves in fresh river water or in devices filled with saltwater. Hardly anyone dipped into the river at the populated lower end of the island, where inhabitants emptied slop buckets at the water's edge, and where, under the southernmost wharves, sewage pipes emptied untreated wastes. Merging with this ever-surfacing sewage was the large amount of human waste and garbage splashed from sailing vessels in the harbor.

Wood was becoming scarce. All of Manhattan's trees had been hacked down by the army for firewood; logs had to be brought over from Long Island and Staten Island. The severe winter of 1779–1780 reportedly caused the water between Staten Island and New York to freeze over, enabling horse-drawn sleighs, escorted by the British cavalry, to exchange food and clothing for wood. Long Islanders were allowed to cut their own timber except spruce, which was used for making beer, valuable in helping to prevent scurvy. This disease was common largely because people had to preserve meat by heavily salting it.

The Wall Street home, used by Samuel for business, had the hustling urgency of a coach station. His diversified responsibilities included supplying passes for citizens leaving the city, aiding newly arrived refugees, and examining intercepted Whig correspondance. A frequent visitor was William Franklin, president of the Associated Loyalists' board of directors, son of Benjamin Franklin, and the last Royal Governor of New Jersey.

Smuggling letters between Philadelphia and New York became increasingly more difficult. In 1780 Pennsylvania's Council resolved that "any person bringing from or carrying any letters to New York . . . unless inspected by some member of this board, or of the Continental Board of War, or Commissary of Prisoners, and such inspection endorsed on the outside of such letters, be proceeded against as offendors." Joseph Scott, who traveled frequently between the two cities, cleverly concealed the letters of Anna, Peggy, and Mrs. Shoemaker. Though he was rarely molested by the British because of his old age, frequent illness curtailed his visits. He died in 1781. Had the family's letters been seized, authorities would not have known who wrote them, for they were neither addressed nor signed, and code names were used when mentioning people. Each letter was numbered so that it could be referred to. The family also communicated by way of newspapers, which were allowed to be sent between the two cities. Messages were written in the margins, the newspapers carefully tied.

All three wrote prodigiously, though Mrs. Shoemaker thought she had little to say. "There is so little variety in our living that you will not be entertained by it. You will see that my conversation is chiefly with men, for the few acquaintances I have made live so distant that little more than a visit passes between us." Reading intercepted Whig letters afforded occasional amusement. "Some curious ones are among them," she wrote. "There are two from a widow lady now in Philadelphia—one of the Carolina exiles—to her very particular friend in Boston, who, she says, has never been one moment out of her mind since they parted, which is eight months. She wrote in a very pretty hand indeed. She will not believe he is unfaithful till she has it from under his own hand. Another from an officer now in Virginia who tells his friend that they have not a pair of shoes in the company, and many neither shirt nor coat. I find these people have been led to believe that an attack would be made upon New York; but none of them think it will succeed."

In the autumn of 1780 the British flagship *Sandwich,* commanded by the crusty Admiral George Rodney, was anchored in the New York Harbor. The supercilious admiral, who rarely listened to the advice of his captains—he once said, "I require obedience only, I don't want advice"—lived onshore. The Shoemakers visited the ship. "We went the other day, to gratify our curiosity, onboard the *Sandwich* of 90 guns, Admiral Rodney's ship. And when I tell you we were there at the time of the salute (on account of the King's accession) you will be surprised. But we did not know till we were onboard that it was so, and it was then too late to come onshore before it began, which was at one o'clock. The *Sandwich* fired 21 guns, and it was returned by every ship of war in the harbour. One can have no idea of the prodigious size of everything onboard, the conveniences, the number of people and length of the ship appear like a crowded street. There is 800 men belonging to her."

Meanwhile, in Philadelphia government officials continued to harass people they considered dangerous. Anna and Peggy frequently sought refuge in the home of their mother's sister, Elizabeth Shoemaker. In June of 1780 the militia broke into Elizabeth's house while the two sisters were packing to leave. "I was frightened," Anna wrote her mother, "and was going down to my aunt and sister, when at the foot of the stairs I observed a man rattling the lock of his gun, as if trying to alarm. I ran up again, and in a few minutes two men entered the room and I soon found their business was to search for arms. They looked in the closet, and desired me, not in the mildest terms, to unlock my trunks. I told them they were already undone. They then put their canes in and by the greatest good luck in the world, the little plate that belongs to me remained undisturbed at the bottom of the trunk. Not finding arms, they went away. They treated my aunt in the same manner, rummaging the closets and drawers and placing a guard at the stairs. One of them said it was to find guns. There was but one or two houses where they treated people with so little ceremony; at other places they took their word."

The whole business of patriotism irritated Anna. She found the women who went from door to door soliciting funds for Washington's troops to be repugnant. She told her mother that the day after she left for New York Benjamin Franklin's daughter (Sarah Bache) and other women rapped on Mrs. Warner's front door. Sarah left suddenly before it was opened. "The reason she gave to a person who told me," wrote Anna, "was that she did not chuse to face Mrs. Shoemaker or her daughters." Women collecting money "were so importunate that people were obliged to give them something to get rid of them." They "paraded about the streets in this manner, some carrying ink stands; nor did they let the meanest ale house escape. The gentlemen were also honoured with their visits. Bob Wharton declares he was never so teased in his life. They reminded him of the extreme rudeness of refusing anything to the fair sex; but he was inexorable and pleaded want of money, and the heavy taxes, so at length they left him, after threatening to hand his name down to posterity with infamy."

Nor did controversial social figures escape her opinionated mind. Nancy Willing "might be set for the queen of beauty, and is lately married to William Bingham, who returned from the West Indies with an immense fortune. They have set out in highest style; nobody here will be able to make the figure they do—equipage, home, clothes, are all in the newest taste,—and yet some people wonder at the match. She but sixteen and such a perfect form. His appearance is less amiable, and the greatest part of his wealth acquired by the sale of some Guinea negroes in the West Indies, that he bought at a low rate. Many would feel disagreeable sensations in using riches gained in that manner, but everybody's conscience is not equally tender alike."

Peggy Arnold was the wife of General Benedict Arnold, who became a turncoat while commanding West Point. When his plot to hand West Point over to the British failed Arnold fled to New York City, leaving his wife and infant son to fend for themselves. Returning to her father, Edward Shippen in Philadelphia, Peggy faced an Executive Council order to leave Pennsylvania within fourteen days. Anna wrote: "they tell strange stories here of her, and strive to blacken her character in a way which her uncommon affection for the general renders improbable." *

February 24, 1781: I sat upstairs. We have a fire here two or three times a week. The chimney is so little that the wood was forced to be cut small enough for a stove, which makes it last longer. Here we sit, sometimes reading or writing, and often talking of New York and of thee, my dearest mother. But today we had an unusual and most pleasing amusement, that of receiving thy diary and letter No. 12. I cannot express the pleasure such a packet gives me; yet, like everything else in the world it has its alloy. That we do not write often is not owing to negligence. Compared to you, "we tread obscurity's sequestered vale," and seldom hear of travellers going backwards and forwards.

Feb. 27: I amuse myself in the evening with Rochefoucault's moral maxims. I had never read them before and was much surprised at the author's opinion of mankind. He attributes every virtue to the influence of some means of selfish motive, and yet, tho' his censures are too general, it must be allowed that he is well acquainted with the human heart, and many of his reflections the unhappy will acknowledge to be just.

March 19: Some people begin to think it probable that the British will be here in the fall. How delightful such a possibility! To see our dear family return to their friends, to their home, and to see them again take possession of what they have been so unjustly deprived, will be the most charming thing imaginable.

March 21: The yearly meeting is just at hand again. How very fast time slips away! I am astonished when I recollect how many months are passed since thee left Philadelphia. Yet I do not regret their flight, for it is not in times like these that one wishes to slacken its pace.

March 22: Upon coming home we had the pleasure of seeing a few lines written by Daddy of 17th of this month, with the agreeable account of your all being well, and that you have not any thoughts of going to England. Very agreeable indeed. I spent the afternoon at my needle. A good deal of talk about what the British have been doing in Virginia. Several families, it seems, have met with considerable loss in their property, but in this destructive war people must expect to suffer on both sides.

March 31: Reading French this morning. We have got into Telamachus, which is more interesting than the little Fables we were reading before.

April 3: Anna and I came upstairs where we amused ourselves in looking over the magazines from New York which Benjamin Shoemaker had brought down in the morning. And here my dear Mammy I resign the pen to Anna for some time between us. We will carry on a journal since tis thy request. I ought to blush at the contrast between thine, and this scrawl of mine. Indeed, I am ashamed of the writing blunders, and other faults, but yet do not improve.

April 14: I spent the forepart of the day reading; writing to thee in the afternoon. In the evening we took our packet up Market Street, sat an hour with them, and returning called at friend Galloway's (met Owen Jones and his wife there). She was more cheerful than I expected to see her, yet very anxious to hear from England. It is ten months since she has had a letter from her husband or daughter.

April 30: Sitting in the parlour at work this morning. Sam Sansom [their tutor] came in soon after dinner. He wants us to continue a little longer at French, but we have given up three months of our time to it already, and it is as much as I can spare. The little knowledge I have of the language I shall endeavour not to forget, and all my leisure hours devote to improving myself in it, by looking in the grammars, of which we have several, and reading such French books as I can procure from the library and other places.

May 4: Continental money is entirely over—at least it goes for nothing but taxes. Some ill-applied remedies from council, it is thought, has occasioned its hasty exit. They say the sailors are dressing up dogs with it and sending them about the streets. It is not so merry an incident with many people; they are provoked instead of being diverted at it.

May 16: Sally Wister came this morning to speak to Caty Neal; she sat an hour here. She was talking of the ball on board the French frigate. Of the ladies they say Nancy Bingham made the

Anna Rawle Clifford /291

most elegant figure, dressed in a suit of black velvet. However, as there must be censurers, it was thought a great impropriety for her to go into so much company when her mother had been dead but three months.

May 17: Samuel Mifflin [a Quaker, and militia artillery colonel] was buried this morning in Friends' burial ground. I thought it was inconsistent to have minute guns firing during the time he was interred. His unfortunate daughter is again the subject of conversation to the town, in a way extremely disgraceful to her reputation; she is either the most injured of women, or the most indiscreet.

September 21: A great many people expect the English here very soon. I heard this afternoon that all the public papers [political documents] were packed up, and that the Whigs were exceedingly frightened. Oh how I wish they would come, and my friends with them! Sure nothing in this world could happen more delightful than such an event as that. Yet some folks think their only business here will be to burn the town, but it's not all probable. A very good Tory said lately he "would take a thousand pounds for his estate" if they came, and he has a very large one.

Sept. 25: At [Friends] meeting. It was a meeting of business. There is a very singular character in town, a Phoebe Smedley, who wears no borders to her caps, nor don't chuse to sleep on a bed, and many other particularities unheard of till now amongst Friends, and very much like the austerities we have been told the Roman Catholics practice. I saw her at meeting today; the manner in which she was dressed made her look very odd, especially about the head.

Sept. 28: The English are coming again and the militia ordered out in a great hurry. These reports are so frequent that it's happy for people they are seldom believed, or many would be sadly disappointed often.

Sept. 29: Becky Fisher was mentioning several things relating to Nancy Emlen. She approves and admires all of what Phoebe Smedley does, it seems, and when she's in town lodges with

Smedley on the floor. They neither of them eat meat, sugar, tea, nor coffee. Nancy's cap is made like her friend's, without a border. This yearly meeting Smedley has applied for a certificate into the country, where she intends to reside. She told the women Friends in meeting that "it appeared odd to them, no doubt, that she should wish to leave so kind and affectionate a mother, but that it appeared to her to be the will of Providence, and she was not free to live here, where taxes were paid." Most people think she carries the matter too far. I have not related half the singularities I have heard of Nancy and Phoebe. Were I to, thee'd think them incredible.

October 6: Two or three uncles called in before dinner. I had the pleasure of receiving thy letter No. 13, newspapers, and book. In the afternoon, writing to thee till 5 o'clock, when I took a walk to friend Galloway's and delivered thy message to her, with which she was much pleased, and desired to be affectionately remembered to thee.

Oct. 16: A great deal of preaching today at meeting; it broke up, however, at a little after eleven, and I called at Caty Hopkin's. From there I went to the shoemaker's; they make one pay three dollars for a pair of common worsted shoes—an extravagant price.

Oct. 19: This morning Juliet, Hannah Fox, her brother, J. Fisher, Peggy and myself took a walk to the glass house, and after staying some time to look at the workman, returned to dinner. The girls brought some singing glasses from the furnace, but broke two of them by the way, for they are so extremely thin that they require the utmost care in handling.

Oct. 21: Uncle Howell, Betsy and Debby Foulke were here after morning meeting. The girls had been to see Judah's family (Jews that were neighbors to them) who are in affliction for the death of their father. There is twelve children, and all of his estate is in New York. A number of elderly people have died lately, more than common.

Oct. 22: The first thing I heard this morning was that Lord Cornwallis had surrendered to the French and Americans [Battle of

Yorktown in Virginia]—intelligence as surprising as vexatious. People who are so stupidly regardless of their own interests are undeserving of compassion, but one cannot help lamenting that the fate of so many worthy persons should be connected with the failure or success of the British army. Uncle Howell came in soon after breakfast, and tho' he is neither Whig nor Tory, looked as if he had sat up all night. He was glad to see all here so cheerful, he said. When he was gone Ben Shoemaker arrived; he was told it as he came along, and was astonished. However, as there is no letter from Washington, we flatter ourselves that it is not true. Nancy Coxe was buried this afternoon; she died very suddenly. Thursday night she danced at Betsy Allen's ball; at noon the next day she went to her Cousin Bird's, where she was taken with a fainting fit, and died yesterday at 5 o'clock. It is usual to bestow encomiums on the dead, whether they deserve it or not, but it is certain she was a very fine girl.

Oct. 24: I feel in a most unsettled humour. I can neither read, work or give my attention one moment to anything. It is too true that Cornwallis is taken. Tilghman is just arrived with dispatches from Washington which confirm it. Ben Shoemaker came here and showed us some papers; long conversations we often have together on the melancholy situation of things.

Oct. 25: I suppose, dear Mammy, thee would not have imagined this house to be illuminated last night, but it was. [Candles illuminating windows were a sign that one supported the Revolution.] A mob surrounded it, broke the shutters and the glass of the windows, and were coming in, none but forlorn women here. We for a time listened to their attacks in fear and trembling till, finding them grow more loud and violent, not knowing what to do, we ran into the yard. Warm Whigs of one side, and James Hartley's of the other (who were treated even worse than we), rendered it impossible for us to escape that way. We had not been there many minutes before we were drove back by the sight of two men climbing the fence. We thought the mob were coming in thro' there, but it proved to be Coburn and Bob Shewell, who called to us not to be frightened, and fixed lights up at the windows, which pacified the mob, and after three huzzas they moved off. A number of men came in afterwards to see us. French and J.B. nailed boards up at the broken panels, or it would not have been safe to have gone to bed. Coburn and Shewell were really very kind; had it not been for them I really believe the house would have been torn down. Even the firm Uncle Fisher was obliged to submit to have his windows illuminated, for they had pickaxes and iron bars with which they had done considerable injury to his house, and would soon have demolished it had not some of the Hodges [merchants] and other people got in back and acted as they pleased. All uncle's sons were out, but Sammy, and if they had been at home it was in vain to oppose them. In short, it was the most alarming scene I ever remember. For two hours we had the disagreeable noise of stones banging about, glass crashing, and the tumultuous voices of a large body of men as they were a long time at the different houses in the neighbourhood. At last they were victorious, and it was one general illumination throughout the town. As we had not the pleasure of seeing any of the gentlemen in the house, nor the furniture cut up, and goods stolen, nor been beat, nor pistols pointed at our breasts, we may count our sufferings slight compared to many others. Mr. Gibbs was obliged to make his escape over a fence, and while his wife was endeavouring to shield him from the rage of one of the men, she received a violent bruise in the breast, and a low blow in the face which made her nose bleed. Ben Shoemaker was here this morning; tho' exceedingly threatened he says he came off with the loss of four panes of glass. Some Whig friends put candles in the windows, which made his peace with the mob, and they retired. John Drinker has lost half the goods out of his shop and been beat by them; in short, the sufferings of those they please to style Tories would fill a volume, and shake the credulity of those who were not here on that memorable night, and today Philadelphia makes an uncommon appearance, which ought to cover the Whigs with eternal confusion. A Neighbour of ours had the effrontry to tell Mrs. Gibbs that he was sorry for her furniture, but not for her

During the early hours of October 22, 1781, a night watchman of Philadelphia cried out "Basht dree o'clock, und Cornwal-lis isht da-ken!!" spreading the news of the British surrender at Yorktown.

Illumination.

COLONEL TILGHMAN, Aid de Camp to his Excellency General WASHINGTON, having brought official acounts of the SURRENDER of Lord Cornwallis, and the Garrifons of York and Gloucefter, thofe Citizens who chufe to ILLUMINATE on the GLORIOUS OCCASION, will do it this evening at Six, and extinguifh their lights at Nine o'clock.

Decorum and harmony are earneftly recommended to every Citizen, and a general difcountenance to the leaft appearance of riot.

October 24, 1781.

Two days later, a broadside inspired Patriots to light candles in their windows. The Rawles, living on a street resembling William Birch's engraving "High Street, from Ninth Street," saw no reason to celebrate.

Anna Rawle Clifford / 297

windows—a ridiculous distinction that many of them make. J. Head has nothing left in his parlour. Uncle Penington lost a good deal of window glass. Aunt Burge preserved hers thro' the care of some of her neighbours. The Drinkers and Walns make heavy complaints of the Carolinians in their neighbourhood. Waln's pickles were thrown about the streets, and barrels of sugar stolen. Grandmammy was the most composed of anybody here. Was I not sure, my dearest Mother, that you would have very exaggerated accounts of this affair from others, and would probably be uneasy for the fate of our friends, I would be entirely silent about it; but, as you will hear it from someone or another, not mentioning it will seem as if we had suffered exceedingly, and I hope I may depend on the safety of this opportunity. People did nothing today but condole and enquire into each other's honourable losses. Amongst a great variety who were here was Aunt Rawle. Next to her sister's, this was the family, she said, whom she felt most interested for. Her visit was quite unexpected. Uncle and Aunt Howell [Becky's sister] went from here to Edgely [their country estate] this morning. Aunt Betsy came to tea. Becky Fisher and her brother came in the evening. *Oct. 26*: Neighbor Waln and Ben Shoemaker were here in the afternoon. Juliet, Polly Foulke, and James Fisher came to see us in the evening; the conversation as usual on the late disturbances. It seems universally agreed that Philadelphia will no longer be that happy asylum for the Quakers that it once was. Those joyful days when all was prosperity and peace are gone, never to return; and perhaps it is as necessary for our society [Society of Friends] to ask for terms as it was for Cornwallis. Juliet says all Uncle Penington's fine pictures are broken; his parlour was full of men, but it was nothing, he said, to Nancy's illness, who was for an hour or two out of her senses and terrified them exceedingly.

* Anna dreaded that her mother and stepfather would have to sail for England. When Becky Shoemaker heard details of the battle of Yorktown from released prisoners she wrote angrily in her diary: "What a fine army to be sacrificed, without a single

effort to relieve them!" Many people in New York refused to believe the defeat. The depressing news, added to acute food shortages, cast a shroud of gloom over the city. Food prices had more than tripled since 1775, and most of the food being shipped from Europe arrived spoiled. Large numbers of barrels and crates, filled with moldy food, had to be dumped into the Atlantic.

The war was virtually over and disillusioned Loyalists were quickly buying all available space on vessels. The Shoemakers, apprehensive of their own safety, cheerfully saw many friends off who took passage with convoys of evacuating British troops. Peggy and Benedict Arnold paid the Shoemakers a farewell visit prior to their own voyage on December 15th. Lord Cornwallis, his suite, and General Arnold were to sail in the *Robuste;* Peggy Arnold and her family in a private ship "more agreeable for her," Becky wrote, "than a man-of-war, yet not safe for him. They gave for the cabin 300 guineas, and then look in what company they chose—chiefly military I believe. I do not hear of any females but her maids." It must have been a stormy, bitterly cold passage. Anna wrote that without a doubt the Arnolds "will attract attention in England, for all who are related to the general excite curiosity—I should not like a winter passage; in the finest seasons we have heard of a number of fatal accidents on the water and to embark in the months when tempestuous weather naturally happens seems delivering oneself to certain destruction."

In New York the winter's first snowstorm in January brought giggles and laughter from the Shoemakers' small son Edward. Carefully bundled, the boy was whisked through the streets in a horsedrawn sleigh. A Grand Ball honoring the Queen's birthday occasioned many women to brave snowdrifts for shops, where they selected imported silk gowns, bonnets, and fans. Prince William Henry, son of George III and later William IV, was the occasion's honored guest. At headquarters on the night of January 17 the musicians were richly frocked in red velvet, elegant lace, and finely powdered wigs; candles flickered from chandeliers and candelabrum. Most prominent among the dances was the minuet; its stately, measured steps required the utmost control and grace. "It was settled," wrote Becky, "that the Prince should dance two minuets, but they must be with married ladies, and the first in rank must be complimented. The two first were B. Elliott and Friend Smith. The latter had not danced in public for twenty years. They both declined. Some other ladies next in course *could not dance minuets.* He danced the first with the wife of Captain Douglass of the Navy, lately married, a pretty woman about 30. The second minuet with Sally Coxe—the first time she was ever at headquarters." Sally, nine months pregnant, gave birth to her child the following day, a few days before a snow blizzard buried much of the city.

In February the Rawles' Laurel Hill estate was sold by the Pennsylvania Council, an action the state justified on the grounds that Mr. Shoemaker had acquired control of the property when he married Rebecca Rawle. Prior to 1782 the Council president, Joseph Reed, used Laurel Hill as his summer residence, Grace Galloway's confiscated house in Philadelphia for the winters. Anna penned a letter to her mother in September 1780 that Mrs. Reed "can never spend another summer at Laurel Hill. Her pleasure there had a melancholy and short termination. She is dead, and of a disorder that made some people whisper about 'that she eat too many of Mr. Shoemaker's peaches,' her husband fainted at the grave." The estate was sold to Major James Parr, who leased it to the Chevalier de la Luzerne, Minister of France, for five years.

The Council allowed Becky to return to Philadelphia, where she remained until a few months before the Treaty of Paris was signed in 1783. The treaty's seventh article provided that "his Britannic Majesty shall with all convenient speed . . . withdraw all his armies, garrisons and fleets from the said United States, and from every post, place and harbour within the same." It was now certain that Samuel would have to go, and soon, to England; without British protection he would be arrested. The city's inhabitants were in a state of confusion and turmoil. Twenty-nine thousand Loyalists, from New York and neighboring states, sailed that year from the New York Harbor, leaving the city with a population of about ten thousand. On the 19th of November Becky remained on the wharf as her husband, clutching little Edward, stood near the railing of a vessel that was disappearing toward the horizon. A few hours after the last British convoy sailed on the 25th General Washington's troops took possession of the city. Three nights later New Yorkers felt a slight shock of an earthquake, becoming more violent toward morning, arousing people from their beds—an event Becky narrowly missed by taking a coach to Philadelphia.

Anna, unaware that her mother would be returning, had married John Clifford, a merchant. The average life span in Philadelphia was forty-five; Anna, at the age of twenty-five, took small pleasure in being called a "spinster," though she relished her individuality and privacy. "I used to say if I ever married I hoped my spouse and I would not be forever together, and I have my wish, for we never are but at meals and in the evening, so that I have plenty of time for contemplation on the duties of the slate. He is constantly engaged at the store and with his vessel that he cannot possibly be much with me." She bore four children, three girls and a boy. All except a daughter, who she had named after her mother, died in childhood.

Anna's brother William Rawle had returned from London, where he had studied law. As soon as he was admitted as a lawyer to the courts of Philadelphia, William brought suit, in his mother's behalf, against the state for the return of Laurel Hill. Though the French Minister's lease had not expired, insufficient funding from his government caused his return to France. Rawle won his case in court, though Becky had to pay the Minister the yearly rent of one hundred pounds for the remaining three years of his lease.

Meanwhile, in England Samuel Shoemaker was gallivanting among London society with his boyhood friend, Benjamin West. The famous painter introduced him to King George III and the Queen. Having spoken to the royal couple for nearly an hour, Sammy wrote in his diary: "I cannot say but I wished some of

Anna Rawle Clifford /301

my violent countrymen could have such an opportunity as I have had. I think they would be convinced that George the third has not one grain of tyranny in his composition, and that he *is not,* he *cannot* be that bloody minded man they have so repeatedly and so illiberally called him. It is impossible; a man of his fine feelings, so good a husband, so kind a father, *cannot be a tyrant."*

Samuel and Edward returned to America in April 1786; the family met them in Burlington, New Jersey. The three Rawle children had families of their own, and Burlington, with its numerous pacifist population, was the safest place for Becky, Sammy, and Edward to live until the animosity against Mr. Shoemaker had cooled. They then returned to live in Philadelphia. Sammy died in 1800, Becky followed in 1819. John Clifford died in 1821, Anna in July 1828, at the age of seventy. ✳

Deborah Sampson Gannett

Boston, August 1, 1786

These may certify that Robert Shurtleff was a soldier in my regiment in the Continental Army, for the town of Uxbridge in the Commonwealth of Massachusetts, and was enlisted for the term of three years; that he had the confidence of his officers, did his duty as a faithful and good soldier, and was honorably discharged the army of the United States.

*Henry Jackson, late Colonel
in the American Army*

✳ State archives have preserved many such affidavits. This one would have been overlooked were it not for the fact that Robert Shurtleff was a woman. Although Deborah Sampson's journal sank to the bottom of the North River (Hudson) in 1783, following the Revolution she helped Herman Mann revise his biography of her, *The Female Review.* The original, she believed, contained many inaccuracies. Excerpts from the revised version are included here.

Deborah's early years were very disturbing. Shortly after her birth in the rustic village of Plympton, near Plymouth, Massachusetts, on December 17, 1760, her father deserted the family. Four of her ancestors were famous seventeenth-century Pilgrims: her father, Jonathan, being descended from John Alden, Miles Standish, and Peter Hobart, her mother, Deborah Bradford Sampson, from Governor William Bradford. Yet Jonathan was so impoverished that he abandoned his wife and six children and went to sea. No one heard from him again, but his wife was later told that he had perished in a shipwreck. When Deborah was five, her mother could no longer nourish and clothe her children, and rather than see them suffer she chose to have them cared for in various households. Deborah was adopted by an elderly woman, a distant relative, who died three years later. A pastor's widow then looked after the eight year old child; unsuccessfully, however, for two years later Deborah was bound out as a servant to the family of Benjamin Thomas, a God fearing deacon and farmer at Middleborough.

In the affluent families of Boston girls were required to cultivate inhibiting social graces. Charm, piety, a delicate self-effacement, and a subordinate attitude toward men were characteristics essential in the development of "young ladies." Scattered on bookshelves were well used volumes of *The Dancing Master, Rules of Civility,* and *The Young Gentleman and Lady's Private Tutor.* Unfettered by such codes of behavior, Deborah developed a peasant-like awareness of her own strength and individuality, an identification with nature, and a strong will. She plowed fields, spread manure fertilizer, milked cows, slashed and stacked hay, fed farm animals, and became skilled in carpentry. She challenged the prevailing Puritan attitudes that a good farm woman never strayed far from the kitchen and that a girl didn't have to be educated. Most New England farmers felt that children should spend their youth laboring at farm work, that nothing was gained by booklearning. The deacon, however, not only allowed his boys hours in the schoolroom, he also let Deborah tag along with them. Younger than the Thomas sons, she devoured everything taught and bullied the boys into teaching her everything they knew. When the war broke out she borrowed newspapers, reading weekly accounts of political and military events, and pestered out-of-towners for additional news.

In 1778, at the age of eighteen, Deborah was legally free from servitude with the Thomas family, though she remained with them a while, doing some of her usual chores, raising her own chickens and sheep, and selling cloth she had spun and woven. She also taught children at the Middleborough school, where she rejected the traditional emphasis upon boys' education over that of girls.

Tired of farm drudgery at the age of twenty, Deborah craved an adventurous life elsewhere. Yet as a woman traveling alone she incurred the risk of being molested and the certainty of being treated as a whore in such pleasurable places as coffee houses and taverns. She, therefore, in a secluded place on the farm, tailored a man's coat, waistcoat, and breeches from cloth she had woven. Having compressed her breasts with a cotton strip, and tied her hair back in male fashion, Deborah made forays into distant towns and rakish taverns. Such excursions were curtailed by a meagre income.

During the winter of 1781–1782 the American Army needed recruits desperately. Of 37,000 men asked for by Congress early in 1781 only 8,000 had volunteered. Few men desired to leave jobs knowing there was little guarantee they would be paid as soldiers. And though cash bounties were offered, it was not uncommon in some areas of New England for men to enlist for a bounty, desert, and sign up elsewhere for a second one. Newspapers were sprinkled with notices for the apprehension of deserters.

In the spring of 1782 Deborah spent a few days with the family of Captain Benjamin Leonard. She shared a bed with Jennie, a black servant, who one afternoon helped her take male attire from the closet of Leonard's son. Slipping out of the home in male garb Deborah walked to the local recruiting office in Israel Wood's house. Enlisting under the assumed name of Timothy Thayer, she pocketed the bounty and strode into a tavern two miles east of Middleborough. There, fuddled in liquor, she behaved raucously. After dusk, when the crickets were churring, frogs croaking, she sneaked back into the Leonard house, and climbed into bed with Jennie. As might be expected, Timothy Thayer failed to appear at regimental roll call. An elderly woman who had been sitting near the fire, carding wool while Thayer was signing up, "whiddled the scrap" (revealed the villainous scheme) by telling authorities the young recruit had the same peculiar way of holding a quill that Deborah Sampson had. Due to an accident, she was unable to use her forefinger properly. Officials descended upon the Thomas farm and forced Deborah to relinquish that part of the bounty not spent at the tavern, with a warning that if she ever came near the recruiting office again she would be punished severely. The town gossiped; worried friends and relatives thought the matter might soon be forgotten if she were married and contained within a home. She disliked the man her mother chose for her: "I did not, in this vernal season of raptures and despairs, escape the addresses of a young man, of whom my mother, I believe, was passionately fond, and seemed struck with wonder that I was not. She considered him regenerated. I had not her eyes to see such perfection in this lump of a man, or that he possessed qualities that would regenerate *me*. I had no aversion to him at first, and certainly no love, if I have ever understood that noble passion. At any rate, this marry, or not to marry, was decided thus: On a certain parade day he came to me, with all the 'sang-froid' of a Frenchman, and the silliness of a baboon, intoxicated, not with *love*, but with *rum*. From that moment I set him down a fool, or in a fair way to be one."

Bolting to Bellingham on May 20, 1782, dressed in men's clothing, Deborah found an agent who, in return for part of her bounty, would sign her up for enlistment in Uxbridge. Using her brother's name, Robert Shurtleff, she was mustered in at Worcester on the 23rd, to serve as a private for three years in the 4th Massachusetts Regiment—commanded by Colonel Shepard, later by Colonel Henry Jackson. Her company commander was Captain George Webb. The Massachusetts State Archives possesses a "receipt dated Worcester, May 23, 1782 for the bounty paid said Shurtleff by Noah Taft, Chairman of Class No. 2 of the town of Uxbridge, to serve in the Continental Army for the term of 3 years." From Worcester the fresh recruits marched for about ten days to West Point, New York. On a chilly, drizzling day along the way Sampson fainted before a roaring fire in a roadside tavern. When she became conscious she found herself in the arms of a woman who kept insisting the young soldier sleep in a comfortable bed with her husband.

Following their arrival at the Military Fortress at West Point, the raw recruits lined up for French muskets, knapsacks, cartridge boxes, cartridges, and infantry uniforms. Sampson, a member of the 1st Brigade, was issued a blue coat lined with white, white waistcoat, breeches and stockings, and black garters, cocked hat, and boots. The hat had a cockade on one side, a plume tipped with red on the other. The soldiers were paced through a military drill each morning, parading at 4 P.M. each afternoon.

Not having plumbing facilities, men cleansed themselves with basin water, took barrel baths, or plunged into the North River (Hudson). Regimental outhouses, or latrines, contained long, raised planks, each having a series of round holes, through which cupfuls of lime were frequently tossed. The scarcity of candles necessitated groping by moonlight or using the facilities by day. Sampson preferred the dark hours for changing clothes and trips to the latrine.

By the summer of 1782 the war was almost over. General Cornwallis had been defeated at Yorktown the year before, and the British Army was restrained to an area in and around New York City. Yet despite a truce between the two armies, heated passions were such that clashes often occurred between scouting parties. Early in June, Deborah was included in a detachment sent southward to spy on British movement. Crossing the river at Stony Point they marched over trails to Tarrytown, a neutral area between American and British lines. The following morning the soldiers split into two groups to cover a wider expansion of territory, before reuniting at Haerlem, within British lines. The soldiers then pulled back to White Plains after cautiously noting enemy troop positions. British dragoons and Loyalists opened fire between Sing Sing and Tarrytown on June 26. When Loyalist reinforcements arrived the enemy fire was so thick the Continental troops, fearing annihilation, retreated to a heavily wooded area. A fresh contingent of Continentals appeared and the enemy fled.

Later in June, Sampson and thirty other soldiers volunteered at the Point to flush out armed Tories in East Chester. Early one morning, while it was still dark and they were encamped at a place called Vonhoite, guard pickets sounded the alarm at the approach of a group of mounted, armed men. Silence was shattered by a barrage of gunfire. When the air cleared, several Tories and one Continental soldier had died. Deborah Sampson was among the wounded. "I considered this as a death wound, or as being equivalent to it; as it must, I thought, lead to the discovery of my sex. Covered with blood from head to foot, I told my companions I fear I had received a mortal wound; and I begged them to leave me to die on the spot: preferring to take the small chance I should in this case have of surviving, rather than to be carried to the hospital. To this my comrades would not consent; but one of them took me before him on his horse, and in this painful manner I was borne six miles to the hospital of the French army, at a place called Crompond. On coming in sight of the hospital, my heart again failed me. In a paroxysm of despair, I actually drew a pistol from the holster, and was about to put an end to my life. That I did not proceed to the fatal act, I can ascribe only to the interposition of Divine Mercy.

"The French surgeon, on my being brought in, instantly came. He was alert, cheerful, humane. 'How you lose so much blood at this early hour? Be any bone broken?' was his first salutation; presenting me and the other wounded men of our party with two bottles of choice wine. My head having been bound up, and a change of clothing becoming a wounded soldier being ready, I was asked by the too inquisitive French surgeon whether I had any other wound. He had observed my extreme paleness, and that I limped in attempting to walk. I readily replied in the negative: it was a plump falsehood! 'Sit you down my lad; your boot say you fib!' said the surgeon, noticing that the blood still oozed from it. He took off my boots and stockings with his own hands with great tenderness, and washed my leg to the knee. I then told him I would retire, change my clothing, and if any other wound should appear, I would inform him.

"Meanwhile I had procured in the hospital a silver probe a little curved at the end, a needle, some lint, a bandage, and some of the same kind of salve that had been applied to the wound in my head. I found that the ball had penetrated my thigh about two inches, and the wound was still moderately bleeding. The wine had revived me, and God, by his kind care, watched over me. At the third attempt I extracted the ball.

"This operation over, the blood was staunched, and my regimentals, stiff enough to stand alone, had been exchanged for a loose, thin wrapper, when I was again visited by the surgeon. In his watchful eye I plainly read doubts. I told him that all was well; that I felt much revived, and wished to sleep. I had slept scarcely an hour, when he again alarmed me. Approaching me on my mattress of straw, and holding my breeches in his hand, dripping from the washtub, 'How came this rent?' said he, putting his finger into it. I replied, 'It was occasioned, I believe, on horseback, by a nail in the saddle or holster. 'Tis of no consequence. Sleep refreshes me. I had none last night.' One half of this, certainly, was true. But I had less dread of receiving half a dozen more balls than the penetrating glance of his eye. As I grew better his scrutiny diminished.

"Before the wound in my thigh was half healed, I rejoined the army on the lines. But had the most hardy soldier been in the condition I was when I left the hospital, he would have been excused from military duty."

Meanwhile, back in Middleborough the First Baptist Church had severed Deborah's membership. Having discussed among themselves her "unchristian like" behavior, clergymen wrote in the Church Record: "The Church considered the case of Deborah Sampson, a member of this Church, who last spring was accused of dressing in men's clothes, and enlisting as a soldier in the army [Timothy Thayer affair], and although she was not convicted, yet was strongly suspected of being guilty, and for some time before behaved very loose and unchristian like, and at last left our parts in a sudden manner, and it is not known among us where she is gone, and after considerable discourse, it appeared that as several brethern had laboured with her before she went away, without obtaining satisfaction, concluded it is the Church's duty to withdraw fellowship until she returns and makes Christian satisfaction."

While Washington's Northern Department of the Continental Army was encamped at New Windsor Cantonment, near West Point, a large detachment was sent north from there to stop Indian incursions against settlements. Sampson marched northward with the troops, along the North River to Fort Edward, where they pushed onward through a snow blizzard. "We came upon the Indians unexpectedly, at the distance of a pistol shot; and our first fire dealt terrible destruction among them. Raising their horrid war whoop, they returned our fire. Three of our party were wounded, but not mortally. Fifteen of the Indians were slain, and many more were wounded. Numbers of the enemy eluded our shots, and made their escape into the woods. Observing one man, light of foot, entering the forest, I happened to be foremost in pursuit of him. I had scarcely come up with him, when he cried for quarter. My first impulse was to bayonet him; but an instant sympathy turned away the pointed steel. My next thought was that his imperfect Indian dialect was counterfeit. Thrusting my hand into his bosom, and making a wide rent in his inner garment, I discovered that he was the child of white parents, while his face, and his heart too, were as black as those of any savage.

"The shades of evening were now settling down about us. Returning with our captive white Indian to the general slaughter ground, a scene of indescribable horror presented itself to our view. The flames had levelled the house [of the supposed white Indian] nearly to the earth. The mother lay dead and horribly mangled a few feet from the threshold. Two children were hung by their heels upon a tree. A fine little girl was discovered by her piteous plaints. She had concealed herself under some straw. She was brought forth, not only stiff with the cold, but having a bad wound in the shoulder from a tomahawk. At sight of her the wretched father sunk down upon the snow, as if never again to rise, exhausted by the loss of blood from his own wound, as well as by the scene that surrounded him."

The soldiers retraced their steps back to Fort Edward, "frequently tinging the snow and ice with our own blood. Our shoes were worn through, and our clothing torn by the thick under growth of the forest." They returned to New Windsor Cantonment in January 1783, and faced another serious threat to the struggling nation. American officers threatened a mutiny unless assured of back pay and retirement pay promised them by the Continental Congress. Congress had neither the funds to pay troops or the power to raise taxes. General Washington averted a rebellion by promising to take action in their behalf. However, in June eighty troops of the Pennsylvania Line in Lancaster, demanding back pay before being disbanded from the army, stormed into Philadelphia, where they were joined by two hundred obstreperous soldiers. Armed with artillery seized from the Philadelphia Barracks, they marched on the State House, where the Supreme Executive Council of Pennsylvania and Congress were separately meeting. An outraged Congress fled to Princeton. General Washington immediately dispatched fifteen hundred troops under the command of Major General Robert Howe to quash the revolt. The day after Howe's soldiers marched southward, Sampson and four others were given leave to join them. But by the time the five of them reached the city the mutineers had dispersed. Two of their leaders were sentenced to be hung—they were later pardoned—and four soldiers were flogged.

Shortly after her arrival Sampson began to shiver and perspire copiously. "A malignant fever was then raging in Philadelphia, particularly among the troops stationed there and in the vicinity. I was soon seized with it. I scarcely felt its symptoms before I was carried to the hospital. I was thrown into a loathsome bunk, out of which had just been removed a corpse for burial; soon after which, I became utterly insensible. It was not long before I came to some degree of consciousness, when I perceived preparations for my burial. I heard the funeral undertakers quarreling about some part of my clothing, which each of them wished to possess. One Jones, the only English-speaking nurse in the hospital, coming in, I succeeded, by an almost superhuman effort, in convincing him that I was still alive. I well remember that he not only threatened these monsters, but used actual force to prevent them from dragging me to the Potter's Field, the place of burial for strangers." A few of Philadelphia's twenty-two cemeteries were in the heart of the city. Potter's Field, at the corner of Sixth and Walnut, contained the remains of foreigners and poor people who didn't belong to any particular church in the city. Surrounding buildings prevented air circulation, causing dampness in graves and in the rotting wooden coffins. During rainy weather, water seeped through this earth, draining into nearby wells, from which the community drew water for drinking and bathing.

In the hospital ward Dr. Barnabas Binney began questioning Deborah. "Though I distinctly heard him, I could make no reply. He turned away for a moment to some other patients. I thought he had left me again to the ravenous undertakers. By a great effort, I made a gurgling in my throat to call his attention to me. Never can I forget his elastic step, and apparently deep emotion, as he sprang to my bedside. Thrusting his hand into my bosom to ascertain if there were motion at the heart, he was surprised at finding an inner vest tightly compressing my breasts, the instant removal of which not only ascertained the fact of life, but disclosed the fact that I was a woman!" The agitated doctor ordered her moved to the quarters of the hospital's supervisor, Mrs. Parker. She was later taken to Dr. Binney's home, where his family, unaware that Shurtleff was a woman, looked after her. "I was introduced by the good Dr. Binney to his wife and daughters as a young gallant soldier who had met in battle the enemies of our country. In their company, I rambled through the streets of the city, attended public exhibitions, sailed upon the Delaware, and strolled in the groves and flowery meads. I was admitted as a guest in many wealthy families; still known only as a Continental soldier." Several women were infatuated by "his" sensitive gracefulness, and beardless face.

Her commitment to the military obligated her to join a contingent of 11th Massachusetts Regiment soldiers on a land surveyance expedition toward the Ohio River. Led by Colonel Benjamin Tupper, the group left Philadelphia in Conestoga wagons. While stopping for provisions in Baltimore, Deborah was given a note asking her to come to a particular mansion. Its author was a seventeen year old woman whom Deborah had spoken to before, who had sent her a love letter and handkerchief filled with fruit while she was in the Philadelphia hospital. Deborah found her fetching, even though the young woman believed her to be a gentleman. "She received me with a dignified and yet familiar air. She apologized with infinite grace for overstepping the acknowledged bounds of female delicacy in making such an overture to a gentleman. She expressed great pleasure and much surprise at seeing me alive; having been led to suppose, from an account that reached her not long before, that I had died in the hospital. She confessed the tender sentiments of her heart, which had led her to seek this interview. What could I do, what could I say, in such an exigency? How should I feel, on receiving such a declaration from the heart? I could not act the hypocrite with such an artless girl; nor could I refuse the affection so warmly proffered, and so delicately expressed. But I could not then disclose to her the secret I was so anxious to conceal from all the world beside. In this state of embarassment I continued the most of two days, and finally compromised the matter by promising to call on her again on my return from the West."

Aided by Indian guides, Tupper's expedition traveled through Virginia's Allegheny Mountains. During this hazardous journey Sampson suffered a recurrence of her past illness. Left in the care of an Indian camp, she rejoined the explorers on their return East. Arriving again in Baltimore, anxieties pressed her to reveal the truth to this young lover. "I resolved to prepare the way for such a disclosure by endeavoring to weaken, without wounding, the passion in her breast. I told her I was but a stripling soldier; that I had few talents, and less wealth, to commend me to so much excellence, or even to repay her regard and the favours she had already conferred on me. I told her, moreover, that I was about to rejoin the army, with a view to receive my discharge, and then to return to my relatives in Massachusetts, and to that obscurity from which I had emerged; but I found I had no power to diminish her regard for me.

"While taking her hand, as if to bid her a last adieu, I observed in her an indescribable delicacy struggling for expression, and mantling her fine features. Never can I forget the tender yet magnanimous look of disappointment she cast on me, yet without the least tincture of resentment, when, still holding her hand in mine, she replied that sooner than wring a reluctant consent from me, she would forego every claim to connubial happiness. But the artless girl continued, if want of wealth on my part were the chief obstacle, I might be relieved from all anxiety on that account, as she was heiress to an ample fortune, it being a legacy which she was to possess on her marriage with a man whose worth should be found in his person rather than in his outward estate. I longed to undeceive her. But the secret I had so long carefully guarded, I could not yet surrender. On parting, she presented me with six fine linen shirts, made with her own hands, an elegant watch, twenty-five Spanish dollars, and five guineas. It is no matter how I felt, or what I thought, said, or did on this occasion. I could not, if I would, describe either. I bade her adieu, and staggered to my lodging and to my bed. But during the greater part of the night my invocations to 'tired nature's sweet restorer' were as useless as though 'balmy sleep' were never intended to refresh the exhausted body, or retrieve a bewildered intellect. At length the resolution with which I started when I went to visit my fair friend the day before—to disclose to her the secret of my sex—returned. I knew that this would be right; it was my indispensible duty. On resuming this intention I fell into a sweet and tranquil slumber." The following day Deborah strode briskly, fists thrust in pockets, back to the mansion. Her friend reacted to the confession with shock and astonishment, yet they parted as friends.

Peace was assured with the signing of the Treaty of Paris in September. Robert Shurtleff had orders to return to West Point, for the 4th Massachusetts Regiment was about to be disbanded. In Philadelphia, where the Binneys saw her off at the coach station, she placed in her knapsack a letter from the doctor to the West Point commander, Major General John Paterson. Arriving at Elizabeth Town, New Jersey, on the 12th of October, she and twelve other passengers climbed on board a North River boat. Fog and drizzling rain changed swiftly to a battering wind and torrential downpour. The vessel capsized. The young private swam ashore, and though drenched and shivering, she had kept her knapsack above water. Her trunk, containing clothes and a daily journal, settled at the river bottom. The stragglers were hauled aboard a small cruising boat, and returned to Elizabeth Town, where they again secured passage for points up river.

Binney's letter to the general revealed her sexual identity, though it praised her moral and intellectual assets. General Paterson and Colonel Jackson refused to believe they had a woman in their army, until she changed into feminine apparel. Deborah was then escorted "over the tented ground, and amidst officers and soldiers, with whom an hour before, I was as familiar as one of the inmates of a family with one another; but none of them knew me. Having furnished the gentlemen with an account of my home, my relatives, and the motives which led me to assume the character of a soldier, I requested them to make the strictest inquiry into my manner of life since I had been in the army. This was accordingly done. The result was a general surprise and, on the part of many, a total disbelief. An apartment was now assigned for my use, and garments for either sex provided. But, in general, I preferred my regimentals, because in them I should be more safe from insult and annoyance. Many of the soldiers, and many of my own sex, were desirious to satisfy themselves as to the truth of what they had heard; but of course it was impossible to gratify their curiosity."

Robert Shurtleff was honorably discharged by General Henry Knox on October 23, 1783. She then tossed her gear into a sloop headed for New York City. There she boarded Captain Allen's packet boat for Providence, Rhode Island. Free of obligations to a family, Deborah journeyed northeast, toward Boston. Along the way, an uncle gave her employment on his farm at Stoughton. Presumably he knew her identity, yet allowed her to assume the name of her youngest brother, Ephraim Sampson. Laboring as a farmhand Deborah enjoyed friendships with women. She wore men's clothing, including parts of her uniform.

Local folks must have thought Ephraim peculiar when, in the spring of 1784, "he" shifted to skirts. Benjamin Gannett of Sharon apparently did not regard her as being odd, for they were married in April in his father's house at Stoughton. Between 1786 and 1790 the piercing cries of babies—Earl, Mary, and Patience—sounded from their parents' bedroom, all three delivered by a midwife. Gannett barely eked out a living as a farmer.

Deborah petitioned the Massachusetts State Legislature in January 1792 for back pay the army had withheld:

> The memorials of Deborah Gannett humbly sheweth, that your memorialist from the zeal for the good of her country was induced, and by the name of Robert Shurtleff did, on May 20, 1782, enlist as a soldier in the Continental service, for three years, into the 4th Regiment, Col. Shepard (afterwards Col. Jackson's) in Capt. George Webb's company and was mustered at Worcester . . . the 23rd of the same month, and went to camp, under the command of Sergeant Gambel, and was constant and faithful in doing duty with other soldiers. Deborah Gannett.

Attached to the petition was a certificate from Dedham, dated December 10, 1791:

> This certifies that Mrs. Deborah Gannett enlisted as a soldier on May ye 1782 for three years and was mustered ye 23rd of the same month at Worcester and sent on to camp soon after and as I have been informed did the duty of a good soldier— P. Elipht Thorp, Capt. 7th Massachusetts Regiment.

The petition passed the Massachusetts Senate and was approved and signed by Governor John Hancock. The General Court of

Massachusetts verified that she had enlisted on May 20, 1782, that she "did actually perform the duty of a soldier in the late army of the United States to the 23rd day of October 1783, for which she has received no compensation. And whereas it further appears that the said Deborah exhibited an extraordinary instance of female heroism by discharging the duties of a faithful gallant soldier, and at the same time preserving the virtue and chastity of her sex unsuspected and unblemished." The Court ordered the treasurer to pay Deborah Gannett the sum of thirty-four pounds.

At the turn of the century John Adams was laboring over an autobiography, Mercy Otis Warren was writing her own interpretation of the war in *History of the Rise, Progress, and Termination of the American Revolution,* and Chief Justice John Marshall was making final changes to the first volume of *Life of George Washington.* Spurred by financial needs, and a desire to justify her enlistment, Mrs. Gannett agreed to speak before audiences in Massachusetts and New York. Boston's newspapers advertised her appearances at the Federal-Street Theatre, where she shared billing with productions of *King Henry IVth, The Will; or A School for Daughters,* and *Columbus; or America Discovered.* Wearing her blue and white uniform, armed with a musket, Mrs. Gannett paced through twenty-seven maneuvers of the Manual Exercise before giving her speech, written in a popular style of the period.*

An Address
Delivered at the Federal-Street Theatre, Boston
Four Successive Nights of the Different
Plays, Beginning March 22, 1802

By Mrs. Deborah Gannett

Not unlike the example of the patriot and philanthropist, though perhaps perfectly so in effect, do I awake from the tranquil slumbers of retirement, to active, public scenes of life, like those which now surround me. That genius which is the prompter of curiosity, and that spirit which is the support of

Deborah Sampson Gannett was known by her friends as a woman who conversed intelligently on theology, politics, and military tactics.

enterprise, early drove, or, rather allured me, from the corner of humble obscurity—their cheering aspect has again prevented a torpid rest.

Secondary to these are the solicitations of a number of worthy characters and friends—too persuasive and congenial with my own disposition to be answered with indifference, or to be rejected—who have induced me thus to advance and bow submissive to an audience, simply and concisely to rehearse a tale of truth; which, though it took its rise, and finally terminated in the

Theatre----Federal-Street.

THE PUBLIC

Are refpectively informed, that Mrs. GAN-
NETT, (late Deborah Sampfon,) the *AMERI-
CAN HEROINE*, who ferved three years as a
private Soldier in the Continental Army, during the War, will at the requeft of a number of
refpectable perfons, make her fecond appearance on the Stage To-Morrow Evening, for
the purpofe of relating her Narrrtive, &c.

TO-MORROW EVENING, March 24, Will
be prefented, (by particular defire) for the
fecond time thefe two years, the much admired
Hiftorical Play, in 5 acts, called,

KING HENRY the IVth,

With the Humors of Sir JOHN FALSTAFF.
Charactere as before.

To which will be added, by way of Farce, an Olio,
confifting of Song, Sentiment, &c called,

THE SOLDIER's FESTIVAL ;
ON THE EVE OF BATTLE.

1ft. In the courfe of which Mrs. GANNETT will
deliver her narrative.
2d. Glee--"How Merrily we live that Soldiers be."
3d Song--" How ftands the Glafs around."
4th Glee--" Here's a health to all true Laffes."
5th Glee-- How fhall we mortals fpend our hours.'

Mrs. Gannett,
Equipt in complete uniform will go through the
MANUAL EXERCISE.
The whole to conclude with the Song and Chorus of
" God Save the Sixteen States."

In 1802 Boston's newspapers, including The Mercury and New-England
Palladium, *advertised Deborah Gannett's appearances at the Federal Theatre.*

splendor of public life, I was determined to repeat only as the soliloquy of a hermit, or to the visionary phantoms, which hover through the glooms of solitude.

A tale—the truth of which I was ready to say, but which, perhaps, others have already said for me—ought to expel me from the enjoyment of society, from the acknowledgment of my own sex, and from the endearing friendship of the other. But this, I venture to pronounce, would be saying too much; for, as I should thus not respect *myself,* should be entitled to none from *others.*

I indeed recollect it as a foible, an error and presumption, into which, perhaps, I have too inadvertently and precipitately run; but which I now retrospect with anguish and amazement. I recollect it as a moralizing naturalist, susceptible to the like fine feelings of nature, recollects the howling blasts of winter at a period when Flora has strewed the earth with all her profusion of delicacies, and whose zephyrs are wasting their fragrance to heighten our sensations of tranquility and pleasure;—or, rather, perhaps I ought to recollect it as a mariner, having regained his native shore of serenity and peace, looks back on the stormy billows which so long and so constantly had threatened to engulf him in the bowels of the deep! And yet I must frankly confess, I recollect it with a kind of satisfaction, which no one can better conceive and enjoy than him, who, recollecting the good intentions of a bad deed, lives to see and to correct any indecorum of his life.

But without further preliminary apologies—yet with every due respect towards this brilliant and polite circle—I hasten to a review of the most conspicuous parts of that path, which led to achievements, which some have believed, but which many still doubt. Their accomplishment once seemed to me as impossible. That I am author of them is now incredible to the incredulous, or wounding to the ear of more refined delicacy and taste. They are a breach in the decorum of my sex, unquestionably, perhaps too unfortunate ever to be reconcilable with the rigid maxims of the moralist, and a sacrifice which—while it may seem perfectly incompatible with the requirements of virtue, and which of course must ring discord in the ear, and disgust to the bosom of sensibility and refinement—I must be content to leave with time and the most scrutinizing enquiry to disclose.

Unlettered in any scholastic school of erudition, you will not expect, on this occasion, the entertainment of the soft and captivating sounds of eloquence; but, rather, a narration of facts in a mode as uncouth as they are unnatural. Facts which, though I once experienced, and of which memory has ever been painfully retentive, I cannot now make you feel, or paint to the life.

Know then, that my juvenile mind early became inquisitive to understand—not merely whether the principles, or rather the seeds of war are analogous to the genuine nature of man—not merely to know why he should forego every trait of humanity and assume the character of a brute; or, in plainer language, why he should march out tranquilly, or in a paroxysm of rage against his fellow man to butcher, or be butchered? For these, alas! were too soon horribly verified by the massacres in our streets, in the very streets which encompass this edifice—in yonder adjacent villas [Lexington and adjacent towns], on yonder memorable eminence [Breed's Hill], where now stand living monuments of the atrocious, heart distracting, momentous scenes that followed in rapid succession!

This I am ready to affirm—though it may be deemed unnatural in my sex—is not a demoralization of human nature. The sluices, both of the blood of freemen and of slaves, were first opened here. And those hills and valleys (once the favorite resort of both the lover and philosopher) have been drunk with their blood! A new subject was then opened to the most pathetic imagination —and to the rousing of every latent spark of humanity, one should think, in the bosoms of the wolves, as well as in those of the sheep, for whose blood they were so thirsty.

But most of all, my mind became agitated with the enquiry— why a nation, separated from us by an ocean more than three thousand miles in extent, should endeavor to enforce on us plans of subjugation, the most unnatural in themselves, unjust, inhuman in their operations, and unpractised even by the uncivilized savages of the wilderness? Perhaps nothing but the critical juncture of the times could have excused such a philosophical disquisition of politics in woman, notwithstanding it was a theme of universal speculation and concern to man. We indeed originated from her [England], as from a parent, and perhaps would have continued to this period in subjection to her mandates, had we not discovered that her romantic, avaricious and cruel disposition extended to murder, after having bound the slave!

Confirmed by this time in the justness of a defensive war on the one side, from the most aggravated one on the other, my mind ripened with my strength. While our beds and our roses were sprinkled with the blood of indiscriminate youth, beauty, innocence and decrepit old age, I only seemed to want the license to become one of the severest avengers of the wrong.

For several years I looked on these scenes of havoc, rapacity and devastation, as one looks on a drowning man, on the conflagration of a city—where are not only centered his coffers of gold, but with them his choicest hopes, friends, companions, his all—without being able to extend the rescuing hand to either.

Wrought upon at length by an enthusiasm and frenzy that could brook no control, I burst the tyrant bonds which held my sex in awe, and clandestinely, or by stealth, grasped an opportunity, which custom and the world seemed to deny, as a natural privilege. And whilst poverty, hunger, nakedness, cold and disease had dwindled the American armies to a handful—whilst universal terror and dismay ran through our camps, ran through our country—while even Washington himself, at their head, though like a god, stood, as it were, on a pinnacle tottering over the abyss of destruction, the last prelude to our falling a wretched prey to the yawning jaws of the monster aiming to devour—I threw off the soft habiliment of my sex, and assumed those of the warrior, already prepared for battle.

Thus I became an actor in that important drama, with an inflexible resolution to persevere through the last scene; when we might be permitted and acknowledged to enjoy what we had so nobly declared we would possess, or lose with our lives—

freedom and independence!—when the philosopher might resume his research unmolested; the statesman be disembarrassed by his distracting theme of national politics; the divine find less occasion to invoke the indignation of heaven on the usurpers and cannibals of the inherent rights and even existence of man; when the son should again be restored to the arms of his disconsolate parent, and the lover to the bosom of her, for whom indeed he is willing to jeopard his life, and for whom alone he wishes to live!

A new scene and a new world now opened to my view; the objects of which now seemed as important as the transition before seemed unnatural. It would, however, be a weakness in me to mention the tear of repentence, or of that of temerity, from which the stoutest of my sex are, or ought not to be, wholly exempt on extreme emergencies, which many times involuntarily stole into my eye, and fell unheeded to the ground before I had reached the embattled field, the ramparts, which protected its internal resources—which shielded youth, beauty, and the delicacy of that sex at home, which perhaps I had forfeited in turning volunteer in their defence. Temerity: when reflections on my former situation, and this new kind of being, were daggers more frightful than all the implements of war; when the rustling of every leaf was an omen of danger, the whisper of each wind, a tale of woe! If then the poignancy of thought stared me thus haggardly in the face, found its way to the inmost recesses of my heart, forcibly, in the commencement of my career—what must I not have anticipated before its close!

The curtain is now up. A scene opens to your view; but the objects strike your attention less forcibly and less interestingly than they did then, not only with my eyes, but with every energetic sensation of my soul. What shall I say further? Shall I not stop short, and leave to your imaginations to portray the tragic deeds of war? Is it not enough that I leave it to the inexperienced to fancy the hardships, the anxieties, the dangers, even of the best life of a soldier? Were it not improper, were it not unsafe, were it not indelicate, and were I certain I should be entitled to a

Deborah Sampson Gannett /323

pardon, I would appeal to the soft bosom of my own sex to draw a parallel between the perils and sexual inconveniences of a girl in her teens, not only in armor, but obliged to perform duties in the field—and those [women] who go to the camp without a masquerade, and consequently subject only to what toils and sacrifices they please. Or, will a conclusion be more natural from those who sometimes take occasion to complain by their own domestic firesides; but who, indeed, are at the same time in affluence, cherished in the arms of their companions, and sheltered from the storms of war by the rougher sex in arms?

Many have seen, and many can contemplate, in the field of imagination, battles and victories amidst garments rolled in blood; but it is only one of my own sex, exposed to the storm, who can conceive of my situation.

We have all heard of, many have doubtless seen, the meteor streaming through or breaking in the horizon—the terrific glare of the comet in its approach towards, or in its declension from us, in its eccentric orbit—the howling of a tempest—the electric fluid, which darts majesty and terror through the clouds—its explosion and tremendous effects!—Bostonians, and you who inhabit its environs, you who have known from experience your houses and your hills to tremble from the cannonade of Charles-town,—your ears are yet wounded by the shrieks of her mangled and her distressed—your eyes swimming in a deluge of anguish at the sight of our butchered, expiring relatives and friends, while the conflagration of the town added the last solemnity to the scene!

This idea must assimilate with the progress of this horrid delusion of war. Hence you can behold the parched soil of White Plains drink insatiably the blood of her most peaceful and industrious proprietors—of freemen, and of slaves! I was there! The recollection makes me shudder! A dislocated limb draws fresh anguish from my heart!

You may have heard the thunderings of a volcano; you may have contemplated, with astonishment and wonder, the burial of a city by its eruption. Your ears then are yet deafened from the thunderings of the invasion of York Town—your eyes dazzled, your imaginations awfully sublimed, by the fire which belched from its environs, and towered, like that from an eruption of Etna, to the clouds! Your hearts yet bleed, from every principle of humanity, at the recollection of the havoc, carnage and death that reigned there!

Three successive weeks, after a long and rapid march, found me amidst this storm. But, happily for America, happily for Europe, perhaps for the world, when, on the delivery of Cornwallis's sword to the illustrious, immortal Washington, the sun of liberty and independence burst through a sable cloud, and his benign influence was, almost instantaneously, felt in our remotest corners! The phalanx of war was thus broken through, and the palladium of peace blossomed on its ruins.

I will not hence urge you to retrace with me (tranquilly you surely cannot) all the footsteps of our valiant heroic leaders through the distraction both of elements and of war. I will not even portray an attempt to reinforce the brave Schuyler [Gen. Philip Schuyler], then on the borders of Canada, where, if the war-whoop of infernals should not strike you with dismay, the tomahawk would soon follow!

Nor need I point you to the death-like doors of the hospital in Philadelphia, whose avenues were crowded with the sick, the dying and the dead, though I myself made one of the unhappy crowd.

You have now but the shade of a picture, which neither time nor my abilities will permit me to show you to the life. The haggard fiend, despair, may have stared you in the face when giving over the pursuit of a favorite, lost child. It is only in this torture of suspense that we can rightly conceive of its situation.

Such is my experience—not that I ever mourned the loss of a child, but that I considered myself as lost! For, on the one hand, if I fell not a victim to the infuriating rabble of a mob, or of a war not yet fully terminated—the disclosure of my peculiar situation seemed infinitely worse than either. And if from stratagem and perseverance, I may acquire as great knowledge in every respect as I have of myself in this, then my knowledge, at least of human nature, will be as complete as it is useful.

But we will now hasten from the field, from the embattled entrenchments built for the destruction of man, from a long, desolating war, to contemplate more desirable and delightful scenes. And notwithstanding curiosity may prompt any to retrace the climax of our revolution, the means, under a smiling, superintending providence, by which we have outrode the storms of danger and distress. What heart will forget to expand with joy and gratitude, to beat in unison, at the propitious recollection? And I enquire, what infant tongue can ever forget or cease being taught to lisp the praises of Washington, and those of that bright constellation of worthies who swell the list of Columbian fame —those, by whose martial skill and philanthropic labours, we were first led to behold, after a long and stormy night, the smiling sun of peace burst on our benighted world! And while we may drop a tear over the flowery turf of those patriots and sages, may she unrivaled enjoy and increase her present bright sunshine of happiness! May agriculture and commerce, industry and manufactures, arts and sciences, virtue and decorum, union and harmony—those richest sources of our worth, and strongest pillars of our strength—become stationary, like fixed stars in the firmament, to flourish in her clime!

But the question again returns: "What particular inducement could she have thus to elope from the soft sphere of her own sex, to perform a deed of valour by way of sacrilege on unhallowed ground—voluntarily to face the storms both of elements and war, in the character of him, who is more fitly made to brave and endure all danger?"

> And dost thou ask what fairy hand inspired
> A nymph to be with martial glory fired?
> Or, what from art, or yet from nature's laws,
> Has joined a female to her country's cause?
> Why on great Mars's theatre she drew
> Her female portrait, though in soldier's hue?

Then ask—why Cincinnatus left his farm?
Why science did old Plato's bosom warm?
Why Hector in the Trojan war should dare?
Or why should Homer trace his actions there?
Why Newton in philosophy has shown?
Or Charles, for solitude, has left his throne?
Why Locke in metaphysics should delight—
Precisian sage, to set false reason right?
Why Albion's sons should kindle up a war?
Why Jove or Vulcan hurried on the car?
Perhaps the same propensity you use,
Has prompted her a martial course to choose.
Perhaps to gain refinements where she could,
This rare achievement for her country's good.
Or was some hapless lover from her torn—
As Emma did her valiant Hammon mourn?
Else he must tell, who would this truth attain,
Why one is formed for pleasure—one for pain:
Or, boldly, why our maker made us such—
Why here he gives too little—there too much!

I am indeed willing to acknowledge what I have done, an error and presumption. I will call it an error and presumption because I swerved from the accustomed flowery path of female delicacy, to walk upon the heroic precipice of feminine perdition! I indeed left my morning pillow of roses to prepare a couch of brambles for the night; yet I awoke from this refreshed, to gather nought but the thorns of anguish for the next night's repose—and in the precipitancy of passion, to prepare a moment for repentance at leisure!

Had all this been achieved by the rougher hand, more properly assigned to wield the sword in duty and danger in a defensive war—the most cruel in its measures, though important in its consequences—these thorns might have been converted into wreaths of immortal glory and fame. I therefore yield every claim of honor and distinction to the hero and patriot, who met the foe in his own name—though not with more heartfelt satisfaction.

But repentance is a sweet solace to conscience, as well as the most complete atonement to the Supreme Judge of our offences: notwithstanding the tongue of malevolence and scurrility that may be continually preparing its most poisonous ingredients for the punishment of a crime which has already received more than half a pardon.

Yet if even this be deemed too much of an extenuation of a breach in the modesty of the female world, humbled and contented will I sit down, inglorious for having unfortunately performed an important part assigned for another—like a bewildered star traversing out of its accustomed orbit, whose twinkling beauty at most has become totally obscured in the presence of the sun.

But as the rays of the sun strike the eye with the greatest lustre when emerging from a thick fog, and as those actions which have for their objects the extended hand of charity to the indigent and wretched—to restore a bewildered traveller to light—and, to reform in ourselves any irregular and forlorn course of life; so, allowing myself to be one or the greatest of these, do I still hope for some claim on the indulgence and patronage of the public; as in such case I might be conscious of the approbation of my God.

I cannot contentedly quit this subject or this place without expressing, more emphatically, my high respect and veneration for my own sex. The indulgence of this respectable circle supersedes my merit, as well as my most sanguine expectations. You receive, at least, in return, my warmest gratitude. And though you can neither have, or perhaps need, from me the instructions of a sage, or the advice of the counsellor, you surely will not be wholly indifferent to my most sincere declaration of friendship for that sex, for which this checkered flight of my life may have rendered me the least ornamental example; but which, neither in adversity or prosperity, could I ever learn to forget or degrade.

I take it to be from the greatest extremes, both in virtue and in vice, that the uniformly virtuous and reformed in life can derive the greatest and most salutary truths and impressions. Who, for example, can contemplate for a moment the prodigal —from the time of his revelry with harlots, to that of his eating husks with swine, and to his final return to his father—without the greatest emotion of disgust, pity and joy? And is it possible to behold the effects of the unprincipled conduct of the libertine, the bacchanalian, the debauchee, and what is more wretched of all, of the emaciated, haggard form of a modern baggage in the streets, without bringing into exercise every passion of abhorrence and commiseration? And yet, happy are those who at the same time receive a monitor which fixes a resolve, never to embark on such a sea of perdition.

I cannot, indeed, bring the adventures, even of the worst part of my own life, as parallels with this black catalogue of crimes. But in whatever I may be thought to have been unnatural, unwise and indelicate, it is now my most fervent desire that it may have a suitable impression on you—and on me, a penitent for every wrong thought and step. The rank you hold in the scale of beings is, in many respects, superior to that of man. Nurses of his growth, and invariable models of his habits, he becomes a suppliant at your shrine, emulous to please, assiduous to cherish and support, to live and to die for you! Blossoms from your very birth, you become his admiration, his joy, his Eden companions in this world. How important then is it, that these blossoms bring forth such fruit as will best secure your own delights and felicity, and those of him, whose every enjoyment, and even his very existence, is so peculiarly interwoven with your own!

* In 1804 Paul Revere, the silversmith, engraver, and copper manufacturer, tried to alleviate her poverty by writing to William Eustis, Massachusetts representative in Congress.

Sir

Mrs. Deborah Gannett of Sharon informs me, that she has inclosed to your care a petition to Congress in favour of her. My works for manufacturing of copper, being at Canton, being but a short distance from the neighbourhood where she lives, I have been induced to inquire her situation and character, since she quitted the male habit, and soldier's uniform, for the more decent apparel of her own sex; and since she has been married and become a mother. Humanity and justice obliges me to say, that every person with whom I have conversed about her, and it is not a few, speak of her as a woman of handsome talents, good morals, a dutiful wife, and an affectionate parent. She is now much out of health. She has several children, her husband is a good sort of man, 'tho of small force in business; they have a few acres of poor land which they cultivate, but they are really poor.

She told me she had no doubt that her ill health is in consequence of her being exposed when she did a soldier's duty, and that while in the army she was wounded.

We commonly form our idea of the person whom we hear spoken of, whom we have never seen, according as their actions are described. When I heard her spoken of as a soldier, I formed the idea of a tall, masculine female, who had a small share of understanding, without education, and one of the meanest of her sex.—When I saw and discoursed with her I was agreeably surprised to find a small, effeminate, and conversable woman, whose education entitled her to a better situation in life.

I have no doubt your humanity will prompt you to do all in your power to get her some relief. I think her case much more deserving than hundreds to whom Congress has been generous.

I am sirs with esteem and respect
your humble servant. Paul Revere

The Congress in Washington granted her the right to be placed on the Massachusetts Invalid Pension Roll. The War Department informed Massachusetts' Commissioner of Loans and Agent for Pensioners that "Deborah Sampson Gannett, who served as a soldier in the Army of the United States during the late Revolutionary War, and who was seriously wounded therein, has this day been placed on the Pension list of the United States, at the rate of four dollars a month," retroactive to the first of January 1803, and paid for by Massachusetts.

This pension enabled the family to build a clapboard and brick house on their hundred acre farmland, and to plant willow trees at the western portion, woodbine on the eastern side. Rosebushes, perennial plants, and flowering shrubs, placed attractively, contrasted with raspberry and barberry bushes growing wild near roughly stacked stone walls.

The cost of such a large undertaking again placed her in debt. "After my unfeigned regard to you and family," she wrote Revere,

> I would inform you that I and my son have been very sick—
> though in some measure better. I hope, sir, that you and your
> family are all in the enjoyment of health, which is one of the
> greatest of blessings. My own indisposition and that of my
> son's causes me again to solicit your goodness in our favour
> —though I with gratitude confess it rouses every tender feel-
> ing, and I blush at the thought that after receiving ninety and
> nine good turns as it were, my circumstances require that I
> should ask the hundredth. The favour that I ask is the loan of
> ten dollars for a short time. As soon as I am able to ride to
> Boston I will make my remittance to you. With my humble
> thanks for the distinguished favour—from your humble ser-
> vant, Deborah Gannett.

In March 1818 Congress passed an Act granting pensions of eight dollars per month to all veterans who had served continuously a minimum of nine months in the land and naval forces of the United States during the Revolution. Veterans already holding state pensions were not eligible under the Act unless they relinquished their rights to them. In September Deborah Gannett petitioned Congress. This time, however, she gave her date of enlistment as April 1781, and said she had served at the Battle of Yorktown. Veterans' pension files in Washington had been destroyed during the War of 1812, when the British burned much of the city. The federal government, therefore, had to rely on state records for evidence in the transferal of pensions. When the Judge of the United States District Court in Massachusetts wrote the Secretary of the Department of War, verifying Deborah's right to a federal pension, he failed to mention her enlistment date. Thereafter, all federal documents listed 1781 instead of 1782. The date, however, had no bearing on whether or not she was entitled to a pension, and her application was approved by Congress. Her acceptance brought an elated response from the editors of *The Dedham Register* in Massachusetts: "This extraordinary woman is now in the sixty-second year of her age. She possesses a clear understanding, and a general knowledge of passing events, is fluent in speech, and delivers her sentiments in correct language, with deliberate and measured accent, is easy in her deportment, affable in her manners, robust and masculine in her appearance."

Mrs. Gannett died April 29, 1827, and was buried in Rockridge Cemetery, one mile south of her Sharon home. Her death may well have been hastened by wounds suffered during the war. Four years later, Benjamin Gannett petitioned Congress for the continuation of his wife's pension for himself. This request was introduced in Congress by John Quincy Adams, son of Abigail and John Adams, and member of the House of Representatives. It was not acted upon at that time because there was no law granting pensions to widows whose husbands had died of war wounds, and had a congressman proposed a bill for the relief of husbands whose wives had died of wounds suffered during enlistment he most likely would have aroused peals of laughter from the floor of the House.

In 1836 Congress passed "an Act granting half pay to widows or orphans where their husbands or fathers have died of wounds received in the military service of the United States." Mr. Gannett, then in his eighties, again petitioned, though the Act specified that the widow would have to have been married to the soldier at the time of the Revolution.

Benjamin claimed that the wounds his wife had received in the war probably hastened her death, that his two daughters were dependent on charity for support. A female friend of the Gannetts testified that she had lived in their home for more than forty-six years, that because of a musket ball lodged in Deborah's body, never extracted, she had generally not been able to do any labor. Other witnesses testified that Benjamin was destitute of property, that he was an industrious man who had to raise a large family, and that he was in debt for heavy medical expenses, due to his wife's war wounds. A physician's bill amounting to six hundred dollars was given as evidence. A sympathetic Committee on Revolutionary Pensions reported to the 25th Congress in 1837 that "were there nothing peculiar in this application which distinguishes it from all other applications for pensions, the committee would at once reject the claim. But they believe they are warranted in saying that the whole history of the American Revolution records no case like this, and furnishes no other similar example of female heroism, fidelity, and courage. The petitioner does not allege that he served in the war of the Revolution, and it does not appear by any evidence in the case that such was the fact. It is not, however, to be presumed that a female who took up arms in defense of her country, who served as a common soldier for nearly three years, and fought and bled for human liberty, would, immediately after the termination of the war, connect herself for life with a Tory or a traitor. He, indeed, was honored much by being the husband of such a wife; and as he proved himself worthy of her, as he has sustained her through a long life of sickness and suffering, and as that sickness and suffering were occasioned by the wounds she received and the hardships she endured in the defense of her country, and as there cannot be a parallel case in all time to come, the committee do not

Deborah Sampson Gannett /333

hesitate to grant relief." By that time, however, it was too late to give Benjamin relief—he had died eleven months before. On July 4, 1838, Congress passed a Special Act for the relief of Deborah Gannett's heirs, directing the Secretary of the Treasury to pay the sum of $466.66, an equivalent for a full pension of eighty dollars per year, from the time of Mr. Gannett's first petition until his death in January 1837.✱

Elizabeth Foote Washington

✳ The early Washington and Foote families emigrated from England to Virginia's wilderness in the seventeenth century. They settled between the Potowmack (Potomac) and Rappahannock rivers, an area broken by myriad, vein-like creeks. The brothers, John and Lawrence Washington became, respectively, the great-grandfathers of George and Lund Washington; Richard Foote, the great-grandfather of Elizabeth Foote. There is evidence that Elizabeth's mother, Margaret Washington Foote, was Lund's aunt.

By the middle of the eighteenth century several of Virginia's tidewater families had pressed northward, to neighboring counties, where they built lavish colonial seats. George and Martha Washington resided at Mount Vernon in Fairfax County, Elizabeth's parents lived near Brent Town in Prince William County. Both families frequently packed their carriages, and rumbled over rough roads to visit the Washingtons and Footes of Chotank Creek in King George County. During such sprees Elizabeth, her sister Catherine, and brother Richard, pleasurably romped with Lund and his brother Lawrence.

On June 15, 1775 the Continental Congress appointed George Washington as Commander-in-Chief of the Continental Army. He took the road north to lead troops in Massachusetts and, other than brief visits enroute to and from Yorktown, didn't return to Mount Vernon for almost nine years. The general's distant kinsman, Lund Washington, managed his estate and business concerns. From Cambridge Washington wrote in November that "it is the greatest, indeed it is the only comfortable reflection I enjoy on this score, that my business is in the hands of a person whose integrity I have not a doubt, and on whose care I can rely." Lund, a thirty-eight-year-old bachelor, was stout, quite frugal, and shrewdly industrious.

George's "little empire" during the Revolution consisted of

five farms, each self-sustaining, on land that increased to eight thousand acres by the war's end. Scattered over the area were thirty-nine dwellings and twenty-one miscellaneous buildings. Roughly five hundred acres surrounding the manor house provided the proper appearance for a "gentleman's country seat": vast, neatly trimmed lawns, tree groves, vistas, and formal gardens. Thousands of varieties of carefully landscaped trees, bushes, hedges, and plants presented an extraordinary view to the numerous guests. During warm months multitudes of brightly colored flowers were visited daily by turtledoves, blackbirds, crimson cardinals, and bright-orange, black, and white-plumed Baltimore orioles. Wind wafted the petals of numerous poppies, though whether or not they were cultivated at Mount Vernon for opium is questionable, despite the fact that it was widely used in the colonies as a medical anesthesia.

Behind the mansion was the spinning-house, where women made cloth from wool, flax, and cotton fibers grown on the estate. Its rooms bustled with activity during the Revolution, when Martha supervised cloth production for American troops. Nearby were the smokehouse, icehouse, bakery, and stables. Professional gardeners, tailors, stonecutters, carpenters, painters, bricklayers, and shoemakers were hired for the week, month, or year. Further afield were forested areas, abundant in geese, ducks, and wild turkeys; pastures, and fields of tobacco, corn, and wheat. Grain was sent to the plantation's mill for flour, or to the general's distillery, where up to twelve thousand gallons of whiskey were bottled each year. Along the clear Potowmack were his herring fisheries. A single draw of the net could bring in thousands of small fish. The heads and tails were sliced off and strewn over crop fields as fertilizer. Garfish, the largest catch, were nearly two feet long. They were distasteful to families of plantation owners, and were generally skinned alive, to be eaten with an abundance of other fish by slaves.

Virginia held over 170,000 slaves, nearly half of the colony's population, and close to a third of all blacks in the colonies. Their life was harsh, and they were treated by most whites solely as property assets. The protests of abolitionists were only faintly listened to. Newspapers rarely mentioned slavery abuse, though the April 21, 1775 issue of *The Virginia Gazette* approved the death sentence of a white man for brutally beating a slave to death, for it served as "a warning to others to treat their slaves with more moderation."

At that time Washington had 188 slaves—men, women, and children who labored at various skills and crafts, in the fields, or as household servants. Although he treated them kindly, and brought in doctors when they were ill, those other than servants lived under deplorable conditions. Their huts were crowded, and pallets so few that children slept on the floor. Alongside each shack was a vegetable garden, and chicken roost. A Polish guest, Julian Ursyn Niemcewicz, wrote in his journal that the general's slaves spoke very good English, and never appeared sad, but that they were more destitute than impoverished Polish peasants.

In 1775 the Potowmack River was vulnerable to a British naval attack. Virginia's Royal Governor, the unpopular Lord Dunmore, took refuge on board a British warship in the York River, and threatened to have the fleet fire upon all the river mansions. Lund, anxious to have Mount Vernon protected, urged that all plantations supply funds to fortify the Potowmack. Plantation owners balked at the expense, and a fortification was never built. Lund wrote Washington that "the common people are most hellishly frightened." In the fall ten companies of the Culpeper Minute Battalion, wearing fringed hunting shirts and trousers, and armed with tomahawks, scalping-knives, and a few guns, marched to Williamsburg to join three Provincial companies in an expedition against Dunmore, then entrenched at Norfolk. Dunmore had the town shelled, and much of it burned, in January. When five British ships threatened the Potowmack, though it was blocked by ice, Lund wrote the general that "Alexandria is much alarmed, and indeed the whole neighbourhood. The women and children are leaving the town and stowing themselves into every little hut they can get, out of reach of the enemy's cannon. Every waggon, cart, and pack horse that can be got is employed in moving the goods out of town. The militia are all up (but not in arms) for indeed they have none, or at least very few. I could wish, if we are to have our neighbourhood invaded soon, they would send a tender or two among us. I want much to see how the people would behave upon the occasion. They say they are determined to fight. Everybody I see tells me that if the people could have notice they would immediately come and defend your property, as long as they have life, from Loudon, Prince William, Fauquier, and this county." Any hope that Dunmore had of launching an attack was thwarted in March when smallpox raged with great violence on board his ships. Particularly affected were numerous escaped slaves, who had joined Dunmore's fleet, having been promised their freedom. Roughly a hundred and fifty slaves died of smallpox, and were tumbled into deep waters infested with sharks.

Elizabeth began her diary in 1779, shortly after her father died. "I have lately promised to enter into the holy state of matrimony and may a blessing of the Almighty attend this momentous step I have taken." She was certain she wanted to marry Lund, then forty-three, but vague as to when they would be having a home of their own. "As there is a probability of my living in houses not my own for some time, may the divine goodness assist me, so that I may study to live in peace and friendship with the family where I live." The Washingtons accommodated the couple at Mount Vernon. Martha often journeyed northward to be with her husband, and on such occasions Elizabeth cared for their two grandchildren, George Washington Parke Custis and Eleanor (Nelly) Parke Custis. The two infants were adopted by the general and his wife after the death of the youngsters' father in 1781.

In April 1781, panic ensued on the estate when an armed British sloop, the *Savage,* crept up the Potowmack, and threatened to open fire. Only a short time before, an enemy boat had devastated a farm near Alexandria. Elated by the unexpected visit, seventeen of Washington's slaves joined the *Savage*'s crew. Fearful that the mansion might be destroyed, and desirous of

Martha and George Washington, their two grandchildren, and an aide stroll over the west front lawn in "A View of Mount Vernon," painted by an unknown artist c. 1790. While Elizabeth Washington was living at the mansion, her husband Lund supervised contruction of the buildings at left.

having the slaves returned, Lund promptly offered food and provisions. He lost the slaves, but saved the estate, though his behavior caused an angry outburst from the general. "That which gives me most concern," Washington wrote, "is, that you should go on board the enemy's vessels and furnish them with refreshments. It would have been a less painful circumstance to me to have heard, that in consequence of your non-compliance with their request, they had burnt my house and laid the plantation in ruins. You ought to have considered yourself as my representative, and should have reflected on the bad example of communicating with the enemy, and making a voluntary offer of refreshments to them with a view to prevent a conflagration.

"It was not in your power, I acknowledge, to prevent them from sending a flag on shore, and you did right to meet it; but you should, in the same instant that the business of it was unfolded, have declared explicitly, that it was improper for you to yield to the request; after which, if they had proceeded to help themselves by force, you could have but submitted; and, being unprovided for defense, this was to be preferred to a feeble opposition, which only serves as a pretext to burn and destroy."

Lund had long wished to manage a farm of his own. As far back as 1776 he had written Washington that "my only wish or ambition has been to save so much out of my wages during the time I have served you and others as would be sufficient to purchase a small farm in some part of the country where the produce of it would enable me to live and give a neighbour beef and toddy." However, as the war years passed, Washington became increasingly more in debt. Land purchases, construction and renovations, and entertainment expenditures for guests had caused large deficits at the central farm, unalleviated by profits from the four outlying ones. To make matters worse, the military commander had refused an officer's salary, choosing instead to be reimbursed for his wartime expenditures. Circumstances were such that Lund chose not to draw his own salary for four years.

In 1782 Washington apparently sold his manager 360 acres of the western property for $15,000. Later in the decade, Lund was given a bond valued at 1,220 pounds sterling, as compensation for his loss in salary. Construction began on Lund and Elizabeth's property the year after its purchase. Vast acres of hay inspired its name, "Hayfield." In addition to the large brick mansion, three farm buildings were constructed and two dwellings to house most of the sixteen slaves. The few servants undoubtedly lived within the mansion. In December 1782, Elizabeth was delivered of a dead child at Mount Vernon, making her even more anxious to raise a family in her own home. Unfortunately, construction costs and Lund's time-consuming duties at Mount Vernon kept the couple from living at Hayfield until 1784.

Virginia's tidewater "aristocracy" regarded the Battle of Yorktown (1781) as having settled the war issue, and they resumed the daily pursuit of pleasure. Entire families flocked to visit one another's estate, traveling as far as fifteen miles or more. Visitors, often strangers, arrived at Mount Vernon so frequently that George described it as "a well-resorted tavern." Dinner guests at Hayfield often included the Washingtons; Lund, Elizabeth, and William Hayward Foote, the son of Elizabeth's deceased brother, mingled with Mount Vernon's guests, and occasionally remained for the night.

Attired in the latest English and French fashion, the "aristocracy" gathered at horse races, particularly at Williamsburg, where large sums of money were bet on thoroughbreds. They relished fox-hunting: the thrill of riding horseback across fields, of sicking hounds against a terrified fox until, weakened and surrounded, it could be slaughtered. It was a favorite occupation of George and Lund, who took to the field with the general's favorite dogs, three of whom he named "Truelove," "Mopsey," and "Sweetlips." Other diversions for Virginians were cock-fighting, gambling at dice or card tables, and crabbing parties. Early in the morning pleasure seekers stepped on board a large vessel on the Potowmack and sailed out to deeper waters where, once the sails were dropped, women lowered fishing lines of hickory bark. When enough crabs crawled over the bait, gentlemen scooped them up with hand-nets.

Following a heavy dinner at two or three in the afternoon, washed down with a choice of punch, cider, toddy (rum, hot water, sugar, and a dash of nutmeg), claret, port, or madeira wine, one gambled at whisk, napped, or perhaps languidly lounged in the library. A family's library was lavishly supplied with beautifully embossed classics and works by the most creative minds of America and abroad.

Religion was generally taken far less seriously in the 1780s than it was earlier in the century. Parish churches were, for the most part, in poor condition. In spite of the general apathy, Sunday attendance was regarded as essential, requiring one's presence at both morning and afternoon services. To enliven the occasion, people who had to travel distances brought hamper baskets filled with delectable food. In the summer the church's green, flowering grove glittered with polished silver laid out on embroidered linen, an idyllic setting made more lavish by India silk petticoats, flowered and plumed hats, and bright male attire. Lund Washington was a vestryman at Pohick Church, four miles southwest of Hayfield.

After a lull of four years, Elizabeth resumed her diary in 1784, shortly before she and her husband moved into Hayfield. ✳

The Summer, 1784: I have now been married better than four years—and I think have had the satisfaction of conducting myself much to the approbation of my husband—and God grant I may continue to do it—hope I shall with the Divine assistance. I can truly say I have never had cause to repent of my marriage. So far from it, that I do think there is not another man scarce to be found that would have suited me so well as my dear Mr. W. And I have reason to think that he is perfectly satisfied with the choice he has made—which surely ought to make me very thankful to my gracious God for his infinite goodness to me—that my prayers and petitions before marriage, and since should be so completely granted. O my gracious God, give me an humble thankful heart for all thy unmerited goodness to me.—God willing I expect I shall go to housekeeping before this year is out; therefore will set myself some rules to go by, trusting in the Divine goodness that I shall be enabled to keep them. His infinite goodness was so great that he came down to show mankind the way of getting to heaven by taking the nature of man, and showing what human nature was capable of doing,—for had he not done that we should never have thought we could have practised all the virtues and graces that is necessary to carry us to heaven. But by his doing them with the human nature about him, shows us we may do them with his assistance—for surely if we do not endeavour to be as much like him as we can, we never shall live with him—for if we are not humble, meek, and of a patient forgiving temper, how can we expect to see the face of one who was all meekness,—who has not only told us we must forgive our enemies,—but we must love them. And yet there are some who will say they cannot forgive those who has offended them,—nor ever visit them—no—never see their faces if they can avoid it. Is it not as much as to say they are determined they never will go to heaven if those who has displeased them should have had the luck to get there before them,—how often do people act as if they thought so,—and perhaps the offence that has been given is the merest trifle in the eyes of everyone who has heard it. I thank God I am not of that disposition. I have been used extremely ill in time past by more than one or two persons, exceedingly ill indeed,—all that have ever heard or seen in what manner I was treated by those persons was amazed, and wondered how I could bear such treatment. But my heart has long been so softened, with meditating on the infinite goodness and mercy of the almighty towards me, and all mankind, that I cannot feel angry two minutes together—not even with those who were using me ill—for at the time of their ill treatment my mind would feel as if it rose above them—and I could look on their behaviour to me with indifference.

I have in some measure strayed from my first purpose of sitting down to write, which was to lay down rules how I would conduct myself in my family—by treating my domestics with all the friendly kindness that is possible for me to do, and never to think they were given me to domineer over by treating them with harsh expressions, because they are in my power,—such as fool —blockhead—vile wretches,—and many other names that I hope I shall ever think myself above using. But on the contrary I will endeavour to do as follows: first, never to scold at a servant if it is possible to avoid it,—but when they do wrong talk to them in a kind and friendly way, pointing out their fault with calmness, —but at the same time with a steadiness that they may know I will not be imposed upon. I will endeavour to make them think I do not wish they should behave well for my sake, but because it will be pleasing in the eyes of the almighty—and that if they will do their business for his sake, I shall be well served if they never think of me. Nothing would give me so great pleasure as having a truly religious family—not led away with Baptistical notions—but a religion that effectually touches the heart—no outside show; second, I will never find fault of a servant before their master—never to let them know that their master has the least idea that their ways offend me by any neglect of their business,—so that they shall never know he knows any of their faults—only just at the time that he may be obliged to speak to them,—as I suppose will be the case sometimes—for I do not expect they will always behave so as never to require his speaking to them. But I expect if they can think I do not tell of all their faults they will be much pleased,—because if they see he takes them to task for some of their faults, they will be apt to think what would he not do if he knew all of them,—so that by this method they may be brought to endeavour to please me, and feel some gratitude towards me for hiding their faults as they will think I dare say I shall hide many of their faults,—for that way of ever-lastingly finding fault and complaining of the worthlessness of servants I do abominate. It must feel irksome to every man who is lied to by such women. It is my wish that my husband should court my company—not avoid it if he can—as must be the case with those men who has those teasing kind of wives—or what else can be the meaning of men being so fond of going abroad, if it was not that they are sometimes tired of their wives' company. Mine, I thank God, has hitherto appeared always pleased with being with me, and I hope I shall never disgust him by any conduct of mine. Though I have known instances of men being very fond of going abroad—or making excuses of business for absenting themselves from their home—when they could have no such excuse to make that their wives were troublesome. But then it was because they had an itching for gaming—so great that they would spend a whole day, or days, in playing with the most indifferent creatures. What excuses, what contrivances will they not make to blind a wife to get to a dice table—or card table. How much do I pity those women who has husbands that loves the gaming table—how often a fine woman is left at home to lament the loss of her husband's company, who is really not worthy of her. Some men who loves the dice or card table dearly, will have a little shame. They will not be forever of it, yet visit those tables pretty often in the course of a week—if they can make any trifling excuse to get from home. O how much have I to thank thee for, my gracious God, that I should have a husband who despises the card and dice table. What a blessing it is that my husband is not fond of the diversion of gaming, a thing I so mortally dispise.

It is time now to return to what I was saying respecting my conduct towards my servants. It shall be my endeavour not to hurt the feelings of my servants. When I am obliged to find fault, I will take care not to find fault of one servant before another— but wait with patience till I have some opportunity of doing it alone. By that means I shall teach myself patience and forbear-ance, and avoid hurting their feelings, and at the same time raise some ambition in their breasts,—for certainly it must be a pleas-ing reflection to a servant if they have committed a fault to think no one knows it but their mistress; thirdly, if I should have children I will avoid if possible ever finding fault of a servant before them. It shall be my true endeavour never to let them see me angry with a servant—and especially to scold—I hope no one will ever see me guilty of that. I trust when we get to housekeep-ing our family will be conducted in great peace and quietness.

I am sure I shall strive after it. I am also sure it is Mr. Washington's desire, and that alone would make me endeavour after it —if I did not feel a principal of religion in me that causes me to desire it. Because it ever has given me pleasure to please him, and I can say with great truth I never took pleasure in anything that I was not sure he approved of.

Should this memorandum book fall into anyone's hands but a child's, it perhaps may be wondered why I should be so particular as to note down what is my intentions reflecting domestic business. I have done it that I may remember what was my thoughts at the time I made the resolutions, and to see whether I put them in execution—and that if it should please God to give me children they may see the method I pursued to live happy with my family,—and God grant it may make an impression on their minds.

I once had a thought of being more particular, and to have kept a journal of my life,—but that I could not have done faithfully, without speaking of all the ill treatment I ever met with, and that I did not wish to hand down. Therefore, whatever memorandums I have made in times past, I now shall destroy them all, and let only this manuscript book remain,—because should I have children, and especially daughters, it can be no disadvantage to them for to know something of my general conduct in my family. And more especially, if I were to leave the world before they arrived at an age to observe my behaviour in my family—or were too young for me to give advice to upon any thing I have mentioned. Daughters generally are very much attached to mothers, particularly if they lose them when they are young—therefore I think whatever legacy in advice a dead mother leaves her daughters, must have great weight with them. I trust, I hope whatever I have said may have the effect that is desired by their mother. I have had a daughter, but it was stillborn, and at this time I expect another child within a few months to come,—heaven grant it may live.

November, 1784: It has pleased God to give me in August last a fine child. It is a girl and its name is Lucinda—a hearty looking child as ever I saw. Should she live, it shall be my true endeavour to bring her up in the fear and love of the Lord,—though I should be reckoned ever so old fashioned for such a notion.

October, 1785: It has been the Divine will to take my dear Lucinda from me, after two or three days illness,—and if she was taken away for the correction of her parents, God grant the affliction may prosper in the design it was sent for. Give me patience O Lord to submit to thy will as I ought.

September, 1788: It has pleased my good God to give me another sweet child. It is a girl, and named Lucinda, and if it lives I will strive to discharge the duty of a parent who wishes to glorify her Redeemer in every thought, word, and action of her life.

Should I leave my dear child before she arrives to the years of discretion, I hope she will read this manuscript more than once,—and whatever other manuscript books I leave behind— I hope she will value—for though I have the books that I have wrote from—yet they being large was not too convenient to carry about me. Therefore, I have wrote some small manuscripts that I can conveniently carry in my pocket to peruse occasionally, which I have received great comfort from.

And let me tell my dear child that there is no real happiness without religion—a religion that effectually touches the heart. To conform to the outward ceremonies of religion is nothing if it does not proceed from a sincere desire to please the almighty being. There is no solidity, no comfort in the outward part of religion if it does not proceed from a real principal of virtue— a sincere desire to please the Redeemer who has done so much for us, has a very pleasing feel. I sincerely hope my child, should she live, will make of her study to walk well-pleasing in the eyes of her Saviour. Never be ashamed of being religious. Never suffer your conscience to upbraid you for the want of sincerity —not only reflecting religion, but of all your actions. Endeavour to live in peace and friendship with every creature. Entertain a good will and fellow feeling for all mankind. Be kind and good to everyone who is in want. Never say or do any thing that will give another pain, though your evil nature should want to do it.

Elizabeth Foote Washington / 347

I can with truth say I have made it my study to avoid saying or doing any thing that would give or cause the least uneasiness to another. Therefore you see I do not advise you to do what I have not practised myself. Should it please God to preserve my child to me, there is many things that will be necessary to give advice upon that I am not so capable of writing down—nor neither have I time to do it—so that if we both live I shall be much more particular. What I have wrote here in this book, was done to let my child see what was my thoughts at the time I was going to change my state, and what was my thoughts at the times that her sister and self was born—also my method of behaviour to my domestics—should I not live to give her direction and instruction thereon.

The Spring, 1789: We have been keeping house going on five years, and I think no one could have put the foregoing resolutions more in practice than I have, or taken more pains than I have to persuade my servants to do their business through a principal of religion. I have frequently told them that it was my most earnest desire they should do their duty as a servant for their Saviour's sake, not for mine. I have instructed them how they were to do it for his sake. As to my two girls, it is needless to say what pains I have taken with their education,—because I have done everything that a mistress could do for them, in every respect. It is impossible to tell what I have done for them, for if they had been my daughters I could not have given them better advice,—and I shall continue to do so as long as we live together. I have taught them to read and write. There is few young ladies ever had the same pains taken with them. I shall have the satisfaction of thinking I have done what I could do towards their happiness in this world, and in that which is to come,—so that they must stand or fall to themselves. They can lay no blame on anyone. I have put good books into their hands. I can do no more for them than I have done, but always to set them and the rest of my servants the best example, which has ever been my study to do, and I trust I have not failed.

Within two years after we came home to live I had prayers in my family, night and morning, never failing to get two or three together—and still continue to do it. But they do not seem fond of it. What is the cause I know not. Human nature I believe is naturally averse to any thing that is good. I believe no family could live in more peace and quietness than we do. I dare believe my servants is much pleased with my treatment of them. I have been very careful in not finding fault of them before their master, or before one another,—nor never did I entertain my company with talking of their faults. We appear to live in so much peace our visitors think we have the best of servants, and that I have no trouble,—because I do not talk of the fatigue and trouble of a family, and am not talking or telling of every fault they commit, or reprimanding them before company for some neglect that they have just been guilty of. But if they are neglectful or careless while we have company, it perhaps may so happen that I may not have an opportunity till the company is gone of speaking to them about it. Indeed it is to me a very painful task to find fault,—and when I am obliged to do it, it is done in as kind a manner as I can. If our servants are better than others, it must be from the manner of the treatment they receive, for when they do wrong, if it is mentioned to them once, there is no more of it. They are not frequently upbraided with the fault they have committed. I believe one reason why servants are not better is owing to their superiors. People in general has a very teasing way with their servants. They will say every ill natured thing that their evil nature can suggest (it can be very provoking when it is suffered to be indulged), yet think their servants are to take it all without one disapproving look. They expect more perfection in creatures of no education than they have themselves.

If our visitors knew how little my servants did they would not think them good—nay there is few would put up with their servants doing so little as mine—and that little I am obliged to follow them to get done. But I cannot get them to do more without scolding and whipping,—and I cannot do either. Therefore, I am often obliged to exercise my patience, and try to be contented. I think there is servants, that was they to meet with the same treatment from their superiors that mine does from me, they would be better servants than any I have,—for to consider how mine has ever been treated they are not such servants as a person would expect—for surely they ought to be the best of servants, which is not the case. But I believe they might be made much worse by being frequently scolded at, which certainly is the ruin of servants. When I consider the blessings the divine goodness has conferred on me, it appears as if my heart could never be thankful enough for them,—such a promising sweet little girl as I have, and so good a husband. There certainly cannot be a more truly affectionate and tender husband than I have. I believe there never was married people who lived happier than we do, nay, I believe there is few lives so happy, so entirely free from any kind of disputing—no—there is no disputes between us,—no angry expressions. In short, there is nothing but perfect peace and harmony reigns in our habitation. There cannot be a better master than Mr. Washington is in every respect. There is no servants who enjoys more of the comforts of life than his does. Their servitude is made as easy to them as it is possible. Were they to do less, they would not live so well, and what they make, they enjoy with comfort. I am satisfied there is no family governed in more peace than ours, their master being remarkable steady in his conduct, so that his servants always seeing him the same man from day to day. They know how to conduct themselves better than when masters is one thing today, and another tomorrow. One of my first resolutions I made after marriage was never to hold disputes with my husband, never to contend with him in my opinion of things,—but if ever we differed in opinions not to insist on mine being right, and his wrong,—which is too much the custom of my sex. They cannot bear to be thought in the wrong, which is the cause why there is so much contention in the married state. The Lordly Sex, they can never be in the wrong in their own opinion—therefore cannot give up to a woman. But I blame my sex most if it is their business to give up to their husbands, Our mother, even when she transgressed, was told her husband should rule over her—then how dare any of her daughters dispute the point. I never thought it degraded my understanding—to give up my opinion to my husband's—that is, not to contend with him. There is no necessity for a woman appearing to be afraid of her husband—indeed I think they err very much when they are so. I think a woman may keep up the dignity of a wife and mistress of a family without ever disputing with her husband. I never could take any pleasure in having my own way. It ever was more pleasing to have my husband's opinion to coincide with mine. I was once told by a very near male relation that I only affected to conform to my husband's will, to be thought an obedient wife,—but this is not, nor never was the case. A much more laudable motive has influenced my conduct, and I hope will always influence it. A desire to do my duty, to conform to the scripture direction given to never has been the ruling principal that has conducted my actions in the married state.

It has also been thought that I should never have been the woman that I am thought to be, had I not had so good a husband. But that is a mistake, because the principal that has directed my conduct I should have had had I never seen Mr. W. Had I not had a good husband my trials, I doubt not, would have been greater, but I trust the power that instilled the desire in my soul to do my duty—because it is pleasing in his eyes that I should—would always have given me strength equal to the trials I should have met with. I do not mean to take any merit from my dear Mr. W.. I shall ever acknowledge him a great blessing. He possesses many good qualities—there is the two following not the least among the number: he is a perfectly sober man—there can be no one who despises drinking more than he does,—not only those who drink to excess, for the world in general despises those kind of men, but he hates to see any one tippling at the grog or doddy through the day, as there is many who will do it without getting drunk,—he disapproves of all drinking except at dinner, and that must be in a very moderate manner. Then no one can despise the dice or card table more than he does. In short, he disapproves of all kind of gaming, let it be little or much,—which I look upon as a very great blessing. It is impossible for me to enumerate all the blessings of Providence,—therefore I will not attempt to mention any more of them, tho' I am sure I look on many things as blessings that others do not think of—but I rejoice that I do look on them as blessings. I can give the glory where it is due.

As well as I can recollect I think I have made a memorandum of what I should wish a child should know reflecting our domestic affairs. Therefore, I shall not write much more, without any extraordinary thing should happen. Should the divine goodness preserve my child to me we shall have many conversations upon what I have written, because I shall enlarge much upon the subject. It has ever appeared to me that the almighty has given me my dear Lucinda to comfort me for the loss of my others. Heaven grant she may be a comfort.

October, 1789: My God—thou hast thought fit to take my dear Lucinda from me—after three months extreme illness. Surely no woman could have felt more than I have for three months past —to see my dear child lay as she did—and poor Mr. Washington greatly afflicted with an inflammation in his eyes at the same time, —my gracious Redeemer support my spirits while under the rod of affliction,—and let me take comfort in this, that whom the Lord loveth, he chastens. My greatest comfort is that the almighty knows it was my sincere intention to bring my children up to glorify him in all their actions—blessed be the divine goodness—that I can take comfort in thinking that their Redeemer should think them worthy to enjoy heaven, without experiencing any of the troubles that attends mankind in passing through this vale of misery. My gracious God, thou hast conferred great honour on me—that thou shouldst think me worthy to bring children who thou hast thought was only fit to live with thee.

The winter, 1792: I have been married thirteen years, and have seen a great deal of trouble in the time—no one knows nor ever will know what I have suffered in the time. My poor dear Mr. Washington for near a year has been extremely afflicted, and remains far from being well. Indeed, I fear he never will be well again, though he is much more mended than the doctors ever expected to see him,—to be deprived of sight is truly afflicting, which has been the case almost ever since his indisposition. He has at this time a little sight, but it is so glimmering that I doubt whether any one else would strive to walk alone, but himself. He certainly has bore the afflicting hand of Providence with all the fortitude and resignation that a creature could do—gracious Heaven—was there not a hope of a better world than this, human nature could not live under the afflictions of this life. But we are taught to believe that every thing is ordered for the best —that nothing happens by chance—therefore it is my study to reconcile myself to the divine dispensations—endeavouring to trust in this gracious promise—that the almighty will not afflict us more than he will enable us to bear. He knows when it is necessary to lay the cross upon us. Then let us be dumb and submit to being made so much like the son of his love—who has shown his poor creatures there is no way of getting to heaven but through the cross.

In July, 1792: I am grieved greatly to have this to set down—that my family is got so Baptistical in their notions, as to think they commit a crime to join with me in prayer morning and evening. I have talked to every one of them separately, and seriously, endeavouring to convince them that they did not commit a crime by joining with me in prayer. But all I can say will not convince them—so that I am obliged to give out having prayers in my family, which has given me great concern. But as I trust that my gracious God knows the desire I had to serve him daily in my family, that I shall not be answerable for not having family prayers. I persevered in it as long as I could, until it was a mere farce to attempt it any longer. I am satisfied there was nothing in my behaviour that caused them to dislike joining me in prayer, but the creatures has taken it into their heads that the prayers I used was too good for them to use—may the Lord direct them in the right way, as they think they are wrong. How I am to discharge my duty I know not. It is impressed on my mind that a master or mistress of a family ought to have daily prayer in their family —but when their servants will go out of the way at the time they are going to be called to prayer, it is impossible for them to have it. And then if they are made to come, they appear quite angry, which must be extremely wrong. Therefore I think it must be best let alone. O my God, direct and influence my heart aright —amen. One thing my poor creatures expected was to be the consequence of my having prayers on my family, that I should never find fault of them, nor ever reprimand them for any thing at all, but when they found that I continued to do it in my way, which certainly is very different from the manners of most people, they thought my religion was all pretence, which is too much the case of the world, the world that loves its own will make great allowances for each other; indiscretions, and even vices, will be charged to the account of human infirmity. But where a person professes to be a believer in Jesus there is no such charity extended to them, but rather all their words and actions will be sifted, their mistakes exaggerated, and if any part of their conduct will bear a double construction it will generally be viewed in the most unfavourable light. Now that it is probable I may not have any children, so of course this book and all my other manuscripts must fall into the hands of some relative, who may laugh at them and think as my servants, and may not give them a reading—but throw them into some old drawer as waste paper, or give them to their children to tear up, as is too often the case with many people, they give their children books to play with and destroy. Tis certain I have wrote and copied together a great deal, an abundance I have destroyed. But what I have now I shall keep for my own satisfaction and comfort. Let them that comes after me think what they will, I do not keep them with an ostentatious view. I can declare with truth that my dear Mr. Washington has never seen any of them, nor even don't know that I ever wrote any manuscripts, so that was it to please God to restore him to his eye sight and take me from him, he would be surprised when he over looked my papers, though I trust he would set great value on all my scribble, for altho my heart has been much taken up with religion, yet very little have I talked about it. Perhaps I may have erred on the other side, and not vindicated religion when I ought to have done it—but I always found myself not competent to speak of it as I should wish, therefore thought it best to say but little, and endeavour to attain the practical part —to hear people everlastingly talk about religion and to see their actions not corresponding with it, is a thing my heart has always started at—and indeed I have ever found a want of words to express my ideas of any thing, much more so serious a thing as religion is. I have ever thought I could think better on any subject than I could express myself—and altho I have wrote so many letters, yet to this day I never feel satisfied with a letter that I write. I always think any one could have done it better, which causes my dear Mr. W. to give me many lectures in his way for being so diffident. He says I am too hard to please or that I am too proud, but I do not think it is the case. My family hitherto has been always thought to be remarkably diffident. I have thought should I meet with a female relation who appeared to think favourable of religion I might give away my manuscripts before my death, as I do not expect my dear partner will ever see again. But should I not do it—who ever you are that they fall into the hands of, I could wish for your own sakes that you would give them more than one reading—who knows but what it may please God to cause a thought to arise in your hearts that you may be better for it ever after. Sometimes it pleases the divine goodness from the merest trifle or accident to work a change in his creatures for the better. Tis certain it would be a pleasing satisfaction had I a relation that I could think would set a value on my religious books of every description, and would read them all through at least once, if not oftener. I feel sorry when I reflect the time will arrive when they will be thrown by. When I take up a book I am fond of, I think and say to myself, the time will come when you will be thrown behind some old trunk or desk for the mice to eat—or tossed up into the garret as old lumber, to make room for books that is more agreeable to the imperfections of human nature—for among those who is thought very good kind of people you will find very few of them that has any idea of reading a religious book any other time than on a Sunday, even among those that is thought conscientious in many respects. They think they do very well if they do not read any other book on Sundays but those that are called good books, but as for the rest of the week they think there is no necessity. But people are as much deceived themselves as they deceive others, who think to use religion as they do their best clothes, only to wear to church on a Sunday, to appear fine and make a show, and with them (as soon as they come home again) lay it aside carefully for fear of wearing it out. But religion is good for nothing that is made of so slight a stuff as won't endure wearing, which ought to be as constant a covering to the soul, as the skin is to the body, not to be divided from it, division being the ruin of both. Religion is a thing much talked of, but little understood, much pretended to, but very little practised—which is a most lamentable case—but so it is. It may perhaps be wondered at, why I wrote so many morning prayers and evening ones, when it is customary to use only one morning and evening prayer through the course of the lives of those who prays in their families. My reason for it is this, when a person is accustomed to say only one particular prayer of a morning and one at night for a length of time, those who join them will be apt to repeat them and not think of them at the same time, having got them by rote, so that instead of praying it is but mere babbling. Therefore, I thought to keep up the attention of the minds of the hearers it was best to have a variety, so that they should not always know so well what was coming, besides human nature is so frail respecting prayer, that it will tire with a constant sameness, without the heart as much affected with religion. I have wrote nine morning prayers and the same number of evening ones for to use in my family. I have nine manuscript books including the three that has the family prayers. I have wrote prayers for a person in private, for I think it is the duty of every creature to pray in private as well as publick, and not only of a morning and evening, but through the day they ought every now and then send up a devout thought to heaven which no doubt the divine goodness will accept as a continual prayer, though a person is not always on their knees—yet that must not be neglected at proper seasons, for although every member of a family joins in publick prayer, yet it is the duty of every member of that family to pray in private, if they have time and opportunity. Joining in family prayer is no excuse for a person not to pray alone, because every creature who sincerely prays will have petitions to make to heaven that cannot be made so well in publick, and for a person who prays regular in their families to think that will excuse them from going to church, is extremely wrong.

Somehow I feel a greater desire to have had some one to have given this book to, than I do of any of the others. I suppose the reason is because this book is all my own thoughts and reflections. Though I am sensible there is great imperfections in this book. Yet I am desirious some one should have it—oh the weakness of human nature is great. But as I do not expect to have children now, if I leave this book behind me after my death, I think I ought before that happens to write it over again, to correct what errors there may be in the diction of it—but whether I shall ever have the time, I cannot say. What pleasure a child would have taken in reading this after their mother was gone—but let me be dumb, and not say another word.

✳ Within hours after Lund's death in 1796, Elizabeth wrote: "O Lord—give me perfect resignation to thy divine will—'tho my gracious Lord has thought fit to take the dear partner and companion of my life from me, after being seven years in the furnace of affliction." In his will Lund requested that his slaves be freed: yet a few wished to remain with Elizabeth. She appeared more frequently at Mount Vernon, where Martha affectionately offered her a candle to light her way upstairs for the night.

On December 12, 1799 George Washington took his customary horseback ride on the estate. Though a heavy snowfall had dampened his clothing and coated his hair, the aging general ate supper that evening in a chilly room, without having changed his clothes. On Friday the 13th he complained of a sore throat, but went out again in the slushy snow to mark trees which were to be cut down. The following morning Washington was unable to rise out of bed, suffering from a bad cold and inflammatory throat obstruction. Instead of resting to regain his strength, George insisted upon being bled, although Martha advised against it. A vein incision was made, and a half pint of blood gushed into a receptacle. When Dr. James Craik arrived, he was bled twice more, the last of which drew a quart of blood. Greatly weakened, the patient was then "dosed with calomel and tarter emetic and sacrificed with blisters and poultices," medication that made it more difficult for him to breathe or swallow. Between ten and eleven that night Washington, in good health earlier in the week, expired "without a struggle or a sigh."

When Washington's will was probated, it revealed a warm sentiment toward several women: "To my sisters in law Hannah Washington and Mildred Washington; to my friends Eleanor Stuart, Hannah Washington of Fairfield and Elizabeth Washington of Hayfield, I give each a mourning ring of the value of one hundred dollars; these bequests are not made for the intrinsic value of them, but as mementos of my esteem and regard." Mourning rings were usually enameled in black and white, and heart shaped. They often contained a lock of the deceased person's hair.

In regard to his slaves—317 men, women, and children—Washington dictated that "upon the decease of my wife, it is my will and desire that all slaves which I hold in own right, shall receive their freedom." For many years he had wished for the abolishment of slavery, having regarded it as an economic evil. Yet he once considered selling his slaves. "The advantages resulting from the sale of my Negroes I have very little doubt of," Washington wrote Lund in February 1779, "because as I observed in my last, if we should ultimately prove unsuccessful [in the Revolution] it would be of very little consequence to me whether my property is in Negroes or loan office certificates, as

I shall ask for, nor expect any favour from his most gracious Majesty, nor any person acting under his authority. The only points for me to consider are, first, whether it would be most to my interest in case of a fortunate determination to the present contest to have Negroes and the crops they will make, or the sum they will now fetch and the interest of the money; and second, the critical moment to make this sale. . . . If these poor wretches are to be held in a state of slavery, I do not see that a change in masters will render it more irksome provided husband and wife, and parents and children are not separated from each other." He finally chose not to sell them.

Virginia's laws were so harsh against blacks that Washington was afraid his slaves, if freed, would not be able to fend for themselves. "I hope it will not be conceived," he wrote the financier Robert Morris on April 12, 1786, "that it is my wish to hold the unhappy people who are the subject of this letter, in slavery. I can only say that there is no man living, who wishes more sincerely than I do to see a plan adopted for the abolition of it, but there is only one proper and effective mode by which it can be accomplished and that is by legislative authority." He mentioned that petitions had been presented to Virginia's Assembly, but "they could scarcely obtain a reading."

In his will he reasoned that he could not free his slaves before his wife's death because a number of them belonged to her. Martha had inherited the slaves of her first husband, Daniel Custis. The issue was further complicated by intermarriages. "To emancipate them during her life, would, tho' earnestly wished by me, be attended with such insuperable difficulties on account of their intermixture by marriages with the dower Negroes, as to excite the most painful sensations, if not disagreeable consequences from the latter, while both descriptions are in the occupancy of the same proprietors; it not being in my power, under the tenure by which the dower Negroes are held, to manumit them. And whereas among those who will receive freedom according to this devise, there may be some, who from old age or bodily infirmities, and others who on account of their infancy, that will be unable to support themselves, it is my will and desire that all who come under the first and second description shall be comfortably cloathed and fed by my heirs while they live, and that such of the latter description as have no parents living, or if living are unable, or unwilling to provide for them, shall be bound by the Court until they shall arrive at the age of twenty-five years." Although Washington dictated that "the Negroes thus bound, are (by their masters or mistresses) to be taught to read or write, and to be brought up to some useful occupation," Virginia's "black-laws" prevented his request from being carried out.

For years Elizabeth had taught Hayfield's black children and servants how to read and write, having considered them as part of her family. When she died in 1812 the family consisted of her adopted nephew William and two servants, Felicia and Daniel. The remaining slaves had either gone northward, or had died. In her will she freed and provided for her two servants. Hayfield she gave to William; ten shares of Potomac Bank Stock, and her investment in the Potomac Company—formed by George Washington for the purpose of building locks and improving the river —to the Washington Society of Alexandria, "to apply to the education of such poor girls as they think proper." She had wished for racial equality in education, impossible nationally because of rampant bigotry. Yet a Rhode Island farm youth, Prudence Crandall, shattered northern prejudice a decade or so later by opening a boarding and teacher-training school for black women in the white-dominated town of Canterbury, Connecticut.*

Selected Bibliography

Published Primary Sources

ADAMS, FRANCIS CHARLES, Editor. *Familiar letters of John Adams and His Wife Abigail Adams During the Revolution.* Boston, 1875.

ALLEN, ETHAN. *A Narrative of Colonel Ethan Allen's Captivity.* Thomas & Thomas. Walpole, N.H., 1807.

ANONYMOUS. *The Laws Respecting Women As They Regard Their Natural Rights.* Printed for J. Johnson. London, 1777.

ANONYMOUS. *Report of the Trial of Richard D. Croucher on an Indictment for a Rape on Margaret Miller.* George Forman. New York, 1800.

BERTHIER, ALEXANDRE. "Alexandre Berthier's Journal of the American Campaign." Marshall Morgan, translator. *Rhode Island History.* The Rhode Island Historical Society. Providence, 1965.

BRISSOT DE WARVILLE, JACQUES PIERRE. *New Travels in the United States of America, Performed in 1788.* T. & J. Swords. New York, 1792.

BRYMNER, DOUGLAS, Archivist. *Report on Canadian Archives.* Ottawa, 1888.

CARROLL, CHARLES. *Journal of Charles Carroll of Carrollton During His Visit to Canada in 1776.* Maryland Historical Society's Centennial Memorial. Baltimore, 1876.

CLINTON, GEORGE. *Public Papers of George Clinton, First Governor of New York.* Hugh Hastings, Editor. Oliver A. Quayle. Albany, 1904.

COLLINS, VARNUM LANSING, Editor. *A Brief Narrative of the Ravages of the British and Hessians.* Princeton University Library. Princeton, 1906.

Colonial Records of Pennsylvania. "Minutes of the Supreme Executive Council of Pennsylvania." Volumes 11, 1776–1779 (1852); 12, 1779–1781 (1853). Published by the State. Harrisburg.

COMMANGER, HENRY STEELE, AND RICHARD B. MORRIS' Editors. *The Spirit of 'Seventy-Six.* Bobbs-Merrill. New York, 1958.

FORCE, PETER, Editor. *American Archives.* Series 4, Volume 3; Series 5, Volumes 1, 3. M. St. Clair and Peter Force. Washington, D.C. 1837–1853.

FORD, WORTHINGTON C., Editor. *Journals of the Continental Congress.* Volumes 2: Appendix (1905), 7 (1907), 8 (1907), 14 (1909). Government Printing Office. Washington, D.C.

FRANKLIN, BENJAMIN. *The Works of Benjamin Franklin.* Volume 7. John Bigelow, Editor. G.P. Putnam's Sons. New York, 1887–1888.

GREAT BRITAIN HISTORICAL MANUSCRIPTS COMMISSION. *Report on the Manuscripts of the Late Reginald Rawdon Hastings.* Volume III. H.M. Stationary Office. London, 1930–1947.

JEFFERSON, THOMAS. *Notes on the State of Virginia.* Thomas & Andrews. Boston, 1801. *Thomas Jefferson Correspondance Printed from the Originals in the Collection of William K. Bixby.* Boston, 1916. *The Writings of Thomas Jefferson.* H.A. Washington, Editor. Volume III. John C. Riker. New York, 1854.

MACKENZIE, FREDERICK. *Diary of Frederick Mackenzie as an officer of the Regiment of Royal fusiliers during the years 1775–1781.* Harvard University Press. Cambridge, 1930.

MANN, HERMAN. *The Female review: or, Memoirs of an American young lady.* Nathaniel and Benjamin Henton. Dedham, Mass., 1797.

MARSHALL, CHRISTOPHER. *Extracts from the Diary of Christopher Marshall 1744–1781.* William Duane, Editor. Joel Munsell. Albany, 1877.

MARTIN, JOSEPH PLUMB. *A Narrative of Some of the Adventures, Dangers and Sufferings of a Revolutionary Soldier.* Glazier, Masters and Company. Hallowell, Maine. 1830.

MORE, CHARLES ALBERT [Le Chevalier de Pontgibaud] *Memoirs du comte de Moré 1758, 1837.* A. Picard et fils. Paris, 1898.

NIEMCEWICZ, JULIAN URSYN. "Under the Vine and Fig Tree." Metchie J.E. Budka, Editor and Translator. *Collections of the New Jersey Historical* Society. Volume XIV. Grassman Publishing Company Inc. Elizabeth, New Jersey, 1965.

Pennsylvania Archives. Series 1 through 6. Published by the State. Harrisburg, 1853–1907.

The Port Folio. Philadelphia, 1800–1809.

RUSH, BENJAMIN. *Letters of Benjamin Rush.* Lyman H. Butterfield, Editor. Volume I: 1761–1792. American Philosophical Society. Philadelphia, 1951.

Medical Inquiries and Observations. Volume IV. Thomas Dobson. Philadelphia, 1794–1798.

SAMPSON, DEBORAH. "An Address Delivered in 1802 in Various Towns in Massachusetts, Rhode Island and New York" *Publications of the Sharon Historical Society, No. 2.* H.M. Hight. Boston, April, 1905.

SCHAUKIRK, EWALD GUSTAV. "Occupation of New York City by the British, 1776. Extracts from the Diary of the Moravian Congregation" *Pennsylvania Magazine of History and Biography.* Volume I, Numbers 2, 3. The Historical Society of Pennsylvania. Philadelphia, 1877.

SMITH, JOHN JAY. *Letters of Doctor Richard Hill and His Children.* Printed privately. Philadelphia, 1854.

STILES, EZRA. *The Literary Diary of Ezra Stiles.* F. B. Dexter, Editor. Charles Scribner's Sons. New York, 1901.

STRYKER, WILLIAM S., Editor. *Archives of the State of New Jersey.* Series 2, Volume 1. New Jersey Historical Society. Newark, 1901.

SWINNERTON, HENRY. "Jane Ferguson's Revolutionary Recollections." *American Monthly Magazine.* Volume XX, Number 4. Publication of the Daughters of the American Revolution. Washington, D.C. April 7, 1902.

Testimonies of the Life, Character, Revelations and Doctrines of Ann Lee. Published "by order of the Ministry in union with the Church." T. Tallcott and J. Deming. Hancock, Massachusetts, 1816.

VERREAU, L'ABBE. "Collection de mémoires recueillis et annotes par M. L'Abbé Verreau." *Invasion du Canada.* 2 Volumes. E. Senécal. Montreal, 1870–1873.

VINTON, JOHN ADAMS, Editor. *The Female Review: Life of Deborah Sampson.* J.K. Wiggin and William P. Lunt. Boston, 1866.

WALKER, MARTHA I'ANS. "The Shurtleff Manuscript No. 153" *New Hampshire Antiquarian Society Collection, No. II.* Contoocook, 1876.

WASHINGTON, GEORGE. *The Diaries of George Washington.* John C. Fitzpatrick, Editor. Published for the Mount Vernon Ladies Association of the Union. Houghton Mifflin Company. Boston, New York, 1925.

WASHINGTON, GEORGE. *The Writings of Washington.* Jared Sparks, Editor. Volumes III, VIII. Ferdinand Andrews, Publisher. Boston, 1839.

WASHINGTON, GEORGE. *The Writings of Washington.* John C. Fitzpatrick, Editor. Volumes 8, 9, 15, 37. Government Printing Office. Washington, D.C., 1931–1944.

WHEATLEY, PHYLLIS. *Memoir and poems of Phyllis Wheatley, a Native African and a slave.* Light & Horton, Boston, 1835.

WILLARD, MARGARET WHEELER, Editor. *Letters on the American Revolution.* Kennikat Press, Inc., Port Washington, New York, 1968.

Newspapers

The Boston Gazette or Country Journal Boston, December 7, 1778; January 4, 1779.

The Boston Gazette Boston, July 14, 1788; March 22, 29, 1802.

The Connecticut Courant Hartford, October 2, 1775; September 10, 1777.

The Continental Journal and Weekly Advertiser Boston, July 30, 1778; April 14, 1779.

The Independent Chronicle and Universal Advertiser Boston, July 27, August 10, 1780.

The Mercury and New-England Palladium Boston, March 23, 26, 1802.

The New-Jersey Gazette Trenton, December 31, 1778.

The New-Jersey Journal Chatham, June 14, 1780.

The Newport Herald Newport, August 19, 26, 1790; September 2, 1790.

The Newport Mercury Newport, March 10, 1781.

The New-York Gazette and the Weekly Mercury New York, April 14, September 22, 1777; November 26, 1783.

The New York Journal; or the General Advertiser New York, November 23, 1775; September 8, 1777; July 20, 1778.

The Pennsylvania Gazette, and Weekly Advertiser Philadelphia, April 14, 1779.

The Pennsylvania Journal; and the Weekly Advertiser Philadelphia, March 1, 1775.

The Pennsylvania Packet, or the General Advertiser Philadelphia, August 22, 1778; October 7, 1779; June 13, July 8, November 4, 1780.

Providence Gazette Providence Providence, August 5, 1780.

Relf's Philadelphia Gazette and Daily Advertiser Philadelphia, April 25, 1804.

The Royal Gazette New York, January 6, November 24, 1779; September 8, 1781.

Virginia Gazette Norfolk, April 20, 1776.

Secondary Sources

ATHERTON, WILLIAM HENRY. *Montreal, 1535–1914.* Volume II. S.J. Clarke Publishing Company. Montreal, Chicago, 1914.

BADEAUX, J.B. "Journal des opérations de l'armée américaine, lors de l'invasion du Canada en 1775–76." *Third Series of Historical*

Documents. Literary and Historical Society of Quebec. E. Senécal. Montreal, 1871.

BALDWIN, THOMAS W., Editor. *Vital Records of Sharon, Massachusetts to the Year 1850.* Stanhope Press. Boston, 1901.

BARCK, OSCAR THEODORE. *New York City During the War for Independence.* Columbia University Press. New York, 1931.

BENSON, MARY SUMMER. "Women in the Eighteenth Century" *Columbia University Studies in History, Economics and Public Law No. 405.* Columbia University. New York, 1935.

BOLHOUSE, GLADYS. "Women and the Battle for Rhode Island" *Newport History* The Newport Historical Society. Winter 1968.

BRIDENBAUGH, CARL. *Cities in the Wilderness.* The Ronald Press Company. New York, 1938.

_____*Cities in Revolt.* Alfred A. Knopf Inc. New York, 1955.

BURT, A.L. "The Mystery of Walker's Ear" *The Canadian Historical Review.* Volume III, Number 3. University of Toronto Press. September 1922.

CALLAHAN, NORTH. *Flight from the Republic: The Tories of the American Revolution.* Bobbs-Merrill. Indianapolis, 1967.

CONWAY, MONCURE DANIEL. *Barons of the Potomack and the Rappahannock.* The Grolier Club. New York, 1892.

COVELL, ELIZABETH. "Newport Harbor and Lower Narragansett Bay Rhode Island During the Revolution." *Bulletin of the Newport Historical Society.* Newport, January 1933.

DEARDEN, PAUL F. "The Siege of Newport: Inauspicious Dawn of Alliance." *Rhode Island History.* The Rhode Island Historical Society. Providence, Winter & Spring 1970.

DOWNING, ANTOINETTE, AND VINCENT J. SCULLY, JR. *The Architectural Heritage of Newport, Rhode Island.* Bramhall House. New York, 1967.

DRINKER, CECIL. *Not So Long Ago.* Oxford University Press. New York, 1937.

EDITORS. "Slavery in Rhode Island" *Publications of the Rhode Island Historical Society.* Volume II. Providence, 1894.

ELLET, ELIZABETH. *Women of the Revolution.* Baker and Scribner. New York, 1848.

FISKE, JOHN. *Old Virginia and Her Neighbours.* Houghton Mifflin Company. Boston and New York, 1897.

FLEXNER, JAMES THOMAS. *George Washington in the American Revolution.* Little, Brown and Company. Boston, 1967.

FOLSOM, FITZPATRICK, CONKLIN. *The Municipalities of Essex County, New Jersey, 1666–1924.* Volume I. Lewis Historical Publishing Company. New York, 1925.

GLENN, THOMAS ALLEN. *Some Colonial Mansions And Those Who Lived in Them.* Volume 2. H.T. Coates & Company. Philadelphia, 1900.

GREENE, EVARTS BOUTELL. *The Revolutionary Generation, 1763–1790.* Macmillan Company. New York, 1953.

GREENE, NELSON, Editor. *History of the Mohawk Valley.* Volume I. S.J. Clarke Publishing Company. Chicago, 1925.

GREENWOOD, ISAAC JOHN. *The Greenwood Family of Norwich, England, in America.* H. Minot Pitman, Mary M. Greenwood, Editors. Rumford Press. Concord, New Hampshire, 1934.

HALL, EDWARD H. *Margaret Corbin, Heroine of the Battle of Fort Washington, 16 November, 1776.* American Scenic and Historic Preservation Society. New York, 1932.

HOYT, JAMES. *The Mountain Society.* C.M. Saxton, Barker and Company. New York, 1860.

HUDSON, DAVID. *History of Jemima Wilkinson, A Preacheress.* S.P. Hull. Geneva, New York, 1821.

JEFFERYS, C.P.B. "An Eighteenth Century Summer Visitor to Newport" *Newport History* The Newport Historical Society. Winter 1969.

JONES, RUFUS M. *The Quakers in the American Colonies.* Macmillian & Company Ltd. London, 1911.

KIPPING, ERNEST. *The Hessian View of America 1776–1783.* Philip Freneau Press. Monmouth Beach, New Jersey, 1971.

LITTLE, MRS. WILLIAM S. "The Massacre of Cherry Valley" *Publication Fund Series.* Volume VI. The Rochester Historical Society. Rochester, 1927.

MCGROARTY, WILLIAM BUCKNER. "Elizabeth Washington of Hayfield" *The Virginia Magazine of History and Biography.* Volume XXXII. The Virginia Historical Society. Richmond, 1925.

MIDDLETON, W.S. "The Yellow Fever Epidemic of 1793 in Philadelphia" *Annals of Medical History.* Volume X. Paul B. Hoeber. New York, 1928.

MORRIS, RICHARD B. *Studies in the History of American Law.* Columbia University Press. New York, 1930.

PIERSON, DAVID L. *History of the Oranges.* Volume I. Lewis Historical Publishing Company. New York, 1922.

PRUSSING, EUGENE ERNEST. *The Estate of George Washington, Deceased.* Little, Brown and Company. Boston, 1927.

ROY, CHRISTIAN. "L'Assomption, foyer de rébellion en 1775." *Histoire de l'Assomption.* La Commission des Fêtes du 250e Anniversaire. l'Assomption, 1967.

SABINE, LORENZO. *The American Loyalists.* Charles C. Little & James Brown. Boston, 1847.

SHORTT, ADAM, AND ARTHUR DOUGHTY, Editors. *Documents Relating to the Constitutional History of Canada.* S.E. Dawson. Ottawa, 1918.

SICOTTE, JUSTICE L.W. "The Affair Walker" *The Canadian Antiquarian and Numismatic Journal* Volume XII, Number 4. Antiquarian and Numismatic Society of Montreal, October 1915.

SMITH, SAMUEL STELLE. *The Battle of Trenton.* Philip Freneau Press. Monmouth Beach, New Jersey, 1965.

_____*A Molly Pitcher Chronology.* Philip Freneau Press. Monmouth Beach, 1972.

STEVENS, MAUD LYMAN. "Washington and Newport" *Bulletin of the Newport Historical Society.* July 1932.

STRYKER, WILLIAM S., Editor. *Official Register of the Officers and Men of New Jersey in the Revolution.* Genealogical Publishing Company. Baltimore, 1967.

TETU, MONSEIGNEUR H. "L'abbé Pierre Huet de la Valiniere 1732–1794" *Bulletin des recherches historiques.* Volume 10. May 1904.

THANE, ELSWYTH. *Potomac Squire.* Duell, Sloan and Pearce. New York, 1963.

TREPANIER, LEON. "L'Affair Walker a Montréal en 1764." *Les cahiers des dix.* Number 27, Montreal, 1962.

WHITTEMORE, HENRY. *The Founders and Builders of the Oranges.* L.J. Hardman. Newark, 1896.

WICKES, STEPHEN. *History of the Oranges.* New England Society. Orange, New Jersey, 1892.

WISTER, CHARLES J. *The Labour of a Long Life, A Memoir of Charles J. Wister.* Volume 2. Germantown, Pennsylvania, 1886.

YEAGER, HENRY J. "The French Fleet at Newport" *Rhode Island History.* The Rhode Island Historical Society. Providence, Summer 1971.

INDEX

Diary, 156–179;
meets General Washington, 168